NELSONS LIBRARY OF THEOLOGY

General Editor
† H. H. ROWLEY, M.A., D.D., F.B.A.

CHRISTIAN ETHICS

CHRISTIAN ETHICS

OTTO A. PIPER

Department of New Testament Literature
and Exegesis
Princeton Theological Seminary

NELSON

THOMAS NELSON AND SONS LTD
36 Park Street London W1
P.O. Box 2187 Accra
P.O. Box 25012 Nairobi
P.O. Box 21149 Dar es Salaam
77 Coffee Street San Fernando Trinidad

THOMAS NELSON (AUSTRALIA) LTD
597 Little Collins Street Melbourne 3000

THOMAS NELSON AND SONS (CANADA) LTD
81 Curlew Drive Don Mills Ontario

THOMAS NELSON AND SONS (NIGERIA) LTD
P.O. Box 336 Apapa Lagos

THOMAS NELSON AND SONS (SOUTH AFRICA) (PROPRIETARY) LTD
51 Commissioner Street Johannesburg

First published 1970
SBN 17 121005 0
© Otto A. Piper 1970

Printed in Great Britain by
Western Printing Services Ltd, Bristol

TO THE MEMORY
OF
WILFRED MONOD
(*1867–1943*)

Stimulating teacher, spiritual leader,
ecumenical pioneer who through his prophetic vision,
in an age of ecclesiastical parochialism
and dismemberment, encouraged a generation to dare
to think and work in terms of
church unity.

Contents

CONTENTS

viii

Preface

In an age in which Christian life is uncritically identified with social action or self-realization, this book aims at giving a description of what the specific features of Christian action are like. The mission which Christianity has in the history of mankind cannot be achieved unless its specific motivation makes itself felt in its actions. That end will not be attained by means of denouncing the Church's failures and short-comings, or by laying bare the evils of our social order. The fact that everybody knows of them does not move people to improve the situation. Rather we want to point out the close and organic connection in which faith stands with the Christian life and thus Christian ethics and theology. Ever since I had discussed the basic problems of Protestant ethics (*Die Grund-lagen der Evangelischen Ethik*, 2 vols. Gütersloh 1928, 1930), students and friends entreated me to expound the practical implications of what I had said about method and purpose of Christian ethics. In retrospect I am glad that circumstances prevented me at an earlier time from complying with their wishes. The conviction has grown with me that systematic presentations in theology or philosophy must be either a young man's outburst of creative vision or the mature fruit of practical experience gained over a long life. I chose the latter way. I am profoundly grateful to the editor of this series, Dr H. H. Rowley, for sharing this view, and for patiently bearing the prolonged delays in the completion of the manuscript.

Contrary to a present fashion, this book goes to the public without footnotes and bibliographical references. In my opinion the great spirits of the past were right in making a clear distinction between research and systematic presentation. The inductive method of research requires confrontation with the details of evidence and the agreements or disagreements with other scholars' views. The systematic presentation presupposes an intuitive apprehension of the whole subject matter. Its correctness is demonstrated by its intrinsic consistency and its agreements with the underlying facts. Likewise, there is a fundamental difference between the historical and the theological use of the Scriptures. In an historical study such as New Testament theology or Pauline ethics, the author has to indicate the passages of the Bible on which he builds his presentation. In a systematic work, however, he starts from the assurance that the Bible proclaims a unified message in and through the diverse views expressed therein. What makes it relevant and authoritative are not the specific views which the writers of its books held at their time but rather the meaning that in the course of centuries Christian experience has succeeded in finding therein. While any mosaic, attractive or absurd, may be formed by a clever arrangement of its details, a particular passage of the Bible cannot be considered relevant for Christian dogmatics or ethics except for the relation in which it stands to the Biblical message as a whole.

For this reason I have most sparingly quoted verses from Scripture, and only for purposes of historical parallels. Likewise I have claimed freedom in using at times Biblical terminology, while on other occasions employing contemporary terminology, when the original English translation was deemed to be obsolete or misleading.

In an ecumenical age it may seem to be strange that relatively little attention has been paid to Roman Catholic literature. The reason is not to be sought in a lack of deference for the sister church in Rome, but rather in the historical situation. Since the Counter-Reformation, the Catholic and the Protestant treatments of ethics have moved on divergent lines. While contemporary 'dialogues' may bring to light the fact that agreement may be found in certain actions to be performed or certain goals to be reached, the contexts in which such agreements are found are quite different. We do hope that eventually the two Churches will enter into a genuine discussion on the problem of Christian ethics, and by doing so will reach agreement. Yet nothing is gained, in the author's opinion, in a mere cataloguing of particular moral commandments held in common.

We see the fundamental characteristic of Christian ethics in the fact that it is governed by a total image of human life. This book is not meant to be a handbook from which the reader is to learn what is the right thing to do in every situation. Rather through the image of man, which forms its centre, the reader is to realize what is the right attitude towards this world in all situations. Since Christian life is to be lived in this world, human life is not depicted in an artificial abstraction as a self-sufficient ego. Rather man's existence is always related to God's redemptive purpose. In order to implement that image in a relatively exhaustive way, it is necessary to present it in various perspectives, as they are offered by the complexity of the image. As a result, a certain amount of overlapping is inevitable. Thereby the reader is reminded that in Christian ethics, man, God and the universe, or existence and time are not independent entities but rather are known to us in their mutual correlation only.

Theologians complain in our days that communication with our contemporaries has broken down almost completely. In my opinion, that is a misreading of the Church's condition. As in all ages, the Church has been given a hearing, whenever it was engaged in emphasizing the facts which form the foundation of its message. The church has been rebuffed, however, when it wanted to convert people to the acceptance of moral theories. That situation has not changed. Yet even when people refuse to accept what we say, yet are thereby hurt, our message has reached them. They realize that by that confrontation their own religious stance has been shaken, and thereby the might of the powers in which they believe has been broken.

I confess that the compilation of the bibliography gave me more headache than any other problem. The literature in the field of ethics is notoriously profuse and of new publications there is no shortage. Completeness is therefore out of the question. I decided to confine the list to titles in the English language, and to concentrate mainly on recent publications, except for the classical works of the past. The selection had to be further limited. The abundance of studies dealing with particular aspects of ethics is so enormous that it seemed advisable to omit them completely. Only its systems and methodologies of ethics were to be listed. In view of such an *embarras de richesse* it is inevitable to employ subjective criteria. The purpose of such a bibliography cannot be an enumeration of the outstanding works on Ethics, but rather to draw attention to books which illustrate the methods of the various schools.

Part One: Prolegomena

1 The Making of Christian Ethics

A. The Problem

By the term 'ethics' we understand the methodical and critical analysis, description and interpretation of human conduct, as it is regulated and determined by the challenge of a worthwhile or true image of human life. It is by its normative confrontation that the subject matter of ethics differs from phenomenological historical and psychological, sociological, or biological description of human behaviour. In those approaches, the scholar adopts a detached 'spectator' attitude towards his subject. He aims at the differentiation, classification and causal explanation of vital processes. In ethics, he identifies himself with his subject. Accordingly, the scholar points out the reason why he is moved to orientate his will and conduct in a definite direction while rejecting other ethics as incompatible with his nature and/or destination. Like other normative disciplines such as logic or aesthetics, ethics occupies a legitimate place in the development of human civilization. The need for a scholarly treatment of ethics is occasioned by the fact that our moral activity originates in the unconscious or subconscious sphere of our life. The ethicist wants to understand the nature and purpose of his ethical actions, in which he realizes an intrinsic contradiction. Our actual behaviour is not necessarily true life. Since man's mind is capable of misuse, error and misunderstanding, a critical investigation of what we aim at in moral action is required. In order to be handled in a scholarly way, ethics like all scientific endeavours must develop a method of its own, that is to say, one which is determined by the nature of its subject matter. It would be absurd to pursue the goal of ethics in the way of such positive sciences as physics or biology. To begin with, the study of ethics must be based on a moral experience which is fit to lead to general statements. Since there are various types of moral experience, however, the teacher of ethics must state from the outset where he stands and why he takes such a stand. The rationalistic and idealistic types of ethics contend that they start from a general moral consciousness. Yet thereby the scholar's position is surreptitiously granted a preferential place. Yet the same danger lies hidden in the uncritical use of the autobiographical method. In all these cases, the scholar presents his own conduct as though it were the norm or model of all moral goodness.

The investigation contained in this volume presupposes the author's conviction that Christian ethics rests on divinely revealed commandments and examples of moral life which are recorded in the Bible and interpreted in and by the life of the Church. Starting from the Church's experience has a twofold advantage. Such approach remains in contact with actual life yet curbs the subjective element of experience through consideration of the Church's past and present life. Furthermore, our method avoids the error of empiricism, in which a desirable good is treated as though it were an absolutely necessary one. Christianity makes the validity of personal experience contingent on the recognition of the central place which God's work in Christ occupies in Christian life.

Christian ethics is closely related to the history of the Church and thus has an intrinsic unity. But unlike the history of dogmatics, which is more or less a continuous stream, Christian ethics is the theory of Christian activity and thus manifests itself not only in a history of moral ideas but also in the actual life of the Church. The textbooks of Christian morals have contributed far less to the development of Christian life than devotional books, the discipline of the Church, charismatic movements like Monasticism, or Puritanism and the examples set by Christian leaders. Hence the history of Christian ethics is not to be understood as the gradual deployment of a basic idea. Rather it is like the march of a crowd which on its way is joined by other crowds, which walk temporarily in several columns in order to reach a pre-arranged common goal, though apparently without appointed leaders the crowd is never unaware of the direction in which the goal has to be sought.

In its amazing diversity of denominations and churches, and in its long history, Christianity has poured out a large plethora of moral emphases and remarkably divergent duties and goals to be reached. Nevertheless, there is the common conviction that all Christians are living their lives in the service of the same Lord.

There are two essential characteristics of Christian ethics. To begin with, God's and man's activities are interrelated. All aspects of Christian life are ultimately rooted in God's purpose of redemption, which in turn supports and illumines the believer's self. Second, while the Christian's moral life cannot be separated from his religion in its cultic and devotional aspects, they are but means by which his moral life becomes articulate. The life of faith has a subject matter of its own, viz. how to believe in God while living in a world that is not divine. Thus Christian life presupposes theological reflection, but unlike theology which points out the ontic basis of faith, ethics rather deals with the practical implications of the Christian existence.

Durkheim and other anthropologists have rightly drawn attention to the close and inseparable relationship in which moral life stands with religion. In the early stages of man's social history, the whole life of the group is determined by its religious view of reality. Social and political groups and institutions are religious communities, too.

These conditions prevail unchanged as long as individuals are unable to assert their own dignity and selfhood over against their group. The transformation of group religion into personal religion took a long while, because from a pragmatic viewpoint, conformity is highly desirable. It is obvious that conformism saves much tribal energy and prevents unnecessary friction. Exceptional courage and self-assurance were – and still are – therefore required, if an individual wants to assert himself as a moral personality over against social mores.

B. The Development of Christian Ethics
1. *The Origin*
Christian ethics is not an absolutely novel phenomenon in the history of mankind. It is rooted in that of Judaism. Israel's religion was originally a tribal religion, but was substantially transformed by the prophetic movement. The latter is an unique phenomenon in the history of religions. Whereas in other civilizations the emancipation of the individual introduces a subjective element into religion, the prophet's subjectivity disappears behind the 'Word of God' that has come to him. The prophetic movement restored, enriched and deepened the traditional religion of the Jewish people. In it the awareness of Election and of divine commandments given to the nation was combined with the obligation incumbent on each head of a household to make the whole family comply with the law of God.

Jesus continued the prophetic line. Yet being more than a prophet himself, he raised Israel's religion to a new level. True religion, he taught, was not in the first place man's work. Rather it gave expression to man's awareness that God was in search of a people to be gathered out of mankind. Thereby God himself transcended the inherent nationalism of Israel's religion and established the universal character of his people. The very fact that, in dealing with non-Jewish nationals, Jesus acted without discrimination was evidence that the Jewish religion served merely as a paradigm of true religion. It could not be considered the only gate to salvation. Accordingly, the moral commandments were no longer to be understood as offering an opportunity for man, to give evidence of his moral earnestness. Rather they would indicate that God was about to call forth the perfection of mankind on the earth. That divine purpose would imply that the individual did not exist for himself but rather was destined to come to the assistance of any person in need whom God would bring to his attention. By designating himself the 'Son of Man', Jesus indicated that he was not just a righteous man obedient to the law of God but rather the realization of the purpose which God had with man. As a result of his perfect goodness other people would be moved also to comply with God's plan. Thus Christ disclosed the deepest mystery of ethics, viz. that in order to realize goodness man needed to have his will illumined and strengthened by God as he acted in history. Thus Jesus could insist on the finality of his mission. He epitomized his ethical message by enjoining love of God and love of one's neighbour, that is to say, the willing acceptance of what God sends and what he demands especially through our fellow man. Finally, through Jesus, God's purpose with mankind would effectually and permanently be realized.

Jesus would be followed by those Jews who discerned in his teaching a deepening of their paternal religion and moral tradition. In turn, those who noticed but his deviations from the official interpretation of the Law would suspect that Jesus was about to dissolve the national existence of the Jewish people. As can be seen from the New Testament, Jesus' own message was passed on by early Christianity in two different directions. As a result of that differentiation the whole future development of Christian ethics would be moulded in various ways. The Epistle of James, for instance, and the Gospel of Matthew would understand Jesus' Gospel as a new Law, aspiring towards higher standards than those of the scribes. Nevertheless its execution would depend on man's moral will. Paul and the Fourth Evangelist, in turn, would expect the decisive change in man to result from the activity of the Holy Spirit. Paul, in particular, will give a good deal of moral advice by means of commandments. But they are practicable because believers have received the Holy Spirit. Thereby, God enables them to perform what otherwise they would be unable to accomplish.

The two tendencies will be found side by side throughout the whole history of the Church; the charismatic one in Ignatius of Antioch

(d. *c.* 110), Irenaeus (d. 202) and Augustine (354–430), whereas the ecclesiastical or mandatory line is found in Clement of Rome (d. *c.* 100), the Apologists of the second and third centuries, Tertullian (*c.* 160–220), Cyprian (200–258), Ambrose (339–397) and Gregory the Great (d. 604). The charismatic line is often assimilated to prevailing Hellenistic tendencies, for instance to Gnosticism in Clement of Alexandria (d. *c.* 215) and to Neo-Platonism in Augustine (354–430) and Makarios (*c.* 300–380). In turn, the Western part of the Church in particular will transform the Biblical concept of a public law like that of the Roman Empire. Thereby a powerful juridical element would invade the Church. Ethics would be tied up with the institution of the Church. Redemption is no longer an unmerited gift of divine grace, but rather a reward that is proportionate to the amount of good works which a person has performed. Platonic influence will prevail in the East, for instance, in the School of Alexandria. There philosophical rigorism will emphasize a moral perfection, which is to be realized through a methodical training of will and mind. Platonism also accounts for a view of Christian life in which the mind seeks to assert itself over against the material world and the body. Moral activity is confined to building up the inner life. Dualistic movements of the age will give birth to ascetic tendencies, especially in Egyptian monasticism. The example of the 'Desert Fathers' will in turn influence the life of the clergy and the congregations. In order systematically to develop the message of Jesus, learned men in the Church would utilize the method and ideas of the classical philosophers. Ambiguities were unavoidable. The terminology borrowed would be fraught with alien associations and connotations, and the goal of moral life would seem to be the same in philosophy and in the Christian religion.

The catechetical instruction of the ancient Church seems to have followed Jewish modes of teaching: strings of commandments or of virtues and vices had to be memorized. Yet it is obvious that the main source of moral goodness was seen in the examples of spiritual life and strict Church discipline. That fact alone explains the rapid spread and effectiveness of Christianity in the Roman Empire. Nevertheless, in the Apologists one notices already a tendency to describe the Christian life in terms of Greek ethics, that is to say, as the result of volitional efforts. That tendency was increased, once the Church had been given public recognition as the religion of the Empire. Stoicism in particular, which placed its emphasis upon civic virtues, seemed to offer a useful model for the new stance of Christianity.

Paganism vanished but slowly and enjoyed a long after-life especially in the upper classes who would read the ancient classics. Consequently, the Christian occupation with that literature would be mainly of an apologetic character. Ambrose, Augustine and Gregory the Great are anxious to show the weaknesses, errors and immoralities of the classical writers, but do not seem to be able to refute them by original moral systems of their own. That tendency lost its importance, however, when the Western Roman Empire began to crumble in the fifth century. During the tumultuous Dark Age the Benedictine rule proved to be of special significance. The re-establishment of the Empire through Charlemagne and the cultural awakening of the northern countries of Europe would not have been possible but for the stress Benedict of Nursia (480–547) placed on cultural work including the preservation of the remains of classical antiquity. The alliance of Christian religion with learning and education was destined to leave a lasting mark on Christian life and ethics.

2. *The Middle Ages*
It is obvious that in the first half of the Middle Ages, roughly until A.D. 900 or so, cultural life was reduced to a minimum as a result of the unstable political conditions, economic poverty and the dislocation of transportation. No original works are found in the field of ethics. By assiduously preserving a fraction of the heritage of antiquity, the monasteries prevented a lapse into complete barbarism. Yet it is an austere and sober-minded world. Though Augustine was widely read, his charismatic view of the life of grace was looked upon with suspicion and the views of Pelagius were commonly held in honour.

Long before the Great Schism (1054), the eastern churches had almost completely lost contact with the Church in the West. The aim of Christian life was seen in spiritual vision. By means of it, the individual would become aware of the way in which God's Spirit operates upon this world and within it. In that way the whole world would be changed into a symbol of the work of the triune God. No direct interest was taken in this world as such. Care for the sick, the lonely and the aged was not neglected, yet served as means by which the Christian took care of the helpless victims of this world.

In the later Middle Ages, Thomas Aquinas' (1225–1274) *Summa Theologica* is by far the most outstanding achievement. In an admirable synthesis Thomas combines dogmatics and ethics. The life of contemplation is preferred to practical activities. The stress falls therefore upon the development of the virtues. They have a rational basis in human nature, yet must be transmuted by faith in order to be in full agreement with God's will. Unlike his predecessor Peter the Lombard (*c*. 1100–1160), Thomas holds that goodness is basically one because rooted in the goodness of God. Accordingly, the final goal of the believer's life is moral perfection, that is to say, the human will assimilated to God's goodness. A similar view of the Christian life, yet with a strong leaning towards mysticism and a methodical gradual approach to the knowledge of God, is found in Bonaventura (1221–1274). Quite different is the approach chosen by Duns Scotus (1270–1308) and Nominalism. Since in that school God is conceived of as unlimited will-power, man is confronted with him through his commandments. The emphasis of moral life falls here on obedience. As a meritorious work it will receive a divine recompense. Duns' approach shows the dominant influence which the Confessional had gained upon the discipline of the Christian life and the theory of ethic. According to the nominalists, good works are meritorious because they are in agreement with the task God has set to man. It is doubtful, however, according to these theologians, whether man's works are intrinsically good. Nominalism was bound to produce a casuistic treatment of ethics, that is to say, the investigation of which features of an action were or were not in agreement with the divine commandments. The emphasis does not fall upon the intrinsic value of the action as a whole, as in Thomas, but rather upon its parts and circumstances. The inevitable consequence was a growing tendency to avoid what was wrong in an action rather than to desire to do what is good.

During the Middle Ages, the moral outlook of the Church was not exclusively determined by the theories of the schoolmen. The dualistic teaching of the Cathars turned many believers away from a static God of Goodness to an active God, engaged in a fight with the Devil. That new outlook resulted in an excessive fear of Hell, the Devil, and the forces of evil and witchcraft. Petrus Waldus (Valdes, *c*. 1170) and the mendicant orders protested against the wealth of the clergy and advocated voluntary poverty as the true Christian life. This praise of poverty was not a mere introduction of a new moral principle. These were the first rumblings of the Reformation. These movements raised the question: Were the claims the Church made for itself as mediator of salvation credible, when the Church itself was so preoccupied with the things of this world? Francis of Assisi (1181–1226) discovered that faith can be a matter of joy and serenity, because God is at work in all things of this world, even in adversity, suffering and death. Finally it was mysticism that in its various forms laid stress on the transcendental nature of the Christian life. Its final goal, those mystics held, was not so much human goodness, but rather visionary union with God or with Christ. No theological background held all these movements together. They were not concerned with details of moral theory, but rather had a common aim, namely man's ontic relation to God.

3. *The Reformation*

The 'autumn of the Middle Ages' exhibits an outspoken tendency to understand morality as something relevant for the individual's whole life, here on earth, rather than something absolutely necessary because commanded by God. Luther (1483–1546) was so disgusted with the ethical works taught by the schoolmen, that in the beginning of his reformation he was inclined to throw out theological ethics altogether. He would be satisfied with mystical works such as the *Imitation of Christ* ascribed to Thomas à Kempis (1380–1471), and similar mystical works. In his early writings, Luther entertains a charismatic view of spiritual life. Faith, he holds, is God's work in the believer. The Spirit makes the believer do the right things and overcomes all opposition of ill will. When he had to deal with congregations and their problems, however, Luther recognized that the mystics had oversimplified the ethical problem. Thus in later writings, for instance in his treatise *On Good Works*, or in his catechisms, he adopted a descriptive method. Though the average Christian was not to be treated as a charismatic, the description was to show him how far he was still behind the goal for which God had destined him. Yet through regular use of Scripture and sacraments the believer would eventually be transformed by the Spirit. Of fundamental importance was Luther's new ethical perspective. The goodness of our actions does not lie in the difficulty or the effort with which they are performed, as had been held by the nominalists, but rather in the fact that they benefit our fellow men. On the basis of natural law, Luther developed a number of social orders, in and for which the believer had to work. Aided by the Spirit, the believer would learn to use the social institutions beyond a purely formal compliance as opportunities for personal love.

Calvin (1509–1564) shared with Luther the interest in the practical nature of ethics. In the assurance of having been chosen by God, the believer can be certain that God will also grant him strength to execute his will. The goods of this world may be used by the believer, yet with moderation, lest the believer should become their servant. Max Weber (1864-1920) has rightly pointed out that this attitude was one of the roots of modern capitalism.

The history of Protestant ethics is from its beginnings determined by the dialectical relationship in which the Protestant churches stand with the Anabaptists. The latter contended that the Reformers had compromised the gospel by ascribing necessity and a divine commission to the body politic. The Anabaptists, and later on the Quakers, refused all participation in political life and the use of violence.

Parallel with the Reformation runs a secular movement, namely Humanism. In contrast to the Reformers, who started from God's work and his purpose with man, that movement is primarily interested in man, his perfectibility and his place in the cosmos. Their method of ethics is descriptive and analytic. It explores the author's inner life, or depicts great men and their ways of action. We mention Pirkheimer and Machiavelli or Geyler in the sixteenth century, and Montaigne, Descartes, Molière, Bacon and Hobbes in the seventeenth century. That literature is of special interest, because it pursues the question, How far is man as a natural creature capable of doing the good? Over against the crude theological anthropology of sin and obedience (or gratitude) those philosophers developed a highly differentiated psychology of ethics. Descartes proclaimed that on the basis of his rational analysis the ego was an autonomous and self-contained entity. The foundation of a new type of philosophical ethics had thereby been laid. The philosophers' secular outlook would eventually be supplemented and clinched by Pascal's psychology of faith.

The churches of the Reformation were for a long while so preoccupied with questions of doctrine that little was accomplished in the field of ethics. Under Melanchthon's influence, the theologians would treat ethics in the way of Aristotle. God is man's supreme good. What are the most appropriate means by which to reach that good? The answer was given by means of a purely rational procedure. For popular instruction, the official catechisms were deemed to be sufficient, and on their basis ethics was understood as the teaching the Biblical commandments. As a result of the Lutheran concept of the 'third use of the Law', ethical instruction was concerned with the secular aspects of life and was but loosely connected with faith. Things were quite different in Great Britain, where the teaching of the Reformers, especially of Calvin, helped to create a new type of faith in which religion and daily life were intimately connected. While, in a narrower sense, Puritanism designates the mode of life of the Presbyterians, their outlook was shared by such influential devotional writers as Jeremy Taylor, John Milton and John Bunyan, and through the Pilgrim Fathers determined the spiritual climate of North America. Over against the intellectualism of Protestant orthodoxy, the Puritans emphasized their experience of a living, holy and stern God. What counts in God's eyes is man's inner life, his righteousness. The test of its genuineness is seen in its practical manifestations, however. Sincere and unsentimental self-scrutiny is therefore essential for the Christian. Hard work, honesty in economic life, desire to furnish quality goods and active interest taken in the life of the community are symptoms of one's love of God and fellow man. An interesting new branch of Puritanism is the Quaker Movement. George Fox teaches that God reveals to the individual what ought by means of the inner light of the Spirit to be done. The formation of a Christian commonwealth in a world of sin, a dream in Cromwell's army, is here successfully realized. Its secret is non-violence and willingness so to assist the fellow man in need that he will become self-supporting. In a different way Richard Baxter (1615–1691) mitigates the rigorism of Puritanism. In order to fulfil God's will, it is not sufficient to fulfil the commandments. Genuine faith is aware of the Grace of God, which enables people to love each other.

4. *The Dawn of the New Age*
The age of the Reformation saw theologians and philosophers commonly engaged in an endeavour to free ethics from its ecclesiastical outlook in order to make it truly relevant. The two groups soon parted company, however. The humanists would conceive the problem as that of a small and select group of outstanding men. Their objective was the development of the valuable potentialities they found in themselves. The reformers, in turn, had the common people in mind who formed the majority of the church membership. Socially that constitutes a shift from the feudal age in which clergy and nobility formed the relevant upper section of national life, to a bourgeois age. Yet while the religious upheaval helped to liberate the laity from the clerical tutelage, the aristocratic claims are raised by two groups in the bourgeoisie, namely the wise man or philosopher and the dissenter. The latter is sociologically an innovation made possible by the Reformation. In the Middle Ages the dissenter was declared a heretic, i.e. one rebelling against the established authority of the Church. With the absence of an absolute authority in matters of doctrine, the Protestant dissenter feels

himself entitled to challenge the Church and to present himself as the true believer. The wise man or the philosopher, too, contends to be the only true man. Nevertheless, in the seventeenth century that type is anxious to prove its usefulness. He will show that he takes an interest in the problem of the majority. Grotius, the Dutch diplomat, will point out the ethical implications of warfare and the necessity of international law. He can point out that war is not to be thought of as a natural catastrophe. Its outbreak depends on the will of men. Hobbes (1588–1679) analyses the nature of public life and contends that government, self-centred as it may be, is indispensable in order to stay the anarchic and egotistic tendencies of the citizen.

No less important is the shift from a purely rational thinking to experience. Thinkers like Machiavelli, Rabelais or Shakespeare boldly describe man as they see him in his diversity, with all his virtues and vices. They no longer clarify them, as Dante had done. Rather they see in the diversity so many specimens of the same species of man, and help to form a very complex image of the true man.

Christian thinking was slow in picking up the new trend. In the seventeenth century, Pascal in France and Johann Arndt and Calixt in Germany are ahead of their age in restating the moral problem in terms of character or personality. They will supplement the original question, What is the commandment of God? with the no less important question, How am I to fulfil the commandments in such a way that it makes sense in my life? That combination allows a highly differentiated code of ethics. In Pietism, and subsequently in Methodism and the writings of Jonathan Edwards, an elaborate mode of self-discipline, a list of pleasures to be avoided, carefully to be observed, is destined to mould the life of the believer in such a way that he is able to enjoy it.

On the whole, it can be said that from the sixteenth to the eighteenth centuries the philosophers assure leadership in ethical theory. Spinoza and Leibniz occupy a mediating position. They try to combine empiricism with religious speculation. Both of them find the ethical ideal in a life of order. Spinoza notices in this world a thorough-going order and co-ordination. Man, too, must live in agreement with the universal order. Leibniz will emphasize that the universals are real in individuals only. Each one must become aware of his place in the universe lest he should act contrary to his destination. The most powerful impetus, however, comes mainly from the Enlightenment of the eighteenth century. The philosophers' thoughts reflect the advance of the bourgeoisie.

They recognize the importance of their role in the economic life of the nation and demand full recognition of their new power. In France men like Voltaire and the cosmopolitan Quaker Thomas Paine (1737–1809) will point out that governments are not to be considered divine institutions. They are man's work and hence may be altered, if they have ceased to operate in accordance with their intrinsic logic. In England Locke discovers usefulness and pleasure as the two principal motives of human action but recognizes the authority of God as moral legislator and a divine reward granted for moral goodness. A similar view is held by William Paley. Hume, however, holds that a purely empirical approach to man's conduct is feasible. He still sees people held together by a common sense of sympathy, we would say class consciousness. Bacon and the Utilitarians contend that in order to be meaningful and relevant, human action must be useful. German philosophers like Lessing teach man's moral obligation to develop from traditional to personal religion. Man is to become aware of the fact that he is a self-contained and self-sufficient being. Notwithstanding its national differentiation, the Enlightenment ascribes to man the use of reason as an innate right. Nothing ought to be regarded as a divine commandment, unless it serves man. Furthermore, the individual is free in the selection of the means by which his goal is to be reached. There is a noticeable tendency to look for the seat of ethical obligation in the individual's nature rather than in a divine will outside of man. This belief in human freedom rests upon an optimistic conviction of man's goodness. Not only the Reformers' stress laid on original sin has been discarded but also Hobbes' warning against the natural wickedness and lawlessness of man as a social being. Adam Smith, in particular, will show that economic life, when freed from all legal and social ties, will not only pay dividends to the businessman but also to the national economy. Bentham (1748–1842) tells his contemporaries that true happiness will be enjoyed, if and when each individual will work for the greatest possible happiness of the greatest possible number of men. Unlike the earlier types of ethics of personality, which were based upon self-observation, the moral outlook of the Enlightenment and its aftermath is based on the infallibility of science. This optimism formed the foundation and was the undoing of all the experiments of socialist settlements in the first half of the nineteenth century. That development is the more remarkable in view of the fact that Zinzendorf was fully successful in founding settlements of the (Moravian) Brethren. His foundations consist of knowledge of God's will, honest recognition of one's sins, unselfish co-operation and satisfaction with whatever is one's condition and undismayed trust in God's kindness.

That development did not proceed unchallenged. The University of Cambridge in particular would cling to a Platonic understanding of ethics. The movement has shown its intrinsic vitality and strength in the fact that it was periodically revived, the last time in modern intuitionism. Likewise, the aristocratic tendency became vocal again in Burke, to whom the democratic element in modern ethics seemed to be the claim of a 'swinish multitude'. The theologians were unable to answer the philosophical development. They tried to show that the Christian ethics, too, was promoting man's happiness, or they insisted that, except for the Biblical instruction, the human reason was unable to know the difference between right and wrong. The humanistic develop-ment of ethics was more or less in opposition to Christian ethics. Yet it was not able to proceed in complete disregard of Christian ethics. Both in method and in forming its specific image of man, the secular views were far from being original creation. It was obvious that Western man's mind is heavily indebted to a long Christian education. Thus the philosophers would content themselves with what they considered supplementations or corrections of the Christian image. From Christian theology, they borrowed the idea of eschatology for their notion of progress or the successful result of moral action. The idea of Election would necessitate the distinction between instinctive animal life and moral decisions. From the idea of the divine law they learned to make a distinction between subjective wishes and objective moral goals. But it had not yet come to anybody's mind to investigate how far philo-sophical ethics could go by itself, on the one hand, and what difference Christianity would make to ethical thought in general, on the other.

C. The New Start
1. *Kant and Schleiermacher*
Right down to the last third of the eighteenth century, theology had either completely ignored the new trends in philosophical ethics or had completely surrendered its identity. The result was equally harmful to philosophy and theology. Almost simultaneously, the development was challenged in either realm by Kant (1724–1804) and Schleiermacher (1768–1834). Kant's contribution to the study of ethics is called forth by the empiricism of the Enlightenment, in particular the utilitarianism of British philosophy, on the one hand, and the claim of supranaturalis-tic theology to teach the only true ethics, namely that revealed by God,

on the other. Kant retorts that empiricism overrates its possibilities. It is able to show what is desirable, and why it should be desired. But whereas the ethical standard makes an absolute demand and hence requires a metaphysical foundation, man's conscience confronts him with two basic demands: the motivation of a particular action must be fit to form a general ethical principle, and human beings should never be used as means for reaching one's own goals. Kant does not present a moral system. The moral decision will depend on particular situations and special interests. Yet my intention to perform an appropriate moral action must be tested by these 'categorical' standards. Characteristic of the moral action is also the freedom of the acting person. Freedom, as Kant understands it, means freedom of motivation in spite of practical obstacles. One must not be motivated by consideration of happiness or success but exclusively by the goodness of the principle selected. The ethical character of an action is determined by one's self rather than by the circumstances or the practical value of the action. Kant's historical significance lies primarily in his 'transcendental' method. He shows that in the ethical action two groups of factors are at work, namely the universal and unchanging structure of 'practical' reason, by which all moral acts are identically determined, and psychological, biological and social factors, which condition a particular moral act. They are subject not only to historical change but also to misjudgement. Kant has wrongly been criticized for his purely formal treatment of ethical life. Over against the rational speculation of the Enlightenment, he stated clearly that all moral action implies a practical element, whose specific character must be considered in the moral decision. Yet the standards by which that is done result from the absolute demand made by man's reason.

Where Kant is weak is in his acosmism. No consideration is given to the fact that the moral urge is dealing with the condition of this world. The moral obligation implies recognition of the fact that this is a world which ought to be changed, and that man is destined so to do.

Whereas Kant and his disciple Fichte (1762–1814) interpreted the self as a creative individual who moves between the extremes of desire and duty, Schleiermacher considers the ego a field of operation in which the Mind conditions Nature. Man lives in a universe by which his life is constantly influenced. According to Schleiermacher, the imperative method, though commonly used in ethics, is incompatible with the Christian view. It presupposes an innate goodness in man by which he would be enabled to comply with a demand whose source is alien to him.

Instead, a descriptive method is required in order to do justice to the fact that the moral will is a gift of divine grace. The teleological element which the philosophers of the Enlightenment had so cherished yet interpreted in a utilitarian sense only, is envisaged in a cosmic perspective by Schleiermacher. Man is destined to live exclusively under the sway of the Mind, or to express it in theological terms; he has to be sanctified by the Holy Spirit. Thereby man is assigned a definite role in the development of the universe, namely to engage in the furtherance of social institutions. One deficiency of Schleiermacher's concept is his view of development. He overlooks the dramatic nature of history. As in the theology of the eighteenth century, the destructiveness of evil is not taken seriously enough. Like Leibniz, Schleiermacher holds that a whole (e.g. the Church) is real in the harmonious co-operation of all its specimens. True unity is unity in diversity and diversity in unity. Thereby Schleiermacher overcomes the rationalistic idea of unity as uniformity. He shows that in ethical action there is not only room for personal viewpoints, but also that without the mark of one's personality the action lacks genuineness.

Both Kant and Schleiermacher exercised a momentous influence upon the thought of the nineteenth century, especially through the Neo-Kantian philosophy which flourished at the end of the nineteenth and the beginning of the twentieth century (e.g. Windelband (1818–1919), H. Cohen (1812–1918), Wilhelm Natorp (1859–1929), Rickert (1863–1936). The idealistic outlook of Kant and Schleiermacher is responsible for the prevalence of individualism in German Protestantism to the present day. Schleiermacher found his main successor in A. Ritschl (1822–1887). He held that the Christian vocation meant that the believer had to transform nature into God's kingdom, i.e. culture. Following the increase of political rights on the part of the bourgeoisie, that practical interest of Protestant ethics shifted from cultural activities, learning and the arts to economic, social and international problems. A straight road leads from Ritschl via Rauschenbusch (1861–1918) to Reinhold and Richard Niebuhr on the one hand, and from Harnack (1851–1930) to G. Wünsch and H. D. Wendland on the other. A self-contained individual is supposed to be moved by his spirit to transform this world, yet the ego is anxious not to lose his identity by merging with that process. Moral action is to be performed for the benefit of the needy rather than in communion with them. Situation ethics is a recent offshoot of those ethics. Yet whereas according to Schleiermacher the difference of personal character provides the principle of differentiation, the modern ethicist hopes to derive a guiding principle from the specific nature of the situation.

Another important development that has its roots in Schleiermacher's ethics is found in the Erlangen theology of Harless (1806–1879), J. C. K. von Hofmann (1810—1817) and Frank (1872–1899). Like Schleiermacher they derive theology and ethics from an analysis of the Christian faith. They hold, however, that in Schleiermacher's system the social institution is treated as a mere product of history. Their objectives would therefore change according to historical circumstances. While there is room for historical changes, the social institutions are implied in man's creation. Hence, they never change their goals and their basic principles of responsible action. Paul Althaus and Elert have revived that type of ethics. Finally, it should be mentioned that Kant's view of the autonomy of the moral sense has been understood in popular ethics as meaning that the voice of conscience was in each man endowed with absolute authority. Thus whatever an individual felt he should do gave him right and obligation to execute, if necessary in contempt of statutory laws. As a result, such opposite attitudes as nonviolent civic disobedience and violent revolution, or enthusiastic participation in warfare and conscientious objection, have been advocated side by side in the name of conscience.

2. *Recent Developments*

a. GERMANY

Strange to say, Kant's and Schleiermacher's critical analyses of ethical action were far from immediately bringing about schools of thought. They stimulated and advanced ethics and thought in general. Yet one might rather say that, more than any previous period of history, the past one hundred and fifty years were a fertile breeding ground of a large number of individual systems. Yet each of them enjoyed a limited following only. In a way such development should not surprise us. It brings to light the fact that the ethical analysis encounters special difficulties. It can never be performed in pure abstractness. The moral action takes place in a concrete world and is the work of individual men. However, the principal reason for that new development is to be found in a radical change of the moral outlook. Originally, the aim of ethics was the individual's desire to be or to become good. Under the influence of eighteenth-century utilitarianism, however, the emphasis is shifted towards the improvement of living conditions in this world. While personal ethics is not completely dropped, it definitely plays a subordin-

THE MAKING OF CHRISTIAN ETHICS

ate role in contemporary ethics or forms a field of its own that is not connected with social problems. Closely related with that shift of emphasis is a shift in subject matter. The overwhelming portion of ethical literature is now devoted to particular problems of social and international reforms rather than to the problems of man's place in the world and its relation to God's Spirit. In Kant's own country, Hegel had described human history as a teleological process, namely the self-actualization of the absolute spirit. The individual ought to act in accordance with the phase of history reached in his time. In his early period until c. 1935 Barth adopted a similar view. Conversely the whole idealistic approach was categorically rejected by Feuerbach (1804–1872) and Karl Marx (1818–1883). They interpreted the ethical phenomenon as a mere extra projection of human hopes and fears, or, in Marx's view, as an ideological superstructure of class interests. Wilhelm Wundt (1832–1920) would contend that the movement of the Spirit could not be described adequately except by studying all of the world's civilizations and ethics. Paulsen (1846–1908) would object to Kant that regard for the personal dignity of his fellow men would not be an ethical attitude unless man felt an innate sympathy with the problems and needs of all men. Nietzsche (1844–1900) asserted that the ethical outlook was symptomatic of a degeneration of the vitality of the human race. In recent times, Max Scheler (1874–1928) and Nicolai Hartmann (1882–1950) would attempt to replace the Kantian criteria of moral goodness by a Platonic intuitionism, which would start from a multitude of values directly evident to the individual. Man's moral effort was discredited by Schopenhauer (1788–1866) and his disciple Eduard von Hartmann (1842–1906) as a vain attempt to improve the conditions of a world which is thoroughly worthless. In the course of the nineteenth century, idealistic tendencies are coupled with a feeling of man's unlimited strength, which rests on the progress of science and the complete freedom of speech. Typical is Pfleiderer (1839–1908). The evolutionary process, as far as man is concerned, is a moral rather than a biological advance. Man grows up to the awareness that through his reason he is destined to restore the unity and freedom which this world had lost on the lower stages of its evolution. In a similar way, Rudolf Eucken's (1846–1926) philosophy represents an objective idealism in which ideas from Goethe are blended with liberal Protestant theology. In order to live a true life man must become aware of the spiritual forces at work in the universe. They help to build up the mental and cultural life of man. The opposite attitude is taken by M. Heidegger

(b. 1889). His existentialism is an avowedly atheistic ethics. In his self-awareness, man finds himself thrown into a universe which proves to be alien to him. In a Stoic attitude the individual must assert himself against that universe by treating it defiantly and with disdain. In that way, the individual frees himself from the fetters of necessity by which the universe had enchained him, and he becomes truly himself.

Just as in philosophical ethics, German theological ethics is represented by an amazing number of original thinkers, yet with the exception of Erlangen and the Ritschlians there are no schools of thought. The explanation lies probably in the complete detachment from church life, which attitude the professor of theology guarded as his most precious privilege. Thus he enjoyed absolute freedom in his interpretation of the Christian message. Nobody had the right to check his subjective excesses. De Wette (1780–1849), e.g., seeks a synthesis of philosophical and theological ethics, in which philosophy will be the guide, while theology helps to implement the ethical ideals. This basic aim is also shared by J. A. Dorner (1809–1884) and Richard Rothe (1799–1867), but their outstanding characteristic is a tendency towards theological speculation, on the one hand, and the desire to grant cultural life a full measure of recognition in Christian ethics, on the other Rothe is the first representative of secularized Christianity. He entertains the hope that Christianity will so thoroughly permeate public life that the Church will become superfluous.

Johann T. Beck (1804–1878), a pietistic biblicist, moves in the opposite direction. From the Bible he wants to derive a psychology of faith, which describes how the believer is sanctified step by step. His successor Adolf Schlatter (1852–1938) moves in the same direction, yet unlike Beck, he wants faith to be applied to church and public life. Bishop Martensen (1808–1884), under the influence of Schleiermacher and Hegel, wants the Church to apply as a national institution the virtues of love and the urge of the conscience to contemporary problems. Martin Kähler (1835–1912) interprets the whole life of the Christian as a process of justification. In it the Spirit gradually sanctifies the individual, that is to say, God renders the individual willing to overcome the forces of evil in his heart and in this world. Wilhelm Herrmann (1846–1922) adopts a similar position. Yet his starting point is the inner life of Jesus. By its image the Christian is gradually transformed into the likeness of Christ. Over against the prevalence of abstract dogma in German Lutheranism, Herrmann rediscovered Luther's original view of faith. Kierkegaard (1813–1855), whose significance was not appreciated until half a century after his death, stressed the significance of subjectivity and personal commitment in Christian life. The believer must be willing to endure the horror of the living God's judgement, rather than fall victim to a notion of God by means of which faith would be rendered pleasant. The social interest of German Protestantism took a new turn, when Wichern (1808–1881) in 1848 proclaimed the Church's inescapable obligation to come to the rescue of its needy, neglected and sick members. Fliedner (1800–1864) and Bodelschwingh (1837–1910) implemented that programme by founding in church homes semi-monastic orders of deaconesses and deacons, who would dedicate their lives to the care of the underprivileged and incurably sick. Yet that work of the 'Inner Mission' did nothing to improve the general conditions of the lower social classes. The 'Religious Socialists' (e.g. Ragaz (1868–1945) and Kutter (1869–1931)) decided to expand the Christian social task by co-operating with political socialism. Out of similar considerations, the Dutch theologian Abraham Kuyper (1837–1920) deemed it necessary to organize a specifically Christian political party in order to render the social teaching of the Church effective in public life.

The deep-shaking experience of World Wars I and II vibrates in the works of Emil Brunner (1889–1966), Karl Barth (1886–1968) and Dietrich Bonhoeffer (1906–1945). Common to all of them is a theological realism. Their starting point is the awareness of God's activity in this world. Man is confronted by an absolute will from which there is no escape. Essential for Christian ethics is therefore the willingness to recognize one's sinfulness and inability ever to be perfect. There is a conservative tendency in Brunner, who sees the Christian's task in preserving the social institutions. Barth, in the latter phase of his theology, prefers a dialectical duality. There are institutions that go back to the creation of man and must be left intact as such. Others are rooted in the redemptive work of Christ. Their purpose is to transform the present shape of the world. As a result of his premature death, Bonhoeffer has not left us a fully developed system of ethics. His aim, it seems, is a Christian existentialism. Ethical life is not so much a compliance with general principles or specifically religious activities but rather life with God as he encounters us in our daily contact with non-Christians.

In the second third of this century, German theology was shaken to its roots as a result of the Church conflict in which the Confessing Church withstood the threats of National Socialism on the one hand, and by the political upheaval following World War II on the other.

Hellmuth Tielicke and Wolfgang Trillhaas are the most characteristic representatives of that development. Trillhaas, whose roots lie in the Erlangen theology, strives to reinterpret the traditional problems of Christian ethics in the light of modern philosophy, especially that of Husserl. Tielicke combines in an interesting and original manner a theological existentialism with a situational approach. Thereby he succeeds in making ethics relevant for modern readers. Yet by doing so he does not always escape the danger of losing the Christian perspective.

b. FRANCE

In France, the radicalism of the Enlightenment gave way in the early nineteenth century to an interest in steady reform of which the thoughts of Cousin (1798–1857) and Lamennais (1782–1854) are symptomatic. Fourrier (1772–1837) and Proudhon (1809–1865) advocated a kind of Christian socialism, which proved to be a complete failure because it was based upon a naïve belief in human goodness. Very popular for a long while was the positivism of Auguste Comte (1798–1867), a strange blending of science and metaphysical speculations. Yet people liked it because it nurtured the hope that with an intrinsic necessity science would bring about sound social and political conditions which the Church had been unable to create. The only counterweight to Positivism was for some while the ethical idealism of Renouvier (1815–1903), who upheld an enthusiasm for freedom and responsibility in a world of scepticism. A new impetus was given to ethical thought in literature and art by Bergson (1859–1941). His mystical appeal to the *élan vital*, in which objective idealism was blended with biological evolution, was apt to let the zeal for reform appear worthwhile. By Teilhard de Chardin (1881–1955), the attempt was made to draw out the lines from Bergson to the Christian dogma by means of a teleological hypothesis. Heavily indebted to Kierkegaard and Heidegger, yet presented in a typically French perspective, is the existentialism of Sartre (b. 1905), Camus, Genet and Simone de Beauvoir (b. 1906). Their basic theme is the absurdity of human life. Man's reason destines him for a meaningful life. But his biological nature and this world's lack of co-operation render the fulfilment of that task impossible. Man is doomed to endure that hell, because there is no escape from it.

c. U.S.A.

Down to the end of the eighteenth century, ethical thought in North America espoused on the whole the mentality of the home country and its various denominations, with a preponderant role played by the Puritans. Yet religious thinking was increasingly tinged by the philosophy of Locke and the Enlightenment. The first beginnings of native thought are found in Jonathan Edwards (1703–1758), Benjamin Franklin (1706–1790) and Thomas Paine (1736–1809). In the nineteenth century, the U.S.A. finds itself confronted with the childhood problems of the Republic, and with the gigantic challenge of a rapidly expanding continent. The relatively quiet conditions of New England did, nevertheless, provide an audience for the idealism of Emerson (1803–1882) and the romantic praise of nature in Thoreau's (1817–1862) ethics. While idealistic ethics were taught in some colleges, they lacked originality and failed to make a noticeable impact. The national mentality, interpreted as that of a 'nation on the march', was finally given adequate expression in the pragmatism of William James and John Dewey (1859–1952). James draws attention to the fact that moral goodness makes no sense unless something is thereby accomplished. Dewey reminds the nation of the fact that settling a continent is impossible except when people trust in their innate resources, and are prepared to co-operate in freedom with each other. Josiah Royce (1855–1916) gave a new impetus to the American brand of idealism by emphasizing its social and political implications. 'Situation ethics' is the most recent attempt to reconcile the moral obligation with a maximum of freedom by deriving the obligation from, and directing freedom towards, the demands implied in a given social condition. The vicissitudes of national history and the many practical tasks confronting the churches explain the scarcity of original theological works on ethics in the nineteenth century. The catechism and the strictness of church mores on the one hand, and the fiery revival movements on the other, served to keep the congregations aware of God's demands.

Characteristic of American church life is a succession of nationwide ethical campaigns, in which the interest is focussed on the abolition of some single evil, for instance the emancipation of the slaves, prohibition of alcoholic beverages, pacifism, or, recently, civil rights for the negroes. A contribution of lasting significance was made by Finney's (1792–1875) insistence on holiness. He did not only denounce the depravity of the sinner, as was common in the revival movements, but also pointed out the blessings of the Spirit's sanctifying power, by which a person's conduct is radically transformed. In turn, the one-sided predilection which Dispensationalism and Fundamentalism showed for theological correctness was not conducive to the development of ethical responsibility.

More in line with American activism is, around the turn of the nine-teenth century, a growing interest in social and international prob-lems. Christian life, it was held, is not and cannot be an end by itself. Rauschenbusch's Social Gospel and the *Christian Century*'s advocacy of social and international justice did much to awaken the nation to the reality of the evils which expected a Christian solution. Yet, on account of the pragmatistic approach of those reformers, their ethics tended towards secularism. That weakness was overcome later through the alliance into which the Social Gospel entered with Neo-Orthodoxy. Reinhold Niebuhr (b. 1892) was the forceful pioneer of that change. Tillich (1886–1965) sought to restore the interest in personal good-ness. Yet on account of his ontological method he had difficulties in doing justice to the historical character of the Biblical events. A real return to the theological foundation of Christian ethics is visible in H. Richard Niebuhr (1894–1962), John C. Bennet (b. 1902), George Thomas (b. 1899), Paul Lehmann (b. 1896) and Waldo Beach. Paul Ramsey (b. 1913) combines the Christian perspective with Natural Law. Over against the quietism, which focusses on moral sentiments and disposition, yet never comes to action, modern ethicists, e.g. George Forell, will emphasize the significance of moral decision. Over against moral legalism, this view points out the risk of erroneous choice.

d. GREAT BRITAIN

In Great Britain, the first half of the nineteenth century is dominated by a utilitarian view of ethics based upon empirical grounds. The naïve utilitarianism of Mill (1806–1873) and Bentham (1748–1839) receives a psychological basis. Over against the earlier assumption that human nature is unchanging, Herbert Spencer (1820–1903) notices a process of historical evolution in which people learn gradually to give up attitudes and actions by which society would be harmed. As by Comte in France, so by Spencer, the moral action is no longer inter-preted as performed by self-contained individuals. Rather it takes place and develops within the social group. Sidgwick (1838–1900) will further refine that method. Man's cruelty and inhumanity can be endured, when one realizes that mankind is on the way to a truly humanitarian conduct. That evolution may be interpreted in an entirely different perspective can be learned from Thomas Huxley (1829–1895). Follow-ing Darwin, he reaches the conclusion that man has by no means over-come or shed the earlier stages of his development. Hedonism must be rejected, because man has learned that like other animals he had fiercely to fight against the encroachments of his fellow men.

Side by side with the utilitarian tendency, one finds an idealistic trend is as a rule growing up upon a Christian basis. Social reforms were advocated by Thomas Carlyle (1795–1881), Frederick Denison Maurice (1805–1872), and Charles Kingsley (1819–1875). Ruskin (1819–1900) propagated a new creative approach to culture. In more recent times a metaphysical school passionately opposed to the prevailing nationalism, pleaded the necessity of a theistic basis of ethics. Its main representatives were T. H. Green (1830–1882), Bernard Bosanquet (1840–1929), F. H. Bradley (1846–1924), Edward Caird (1835–1908), G. E. Moore (1872–1958), A. E. Taylor (1869–1945), and Seth Pringle-Pattison (1856–1931). While these philosophers offered a moral proof for the existence of God they did not go into the details of practical life. They confined themselves to advocating moral goodness in general. Pointing out their lack of reality in idealistic ethics, nevertheless the logical positivism of Wittgenstein (1886–1951) and Ayer (b. 1910) itself also remained sterile in the field of ethics. The linguistic approach to moral theory remained on the whole confined to the Anglo-Saxon world. It originated in modern times with G. E. Moore (1875–1958), and was espoused and in various respects modified by Charles Stevenson (b. 1908), R. M. Hare (b. 1919), Stephen Toulmin (b. 1922), A. J. Ayer, and others. The linguistic analysis of ethics proved to be unsatisfactory, because it dealt with verbal utterances only, which as commandment, explanation and judgement may accompany the ethical act. They did not get the moral act itself into focus because the latter is non-verbal.

In the field of theological ethics, Great Britain for a long while adopted an apologetic approach. The utilitarian views were modified rather than rejected, e.g. by H. Rashdall (1858–1924), and the traditional teaching was shown to be superior to empiricism because established on Revelation. The bishops, e.g. K. E. Kirk (1886–1954) and H. Hensley Henson (1863–1947), will emphasize the value and necessity of church life and church discipline, while the laity is inclined to adopt the evangelic line of personal goodness. Typical of the Free Churches is B. J. Dale, who indicates the shift from Puritanism to Evangelicalism. That tendency was continued in greater depth by P. T. Forsyth (1848–1921) whose Christocentric theology did full justice to the Incarnation as the foundation of Christ's presence. Symptomatic of a widespread trend in British theology was the teaching of A. M.

Fairbairn (1838–1921). In order to safeguard the absolute character of Christian ethics, he proceeded from philosophical theology and ethics which were to be supplemented by theological elements.

While such approaches to Christian ethics won followers, the efforts of Carlyle and his friends to engage the churches rather than individuals in social activities had originally a rather limited success. Likewise the Ritschlian theology, which was brought to Great Britain in the beginning of the twentieth century, e.g. by A. E. Garvie (1861–1945) and W. F. Lofthouse (1871–1966), was too academic to arouse great enthusiasm.

Throughout Europe one finds in the late nineteenth century a growing awareness of the cleavage between the ideas and social movements of the modern age on the one hand, and the traditional Christian attitude on the other. Whereas on the Continent that development led increasing numbers of people away from the Church, one notices in Great Britain after World War I a firm determination to bring the Christian moral patterns up to date (e.g. Gore, Streeter, Dean Inge). The strongly evangelic undercurrent in the Labour Movement, the problems of the mission field (William Paton, George Oldham), early ecumenical contact, and a keen interest taken in social problems, especially by the Student Christian Movement, led in 1924 to the Copec Conference under the leadership of Bishop Charles Gore (1853–1932) and Bishop (later Archbishop of York and then Canterbury) William Temple. That 'Conference on Christian Politics, Economics and Citizenship' resumed on a broad basis Carlyle's vision of concerted social action on the part of all the churches of Great Britain. This comes within social ethics. Yet over against the former tendency to choose a single doctrine (Incarnation, Church, New Life, or Holy Spirit) as starting point, efforts are now made to see the moral task in the light of the Christian faith in its totality.

D. Conclusion

A survey of historical developments like the one given above is bound to bewilder the student by its amazing multiplicity and diversity. What right do we have to speak of 'Christian Ethics' in the singular, when every writer on the subject seems to be proud of his ability to give a unique and original presentation. Where do we find the unifying element?

Furthermore, our survey shows the close interrelation of philosophical and theological ethics. In that process, theologians on the whole have shown greater open-mindedness than their philosophical colleagues. Our survey should also make us aware that in the confrontation of the two types or methods, a number of questions have been asked on either side which thus far have been left unanswered. For instance, Leibniz had already stated that the only way in which a universal can become real is through the operation of its particulars. On our side, theologians have objected, however, that in the case of the Christian religion any pluralism would be a betrayal of its absolute claim. Another question concerns the quality of man's nature. If man were substantially good, he would not feel challenged by moral demands. In turn, however, if he were entirely depraved, how could he ever be able to do what is good? How evil and how good then is man? Furthermore, man is able to increase his knowledge and to improve his abilities in the process of time. Would the Bible be an exception from that rule of growth and obsolescence? In turn, does the historical nature of human life preclude a divine revelation of unchanging truth? Or take the fact that we live in a world full of evils. Yet there is also good reason to give thanks to God for many benefits. Is evil a mere illusion? Or, to accommodate the pessimist, are the world's goods but disguised evils? Again, how do we reconcile the unconditional character of the moral commandment with the fact that moral actions which do not serve a useful purpose are meaningless? Moreover, throughout this world we notice the operation of a Mind or Spirit. But how is that Spirit related to the Holy Spirit of our redemption? Are there two spirits, one created and one uncreated? Or, if there is but one, does he work redemptively and with equal strength and effectiveness everywhere in nature and human life? But then, what significance does the work of Christ have? Finally, what do we mean by 'real'? Only the objects given to sense experience. But what about the determinants of our earthly life such as time and space? Or, also, such determinants of our existence as the order or the equilibrium of the universe, and the urge to grow as found in animal life? Are they not real, because not sensually perceptible? Is God not real, although he is the supreme determinant of our life? These and similar questions must stand before our mind, as we proceed to our presentation. Our first question will be, Is there any hope of avoiding some of the limitations enumerated above by choosing an appropriate method?

2 Methodology

A. Perspectives
1. *The Problem of Method*

As the modern age dawned, a cleavage developed in the treatment of ethics. Protestant and Catholic theologians alike continued the authoritarian method of the Middle Ages. They disagreed essentially in one respect only. The Catholic divines would place the commandments of the Church on the same level as the commandments directly revealed by Gcd, whereas the Protestants denied spiritual significance to Church law. Outside of the official teaching of the churches, a new type of ethics was advocated whose goal it was in a practical way to instruct people how to become truly human. It was Spinoza and Grotius in particular who insisted that in order to have cogent authority, ethics had to be worked out in a scientific way. They were horrified by the inhumanity that was possible in people who made every effort to keep God's commandments. Right through the Enlightenment of the eighteenth century that Humanism was conceived of by most philosophers as a system of ideas derived in a deductive way from supreme and self-evident premises. Yet, since ethics has to do with actions, thinkers of the second half of the eighteenth century would emphasize the importance of adequate motivation. Practical usefulness, happiness or pleasure seemed to be goals worthy to be pursued. The new outlook required a shift in method from the deductive to an inductive method. One had to start from given situations or needs, and to ask oneself in what way the desirable goal might be reached in the most satisfactory and sufficient manner.

In his transcendental method, Kant offered an entirely new approach to ethics. Neither of the traditional views was certain to attain to the truth as long as all the elements which formed moral action had not been clearly defined. For that purpose a careful analysis of ethical life had to lay bare the structure of the mind. It would show that ideas as such had no motivating force. One might admire the consistency of a system of ethics without feeling the urge to live accordingly. In turn, it was of the essence of moral life to make itself felt as a categorical imperative which addressed itself to one's will and demanded unconditional compliance. According to the utilitarian or eudaemonistic view the goal to be reached would be chosen according to the individual's wishes or needs. Yet an empirical factor would not suffice to give general validity to the obligation. The motivating power, according to Kant, was not to be sought in subjective conditions or needs, but rather in the approval of the individual's practical or moral reason. Self-respect would impel the ego so to act that any conflict between his true nature as a person, on the one hand, and the practical consequences of his action, on the other, would be avoided. While the practical necessity to act would lie in the individual's needs as a citizen of this world, it would be up to his moral reason to decide which motivation should be adopted. This understanding of the 'autonomy' of practical reason would also separate Kant from the authoritarian method of the teleological ethics of his time. Kant's critics objected that his reliance upon the power of man's moral faculty would lead to a mere formalism. It would demand of man to be good in general while leaving it entirely to his discretion what in particular ought to be done in a given situation. That is the main problem which besets the 'ethics of decision' or situation to the present day. Does the analysis of the moral mind suffice to explain the nature of the moral action?

2. Modern Approaches

Schleiermacher noticed sagaciously the basic weakness of Kant's approach. The philosopher's 'autonomy of reason' would end in subjectivism as long as God was a mere transcendental idea in man's consciousness, as Kant contended. Schleiermacher gladly recognized the value of Kant's analytical method. But whereas Kant was eager to expel all vestiges of metaphysics from ethical life, Schleiermacher would take his departure from the metaphysical presuppositions of moral life. Since ethics is dealing with things to be done, the basic approach must be an ontological one rather than an epistemological one. Apart from the assurance of a universal power by which the universe is kept going, and man is integrated into it, there would be no sufficient motive for man to act morally. Schleiermacher had learned from Kant that the moral obligation would be compromised if one started from practical needs which man pursues in this world. The theologian must rather start from the gracious operation which the Holy Spirit performs in the hearts of the believers. Like the Kantian, such an approach would find the specifically moral quality of action

27

in the awareness of the privileged role which the believer was able to perform through the indwelling Spirit. In agreement with this pneumatological approach moral life could not be confined to the performance of duties, as was held by Kant. Rather, in addition to commandments, moral life was also concerned with attitudes taken, goals aspired for and values acknowledged. Schleiermacher succeeded in combining the theonomy which characterized the ethics of Protestant orthodoxy with the Kantian autonomy, by discovering a synthesis of those aspects in faith.

The significance which Schleiermacher had for the development of modern Protestant ethics can hardly be overrated. There are, nevertheless, some aspects of ethical life which had been ignored by the great theologian. It was especially man's predicament, as caused by the conditions of this world, that was emphasized by the philosophers of the nineteenth century. J. S. Mill pointed out that Kant's moral absolutism had lost sight of the fact that, in order to be meaningful, moral deeds must have a practical significance, too. The utilitarian character was not an incidental feature of moral action but rather its presupposition. Herbert Spencer will draw attention to the importance which the historical process has for ethical theory. Far from remaining the same throughout the ages, as the theory of natural law no less than Kant and Schleiermacher contended, the moral life of man is subject to evolution. Human life runs through successive stages of gradual improvement and deepened understanding of its purpose. Hence people have a right to rebel against traditional ethics by which the *status quo* is galvanized. They may proclaim new attitudes and duties appropriate for their age.

In a different vein, confessional Lutheran theologians like Harless will remind the Church that the world in which we live is not a mere neutral raw material to which God's commandments are to be applied. Rather, this world has a definite structure given by God, the so-called 'orders' or 'ordinances of creation'. They manifest themselves especially in social life. Objective idealism as taught by Hegel and his followers would go even further by interpreting this world in all its aspects and areas as the necessary manifestation of Absolute Reason. Man was not to consider himself free to mould this world as he pleased, but rather had to treat it according to its nature and intrinsic rational tendency. Whereas Hegel asserted that true reality could be found in general phenomena only, never in particular facts, romanticists such as Kierkegaard would contend that one could not consistently assert the meaningfulness of this world as long as it was seen in its general structures and its species only. Each particular entity was also meaningful in itself. As a result naturalism, rendered most popular by Thomas Huxley and Freud, would proclaim it to be the individual's moral task to assert himself over against repressive influences. In a different way the individual's right of identity was understood by subjective idealism. It was held to imply the obligation to develop one's potential nature into full actuality. Whereas the idealists interpreted that potentiality in purely ethical terms, existentialists like Heidegger and Sartre discern in the individual a conflict between the Ego and this world into which he had been 'thrown'. Heidegger, as well as Christian existentialists like Bultmann or Gabriel Marcel, expects 'authentic existence' eventually to triumph over the cosmic forces. However, the French school of the Absurd (e.g. Sartre, Simone de Beauvoir or Camus) would hold that in spite of the transcendental necessity of individual self-assertion no ultimate meaning could be found in human life.

That resignation was the final phase of a pessimistic trend in modern ethics. Its roots may be found in the Christian dogma of the Fall. In opposition to that view, Rousseau believed in the basic goodness of human nature. He would explain the unsatisfactory character of present social conditions as the result of an unfortunate lapse of our ancestors. Its consequences might be remedied, however, by means of a return to the original state of social relations. In a similar vein, the Romanticists, e.g. Görres, Byron or Victor Hugo, would propagate a return to the splendid conditions of past epochs or periods of history. Over against the optimistic belief in man's power to bring back the original state of things, Schelling was so moved by the prevalence of evil tendencies in this world as to postulate a permanent cosmic dialectic between good and evil forces. As a result man's ethical life was permanently wavering between constructive and destructive actions. That view was brought to life again in our day by Tillich. In a different way, Schopenhauer started from the insuperable contrast between the rationality of the human mind, and the utterly irrational character of this world. He refused to see goodness in a world of suffering transitoriness and decay. The only hope he indicated for a meaningful life would consist in the individual's flight from practical life into aesthetic contemplation of beauty. Under the influence of scientific determinism, finally, Spengler would expound a fatalistic type of ethics. According to him history was dominated by an intrinsic necessity of self-destruction. Its pattern was beyond man's control. The only possibility to live a truly human life would consist in man's willingness to adjust himself to the demands of his epoch, even though he realized his inability to influence its deadly course.

An exit from the impasse into which ethical theory had manoeuvred itself is offered by the advocates of situational or contextual ethics (e.g. Brunner, Joseph Fletcher, Paul Lehmann or Harvey Cox). They realize the inadequacy and the practical failure of the older types of imperative ethics. Preaching ethical commandments has hardly ever changed people's hearts, let alone made them act contrary to their interest. Yet equally unsatisfactory is Christian existentialism, which identifies 'authentic existence' with a vague concept of love. As a remedy, it is suggested by the situationalists that the individual give up the idea of being a self-sufficient ego and recognize himself as standing in a fellowship with other individuals, or in the community of the Church. Love, that is to say the recognition of such ontic relatedness, would then eventually lead to a harmonious relationship in which the interests of all the partners would also be fostered. Quite apart, however, from the vagueness with which the concept of love is used in this and similar types of modern ethics, the awareness of relatedness will not by itself prompt people to promote the well-being of non-Christian institutions.

In the light of these developments, it should be obvious that neither the deductive nor the inductive method, nor the transcendental analysis of ethical life, is sufficient to explain the nature of the moral attitude. We have to realize the fact that underlying all moral actions is an ontology or a myth of a transcendental reality by which the moral urge is explained. Unless that presupposition of moral life is recognized, the moral demand cannot be adequately interpreted. That objective cannot be attained, however, except within the context of the reality in which we live ourselves. We cannot start from a general concept of Being, as is done, e.g., by P. Tillich or H. R. Niebuhr. It is necessary not only to analyse all the areas, dimensions and tendencies of the social reality in which ethical life takes place in order to ascertain the specific obligations which accrue to man from each of them. No less important is a study of the determinants of human existence, because from them depend the limits and the direction of ethical action. In turn, however, ethics is not ontology. We must discuss such topics as man's function and predicament within the universe, the nature of this world and of time, the redemptive work of God, and so on, in order to state why moral life is possible and necessary. But we only use what dogmatics and experience have taught us.

3. Ethics and Theism

All ethical life, in order to be meaningful, requires satisfactory answers to be given to two questions. First, what is the reason that moral activity is an indispensable part of human existence? The reason cannot be found in human nature, for people may live in disregard of morality. The very fact that the individual is free to reject the moral urge is a constitutive element of moral life. In turn, the necessity implied in oughtness differs essentially from causal, logical or aesthetic necessity and cannot be derived from any of them. Likewise, when materialism contends that moral life is the necessary reaction of the ego to a chemical or physical stimulus, the fact is disregarded that equal stimuli can produce opposite reactions. Materialism wrongly substitutes conditioning factors for effective causes. The second question is this. How do we explain the fact that ethical action produces tangible effects in this world though it is not a working cause in this world? How to explain the fact that man is capable of making the transition from seeking what is advantageous, as do also the animals, to pursuing moral goodness? When Sartre contends that the transition is never made, he simply misinterprets the facts. True enough, man finds it difficult fully to overcome his egotism. There is a wide gap between our attitude by which we pursue nothing but our own interests, on the one hand, and a moral outlook, no matter how much it may be marred by the wish to earn thereby pleasure and happiness or by the hope that its outcome will be profitable.

The ancient philosophers were intuitively aware of the fact that moral life cannot be understood as the natural outcome of man's being a part of the animal world. They tried to explain the uniqueness and ontic peculiarity of the moral obligation as the result of man's special relation to the deity or at least to a cosmic condition arranged by the gods. The conviction that moral life should have a transcendental basis was held as the unquestionable axiom which determined the ethics of Western philosophy down to the age of the Enlightenment. Kant's profound analysis of 'practical reason' led him to the assurance that apart from the idea of God, ethical life would lack objective meaning. The empiricism of the British philosophers since Hobbes, however, was in striking contrast to the traditional view. Though Kant had pointed out the intrinsic contradiction of moral empiricism, it remained a potent factor in the ethics of modern times. Kant showed that the imperative character and the absolute demand of man's moral consciousness could not be understood as commandments which he was giving to himself.

In turn, Kant did not deny that the human wishes which formed the subject matter of eudaemonism, hedonism and utilitarianism may at times be very powerfully felt. But man would sacrifice his dignity as a human being if they were allowed to make an absolute claim over other ethical values such as truthfulness, compassion or fidelity. Furthermore, as Kant argues, truth is not, and cannot be, man's creation. His mind only tells him the difference between true and false notions. That, unlike the limited validity of scientific knowledge, the moral values should claim absolute validity, points to a transcendental origin.

Yet, paradoxically, it was Kant's idea of the autonomy of moral reason that encouraged the modern philosophers to continue their search for an empirical foundation of ethics. For Kant, however, the autonomy of practical reason meant that moral consciousness must be consistent with itself in order to make valid demands because it is a specific faculty of its own. It must not be influenced by practical considerations of expediency or self-interest. Autonomy did not mean, however, that the individual or the social group is able to be its own lawgiver. Its function is purely critical. The practical reason's authority lies exclusively in the right and ability to decide about the validity of commandments which pretend to be moral.

Kant did not discuss the way in which man is rendered capable of making such decisions. The distinction he made between things by themselves and things of experience points to the way in which he reasoned. In order to be able to judge the moral validity of a commandment, man must be related to a reality by which the realm of action is both transcended and determined. However, ethics is not concerned with the theoretical knowledge of such determinants or values. Theoretical reason or science may tell us in an objective way that moral actions exist and are appreciated by some people. Such knowledge may lead us to admiration or even imitation, because we are ambitious and would like to see ourselves on the pedestal of perfection. The demand implied in the moral consciousness belongs to a different dimension. It directs the individual towards a goal to be reached or a claim to be acknowledged. Hence the transcendental reality that determines us in moral experience must be seen in a teleological perspective. This important distinction is overlooked in the ethics of the Cambridge Platonists, by G. E. Moore, or by Max Scheler. Ethical values strike us as being evidently good, and thus having universal validity.

Humanists and subjective idealists seem to heed that aspect of moral experience. According to them a distinction has to be made between man's actual condition, on the one hand, and his true or final nature on the other. By means of an intrinsic dynamic or acts of man's will the final goal would be attained. The moral imperative would be the awareness of the way in which that goal enters into man's consciousness. However, if man's goal is identified with the image he formed of himself by means of his wishes, it will be purely subjective. There is no cogent reason why other people should adopt my image, nor why reaching it should be considered a necessity for me. It is true to say that in their actions people are guided by an image of themselves. Yet there is a fundamental difference between the image which is the product of wishful thinking fed by our ambitions and imaginations, on the one hand, and the guiding moral image formed by the moral values apprehended in my moral life, or my *Wunschbild* and my *Leitbild*. If, as the idealists postulate, an intrinsic dynamic transforms man into his ideal image, the moral obligations might be considered the implementations of that image. However, that transforming urge could not be identified with the ego or the genius of mankind. It rather would be the operation of a transcendental force. For the ego comprises man's biological nature no less than his mind. Hence, human life is characterized by the conflict of moral and biological reality. In the order of nature, the satisfaction of our biological needs must take precedence over man's mental and moral aspirations (*primum vivere, deinde philosophari*).

Likewise it is hardly feasible to build ethics upon man's superior stance in the universe. It is true that the categorical character of the moral claim demands that the good should be done irrespective of the intrinsic trend of nature. Yet although man has amazing discoveries and technological achievements to his credit, he is in his moral life permanently harassed by the forces of nature. Defying nature could therefore be a futile and meaningless enterprise, unless man could be sure that he was himself part of a cosmic plot, by which his moral activities would eventually prevail over the cosmic forces. Nietzsche attempted to build moral life upon the individual's will to live. All that was apt to develop him biologically would be called good. The traditional systems of ethics with their reliance on a transcendental reality were, according to him, evidence of a debilitated will to live. Nietzsche was aware of the destructive element implied in vigorous vitality. His hope, therefore, that in the evolutionary process 'superman' would eventually come out on top was based on the wisdom and power of the evolutionary impulse. Yet, his belief that evolution was controlled by acts of the individual will, and that superman would be able to employ his strength at the expense of the weak without destroying himself, is contradicted by the research of biology.

The transcendental reality, whose existence is presupposed in the moral act, has been interpreted in two different ways. The pantheistic and panentheistic systems from Neo-Platonism over the mysticism of the fourteenth century to Hegel and Bergson explain the moral attitude in an epistemological way. While the cosmos is constantly in motion, the individual is inclined to regard himself as an independent entity. Moral life is concerned with the apparent contrast between what the individual thinks he is like, on the one hand, and his existence as an element of the cosmos, on the other. Life remains meaningless until the individual is fully aware of having his being in the cosmos rather than in his particular existence. Yet such correction of one's self-awareness is not the moral act itself. It is but its prerequisite. The real problem is to be seen in the distance between what I am like and what I ought to be like. That distance differs essentially from the temporal distance between the now and the not yet, the effectual distance between cause and effect, or the axiological distance between partial worth and perfection. Unlike those distances, which may be overcome by an intrinsic cosmic movement, the moral distance presupposes a transcendental will by which irrespective of man's approval a necessary goal is set before man which man nevertheless ought to realize. If the goal had already become real in our life, the goal would not manifest itself as an obligation but rather as a privilege. If we adopted Tillich's idea of man, for instance, human life would be a dialectical process alternating between demonic and numinous impulses. In the interest of man's happiness, it might be wise to prevent either tendency to move to its full extreme, but so to do would not be morally necessary. Tillich assigns a central position to love. Thus, it occupies a point of indifference. It may manifest itself constructively, yet also destructively. Yet love is then used in an ambivalent way; which direction to go would therefore be a matter of prudence rather than a moral decision.

We conclude. In order to be meaningful, the moral obligation presupposes a transcendental deity, which determines the goal of human existence. In view of the interdependence of man and the universe on the one hand, and the autonomy which the moral obligation enjoys over against nature on the other, the deity must have a worldwide purpose and be in control of the whole universe. These requirements are met by the God proclaimed in the Bible. The reason for the superiority of the Biblical religion is not to be sought in the supreme consistency of monotheism, but rather, in the unique manner in which the moral obligation manifests itself as originating in the personal relationship of God and man. God manifests himself as redemptive will, and man recognizes himself as destined for the service of God.

The question now arises whether the trinitarian view of God as held by Christianity offers any advantages for the understanding of ethical life which are not found in the strict monotheism of Judaism or Islam. The answer should be a categorical Yes. As Jesus rightly pointed out, if this world and human life are understood exclusively in terms of a creator God, existence at all times must be accepted as it is because it is willed by God. The outcome is either a fatalism as in Islam, or a particularism as in Judaism. Either position implies an inconsistency, however. The God of Islam is the almighty maker and ruler of this world and often hardly more than the power of nature. His commandments must be accepted as they are given. That view satisfies the categorical character of moral consciousness, but no room is left for the subjective aspect of moral life. Judaism, in turn, proclaims a God who made all men of one blood yet who grants a special hope to the Jewish people. The Pharisaic expedient of explaining such exceptional privilege as a reward for the moral goodness of the Jews is blatantly contrary to experience and the Biblical message. The God of the Old Testament deals in a seemingly inconsistent way with his people. He insists on the one hand on obedience to his commandments, while on the other hand he is ready time and again to forgive their trespasses and sins. If explained as rooted in the lordship of God, such behaviour appears to be an arbitrary attitude. In turn, there would be no reason why a God who was but grace should ever have created a finite world and singled out a people for himself. These seeming inconsistencies are overcome in the New Testament.

Viewed from the trinitarian perspective of the New Testament, the moral phenomenon makes full sense, however. The uniqueness of the absolute demand corresponds to the unique role played by man in this world. The demand is not rooted in the uniqueness of man's physique or mind. Rather they are expressions of the fact that man is destined to perform a unique function in this world. Though by nature man is a member of the animal world, he is reminded by the voice of his conscience of the fact that he has a unique role assigned to him in this world: whereas his mental life differs but in degree from that of the animals, his moral conscience is evidence of his being lifted above all other earthly creatures. That distinction does not result from the special

35

effort which man has made in history in order to improve human nature. Rather, it is the prerequisite of human nature. God's kindness may be seen in the fact that God created him for that function though by nature man was not equipped for such a task. That man should be able to act in accordance with his conscience may be explained as an outcome of the evolutionary process, but it is not brought about by a natural energy. Rather, it is an indication that man has been endowed with a special faculty, namely the Spirit.

Notwithstanding his moral consciousness, however, man is inclined to disregard God and his demand. Yet, in spite of the moral rule of God, mankind has not been exterminated. Seen in the light of the New Testament, human life as such implies a contradiction: namely, man's disregard of the Creator's will on the part of his creatures. Only God himself is able to change that condition which man has brought upon himself. Yet a universalism of redemption based upon the fact that all men are created by God would be inconsistent. It would mean that God who had proclaimed his sovereign will to mankind had then completely ignored man's disobedience. Salvation is not the necessary outcome of the creation of this world. In Jesus Christ, God reveals the fact that he has a saving plan with man and that with that plan in mind he created man. Human existence is not an end in itself. In the execution of that plan it is God who takes the initiative. In sending Christ, God also indicates that salvation, far from realizing itself automatically and universally in all men, presupposes faith on man's part. Thereby man shows his willingness to overcome his rebellion against God's plan and to accept God's offer of redemption. Such willingness would remain wishful thinking, however, but for the fact that in faith the spiritual power of life is set free and operates in the believer. By this trinitarian view of the different 'works' of God, God and human spontaneity are brought into a relationship in which both God's sovereignty and human will, as also a cosmic purpose and ethical activity, are brought into a satisfactory and consistent relationship. There is a close correlation of the moral experience and the work of God as described in the New Testament. The moral life is not a mere preoccupation of man with himself. Since it reflects God's will, the moral action is never without consequences. It is subject to the moral order to which God has subjected human life. But those consequences have a provisional significance only. Disobeying the will of God does not immediately bring about the extinction of the individual. Rather, man is allowed morally to make a new beginning as a result of which his destructive impulses are curbed and social order is rendered possible. Therein, we have a sign of the kindness of God. Creation is not for the mere purpose of giving evidence of God's unlimited power. It manifests also the interest God takes in his creatures. God's nature reflects itself in this world, or to use the New Testament language, this world was made by God, yet through the Son. For that reason man is not discouraged by his constant moral lapses. He feels intuitively that whatever he does in response to God's will makes a contribution to God's cosmic plan. In other words, in the continual response to the moral demand, we experience the operation of God's Spirit active in our hearts. The divine foundation of moral life explains the paradoxical fact that man takes morality so extremely seriously, yet rejects moralism. Moral life is not an end in itself. It is both the way in which God uses man for the execution of his plan, and also man's response to God's demand.

B. The Descriptive Method

Thus understood, Christian ethics is intimately connected with Christian faith. The latter is the awareness of what God is doing redemptively for man, while ethical life is concerned with man's response to God's self-disclosure in man's life and human history. Since both aspects of the Christian life are dealing with interrelations of man and God, neither the imperatival nor the transcendental method will be appropriate for the presentation of Christian ethics. For it is concerned with the means by which the moral obligation is realized no less than with its recognition of God's demands. Experience should have taught us that the imperative method, that is to say the enumeration of the divine commandments or man's duty, lacks motivating power. It is true that the imperatival method has proved to be highly effective in the catechetical instruction of the Protestant churches. But the result was not due to the intrinsic power of the Ten Commandments and other Biblical instructions, but rather to the authority and the example of the teaching churches. No wonder that with the disintegration of that authority the catechetical method was abandoned.

The transcendental analysis, which since Kant's days has become rather popular, has its serious shortcomings, too, no matter whether it is practical from the epistemological, logical, sociological, anthropological or psychological viewpoint. While it produces criteria by which genuine moral statements may be recognized, it does not deal with ethical phenomena, as they concern us, but merely with our knowledge about them. The method which in such a situation commends itself is a descriptive one, which deals with the moral experience as a reality in whose midst we stand, or as a divinely inspired process in which we participate in a responsible way. The technical difficulty of such a method lies in the fact that the description must concern itself with the whole of Christian experience. In order to bring out our own commitment we have to choose our personal experience as our starting point. Inevitably, our image of the Christian life will be conditioned by our cultural affiliation as well as our denominational membership, and most likely also our specific ideas derived from the scholarly treatment of dogmatics and ethics. By means of historical research and comparison, we must attempt to ascertain the divinely wrought facts which underlie the whole Christian history. Since all our religious knowledge rests upon God's self-disclosure and since God does not change, we may confidently assume that certain aspects of God's work will come to light, which determine the bewildering diversity of Christian history. This does not mean that we attempt to formulate a kind of ecumenical theology or ethics which would replace the manifold types of Christian life. Rather, we see in the denominations and theological systems more or less adequate expressions of Christian understanding of God's self-manifestation. What guides us in such an enterprise is the vision of the plan which God pursues in the history of Christianity, and which determines our own life of faith, too. This telic outlook characterizes the comprehensive and transforming activity of the Spirit. It distinguishes our description from an historical description which merely enumerates the facts and events in their chronological and causal relationships. It is inevitable that in such an enterprise a subjective element should be found. The collection and selection of the material to be used for this picture is in each case conditioned by the theologian's own experience and outlook. Such subjectivism is tempered, however, by two factors. The material which forms our picture has been recognized by the Church as genuine manifestations of the faith, and thus as the work of the Holy Spirit. Moreover, the extraordinary consequences of many of those acts will in their objectivity set limits to the theologian's subjectivity. The selection of material will be further facilitated by the fact that unlike dogmatic theology the subject matter of Christian ethics is but slightly dependent on denominational or historical positions.

At first sight such a picture of the Christian life may appear to be inconsistent. For it embraces the ascetic ideal of the Coenobites of the Nitric Desert as well as the Episcopalian business man living in one of

New York's desirable suburbs, the Baptists in Soviet Russia no less than the people of the well-to-do middle class who form the mainstay of the established Lutheran Church of Sweden. The very co-existence of those seemingly diametrically opposed types will lead us to the realization that what they have in common in spite of their manifest differences is not to be sought in certain ideas or dogmas, on which they are all agreed. Rather, they are held together by the common influx of God's Spirit who directs them from the diversity of their spiritual and theological stances to God's ultimate goal. The purpose of the picture presented by Christian ethics is not meant to inform the Church about the diversity of ethical experience. Rather, it states what it is that leads the Church into the depth of spiritual understanding of its commitment.

In the light of that purpose the relationship of philosophical and Christian ethics should be discussed. It is obvious that for its scholarly treatment, Christian ethics may learn a lot from the viewpoints and methods of philosophical ethics. The philosophers have been able to draw the theologian's attention to areas and aspects of ethical life which had been neglected or overlooked in theological research. Conversely, however, the theologian will point out to the philosopher that as a result of the disregard for, or the misinterpretation of, the transcendent God and his purpose, he fails to pay sufficient attention to the spiritual depth of ethical experience. Hence the philosopher's view of human life is doomed to remain a provisional one.

Assigning to Christian ethics a purely descriptive role may seem to be absurd in view of the many commandments found in the Bible. But the grammatical form in which the will of God is expressed should not conceal its true intention. It was Paul and John especially who pointed out that in the Old Covenant it was natural that God's will should be understood as demand. God had manifested himself in Israel's history primarily as infinite and unlimited will. It was hard to tell whether in dealing with his people God was motivated by kindness or whims. With the coming of Jesus, however, a radical change took place. Through the Incarnation God disclosed what by faith in Christ man is able to become. The imperative form is still retained, yet does no longer express that man is under orders to work towards his perfection. Rather a promise is hidden in the commandment. The imperatives give expression to the fact that the goal which man is to reach has been rendered accessible by God. Thereby, people were driven to the admission that Jesus described what in God's eyes is the true human life. The message presupposes a radical change in man's relationship to God which has been brought about by fellowship with the Son of God. A new operation of the Spirit has been initiated by the messianic work of Jesus. While the average Christian is aware of the fact that his belief in God's redemptive work must have its repercussions in his conduct, he is not always certain of what that means in his actual life. The assistance which the theologian offers to him in that respect—usually through the medium of sermons and church instruction—will not immediately move him to action unless, as a member of a church, he is convinced that those who teach him have right and authority to do so. The situation is relatively simple in the Roman Catholic Church. There the dogmas proclaimed by the bishop as infallible teacher, bearer and dispenser of the gifts of the Holy Spirit have an undisputed and unquestionable authority. Attempts made at the Vatican II Council and afterwards to modify that dogma have been unsuccessful.

The case is more complicated in Protestantism, because we lack an official teaching office. However, the Protestant confessions of faith point to the divine authority of the Bible as God's revelation. Its inerrancy as the revealed Word of God obviously places it above the authority of the Roman hierarchy. Unlike the Roman Church, by which the Bible is treated as an extraneous lawbook, the Reformers have indicated that faith places a man voluntarily under the Scripture. Thereby he becomes himself part of the revelatory process, of which the Bible is the most conspicuous aspect. The Christian employs the Bible as the Word of God which God addresses to him personally, and from which he is anxious and willing to learn divine wisdom. Unfortunately, however, the Bible needs interpretation. Jesus himself demonstrated that necessity through his powerful re-interpretation of the Old Testament laws. The history of Biblical exegesis teaches that there is great and disquieting diversity in the interpretation and comprehension of the Bible. The reason is not to be found in the ambiguity or obscurity of the Biblical text or in the arbitrariness of the exegetes, though both factors have never been completely absent. The main reason lies in the fact that, as God's self-disclosure, the Bible must be understood as an organic whole. Doing so depends not only on one's spiritual experience, but also and above all on one's spiritual depth and maturity. One might even be tempted to contend that the transcendence of God would render all knowledge of God impossible. In fact, however, Christianity has always held that God's factual revelation enabled man to have at least an analogical recognition of God. Thus, in spite of their divergent interpretations, believing exegetes may legitimately claim that their exegesis points to the truth, though none of them has a right to call for sole and exclusive teaching authority for himself. That situation does not lead to relativism, however. As any Christian, the theologian will subject his views to the test of experience. The consequences of his interpretation will bear testimony to the spiritual origin of his views, or to their lack of genuineness. His experiences will not only verify his being on the right path, but also the correctness of his particular insights. Thus, the theologian is a witness of the ethical truth. That testimony, in turn, will enable those whom he teaches to assess the credibility of his statements.

Notwithstanding the normative role which the Bible plays as instrument of God's revelation, its historical character must not be overlooked because it is constitutive for the formation of Christian ethics. Since God has a redemptive purpose with mankind, which is executed in the course of history, God's ongoing self-disclosure will imply references to the progress of God's work and to the spiritual significance of our age. In that process, as J. C. K. von Hofmann and G. von Rad have rightly pointed out, there is a succession of events through which, in ever-widening and deepening degree, God not only carries out his purpose but also discloses its progress. Thus, as phases of his total plan, the events of the past do not become obsolete when new events happen. It is in that sense that we use the Old Testament no less than the New Testament. While it does not represent an absolute truth, we recognize its authority as the record of the first stage of God's redemptive history.

C. Subject Matter
What exactly is it that we are to describe in Christian ethics? In a most general way we might say Christian ethics expresses the self-consciousness of Christianity as it responds to the disclosure of God's redemptive will. For that purpose Christian ethics refers constantly to God's activity as it manifests itself in personal experience and in holy history. Those references are not used as illustrations of an unchanging principle but rather as disclosures of the presence and dynamics of the Spirit in Christianity. Schleiermacher had adopted a similar method, but failed to do full justice to the purposive character of the Spirit. According to that great theologian the work of the Spirit moves from primitivity to perfection, whereas in the New Testament ethics is in the service of a process which leads from a world unredeemed and in need of redemption to a comprehensive redemption. What is recorded in the Bible, and what we gather from the history of Christianity, are therefore events which point beyond themselves to the goal which God

wants to attain to through the activities of Christianity. As a result of that telic self-consciousness, Christian ethics differs essentially from any other kind of ethics in structure and content. Something is happening in Christian life as it stands under the influence of Christian ethics, both on the part of God and of the believer. Hence, its subject matter cannot be reduced to a few value judgements as is done by Herbart, or to a few theological concepts, as suggested by Joseph Fletcher. For in such cases sight has been lost of the divine activity to which man may react. Likewise the interrelation of Christian experience and ethics cannot be reduced to an ontological framework, as is done at times by Tillich. The Biblical material introduced by Tillich, for instance, serves merely to illustrate the attitude of faith. Ultimate being is not described as taking the initiative in the process of redemption, and hence is unable to set a goal to man. As in Aristotle, God is merely the cause by which reality is kept in motion.

Also unsatisfactory is the identification of Christian ethics with Biblical ethics. Of course, Christian ethics is impossible to describe unless constant reference is made to the Scriptures, and certain Biblical passages such as the Decalogue, the Sermon on the Mount, or I Cor. 13, will recur time and again in all types of Christian ethics. But the aim of Christian ethics is not reached by a mere enumeration of Biblical commandments or attitudes. It was in a process of dynamic self-disclosure that the Holy Spirit was at work in the making of the Bible. Likewise the meaning of the Bible is not grasped by merely describing its place in history. Its contents must be related to the spiritual experience of the reader and the Christian fellowship to which he belongs. In that way, Christian ethics has its centre in God's work rather than in man's. It is not the historical description of a dead past, but rather the proclamation of the power of the Spirit as he acts in us as members of God's people.

Part Two: Foundations

3 Man

A. Createdness and Creatureliness

A theological description of Christian life, it would seem, should begin with the role played by God in the believer's life. Yet ethics has a practical function which cannot with impunity be disregarded by the theologian. It is to lead people to a deepened understanding of their nature and their place in God's universe. That is the reason why all the great teachers of Christian ethics deemed it advisable to start with anthropology. They agreed in that respect with the sages of ancient Greece, who held that in order to act rightly, man must first know himself as an ethical being. By proceeding in the same manner, we do not fall into the traps of humanism, for in the Christian perspective, man and God are correlated in an inseparable association.

What man is like can be studied by biology, psychology, sociology, anthropology, and a dozen or more branches of science. All of them, however, provide but fragmentary sights of man. While all of them furnish valuable insights to the student of ethics, his principal attention must be directed towards man's relation to God. Man's capacity to act ethically rests in his being a creature. That is to say, the existence and history of the human race is not the incidental outcome of organic life here on earth but rather owes its origin to an all-embracing purposive will. God's creative work accounts for the createdness of man, that is his ontic primacy and dignity, yet it also implies man's creatureliness, that is the limits that are set to his will and development. As a creature man has from the moment of his origin his nature and his goal assigned to him by God. The meaning of his life, while influenced by what he is and does, nevertheless is derived from his ultimate destination, which is to be God's agent in the spiritual transformation of this world. That destination explains man's sense of self-transcendence. Unlike plants and animals, which acquiesce in what they are, man is unable to content himself with his actual condition. Apart from the Christian faith, he has no clear idea of the 'beyond' of his existence. He may seek it in what goods he acquires, be it wealth or power or renown, or in what he makes of himself, for instance wisdom or strength or skills or goodness. For the Christian the self-transcendence consists in his ability to be used by God as his agent. Thus man proudly recognizes that he has been placed high above all the other creatures, but he is also aware of the fact that in order to reach his destination he depends on God for opportunity and strength.

In turn, his creatureliness places man on a level with the rest of this world. He has not been made of a special supernatural substance, but is made of the same stuff as plants and animals. In the awareness of his primacy, he seeks the source of his strength in himself. That is his undoing. He tries to act as though God and his plan did not matter and man were able to make himself the master of his destiny. It is this attempted disregard of God which the Bible calls sin. Yet such emancipation does not deliver man from the ties by which he is attached to the rest of the universe. Instead of being an act of liberation, sin fetters him. The more vigorous and comprehensive his attempts to assert himself in this world, the more man becomes the slave of the limitations which characterize the creatures of this world. Createdness and election impart to man the power to dominate this world, while his creatureliness makes him dependent on divine support yet leaving him freedom to make or not to make use of God's aid. Thus man has an enormous power. He is capable of disturbing the order and balance of the universe. As a result of his sinfulness, man is not only in a position to harm other creatures; he has also become the permanent disturber of this world.

Man seldom becomes aware of the inner contradiction into which sin has thrust him. By the grace of God, man's createdness is not withdrawn from a sinful mankind. Man differs from all the animals by the awareness of his ability to transform natural objects and materials into goods of civilization, for instance tools, weapons, household implements, and by possessing a unique faculty, namely the intellect by means of which he is enabled to proceed from the sensual perception of particular things to the awareness of general features. Thus human life has a telic character, that is to say, it is preoccupied with attaining to goals. Thus man and man alone, has science and technology, and on a higher level art, philosophy, religion and ethical aspirations. Yet whereas Greek philosophy, for instance, held that man's specific equipment is the basic datum and that man's destination consisted in bringing about a civilization, Christianity considers both equipment and attainments as mere means. Their provisional character is seen in the lack of final satisfaction that accompanies civilizatory enterprises. Yet apart from the Christian faith, people will seek the reason for their lack of satisfaction in the nature of things or circumstances rather than in the wrongness of their understanding of man's destination. On account of his self-inflicted imprisonment in the things of this world, man in his sinfulness is unwilling to recognize the wrongness of his life. As can be seen, for instance, in Hinduism and Buddhism, even when he turns away from civilization in the narrower sense, religion itself becomes a means of self-assertion. Only God alone in his redemptive work is capable of enabling man to reach his destination. In turn, however, the fact that God himself has to come to the rescue of human life, indicates that the inner contradiction of man is not a mere paradox, as Sartre holds, but rather an intolerable contradiction. Its 'absurdity' does not lie in the nature of moral life, as the French existentialists contend, but rather in man's attempt to treat means as an end. Sartre hopes to render the 'paradox' acceptable by the fact that the un-good man who in the moral act wants to be good, sets to himself that goal, thus overcoming his lack of goodness.

Yet sinfulness is not to be understood as an inescapable fate, for instance in a dualistic way as the work of evil forces against which God himself is unable to prevail. Such a view is incompatible with the Christian idea of God as creator of all things. Likewise, sin cannot be interpreted, as Tillich does, as the result of man's finitude. Our finitude is the reason of our imprisonment, not of our sin. It is of his own accord that man wants to live his life irrespective of God's will and work. Yet since he relies on the infinite possibilities of his mind and will, he is helplessly trapped by the immensity of the universe, to cope with which his limited strength is entirely inadequate.

Since human life implies both the primacy of man's createdness and the limitations of his creatureliness, the life of faith, too, is characterized by a strange ambivalence. In his condition, his nature, actions and achievements the Christian finds much to deplore and to condemn. Grateful as he is for the support by which God's Spirit enables him to acknowledge the wrongness of sin, he finds himself thoroughly conditioned by the practical outlook of his environment. Thus even Christians are tempted by the wish to reconcile the will of God with the pursuit of their own interest, and often succumb to such a temptation. There lies the error of synergism by which Christian life is so frequently vitiated. Instead of realizing that God had to do what man is unable to do, viz. to render man God's agent, Pelagius and his modern followers consider goodness as a value which man realizes by his own initiative and goodness, to which enterprise God is bound to grant success. Contrarily, the theology of Pelagius is probably the clearest evidence of the fact that man never really loses sight of his createdness. As a result the awareness of the ambivalence of ethical life may lead to a pessimistic or nihilistic view of man, yet people do not destroy their lives for moral reasons. Wherever that seems to be the case, closer scrutiny will discover a mental or physiological defect, which is disguised as moral scrupulosity.

B. Essence and Relatedness

In order to emphasize the specific character of ethics, Greek philosophers would describe ethical life as a process that was concerned with the inner life of man. Goodness was defined as the control which man's mind or reason held over his physical life or his passions. Since the body was only to be employed as the mind's slave, little or no attention was paid to the specific life of the body and its relation to this world, in which it moved and worked. Helpful as this outlook was in focussing the centre of the moral decision, it proved to be fatal in other respects, especially when applied to Christian ethics. That man in his totality of body and mind had been created by God, and that he had to live in this world, was strongly emphasized in dogmatics as constituting the human predicament, but seemed to have little or no significance for Christian ethics.

This condition was not substantially improved, however, by those theologians who patterned ethics after the model of 'natural ethics'. It was based upon the fact that there are values embedded in the nature and structure of this world. Moral goodness was supposed to consist in respecting and safeguarding them. That method proved to be unsatisfactory, too, because the 'natural law' would thus confront man from the outside, whereas Christian theology was inquiry as to what meaning there was in man's being placed into this world by God. When carried out consistently, the 'natural law' sees goodness realized in the world of things, and man's task is confined to recording that goodness. What ecology describes for biological life, namely that a certain species is unable to live to its own satisfaction and to thrive except in a suitable environment, applies to ethical life, too. Man is doomed to engage in futile mental exercises, unless his ethical life is lived in the place assigned to him by God. For his ethical life man needs an appropriate environment in time and space. In time, it depends on tradition, heredity and opportunity. Human life would never advance, but rather stagnate and simply repeat itself as in the case of other animal species, unless there were a living past making itself felt as a determinative impulse in the life of the present generation. Equally essential is the presence of a world of his own consisting of objects within which he proceeds, upon which he is able to act meaningfully and whose characteristics condition his modes of action and thinking in a sensible way. Imagine a world whose nature were so strange and inscrutable that the human mind lacked all faculty to investigate it or to respond to its moves in an appropriate way. You will soon realize what deep wisdom lies behind the stories of the Creation, in which man is depicted as God's agent appointed for useful and responsible work in this world. In Christian thought, no room is left for a self-sufficient man who existed detached from his world, or related to it incidentally only. Not only was he created in connection with the rest of the universe, but also, on account of God's purpose, he was given full use of it and in turn he was destined to enable the rest of this world to participate in God's redemptive work. Thus the Christian will not only experience with a sense of gratitude and wonderment that he has a world of his own, but also feel responsible for the attainment of its destination. Somehow, man is aware of his guardianship, and by caring for and developing nature he transforms it into a civilized world.

The relatedness of human existence is also conspicuous in our relationship to other people. No human action is performed in a vacuum. Sooner or later it will affect the lives of other people. In turn, cut off from all human contact the individual is in the long run unable to live a human life. Without Friday, Robinson Crusoe would increasingly lose his mind and his humanity, even if he were able to support himself. It is only by dealing with his equals by means of speech and social intercourse that the individual is able to develop the properties and social institutions by which he differs from the animals. This interdependence of human beings is the reason why individualism is not only unrealistic but immoral. For it is an attempt one-sidedly to exploit interdependence for one's own benefit. Self-centred individualism, however, is almost unavoidable in social life, and especially in institutional relationship. For what people seek is in the first place a goal to be reached, with which they identify themselves. In political life, for instance, we strive for stability and security in public life, no matter what the condition of our fellow citizens may be. In the PTA (Parent-Teacher Association) we make a stand for good schools, yet are not interested in the headaches of the other parents. Thus we act as though the presence of the other people were only in existence as supporting factors for our own aspirations. This illusory perspective is almost inevitable as long as we consider our own existence a purely secular matter. Christianity insists upon the fact, however, that our relatedness to this world and other people are ethically relevant, if and when they are seen as aspects of God's redemptive purpose. The basic difference between secular and Christian realism is to be found in the fact that according to the biblical view all earthly reality is truly meaningful only when it stands under the will of God.

Whereas the secular approach to reality is a bilateral one, that of theology is a triangular relationship. In secular mentality subject and object, man and his partner, individuality and collectivity, and so on are supposed to stand on the same level. In the field of knowledge, the result is doubt and uncertainty, and in the field of action, likewise, one must content oneself with a compromise, all other factors being equal. The result is that in non-theological ethics one of the component factors is arbitrarily or without sufficient reason described as superior, and there is no way by which the prejudice can be overcome. In theological thinking both earthly factors are related to the will of God, with the result that not only each earthly factor but also their mutual relationship are rooted in God's will. Accordingly, man does not simply happen to find himself in this world. Rather he has a field of action assigned to him and so a determined sphere of operation. Similarly, the people whom I meet in my field do not encounter me as strangers. Rather they are my fellow men or neighbours, that is to say the people entrusted by God to my care.

The relatedness of human existence explains the nature of man's self-consciousness. It is not simply the awareness of being an *ens cogitans*, that is to say the subjective source of his mental processes. Human existence implies also the awareness of one's specific dignity. People may not be cognizant of the fact that their wish and demand to be treated as human beings, who differ essentially from animals and stones, is founded in their createdness and election. As a result self-consciousness may express itself as tribal or racial pride, as militant class consciousness or as the haughty contempt of an uneducated or unsophisticated mob. But its origin manifests itself clearly. People insist that their sense of dignity be given unconditional recognition. Also, the relatedness to this world manifests itself in the assurance that living in this world as a human being makes sense. The individual may be in doubt as to the reason why he has come into being at all. But he feels certain that being real, his life in this world is meaningful. All human beings, even primitive man, are endowed with this feeling of dignity.

Finally, as a result of his election, man has a sense of obligation. He is full of unrest, because he is unable to accept his stance and his actions as something final. In that respect, too, the interpretation he gives to that urge may seem to be absurd. But when the African, who has hurt his feet, does not content himself with taking cognizance of his injury but feels an urge to act upon a Spirit, he does not intend to prevent the ghost from continuing to do him harm. To do that he would be unable. Rather he feels that a relevant event has taken place in his life which requires an adequate response on his part.

Joy of life is another element of self-consciousness. Although life is directed toward a future, which is unknown to us, people live with the certainty that there will be enough not only to sustain life but also to enjoy it. Fear of starvation or inability to live is found as a momentary feeling only. That certainty and joy is based upon the assurance that by creating this world God had a purpose and that he is therefore not likely to drop it and let this world perish. The principal difference between the concept of self, as held by idealists and existentialists on the one hand and Christian realism on the other, lies in the fact that as a result of his creatureliness, man's self recognizes the determinants of this world. For instance, there are spacial expansion, the principle of equality through diversification, the interrelation of inorganic things and organisms, or the telic nature of the universe as willed by God and therefore as appropriate for the attainment of God's goal. Full selfhood is not to be reached, as in mysticism, by a flight away from this world, nor, as in Kant's philosophy, by considering man the creator of his categories and moral standards. Rather we approximate our selfhood in some measure as we accept this world, including its evils, as manifesting God's will, and ourselves as made for the service of God by means of our actual abilities and earthly resources. The limitations and distortions of our selfhood are not to be sought in outside influences by which our spontaneity is curbed but rather in an erroneous idea we hold concerning the nature of selfhood. That fact is most conspicuous in idealism. By ascribing his originality to himself, the individual fails to heed the divine signs, which are meant to lead him to his goal. Unlike God, whose selfhood consists in his unlimited creativity, the human self is bound by man's creatureliness. He may choose the way of action which promises to be most useful or effective, but the individual has no control over his own nature. Likewise, man may utilize and transform all that forms his field of action, yet he is unable to alter the direction of the cosmic process or the structure and composition of the universe. As a Christian he will accept that fact as the outcome of God's wisdom and compassion. For through that arrangement he is protected against losing himself in the vastness of the universe. The 'practical' or 'scientific' view, in which these determinations of human life are ignored, may suffice for classification and practical pursuits. It is a mutilation, nevertheless, of the true picture of man and hence unfit appropriately to deal with the problem of the meaning of life. There is every reason to surmise that the trend toward self-sufficient selfhood, far from being the mainstream of human evolution, as Erich Fromm suggests, is rather one of those terminal sidebranches of evolution which 'nature' uses in order to get rid of useless or unfit hereditary elements.

In modern religiosity selfhood is raised to the point where God and man seem to co-exist side by side. Hence it is man who decides on his own accord whether or not he is to enter into friendly relations with God. Conversely, in the Christian view God takes the initiative. Man's selfhood consists in replying or reacting to what God has done. The Bible uses the metaphors of 'son' and 'image of God' in order to characterize that relationship. These metaphors indicate that what is in God as creative power and purpose, becomes actual 'worldly' reality perceptible to human beings. In other words, the creation of man, far from being a terminal event, is a process which begins in God and will not end until God's goal has been completely realized.

C. Interdependence

Interrelation is not a mere co-existence. It implies interdependence. Whatever exists, exists through and for each other. Nothing in this world is an absolute beginning, nor is it an end in itself. The world in which we live is a whole in which each part exists for the sake of the whole in general and of certain things in particular. Likewise nothing is able by its own strength and resources to keep itself in existence. It would disintegrate but for what other things do for it. That interdependence is not only found in the mutual relations of particular things, but also in that of the whole and its parts. Even the most infinitesimal speck is needed for the equilibrium of the universe, and in turn it is the cohesion of the whole which safeguards its component parts from dissipating themselves in the vastness of the universe. The Christian view is not afraid to ascribe this interdependence even to God. By defining the divine essence as love, it gives expression to the fact that God and world must be thought of as depending on each other. God could not be love without having something to be loved. In turn, there could be no world, unless God had given it origin and kept it in existence.

The function of interdependence is primarily one of supplementing the deficiencies of all particular beings. No thing is by itself what it is destined to be. In order to become truly itself, it must come under the influence of other things. By calling his disciples the light of the world and the salt of the earth, Jesus indicated that a thing does not depend on other things in their totality. It may be only a relatively small element that is lacking in the deficient thing and is supplemented by the other. The disciples were related in a number of ways with their environment, for instance politically, historically, commercially, or culturally. But what made their existence relevant not only to their environment, but also to mankind, was the least conspicuous feature of theirs, viz. that they were able to serve as spiritual light to others. By this interdependence the benefits we convey to others are rendered relevant. They are not mere expression of our compassionate sentiments, but can become a real service to others. In turn, these services are so important, because all men have certain deficiencies which they are entirely unable to fulfil, yet which other people are able to remedy. That is the reason why spontaneous acts of kindness or assistance fail so frequently to help the other person. They are acts of sentimentalism. True love demands sensitivity of what is the real nature of his deficiency. Such search is not in vain, because it is done in a world whose wholeness presupposes the availability of all the goods necessary to overcome all deficiencies. This does not mean that it is in our power to satiate all the hungry people of the world or to wipe off all tears. Yet, neither must our insufficiency be interpreted as though caring for the needy people were a hopeless task.

In view of that universal interdependence, no human life is doomed to be utterly useless and futile. No matter how low one's station in life may be or how primitive one's level of education, there are always people around the individual, to whom he can show kindness and in whose life he may take an interest. A friendly greeting given to a distant acquaintance may make in his life the difference between despair and the courage to begin afresh. Human life offers many opportunities for interdependent relationships but also great and variegated deficiencies. While some of them are taken care of by the general course of nature, for instance in the mother–babe relationship or in the healthy effect which sunshine and fresh air have in the growth of our body, more of man's deficiencies require diligent search and effort. Delivering the solitary person from his prison is so difficult, because he is inclined to hide the discomfort of his solitude, and often an excessive sense of inferiority will deceive his environment about the true character of his ill by manifesting itself as aggressiveness.

Realizing that this is not only a world of deficiencies but also of interdependence gives us hope and confidence in difficult situations and reconciles us with the present condition of this world. That interdependence serves the preservation and improvement rather than the disintegration of this world. Its perfection will be approximate in proportion to the degree in which the hidden opportunities for interdependence are discovered and used. In turn, it is the ubiquity of the world's interdependent structure that makes us aware of our opportunity to participate actively in the process of redemption. The readiness to act accordingly is what the New Testament calls *agapé*. It is the willingness to come to the aid of another person in a situation of deficiency which he is unable to master and in which I am able to supplement what is lacking in him. Unfortunately there is no English word by which the meaning of *agapé* is unambiguously and adequately rendered. Neither love nor charity, compassionate sympathy, nor solidarity will designate an attitude by which, irrespective of our own needs and deficiencies, we feel destined to come to another person's assistance merely because we are able so to do. Its only motive is the fact that we were created with the ability to work for each other. We contradict our own nature when we allow our own pains or loss or want to stymie us and render us callous toward the needs of other people.

The fact that we are willing to relieve somebody's needs and to relieve it irrespective not only of his sex, religion, social status or education, but also irrespective of his worthiness, is tantamount to the recognition that interdependence is a basic structural element of human life, and wholeness its goal.

D. The Ego
1. *Ego and Selfhood*
Human life is a paradox. Though we may be fully aware of our relatedness to other people, this world and God, we also feel ourselves as being endowed with self-determination and thus capable of preserving our identity in the midst of, and in spite of, all those relations. The

sense of personal selfhood has emerged only late in human history. Even in the Old Testament, it seems to be lacking until the end of the seventh century. Yet that human self-consciousness should originally have been a tribal or national consciousness is not surprising in view of the basic role of interdependence. What that individual self is like has long remained a puzzling problem. In view of the clashes between collective consciousness and individual self, Socrates seems to have seen in it a *daimon*, that is to say, a supernatural intruder, though one whose promptings must be recognized. The experience of prophetic ecstasy seems to point in the same direction. In a slightly rationalized way, Plato identifies it with the *logos*, a superpersonal energy which speaks to man's mind and must be obeyed. Fully rationalized, it is in Aristotle and subsequent Greek philosophy reduced to the spontaneity of the human mind which prompts the individual to assert his rational power over against the onrush of his passions.

This view of the individual which has survived for a long while actually substituted a general principle, namely reason, for the self, while the individual's particular features, his individuality, was considered an incidental element, seated in the 'lower' life of the body. The Biblical writers were spared these inconsistencies. They recognized that selfhood was not just a faculty of the individual but rather the sovereign power of self-assertion and self-determination, which were implied in man's createdness. When Jesus, following Jewish usage, contrasts the heart of man with his 'body', or when Paul contrasts the 'flesh' with the spirit in us, they mean what today we designate as self. 'Body' and 'flesh' are terms used to denote the individual as part of this world and therefore conditioned by it, while 'heart' or 'spirit' indicate the individual's ability to regulate his relations with this world in agreement with the purpose God has with man. Thus the self is not an alien factor in man or merely the operation of the *humanum* in man, but rather his individual existence, as it is aware of his dependence on God. It is in that respect, and only in it, that the self has the freedom of self-determination. While the individual is capable of taking decisions, they are conditioned by his uncritical conformity with the circumstances in which he lives. Thus in spite of the formal freedom of of decision, the individual remains the prisoner of circumstances. This applies in a special sense to man's sinfulness. Even apart from faith man possesses freedom of action. But by accepting his sinfulness as a matter of course, he is unable to direct his actions toward the goal of his destination. Like the animals, he uses his freedom for the satisfaction of his personal or collective needs. The true freedom of decision, in turn, is not man's own work, as the idealists understand it, who contend that by his own strength man is capable of extricating himself from the fetters of Fate or Necessity. Our freedom depends on God's taking the initiative and intimating to a person that as a member of the human race he is destined to live and act as God's agent in the realization of a cosmic task. Freedom alone without that divine appointment as it is understood in liberal Protestantism and the modern 'secular' theology, is bound to end in a self-defeating relativism or the glorification of brutal power and the reign of passions. In turn, any sense of freedom which is not a divine gift will by the presumptuousness of a self-chosen cosmic mission be driven into despair. For the task is too enormous when man is to rely exclusively on his own strength. It is only by the combination of freedom and destination as implied in man's election that freedom is possible and the task meaningful. Its execution is assigned to God's people in an historical and eschatological process, and God himself supports the frailty of man by granting success. Hence, Christian freedom, while rendering us proud of the divine gift and its cosmic perspective, fills us at the same time with deep humility because our strength lies in God's kindness rather than in our innate strength.

Understood in this way, self-determination is the prerequisite of faith as Protestantism understands it. When faith is understood as an act of assent given to a confession of faith or to the Bible, it is an act of the intellect by which the agreement between the individual's convictions and the authoritative texts is recognized. The result is a legalistic concept of ethics, by which the assent is extended to the commandments found in the Bible or given by the Church. Faith, however, as the Bible understands it, is not merely a mental faculty but rather an act in which the individual surrenders himself, to the God by whom he was created, as the supreme determinant of his life. The Christian refuses to recognize all the other urges that work upon him as ultimates. Faith then is an act in which the self recognizes voluntarily the supreme authority of the Creator. It is not an act by which, as in fatalism, the self is extinguished, but rather in which it becomes truly itself by acknowledging its relatedness to God.

The self is the spring of life by which the individual is given its specific character as a human being. That we are able to distinguish between truth and falsehood, goodness and wickedness, importance and irrelevancy, usefulness and uselessness or futility, is not the result of experience but rather of the fact that, no matter how dimly, the individual is aware of itself as God's creature. Thereby all reality is given its basic pattern and co-ordinates so that we are able, whenever a new thing, mental or material, enters our mind, to relate it to them immediately. Subsequent verification will serve to fix the place which the new thing is to be accorded in our mind. Therein lies the element of truth implied in Kant's view of the autonomy of reason. Yet his view would interpret the intellect or the moral sense of man as general human feature and thus place them into the neighbourhood of hereditary abilities, rather than seeing in them a manifestation of man's election. Thus alone is the individual capable of asserting itself over against man's *bios* and to resist the *nisus* which self-consciousness has toward the biological side of human life.

Greek philosophy never attained to a full understanding of the self. The reason is simple. The Greeks were afraid of selfhood; they considered individuality as the incidental result of man's material existence and sought true existence in the features all people have in common. Individuality was interpreted as the source of falsehood and of discord. They ascribed selfhood to few persons only, and they meant thereby that those people had all that is required for true human existence and nothing else. Body and mind (or soul, *psyché*) were regarded as artificially and incidentally joined together. The body would perish, the mind or soul alone would survive. One should not be surprised that under the influence of that philosophy theologians of the Middle Ages would identify that immortal soul with the self. Unlike their Greek teachers they ascribed individuality to the self. Yet, in accordance with them, they considered the life of the body as non-essential for true existence. That view implied a shift of perspective. The true life was to be the disembodied life of the soul in heaven, whereas life on earth was regarded as a mere preparation for the life to come. Neglect and even mortification of the body and detachment from secular preoccupations were the means by which the self would learn to assert itself. Christian life that had been nurtured by the spirit of the Bible, especially the Old Testament, moved in a different direction. Principal emphasis was laid upon life here on earth, for which the life to come would be the natural sequence. Starting from the Creation of man, this view would underscore the significance of individuality. What mattered ethically was not the generally approved goodness of one's action, but rather the willingness of each individual to assume full responsibility for one's deeds.

Such an outlook would inevitably raise the question, What then is the significance of our living in a body? The answer was like this. The body, or rather an earthly life of body and mind, is the instrument by which the individual is enabled to act as God's agent here on earth. Through the activity of the self, body and mind are tied together and form a unity of which the self is the directing centre. Truly understood, such unity implied, as Jesus pointed out, that the ethical value of an act lies in the attitude of the self. The intention is accountable, no matter whether or not the individual had an opportunity to execute it.

2. *Inclusiveness*

One of the main obstacles to get a clear and adequate vision of our ethical situation lies in what we might call the inclusivness of existence. We know existence merely as the existence of particular things. Yet scientific knowledge would not be possible unless certain particular things had features in common, by means of which they could be treated as specimens of a certain species, and thus not fit for being ascribed to another species. But what gives us a right to classify things in such a way? Outward appearance can hardly suffice. We know how deceptive it is.

As far as man is concerned, the problem is concealed by the fact that individual self-consciousness is easily misunderstood as indicating the self-sufficiency of the individual, and hence his autogeny. However, the individual is also aware of his belonging together with other individuals in his capacity as a human being.

Philosophers have emphasized that, in speaking of general features, we assume that underlying particular existence are formative principles or forces which Plato called 'ideas' or 'images', and for which Kant preferred the designation 'thing in itself'. They wanted thereby to point to an ontic foundation of particular existence which cannot be given directly by sense perception, yet which is nevertheless presupposed or 'included' in any sense experience. In turn, whatever is perceived by us is never an absolute particular, but rather a specimen of a species, for instance a rose, a cow or a man. In discussing the Biblical notion of Adam, it was pointed out that mythical language is one way in which knowledge of such formative principles may be given expression in a religious context. Another method consists in forming a kind of synthetic 'image' of what is meant by a specific thing. The particular thing and its formative power cannot be separated. We cannot know of the existence of a species unless it manifests itself in particular objects.

That fact implies, however, that all particular specimens are manifestations of their formative power. Hence, in order to know what man is like, it is not sufficient that I should look at myself and describe human nature in terms of my particular features. All other beings which my mind tells me to be of the human race are as authentically indicative of human nature as I am. In turn, we would relapse into the error of a classificatory nominalism, if we would confine our 'image' of man to those features which all men have in common, while ignoring individual differences. What greatness we see in other individuals is a manifestation of human nature and hence has a disposition in ourselves. Even though it may never be realized in our non-historical existence, seed of such achievements lies dormant in all of us. In that fact we see the ethical significance of Jesus. His life shows what by the Will of God man is destined to become, and what by the grace of God is possible to man. Thus what I am may not be considered the limit of 'what I may become'. The New Testament speaks of the 'man of wickedness or lawlessness' (2 Thess. 2:3) as an historical reality which serves as a sign indicating the extreme to which sin may be carried and in turn presents Jesus as the sign and example of the goodness for which mankind is destined. In turn, while we are inclined to look down contemptuously to the depth of degradation reached as a result of sin, we should also realize that it is 'human nature' that is manifested therein. It is not by any merit of mine but rather by the grace of God if my own sinfulness does not manifest itself in the most terrible way. Looking at what sinful man is capable of being gives us an idea of the weight of sin and shows us what destruction it may carry out in man. The relationship between humanity as a formative power and its manifestations in human individuals does not reduce the latter ones to mere pictures, while the formative power would be the true reality, as would be the case if we followed Plato. Rather, the earthly existence and the relations of human beings are the way in which the operation of the formative principle makes itself perceptible and known.

If the empirical existence of human beings were the whole reality of man, the contacts between human individuals would be from the outside, puncticular and fortuitous only. Phenomena such as speech, conscience, institutional life and history, far from being explained by incidental contacts, presuppose a collective interrelation, rooted in a supra-empirical energy. How real it is in all of us may best be seen in the fact that without pangs of conscience we tolerate and even commit collectively actions such as the abominations of total warfare or racial oppression, although we abhor them in personal relations. Likewise, what we approve as standards of a truly Christian life by far transcends the standards by which we actually live. This phenomenon is misunderstood when interpreted as hypocrisy of 'double moral.' It rather indicates that the goodness with which God has endowed mankind, rather than being the sum total of individual goodness, is an energy working upon the minds and wills of the individual in such a way that we are unable to ignore its claims.

The presence and operation of the formative principle of mankind explains the otherwise puzzling fact that in the history of mankind an accumulation of mental and spiritual achievements takes place, whereas from a purely individualistic vanguard point we would expect that all of man's accomplishments would soon be wiped out by the power of oblivion. What amazes us in that process is not the fact that documents of the past are preserved but rather that people should be anxious to appropriate the wisdom and experience embodied therein and to use them as helps for their own life, and that notwithstanding the difference of historical circumstances the past should prove to be useful and beneficial for subsequent generations. Apart from the reality of human 'nature' there could be no historical continuity. In turn, since 'Adam' is real, there is progress not only in the history of civilization – the advances of the Western world, for instance, are communicable and actually communicated to the less developed nations – but also in spiritual life. The development of religious thought and the experience of the practical implications of Christianity have successively enabled churches and denominations to become messengers of the good news to people living in spiritual ignorance or misconceptions. Conversely, the 'quest for the historical Jesus' would lack theological interest except for the fact that his historical work marked a decisive advance in the existence of 'mankind' and in turn enabled his followers to give historical expression to that progress. He is our peace and comfort, because he is the 'Son of Man' rather than a 'great man of history'.

3. Self-consciousness and Conscience

Individuation is the general pattern of earthly reality. The species or formative powers are perceptible only in particular specimens. Of all the creatures, man is to our knowledge the only one in whom individuation is combined with selfhood. Plants and animals are determined by their specific form, and the latter is preserved in their metamorphosis and in spite of all the changes that take place in their environment. But in turn, they are not in control of their existence. Rather, it is constantly modified by environmental factors. Man alone possesses self-awareness and self-determination. Animals, as far as we can see, have an awareness of their existence. Yet, they are merely aware of their existence in a given situation, just as I am aware of my pain or hunger in a given moment. It is hardly exaggerated to state that plants and animals are being lived. They do not give their own life.

What man has as his exclusive privilege is the awareness that he remains the same throughout his life. In his recollections he is able to state, 'I did it', or 'I experienced it, notwithstanding the radical replacement of the cells which formed my body at the time of the event remembered, and in spite of the numerous new experiences which I gathered in the meantime.'

This awareness of selfhood points to the special role which by God's will man is destined to play in the history of the universe. In the execution of the divine purpose he is not somebody who happens to be at a place of action and who therefore performs some deed. Rather, man is destined to act as precisely this person and in this specific way. Plants and animals are used as available material in the process of universal causality. They have no role of their own to play in this world. For that reason man is not to deal with them in the same personal manner in which he approaches his fellow men.

In an age in which the psychologists attempted to fragmentize human existence into a succession of momentary and passing experiences that were precariously held together by incidental associations, it was Freud's merit to rediscover the unity and permanent identity of the Ego. Yet, like his contemporaries Freud was fettered by his materialistic philosophy. As a result he understood his Ego as being moved by the biological *nisus*, especially sex. In fact, however, man's self-consciousness manifests itself as an active and spontaneous function, which accounts for man's ability to think, to act as man's conscience, to remember the part and to be willing to assume responsibility for what one has done in the past. Thus, man's basic awareness is not one of being passively doomed to living on the good graces of the forces of this world, as Heidegger interprets human self-consciousness; man's basic attitude is one of actively dealing with this world. Conscience is not, like Socrates' demon, a mysterious voice by which we are told what we ought to do and what to shun. Rather, it is the concrete awareness of our createdness, that is to say, of the fact that not only our essence and existence; but also the circumstances of our life do not depend on our own will, but rather are determined by a supreme reality. Hence, we realize that life contradicts itself when it neglects that supreme and comprehensive determination. Thus the voice of conscience is not so much a legislator speaking from outside of ourselves and telling us what to do, but rather a function of our self-consciousness by which we are reminded of our origin. That function implies a mandatory element, yet not that of an autonomous legislator, as held by Kant. The mandate results from man's createdness. It operates on levels of human evolution which antedate the development of a specifically moral sense. Even then human life implies the distinction between things to be shunned and things that may be tolerated.

In Christian experience our conscience makes us aware of our being God's creatures and thus being subject to certain limitations of our conative will. Yet what those limitations are like is not to be learned from our conscience, but rather from Christian experience. Hence it is not surprising that even Christians are not agreed on the demands made by their conscience. But that diversity does not by itself indicate inconsistency, nor does it give Christians the right to contend that the fellow Christian lacks the true faith. From a Christian viewpoint, a man's conscience is mistaken if and when particular values or realities, such as national honour, the progress of human civilization, or the individual's self-realization, are substituted for the supreme reality of God by which we are determined in our createdness. In this most general sense, the voice of conscience forms the basis of all decisions on values.

Even in Christian experience, conscience does not act like a catechism. The basic decision with which it confronts the individual is so broad that it has to be implemented by experience, common sense and moral sensitivity in order to be helpful in practical life. According to age, people and circumstances, its interpretation will vary greatly and would end in utter confusion, but for the fact that its diversity is integrated in the example set by Jesus. Thus, conscience is not supernatural manifestation in man's mind but rather a function of his self-consciousness. In the Augustinian tradition, and thus especially in the Reformation, that function has been understood as making us aware of our transgressions and their dreadful consequences. Such over-emphasis laid upon guilt and damnation was probably inevitable in an age where the believer's conduct was interpreted as a transaction between the individual and the Church. In such circumstances it was necessary to remind people that in the life of faith they were confronted with an angry God. In our age, on the other hand, where people have lost sight of an absolute obligation, it is advisable to lay stress on the basic decision with which our conscience confronts us in order to give us direction and guidance in our life. The function of conscience is completely misunderstood where it serves merely in retrospect, as an evil conscience that accuses us. Of course, there will be more than one occasion when our conscience warns us against believing that what we love best must be in keeping with God's will. Even more frequent will be the instances in which our conscience reminds us that we have neglected to foster God's plans in a constructive and co-operative way. But in such cases it is the very voice of conscience which tells us that our createdness is rooted in God's plan to render us his agents and children. Thus we have a right to ask for his forgiveness in the assurance that he is willing to grant it. Some people suffer from an excessive sense of guilt which does not result however, from moral hypersensitivity, but rather from the individual's desire to straighten a wrong out by one's own efforts, or from an obstinate denial that there could be pardon for one's misdeed. In either instance, the genuine voice of conscience is muted. The individual is not willing to accept his createdness. It is at this point that the difference between the Christian view of self-consciousness and that held by psychoanalysis is most evident. The psychotherapist is inclined to tell his patient that his sense of guilt should not be taken seriously, because what seems to be wrong is measured by social conventions, to which no general authority should be ascribed. The Christian counsellor would tell that same person that his sense of guilt was justified, but that his was not a hopeless case because he might turn to God for pardon.

4. *Adam*

a. THE PRIVILEGE

In the theology of the last two hundred years enormous confusion has been wrought by substituting biological, psychological and sociological categories for theological ones. On account of the use of statistical method, the image of modern Western man replaced the Biblical view of mankind, and the notion of ethical life was watered down to the average activities of people in a given group. Thus the idea of oughtness had to give way to the urge of biological, psychological or sociological needs.

In the Bible man is frequently referred to under the mythical figure of Adam. Adam is not a fictitious person. By calling him a mythical being we simply want to indicate that, as in other religions, the Old Testament adopts a form of speech in which the permanent is described by means of a particular action or event, and the divine appears under the guise of an earthly agent. Freud and Jung use the term 'myth' in order to designate a psychological pattern. But the descriptive element is secondary in the myth. Its principal function is ontological. It is to explain the origin of the specifying nature and the permanency of relevant novel features in nature and history. That in such case the form of the myth is chosen has two reasons. Firstly, people realize their inability to explain the origin of the relevant phenomena as resulting from the regular or 'natural' course of events. Their origin implies a mystery; people are amazed that it should be in existence and prove to be so relevant. Secondly, by choosing actions of human or otherwise rational beings, people express their belief that the explanation of the specific origin presupposes the operation of a man-like agent, yet one that transcends the abilities of ordinary men.

When in the Old Testament, a person is given the appellation 'son of Adam', the term implies that all men share the same nature, and that to have that nature is not an incidental event. It is so by the will of God. Thus, mankind is characterized as a homogeneous collectivity which reproduces itself, and within which no individual is capable of being anything but a human being. The reproductive ability does not depend on the individual's will. Rather, it is a determinant which affects the individual's physiological and mental life. Whatever differences there are among individuals – and they are innumerable – are nevertheless within their human nature. The origin of which the myth speaks is invisible. It is only by means of its specimens that it is able to manifest itself. Yet, it is also obvious that the relationship of originator and its specific manifestations is not a causal one. Rather it is a determinative one. It imparts to the beings their specific form or *morphé*, yet also sets the limits to them. As originator, 'Adam' designates the fact that human beings are unable to change into specimens of another species, as also that each man has certain characteristics by which he differs from all other beings yet is known as a member of the species *homo sapiens*. Man, and man alone, has reason, and hence is capable of using articulate speech and of moulding and employing all that is in accordance with his plans and will. Thus, Adam symbolizes the power by means of which mankind is one throughout the ages and irrespective of their domicile. As a theological appellation, Adam refers to human nature. At first sight it might appear as though the Biblical Adam designates the same reality which the Romanticists and more recently W. Wundt had in mind when referring to the spirit or genius of a nation or what is intended by our contemporaries who talk about *Deutschtum* (Germany) or *négritude*. Yet Adam designates a basic ontological determinant of reality, whereas the modern authors think of historical formations, to which, however, ultimate authority may be ascribed. In turn, the various human races are not to be considered as purely subjective classifications. They are manifestations of the specifying power of 'Adam' or 'human nature'.

References to Adam are not meant to describe when and how the human race came into existence. To answer such questions is up to the scientist. The way in which the Creation of man is described in Gen., ch. 1-2, indicates two aspects of the oneness of mankind. But describing the creation of man as taking place in a special act apart from that of the other creatures, man is characterized as a unique being which by the Grace of God, and for no merit of his own, has been chosen by God as agent for the execution of his redemptive plan, expressed by man's commission as gardener in God's service. Thus, man's createdness implies that the races as a whole and each of its members are destined for a divine design. In its light all differences found among men are of secondary significance. Moreover, the fact that mankind is described as descended from a single couple is meant to bring out the intrinsic unity of all men. They are all interrelated and interdependent. While the biologist may be able to modify human genes, the beings thus produced will not differ from the rest of mankind in their attitude towards God and his dealing with man. Thus, what gives man his unique position among the creatures is not to be sought in the fact that man and man alone has reason, as is held by idealists and rationalists. While thereby he differs from other animals, the differentia may be compared to the bat's ability to 'sense' distant objects and other specific characteristics in the realm of organism. Rather, it is his destination for participation in God's redemptive work by which man is assigned an absolutely unique position in this world. Reason is one of the abilities by which that task is to be performed.

By thus combining man's task with his creation the Bible ascribes to all men without exception this dignity and obligation. By failing to comply with it people deprive themselves of what makes them truly human. Yet, at first sight, it might seem as though such a view would so one-sidedly treat man as a generic being that no room were left for individuality. Of course, as everywhere in nature, each individual person is determined by its species. What makes the human phenomenon so confusing, however, is the fact that mankind's specific dynamic manifests itself most conspicuously in the spontaneity of individuals, whereas the overall changes in the life of the specimen can be noticed only by covering long periods of time. Thus it looks as though the individual were his own creator and, as Nietzsche contended, an absolute beginning. In fact, however, the actions of the Ego are not only to a large extent determined by hereditary factors and by human sinfulness; the individual is also in an inescapable way conditioned by his environment, even when he rebels against it.

b. DISREGARD OF GOD

The mythical story of Adam's Fall is not meant to describe an historical event in the life of a primitive couple, or merely to characterize what takes place in every man's life, as Brunner suggests. Rather, the story draws attention to the paradoxical fact that though sinfulness is a common feature found in all people yet it implies each one's accountability. Sin is not a mere congenital weakness caused by man's finitude or mortality. Considerations of such concreated limitations may occasion sinful thoughts. But sin itself is man's desire to be his own master irrespective of whether or not there is a God. In placing Adam's Fall after his commission, the Genesis story characterizes sinfulness as a rebellion against man's obligation to serve his Creator and a perversion of his true nature. In view of the spontaneity of his mind and the broad scope of his will, each man considers that disregard of God as a legitimate and fitting attitude for himself, if not for his fellow men. He holds that by heeding the claims of an absolute will, he would jeopardize his own freedom and dignity. What renders Adam's sin, and all sin, wrong, is not its specific content, for instance the eating of a fruit, but rather that by doing so man questions God's Lordship.

Sin, rightly understood, is not so much open rebellion against God's will as rather doubt. The awareness of his createdness and creatureliness is but dimly apprehended by many a person. Nevertheless, there is in all men a certain 'sense' or 'feeling' of self-transcendence which makes it impossible for a person to ignore his obligation and dependence. The order in which in Gen. 1–2 Adam's commission and fall follow each other indicates that the sinfulness of sin is not to be seen in particular acts of disobedience against certain commandments. Rather, it is man's presumption by which we question God's Lordship and the wisdom of his plan. As self-contradiction, man's sinfulness threatens the very meaning of his own existence. His only hope lies in a redemptive action on God's part. The Bible characterizes our sinfulness as a disease. It is a deficiency of whose presence we complain, yet without being able thereby to remove it. This paradoxical nature of sin has been interpreted in the western world as the tragic sense of life. Man finds himself entangled in a maze of contradictions which eventually lead to his ruin. But thereby the real issue is dodged. No matter how sinfulness may originate, the fact is that the individual identifies himself with it.

In a Christian the realization of his sinfulness will call forth repentance. Thereby we acknowledge that we are accountable for our disregard of God, yet also that we desire to receive his forgiveness. Thus, faith differs essentially from the tragic sense of life. The Christian assumes responsibility for his predicament, while in the tragedy the fault is found in some mysterious force outside of the individual. Moreover, while the 'tragic sense' is fatalistic and despairs of deliverance, faith trusts in God's kindness by which he will overcome the consequences of our sinfulness.

Protestant orthodoxy expressed the gravity of sin by ascribing to it a total depravity of human nature. That characterization should not be understood, however, as though apart from faith man's mental or physiological equipment were deficient. Logically such a view would imply that Christians were better athletes, scholars or artists than the rest of man. Rather the term gives expression to man's inability to engage in the service of the task for which he is appointed.

5. *Wholeness*

The interdependence of existence is particularly manifest in the case of the human individual. No other animal is known to us that depends for such a long while on its parents for food, shelter, and protection. That dependence, instead of decreasing as the individual comes of age, is rather augmented. For even in the stage of maturity man is not able to live a truly human life except within human institutions. The question may therefore legitimately be raised, Is man ever in a position to assert his selfhood? Or is belief in selfhood a delusion? Is his whole life perhaps, as the Behaviourists contend, nothing but a series of responses to stimuli coming from the outside? This and similar errors are based upon the assumption that selfhood is identical with our vital functions. While we are aware of our being spontaneously acting individuals whose selfhood is manifested through physiological, nervous and especially mental processes, none of them is the self. In turn, the infant, notwithstanding his total dependence on others, is capable, nevertheless, from the first moment of his life outside his mother's womb, to distinguish between what he is himself, and what comes to him from the outside. As the child grows up, self-consciousness is supplemented by self-determination. While dependent on the outside world for food, shelter and social intercourse, the child grows in his ability to select the means for those ends and purposes for which the things which form his world, are to be employed. Nevertheless, that is a rather limited selfhood, not considerably larger than that found in mammals, birds and reptiles.

At this point it is well to remember that selfhood is not to be equated with maturity. Maturity is the final stage of the biological process of growth. It takes place with an intrinsic necessity, though it may be retarded or prematurely stopped in some individuals. Maturity is the condition in which the individual is capable of making deliberate choices for the satisfaction of vital needs. Making maturity a prerequisite of moral action, as is often done in modern naturalism, is misleading. Not only is maturity a vague concept, for the level reached differs immensely in various individuals. It is obvious that maturity, be it physiological or mental, can hardly be considered a ground on which sexual relations are morally justifiable. At the best it is the indispensable prerequisite for weighing the moral character of a sexual relationship.

Genuine selfhood is seldom reached prior to biological maturity, yet is not its result. Independent of biological growth, it is through reflection, discipline and regular practice that the individual's ability of self-determination is developed. That process does not take place with an intrinsic necessity. Rather the self cannot attain to itself except by flexing its own muscles. Whereas biological growth cannot advance beyond a certain point, after which there is no further progress, but rather gradual disintegration, the self-realization of the human individual is a process which may go on right until a person's death. Its goal is not so much to be seen in shedding off all the factors by which the ego is rendered dependent on its vital functions and the goods of the non-subjective world, but rather in bringing all of them under the control of the supreme determinants of human existence and thus to make them subservient to the goal for which man was made by God. The ego is entangled in a comprehensive and seemingly irreconcilable contradiction. Tactile, visual, acoustic and other experiences give the impression of an 'objective' world which sets an absolute limit to man, seemingly confronting him with an irreducible supreme reality. Yet, the ego is unwilling to recognize the superiority of the objective world, and by means of knowledge, especially science and philosophy, as well as by art and social order, the ego seeks to subject to itself the world on which it depends. The result is a constant oscillation within the ego between bondage by an objective world and the freedom of an ideal subjective world. The situation is the same, no matter whether it is interpreted as demanding a compromise or made tolerable by a fictitious elimination of one of the two factors, that is to say, either through materialism or idealism.

Neither view is able to give the ego real satisfaction, because it wants to be truly itself, that is to say, its own master. That goal cannot be reached except by fully integrating the subjective and the objective sides of reality into a whole which is both flawless and realistic. Thus the ego is not self by nature nor is its true selfhood attainable through a natural process of growth. It is possible only by faith, that is to say, by accepting both one's spontaneity and the world in which we live as willed by God. In their correlation they are destined to serve his purpose rather than being ultimates. The total and unchallenged selfhood of man is not a datum of his life but rather the final outcome of a process of integration performed by the ego. In this life we seem never to be able like Jesus, whom John calls 'himself' (*autos*), to terminate that process. Hence, Christian faith necessarily implies our receiving a new 'body' or a 'white garment' to cover our 'nakedness'; that is to say, we are looking forward to a condition of existence in which we shall be entirely masters of the things on which we depend.

That goal would not be reached, however, if we followed the acosmistic view of Plato and his idealistic successors. For by ignoring the existence of the objective world around us we are not able to undo it, and its existence must constantly disturb us as an insoluble mystery. We are not able to dodge the nagging question, Why is it that the world which surrounds us seems to be relevant, if in effect it is not? In other words, the quest of self-realization which is inherent in human existence cannot be satisfied successfully unless it is the same God who has created both man and this world and who has destined them, either of them in its own specific way, for bringing about a 'new' world.

What then is the ethical significance of man's longing for selfhood? Positively such aspiration confirms the dignity of man. Unlike the animals, which are unable ever to attain to genuine self-determination and whose life is confined to permanent adjustment to the things on which they depend, man in the interdependence with this world is able to play a dominant role, and one which is not gained by a trick but rather by confronting this world with true humanity or at least the longing for it. That I should yearn after so lofty an end of human existence is the work of God who reveals himself to us as our God. Hence, we rightly feel pride in our election by which we are singled out from all other living creatures. Yet, the very ability to aspire for self-determination indicates also that the goal cannot be reached apart from the individual's own efforts. In making them, man evidences his eagerness to reach the end for which he is destined. Implied in that aspiration of faith is the realization that what I want to become in actual life is not in the first place the development of my particular individuality but rather my share in the task assigned to humanity. Hence the final aim of my concern for my fellow men, too, must be to encourage and assist them so that they will strive after wholeness. Such intention does not preclude practical help; nevertheless the fellow man is stopped rather than furthered on his way to a worthwhile life, unless my help is received as a means for practising self-determination. In turn, the role which faith plays in that process of self-realization reminds us of the impossibility of obtaining true selfhood by means of science, art or social order. Paradoxically, those factors have the opposite effect. The more intensely we cultivate our intellect, for instance, the longer grows the number of facts, views and arguments to be taken into consideration. The rapid growth of our libraries is the nightmare of scholars. The broadminded scholar of the Renaissance, who could proudly call himself a humanist, has been reduced now to the unenviable role of a specialist or expert, who even in his self-limitation is no longer capable of keeping track of the literature in his narrow field. Similarly in the area of political order there is a proliferation of laws and decrees which even the head of a department of the government is able to apply only with the aid of numerous specialized assistants. In other words, when the cultural sphere of life is regarded as the final goal of human development, man constantly increases his dependence on his environment and is far from moving on toward genuine selfhood. In that respect, man's yearning for wholeness will bring about some kind of harmonious or systematic arrangement of the vital functions and their products, and thus a certain degree of co-ordination of the activities. But in the hustle of cultural activities modern man feels increasingly dehumanized, unless by faith he is enabled in the multitude of cultural goods that are at his disposal to orientate his life towards the divine goal.

4 This World

A. The Nature of This World

1. *Cosmic Laws*

As has been shown in Chapter 1, the spiritual interpretations of the faith are usually acosmistic. Yet all life presupposes a sphere in which it is to be lived and upon which it can draw for support. The Jews would originally identify their field of action with the territory in which they lived. Yet with their distinction of clean and unclean, or between Jew and Gentile, they transcended their original naïve realism. Jesus re-emphasized the prophetic view that, being the children of the God who had created heaven and earth, his people had to conceive of its field of action as being co-extensive with the whole universe. In turn, however, that universe, while comprising all things, was religiously relevant because God had a purpose in making it. The basic question of human existence should not therefore be, What ought I to do? but rather, What is the place that has been assigned to me in the totality of creation?

The world in which we live is not a nascent world but rather a complete one on its way to a divinely fixed goal. In the former case, the openness of the universe would be unpredictable, for it would leave room for any kind of development. From the Christian point of view it is moving in a definite direction so that it is possible for man to adjust himself to its course. Such an outlook is geocentric merely in the sense that the problems of which man is aware are by the will and power of God moving towards their complete solution. That is the case even though man, in his expanding field of action, may encounter new problems in outer space which at present are unknown and inconceivable for us.

In many pagan religions it is held that in order to bring this world into being, the gods used some pre-existent material which proved to be inadequate for their purpose. As a result, this world is substantially imperfect and imperfectible. The Christian notion of creation implies that God made this world entirely appropriate for the purpose he had with it. Thus it is a world which exhibits the wisdom and glory of God.

It is a world which remains under the Creator's control and which can be enjoyed by man. That the universe is God's work can be seen in its determinants. That is to say, the fact that this world and the things of which it is composed are subject to necessity and unchanging order, as well as that the universe remains in a state of equilibrium. Besides the laws of nature there are many other cosmic determinants, for instance the indestructibility of the universe, the constancy of the nature of things, the limited length of time in which things may be in existence, the rhythm of the seasons and the regularity of the stellar revolutions. Their dominant and inescapable character bears witness to the fact that this world did not bring itself into existence. The operation of these and many other cosmic determinants gives us the assurance that this is a dependable world, in and upon which man may act methodically towards a goal and in the awareness of the consequences of his actions.

2. *Oneness and Diversity*

If God were thought of, as in classical philosophy, as a prime cause or pure substance, its meaning would consist in a tendency to bring about uniformity or mechanical unity. But the Bible describes God as the living God or the God of life, thereby intimating that he carries in himself the unlimited multitude of diverse possibilities. He remains nevertheless one, for in him is no inner contradiction or tension. That fact explains why it is that the world in which we live is full of diversity: diversity of quantity and quality, of energy and direction, of genera and species and above all of an infinite number of particular objects and beings. Ancient philosophers interpreted particular existence as an ontic weakness. Their interest envisaged the general. Christian religion, conversely, turns toward the particular things, and in ethics we are dealing with particular persons and situations.

The particularity of a person or thing is not valuable by itself, however. It rather serves as a divine device by which the plenitude of a species is given outward expression. Situational ethics is grossly mistaken in treating the specific features of the individual or a particular situation as the motive of ethical action, while it should be a modifying factor. Yet equally mistaken is the mechanical application of a general principle to a given situation. In turn, the emphasis which Christian ethics places upon the particular is derived from the fact that the particular specimens of a species do not result from fortuitous mutations. Rather God uses all of them in order to attain the goal for which the species exists. Hence particularity may not be interpreted in terms of social pluralism. The latter attitude is symptomatic of relativistic indifference. One form or mode of existence is considered the equivalent of others, irrespective of the goal for which they aspire. The fact, for instance that Judaism and Christianity confess an ethical monotheism does not mean that they pursue the same objective. The fact, however, that I differ from all other human beings provides evidence for the wealth of God's creation.

Yet notwithstanding the diversity which characterizes this world of particular things, it is not an atomistic world in which each person or object exists by and for itself. There is, as has been shown, interdependence and inclusiveness by which the texture of reality is held together and given structure. Thereby we are given intimations of the way in which we can work for harmonious co-existence and wholeness. Above all, however, there is the will of God, by which this world not only has been brought into being, but also given its telic nature, by which we are enabled to work for an ultimate goal. The unity of this world is not to be seen in the material out of which it is made or the dynamic which keeps it moving. By themselves they would not prevent this world of diversity from disintegrating and moving toward all sides in a centrifugal process. It is the telic will of God, which gives us the assurance that whatever we do in a particular way or situation will contribute, with all other acts of faith, to the attainment of a common goal. Conversely, where people hold a non-theistic view, they will be told by an honest analysis of their activities that there is no reason why they should expect lasting consequences from them. Summarizing, we could say that this world, as seen with the eyes of faith, is not a mere agglomeration of co-existing things and events but rather a systematic whole of inter-relations, in which each particular fact not only influences directly adjacent facts but rather by doing so influences the whole. The significance it has determines its value. Hence the idealistic bipartition of facts and values projects a duality into the universe which has no basis in reality. That it should be made has its reason in the complex multi-dimensional structure of the universe. Just as the moon by orbiting around the earth shares its orbiting around the sun yet in its own plane, thus also both moon and earth participate in the cosmic movement of the sun within our galaxy, so the things of this world are dependent on a hierarchical system of determinants. The modern sociologist and anthropologist try to describe man as moving within a particular system of determinants, whereas faith is anxious to see him in the totality of the world's dimensions.

3. *Teleology*

When individual persons and particular things are considered as ultimates, this world, far from giving the appearance of a unified entity, seems to be closer to chaos. To the positivist, that co-existence of order and disorder is evidence of the universal rule of probability and chance. Consequently human activity, as William James and the Pragmatists advise us, is to be guided by considerations of usefulness. Since the course of things does not follow any general rules, life is bound to be a never-ending experimentation. To theologians who adopt the pragmatist position, God himself is an experimenter who is not too sure of what is best or who is unable to manipulate the world stuff in a consistent way. The notion of God is in that interpretation but a symbol for cosmic chance. Apprehended in the light of the Bible, however, this world appears in a different light altogether. Notwithstanding the role of cosmic determinants, this world is not a stationary one. Rather it is permanently in motion. But its movement is a complex process in which creaturely freedom and divine purpose are found united. The things of this world are not to be understood as God's puppets, whose spontaneity and changeability are mere appearances. Yet definite limits are set to their changes by the nature of the species to which they belong, and in general by the cosmic determinants.

Above all, however, it is the purpose which God pursues in this world that explains the seemingly contradictory texture of this world. The phenomenon of novelty, which is most conspicuous in biological evolution and in human history, indicates that supreme reality implies directionality and the possibility of the creatures either to move toward the cosmic goal, or to disregard that tendency. Hence the distinction between good and evil has an objective basis, and moral decisions can be made on a solid foundation. The goal of God's purpose is called the kingdom (or the kingly rule) of God: that is to say, a condition of this world in which all its spontaneous movements in their particularity serve the whole so that the wisdom, goodness and power of the hidden creator, or God's glory, are manifested in and through the world process. Accordingly, the contradistinction of ethical and practical activities is rather misleading. All of man's activities, artistic ones no less than industrial or commercial ones, are to be evaluated and judged in the light of God's ultimate goal. In turn, the operation of the divine purpose stimulates man never to be satisfied with the *status quo* but rather to be guided by the vision of far distant goals. In that way, progress toward perfection is possible in this world, yet it is not a movement of intrinsic improvement. It is as God's agent or steward that man participates in it.

4. *The Powers of Evil*

That the aspect of this world should be so bewildering has been explained as resulting from the creaturely finitude and ontic imperfection. Such explanation is unsatisfactory, however. It would imply that this world is forever doomed to remain what it is like. For since, in the millions of years in which this world has been in existence, such creaturely weakness has not been overcome, we had to infer that God either does not want it to improve or is unable to change it. Such a pessimistic view is precluded, however, by the life of Jesus and the operation of his Spirit in the Church. They are evidence of the fact that in this world an effective movement takes place toward a perfect life.

Yet granted the irrefutable evidence of those facts, it is equally and overwhelmingly obvious that the world in which we live is filled to the brim with moral and physical ills. Most incomprehensible and confounding are probably two facts – viz. the irregular and irrational distribution of natural endowments and the loss of things and people we love. They give us the impression that, in this world, forces are at work which thwart the cosmic teleology. That impression is confirmed by the Bible, which points to the enmity with which Satan and antiteleological forces of evil interfere with the course of this world and human life. Such a view contradicts the naïve belief that we are living in a neutral world free of values into which man infuses his values. If that picture were right, it would be amazing that after so many millennia of civilization no noticeable improvement of the human predicament had been accomplished. On the contrary, increased comfort has also strongly augmented the number of ills.

Buddhism tries to cope with the problem of evil by ascribing it to a wrong attitude of the will. When the evils of this world are disregarded, because in fact they are but self-created illusions, the individual will feel unlimited and pure happiness. Such an attitude is not possible, however, except by ignoring the condition of one's fellow men, as is evident from a study of social conditions in South-East Asia. In the Western world, an optimistic hope is widely entertained for a radical improvement both of living conditions and human nature. The ameliorating factor would be found in the development of man's intellect, and especially of science and/or in a new social order which would take care of all of man's problems. Yet to the present day such expectations have not left the stage of wishful thinking. To mention only one or two instances. While certain endemic diseases, such as tuberculosis, for instance, have been successfully combated, the incidence of nervous and mental troubles has greatly increased in recent years, and since their main cause is to be found in our modern civilization, it is most unrealistic to regard them as a passing phase of modern life. Likewise, the contention that crime, vice and unethical behaviour have their roots in unfavourable social conditions, and that the moral level would be raised in proportion to social and economic conditions, is strikingly contradicted by the police reports. Similarly, while it should not be denied that communism has substantially improved living conditions for millions of people, the frightening tension in Sino-Russian relations is evident proof that the new social order does not guarantee the peace of the world.

In view of the ubiquitous and inevitable presence of evils many modern people still espouse a naïve optimism. They live on the assumption that ours is basically a good world populated by a host of good people. The exceptions from this rule are supposedly few only, and man is allegedly capable of taking care of them. To an affluent society, it serves as a tranquillizer that saves a lot of worries, and the prophets of doom are not taken seriously. But it can be confidently stated that there will be a gruesome awakening.

In order to explain the present state of things in this world, the New Testament speaks of powers (*archai, exousiai, dynameis*), that is to say, cosmic tendencies which attempt to thwart the purpose of God and, if possible, to destroy this world. In that group, enmity, want, error, appearance, disintegration, and death are found.

A further group of evils is usually referred to in the Bible as Sin. The term designates the ontic iniquity of man. In the Old Testament, Sin is mainly described as transgression of God's commandments. However, already by the prophets of Israel, Sin was denounced as disregard for God's lofty intentions and his redemptive work in history rather than as transgression of special divine precepts. Augustine discerned its root in pride (*superbia*), that is to say, man's overrating his significance and power.

Man is aware of the fact that on account of his mental abilities he has opportunities and possibilities which all animals lack. He alone is capable of transforming nature according to his plans and for his well-being. Realizing his exceptional place in this world, man is disinclined to accept his createdness and his creatureliness as the ultimate determinants by which his life receives its direction. Thus he looks for a source of authority in himself, by which he would be enabled to arrange his life in complete freedom. The consequence of such an attitude is a thorough disturbance not only of the cosmic order but also of the redemptive plan which God has for this world. The results of Sin may be seen not merely in vice, gross immorality, violence, or brutality but also in the damage done to one's own destination. It will manifest itself, for instance, in wilfully ignoring God's presence and purpose, that is to say, in secularism, or in worries and refusal to notice the world's good things, in greed or in unlimited thirst for pleasure, power or renown. All these ways of denying the existence of God are compatible with an otherwise 'moral' life. Yet in the long run Sin will stop the individual's spiritual growth and debilitate his spiritual energies, unless he realizes the falsehood of his aspirations.

Theology has been at pains to explain how these evils came into existence but has left no doubt as to their purpose. One thing is certain, however. Evil is not able to come into being unless there is positive goodness. The Zoroastrian or Manichaean dualism, for instance, contradicts itself by positing a power of evil which is contemporary with that of goodness. By itself and apart from goodness evil is not able to exist.

Thus understood, the world in which we exist is basically a good world, as can be seen in its order and balance. In it, however, dysteleological forces are at work which try to stop the execution of God's plan by using the things of this world for their purpose. Thereby, man is deceived. He holds that the direction which the forces of evil attempt to give to this universe is the final outcome of reality. The forces of evil are not therefore to be identified with the specific nature of things or with the laws of nature. They are superior determinants, by which all earthly forms, laws and principles are subjected. Yet their adversity is ultimately directed against the heavenly powers, by which things are held together, and are granted prosperity and growth. That is the reason why, by his natural abilities, energy and resources, man is unable successfully to fight the ills of the universe.

Man's is not a hopeless predicament, however. There is no ground for despondency and despair. Asserting himself as a truly human being in the universe is difficult but not impossible. It is an impossible endeavour for those who disregard the presence of God. They may be able to acquire power, renown or wealth but will become the slaves of their acquisition. Of one thing we may be sure. The forces of evil will never be able to destroy this world because they derive their strength from its existence. As Christians, we may go a step further and hold that our inability to get into control of those powers may be overcome by turning to God and relying on the means which he has put at our disposal in order that we should participate in his lordship. Even so it will not be an easy task. Rightly is the Christian life compared to warfare. Nor will the battle end before this life is over. But Christians have no right or reason to despair or to give up the fight against evil in themselves or in this world.

B. God's Good World

1. *The Realism of Faith*

That God's redemptive purpose should have a share in the constitution of earthly and cosmic reality must remain a mere assertion as long as the Christian faith is a mere message mediated to us through the historical agency of the Church. Not until God's redemptive activity has been experienced in some particular situation are we capable of distinguishing in this world between forces of evil and the manifestations of divine goodness. Man is bound to misunderstand the nature of this world as long as he takes it as a stationary world in which each person and thing have their meaning in themselves. In truth, however, their meaning lies in their being the means by which God's goal is to be actualized.

First of all, plants and animals have but a small share in the things of this world, namely as much as they are capable of using for food or shelter. Man however realizes that there is nothing in this world that is not at his disposal and of which he is unable to become the master. There is nothing in human nature or in man's accomplishment by which he had become worthy of such power. All things of this world are God's property for he made them exclusively himself. It is by sheer kindness that he lets man partake in his lordship; that is to say, in learning their nature and function and in using them for the benefit of all men. Thus all things in this world are good, since they are fit to serve God's purpose. The beneficial effect may imply happiness or success, but incidentally only. Above all it means that this is a world in which man may become truly human. The basic question of life is not therefore, What ought I to do? but rather, What is the relationship with God, for which he has destined me in this world? It was the priceless rediscovery of receptiveness as man's true relation to God that gave the Reformation its momentous significance. Assigning priority to the question, What ought I to do? is tantamount to postulating that it is man who through his activities imparts true meaning to this world. It is only with that attitude and the corresponding vision of a divine teleology that I am able to act in accordance with God's will.

We rebel by nature against assuming such a receptive attitude toward this world. For it implies the recognition that everything in this world serves God's plan. That does not mean that everything is morally or ontically good in this world. Yet paradoxically God allows the forces of evil to do their work in this world. Because they are evil they succumb eventually to his judgement; because they are real, they, too, must make their contribution toward the execution of his plan. Thus the things of this world which harm us and hinder us, are nevertheless willed by God. He offers them to us as means to develop our faith and to disclose their ambivalent nature. This teleological view must not be confounded with the naïve belief that evil is necessary as a stimulus for goodness. People will point out, for instance, that in warfare people show a sacrificial attitude, heroism and comradeship, which are rarely exhibited in peace-time. That observation is true. But the fact that these virtues are hardly brought home, when the war is over, should open our eyes to the fact that what is done under the dire pressure of necessity is no real virtue but rather attitudes required for collective self-preservation.

In turn, when we are willing to receive this world out of God's hands rather than as a lost property which we pick up stealthily, we discover a consistency and relatedness of life, within it, yet of a paradoxical nature. For seemingly its teleology has nothing to do with the causal and pragmatic connection of things. Apparently unrelated events form a pattern of divine guidance and education by which we are made ready more effectively to serve God's cause. Thus understood, the receptiveness of faith is an aspect of our love of God. Faith does not fatalistically acquiesce in what happens to us by the will of God. Yet it would also be naïve if we believed that all that God does to us must be pleasant. By faith, we love God himself rather than that particular work of his. We are sure that God's ultimate goal is good, and that the means he uses are in agreement with his goal. This assurance implies that God has so arranged this world that eventually our self-will is rendered capable of making a lasting contribution to the execution of of God's plan with this world. Love of God then is an attitude, in which we trust that notwithstanding all appearances to the contrary this is a good world, in which to live makes sense even though we are unable fully to understand the significance of each phase of it.

2. *Manifestations of Goodness*

While this world is far from manifesting its teleological goodness in every place and at all times, the trust we put in it is not based upon an arbitrary guess. By faith we are enabled to pick up manifold evidences of its goodness. The telic nature of this world makes evident that this world is not the work of a heavenly artificer who having created a work leaves it to itself. Rather, through this world God shows that he is a living God. The classical distinction of immanence and transcendence can therefore hardly be applied to the God of the Christian faith. While as the origin God is the ultimate determinant of all that is, he is at the same time present in this world as the dynamic by which it is directed toward its final goal. As a result everything in this world partakes of its teleological character. The telic nature of the universe is probably most conspicuous in the permanency of its orders. For billions of years the cosmos has existed as a system whose parts have always stayed in a harmonious relationship. If ever at some point the equilibrium of the cosmos is disturbed, it is for a moment only and never to a serious degree. The universe has proved to be capable of engendering life, not fortuitously, for then life could not have remained in existence and have developed increasingly higher realms and families and species. Furthermore, the things that have originated in this world are not simply destined to exist for each other, but also to bring about something new that points to the eventual realization of the final end. From a purely rational viewpoint, the fact that change should be found in this world is a mystery. Why did it not remain unchanged in its original state? And if you start with a primeval amorphous matter, how is it explainable that it developed into a universe of shaped bodies and permanent forms? And that such a process did not end with the formation of the stars and suns but rather manifested its unbelievably rich capability to diversify. It advanced and brought forth all the species of organic life, and eventually man, into being. These facts do not furnish a complete demonstration of God's work in the universe. They suffice, however, to show that all attempts to prove the origin of this world as an incidental development from an original stuff without qualities or as the mere result of hazard are far less cogent. Christianity is not interested in the hypotheses by which the origin of our universe is understood as condensation of formerly diffuse energy, or as the result of a primeval explosion of a field of energy. The fact remains that all such hypotheses must take their start from something that is capable of eventually developing into the universe in which we live.

The harmonious balance of the universe is not a mechanical one only; it also manifests itself in the sufficiency of supply needed to support the innumerable host of living creatures. Drought, diseases, natural catastrophes and other causes may temporarily limit the resources available. Whole species may die out, but life proves to have an amazing resiliency and quickly restores its losses. The universal co-operation and co-ordination, which we notice throughout this world and in particular here on earth, makes us therefore bold to speak of a divine Providence which presides over this world. We are thereby enabled to act in a rational way because we can count on the dependability of the things of this world, whereas the devotees of primitive religions live a precarious existence from moment to moment.

A further root of ethical behaviour is to be found in man's relationship to nature. Both the belief in *mana* and primitive animism show that man is aware of a reality that confronts him in his contacts with this world yet is in a mysterious way superior to, and more valuable than, his existence by itself. This sense of the numinous, as Rudolf Otto called it, is constitutive of man's awareness of himself, notwithstanding the fact that in the history of religions various realms of nature and various objects have been experienced as carriers of the numinous. As a result, man feels that all reality, or at least portions of it, must be approached with reverence. Thereby man is reminded of the fact that no matter how highly he thinks of himself there is a reality above him, disregard of which would devaluate his life. This sense of reverence provides the perspective for ethical action. No matter how dim and indefinite our idea of the reality to be revered may be, it enables us to realize that in order to be genuine, our life must reach into a sphere that transcends what we actually are.

More than any other religion, Christianity emphasizes also the fact that the mere awareness of a transcendental reality does not establish a real relation with it. On the contrary, man's sinfulness, that is to say his disregard for God's will, would doom his moral efforts to sheer futility but for the fact that the repentant believer may count on God's pardon. Thereby the destructive consequences of sin are neutralized. Nevertheless, the believer will be aware that by itself his moral life is insufficient to make his existence meaningful. Consciousness of our sin compels us to realize that God has not destined us to create a perfect world by means of our own goodness. Rather he is willing to use us in spite of our failures, as instruments for the execution of his purpose. Paradoxically, the Christian life is accompanied by a sense of dignity and election. Yet also with a sense of humility by which we recognize that it is not we, but rather God, who builds up the new world. Thus the Christian view of man precludes any idea of innate moral sufficiency or of power in our own strength to build up a new world. What goodness we have is donated by God. Yet the Christian is also certain that by the kindness of God that power works in him. He can point to the changes which God's kindness works in the life of the Church.

3. *Appropriations*

Our survey has shown that a clear distinction must be made between the ontic goodness of this world, that is to say its fitness for the execution of God's purpose, on the one hand, and its practical goodness, that is, its usefulness for a pleasant life, on the other. The former is unlimited, whereas the latter is restricted at many occasions. Yet the two perspectives may not be completely separated, as in Buddhism, nor may the latter one be interpreted as mere appearance, as is done in Hinduism. Rather the ontic goodness of this world implies the promise of a development, in which the errors and shortcomings of the latter sphere will be overcome. The attitude that Christians take toward this world is therefore neither an optimistic nor a pessimistic one. In either case, goodness or lack of goodness would be a stationary condition that is rooted in the nature of things. In fact, however, the correlation and interdependence of things is at times interfered with by destructive forces, while in other instances they are used as the starting point for the bringing into existence of higher values, as is the case in biological evolution and in the products of human creativity, for instance in the works of art and the discoveries of scholars.

Our faith has nothing to do with that gloomy apocalypticism which erupts from time to time as a neurosis. Its devotees take delight in the idea of an imminent destruction of this world. Yet Christian faith holds that even through a cataclysmic change of this world God would renew rather than destroy what he had created as expression of his wisdom and kindness. Because this world is basically good, we have a right momentarily to forget what damage is caused by the forces of evil, and to engage in jests, gaity, play, entertainment and exuberant hilarity, or to mock the evil powers by means of humour. There is a deadly seriousness which is a caricature of faith, because man takes his awareness of possible losses and failures more seriously than the way in which God has constituted this world. The funny way in which demons and the Devil are treated in the statuary of the medieval cathedrals, far from being an indication of secularization, is rather evidence of a triumphant faith.

Nevertheless, Christian faith is not a joke. The very fact that the ontic goodness of this world is indestructible, tends to conceal to the careless eye the stealthy operation of the destructive forces. Constantly we have therefore to be on our guard, lest what seems to be a matter of indifference should become the beginnings of a dangerous and destructive process. When the Christian ethos is identified with the mores and social practice of our nation, as is largely the case in the Western world, people's activities are soon dominated by the pursuit of the political and economic interests of the nation or its ruling group. It is of paramount importance for our life of faith that time and again we should set before us the goal for which God has destined us. Even in countries in which the majority of the population belong to Christian churches, it is not to be taken for granted that what is good for one's country is good for the whole world. The fact that the critics of the Church do often exaggerate the faults of the Church should not tempt us to take them lightly. Their exaggerations may be understood as being a divine device, by which a sleepy church is to be awakened in order to become more zealous in the pursuit of its true goal. The danger for us does not lie in the nature of things, so that abstaining from them was the solution of all moral problems. On pragmatic grounds, a good case may be made for abstention from alcoholic beverages, meat, movies, or participation in warfare. But useful as such attitude may be for an individual or his environment, it can never be understood as the final goal of human life. It may even become blasphemous, when it is exaggerated and abstention is blown up into a prerequisite of redemption, or when the individual holds that the things he shuns are the only manifestations of the forces of evil.

Evil is not truly explained when considered a purely mental phenomenon, namely an inordinate movement of our will. Forces of evil are at work in our field of action, and it is so ubiquitous that the true life cannot be found in a discipline of the will, by which all evils are shunned. The inordinate nature of our will lies in our unwillingness in an act of the self to detach ourselves from the claims of all earthly things to have ultimate significance for our life. As we look in that direction, we realize that the forces of evil are using all earthly things to turn people away from God. Not only are they dangerous when they present crime, vice and bad habits as useful or pleasant, but also when learning, art, morality or even religion prompt us to treat them as ultimates and ends in themselves.

The two perspectives of goodness explain the twofold nature of human activitiy, which is both a controlling and a transforming one. The myth of the Garden of Eden and the expulsion from it describe these aspects graphically. Gardening is work performed for the joy of it, as distinct from what we must do in order to satisfy our needs and to assert our dominion over nature. Even in a world entirely free of evils man would not be doomed to idleness. Not only could he enjoy and exercise his abilities in sport, artistic activities and rational pursuits, but also would his vocation as God's agent demand of man that in the biosphere of the earth he should exercise control of rank growth in order to render this world subservient to his own pleasure and make it enjoyable.

There is no wrong in man's engaging in activities which lack practical value. The goodness of the universe implies that apart from his special efforts and active participation man will be taken care of, and that the evolutionary process of the biosphere will continue by itself. But since man is destined to be God's agent and not the mere beneficiary of his kindness, he cannot leave things to themselves. In order to become fully human, he must transform the world by which he is surrounded, and on account of the evils which beset him from all sides, he must attempt to reach his goal through toil and sweat. Hence human life alternates between leisurely enjoyment and hard work, and as the arrangement of the week indicates, considerably more emphasis must be laid upon the working portion than of that of relaxation. Yet the man who prides himself on keeping busy all his life and who takes no time out for leisure, merely shows that he does not believe in the ontic goodness of the universe, just as the playboy's permanent enjoyment of life discloses his unwillingness to accept his vocation. In view of the shortening of the work week, which results from technological progress, some people have worried about the right use of the increased leisure time. The fallacy of such reasoning lies in the view that work is necessitated by man's economic needs rather than by man's divine vocation. Looked at from the latter perspective, the shortening of the work week should be understood as a God-given opportunity to employ the additional free hours for fight against the powers of evil outside the economic zone.

The enjoyment of the ontic goodness of this world will miss its mark, however, when it is understood in an egotistic way. Certainly it is due to God's kindness and love, that life on earth is not a mere succession of hardships and sufferings. But in order truly to enjoy it, man must recognize that attitude of God, which is done in prayer and religious meditation. Thereby we acknowledge the gratitude we owe to God, the wisdom with which he has arranged this world for the benefit of his creatures, and the power with which he asserts his purpose. People who are unable to feel awe, admiration and thankfulness and take the goodness of this world for granted, thereby prove merely the shallowness of their thinking and an utterly unjustified conceit.

Art has been from the beginning one of the media by which man gives expression to his recognition of the goodness of the universe. It does so either by adorning the objects of daily use or by reproducing nature in such a way that the ontic goodness rather than the exact look of things is emphasized. To say that art distorts reality is a complete misunderstanding of art. It does not intend to copy nature but rather is anxious to bring to light the mystery of its God-given goodness. It is not surprising, therefore, to find art closely related to prophecy. In turn, it may be said in criticism of modern abstract art, that it fails to notice the transcendental background of nature. What is wrong with it is, not its desire to show the discontinuity and intrinsic contradictions of modern life, but rather its failure to present them against the background of the world's goodness. It would seem that in a similar way modern painting is anxious to emphasize the element of order in our world but fails to show that it is an expression of God's kindness and concern for his creatures rather than a dictatorial rule.

In conclusion, it may be said that the Christian view of the world differs from that of modern science yet is not incompatible with it. The latter studies the causal relations of things and events, whereas the Christian faith is concerned with its teleological nexus. In a way, both approaches are interdependent. Faith must have a clear view of the things whose telic role it is concerned with, and science will assist it to a certain extent in that endeavour. The scientist, in turn, will be confronted with teleological problems, especially in biology, psychology and sociology, as also in the philosophy of nature. When it is a matter to understand the universe in its totality, the question why and for what end it is in existence will arise inevitably. Yet no synthesis of science and faith is to be hoped for. The scientist will insist on his inability to explain this world; he must be satisfied with a description. In turn, the theologian will categorically refuse to reduce the teleological character of the universe into a merely causal nexus, whereby the telic movement is ascribed to the nature of the things engaged in the process.

5 Time

A. The Nature of Time

Inseparable from the place which man occupies in the universe, is the temporal character of earthly reality. According to Christian faith, the temporality of existence exerts a decisive influence upon the evaluation of man's activities and of the world with which he is dealing. All religions do not ascribe such significance to time. The great religions of the Far East, for instance, either ignore time or advise their devotees to escape from it. Primitive religion in its various forms seems to be one-sidedly concerned with the beneficial or harmful effects which particular things have on their individual or social life without caring for their temporal function. In ancient Greece there was a remarkable awareness of the temporal character of this world. Special emphasis was laid, however, on its disturbing character, and it was closely associated with instability and disintegration. In the modern Western world, especially under the influence of science, time is often regarded a kind of vacuum in which things move, similar to the popular view of space. Yet time does not exist apart from things; it is the process in which they change. Accordingly there are as many kinds of time as there are modes of change in this world. The chronological time by which we measure our years, for instance, is originally planetary time. It takes its measure from the revolutions of the earth around its own axis and around the sun. It proves to be very convenient for all processes which take place in the earth's biosphere and the sphere of civilization. There are, however, as Bergson has shown, other types of time, such as mental or biological time.

The various perspectives in which time is seen points to its ambivalent character. Looking at the objects in time, one notices change and eventual disintegration and disturbance in the biological sphere, whereas the temporal process in which the objects are changed manifests the regularity of a causal or teleological succession of phases. Similarly there is the apparent contradiction between obsolescence, on the one hand, and the origin of progeny from perishing individuals as also of novel phenomena in our apparently permanent order of species, on the other.

Finally, we mention the paradoxical difference found in the fate of the author and his work. While the personal influence he has on other people wanes quickly after his death, his work may have a long lasting or even permanent influence upon mankind.

The attitude we take to these ambivalent features of time will depend on the relation in which we see them to God. That we have to live in time cannot be completely separated from the will of the Creator. Any existence that was entirely independent of God would seriously curb his power and sovereignty. But if temporality in the way in which we notice it in this world were the unambiguous expression of the will of the Creator there would be no meaning in his work. Like the Greek Kronos or the Gnostic Aion he would bring forth his creatures merely in order to have what he might devour and destroy again. If we believe that God loves his creatures – as has been shown, there are good reasons for believing so – a radically different view must be adopted. That the world in which we live is a temporal world is best explained in this way. In the fact that an objective world is in existence, we see the power of the Creator at work. That the existence of the universe is a temporal one is an indication of the purpose which God has with the world that he brought into being. The ambivalence and apparent inner contradiction of the time process has its root in the operation of forces of evil. They are capable of here and there, now and then disturbing the cosmic order but incapable of effacing its original harmony. The goal which God has in mind in creating this world will eventually be reached.

Accordingly, there is no point in seeking relief by means of a flight into a timeless reality. That goal can be attained in our imagination only, not existentially. In turn, the pessimistic view of time results from an unbalanced approach to time. Man clings to life, because his self-consciousness is in an undeniable way aware of the power of his vitality. In addition to obsolescence and disintegration, life is also the source of growth, of the enjoyment of increasing vitality and creativity. Above all the temporality of our existence offers opportunities for action and of leaving behind the marks of our mind in the works we perform and create. Not only discoveries and inventions linger on long after our physical existence has disappeared. Our deeds, too, affect the lives of others for good or bad through the generations.

Yet strange to say, while change is such a manifest characteristic of temporality, its domain is strictly limited. Times does not change the nature of man or of anything in this world. It is true that novel features make their appearance in time, in place of, or in addition to, existing ones. But there is no transformation of a species into another one. Nor is man in a position to shed his nature. Yet notwithstanding its positive side, life as a temporal process has also irritating and saddening features, above all its elusiveness. Life runs through our fingers like water and makes us aware of the futility of our attempts to hold the fleeting moment. Even its pleasures have but a limited possibility of enjoyment. The more frequently they are repeated, the more quickly their charm is dulled. Thus time as the power of change is one of the most powerful determinants of our existence, both in changing us willy-nilly and in setting definite limits to our own plans and desires. There is no reason for fatalism, however, for the course of time does not run in the same direction all the time. On the contrary, time offers new opportunities from time to time. We are not entirely its slaves. Thus, man's reactions to his experience of temporal existence are strangely divided. He feels both gratitude for the new gifts it offers constantly, yet also humbled by his limitations and the futility of his attempts to get control of it, and he is saddened by the awareness that notwithstanding his toil and discipline his physical existence will be eventually a total loss.

In addition to these reactions, which the Christian shares with the rest of mankind, there are specifically Christian attitudes toward time, once it is realized that through the time process the Creator manifests the purposiveness of his work. First of all there is a feeling of gratitude for the gift of life as an opportunity to act spontaneously and in the awareness of the meaning of his temporal existence. Furthermore, there is the glad awareness that temporality is not the ultimate determinant. By means of faith man is able to discover the way in which God diverts time toward his final goal and enables man, too, to embrace it and thus to triumph over the limitations of temporality. While that goal does not realize itself automatically but rather requires man's readiness to adjust himself to it, it is nevertheless not beyond his reach. That experience guards us against contempt of life and cynicism, and enhances our gratitude even for the things and events which, apart from God, seem to be burdensome. What appeared to be without design is then given ultimate significance. Temporal happenings do not fall into the abyss of nothingness, but work upon the substance of time. If that substance were identical with the mass of the material universe, temporal movements would be indications of mutations only and lack true meaning. We are aware, however, of the privilege of contributing to the realization of God's design. In it all that happens in this world is never lost, but rather makes its permanent contribution to God's work.

The Christian view of time is most authoritatively expressed by the church calendar because it is universally observed in Christianity. Conspicuous therein is the role assigned to the week and the year. Both of them have lost their original planetary association and their agricultural function, which they originally had in Mesopotamia and Israel. Instead they have become impressive symbols of God's dealing with this world. As the last day of the week, the Sabbath reminded the Jews that God was the end and goal of all of man's ways, yet also that in his kindness God provided so generously for the support of human life, that six days of work would suffice to gather enough food for seven days. Thus, time was not an incidental natural phenomenon. The system of the week manifested the divine origin and function of time, which is reverently to be hallowed. The observance of the week as a divine institution was taken over by the primitive Church, yet with a remarkable shift of emphasis. The accent fell on the first day of the week, which was associated with the Resurrection of Jesus. Thereby time was shown to be the medium through which the risen life of Christ would be instilled into the ordinary course of time. The Sunday symbolized the new beginning that God had made in dealing with this world. In spite of all the limitations and setbacks which temporality carried with it, it stood under the blessing of the Saviour. By making the Sunday the day of common worship, Christians indicate that in their workday, too, they act as God's people. That the week is a divine institution rather than a human device may be seen in the fact that it has been adopted by non-Christian and atheistic countries, too. Its effectiveness lies in the favourable ratio of resources and human abilities, which is God's arrangement made to safeguard the permanent existence of the human race. Thus the Sunday reminds us not only that the whole universe is under God's faithful care, but also that his care implies the work of Christ, that is to say the spiritual destiny of mankind.

The religious observance of the year was originally geared to the successive phases of agriculture and their regular recurrence. Post-exilic Judaism had already overlaid its seasonal character with the commemoration of the great deeds Yahveh had performed in Israel's history, and the Church completed the process by giving a strictly Christocentric character to the ecclesiastical year. By interspersing Christmas and Easter as the highpoints of the year, its former cyclical view of time was supplemented by a linear and teleological perspective. As in the case of the week, the Christian festivals gave emphasis to Christ's function as giver of new life, and his triumph over the forces of death and evil, by which temporal existence is normally marred. The regular recurrence of the year implied the assurance that what had happened in the life of Jesus was not a merely incidental event, but rather gave expression to God's unchanging will. Thus, through its calendar the Church bears witness to its triumphant assurance that the power of life was not exhausted in its biological and historical manifestations. They formed but the foundation of a new life in the power of the Spirit. Thereby God is proclaimed as the Lord of time, and all fatalism is overcome by the assurance that whatever man does by faith will be led by God to a good end.

The Jewish calendar never overcame its original cyclical character according to which the time process repeats itself. Hence the goal of history was seen in the return of the Paradise to the earth, or, in a more political way, in a final restoration of the glory of Judaism, as it had been in the days of Solomon. With the emphasis laid upon the Resurrection of Jesus, Christian experience is geared to a goal in which past and present events will be essentially transcended. The regularity and unbroken ongoingness of the succession of weeks and years was felt to be a confirmation of the power of life. It was not to be understood as the outcome of the intrinsic energies of earthly creatures but rather the confirmation of the belief that Yahveh was the 'living' God, that is to say, the very origin of life, a restoration of original bliss, either of the paradise, or of the political grandeur and affluence of Solomon's reign. Christianizing the Jewish calendar was a revolutionary deed. Through this Christocentric character, the festivals of the year pointed to the novel age brought about by Jesus. His birth and resurrection marked the beginning of a process which aimed at a transformation not only of man but also of the whole universe. It was but consistent with such a view that eventually the Church repudiated the chronological systems of its pagan environment and adopted in 525 a chronological scheme of its own. In it the birth of Christ was treated as the beginning of a radically new era, by which all events prior to it were demoted to a preparatory role.

The element of truth embedded in the cyclical view of time was not thereby disregarded. Rather it was subordinated to the teleological outlook of Christian eschatology. The goal which God has in mind in history, and whose realization has been initiated through the birth of Christ, will not be reached in a haphazard and irregular manner though the eschatological process will imply catastrophes. Rather it will work itself out through the cosmic order in time and space.

B. The Course of Time

1. *Faith and History*

Thus far we have discussed time in general and the attitude taken by Christians toward the temporal character of human existence. But unlike all other living creatures, man stands in a temporal process which is quite unique, viz. history. Man is not only capable of being aware of time, but also acts in response to time and modifies the temporal nature of his environment by means of a rational or spiritual approach. Thereby man creates a special sphere of life, viz. civilization. Animals, too, are engaged in search of food, and may even hoard it, yet man is the only creature which builds storehouses and cultivates animals and plants for regular and methodical production of food.

Guided by the awareness of a divine design, the ancient Hebrews were able to discern within history a special strand which contributed in a special and direct way to the execution of God's redemptive purpose. It has become customary to designate it history of redemption, or holy history, translating the German *Heilsgeschichte*. Man is not yet man as long as he lives outside of history, that is, without the awareness that he is destined to assert himself over against the temporality of existence by means of his own works. Unlike the animals he must not allow his biological origin and heredity to determine his outlook and actions. The urge to act historically and to create civilization is felt by all men, yet the realization of the goal depends on the presence of individuals, who possess a special creative ability.

Election is a basic pattern of the life of mankind. Not every man is a philosopher, an artist, a statesman, or any other leader of men. This fact implies that all men are destined to participate in historical life, yet not everybody is destined to be an independent agent. Even the best type of democracy, for instance, requires political leaders and while all are called upon to make their specific contribution in a responsible manner, in their majority they cannot do so except by following their leaders. Such attitude does not preclude a critical attitude on the part of the followers, but it debars the critic from usurping the role of the leader.

The principle of election applies also to the historical role of nations and religions. Israel believed confidently in its election as the protagonist of the true faith, because the insights given to it proved to be more profound, comprehensive and plausible than those found in other religions. The followers of Jesus, in turn, were assured of two things. Through him all want and suffering of mankind had lost their harmful power. Also he had expressed his insights in such cogent manner, that they needed not and could not be surpassed. Since in creating man God had indicated that he had chosen him, and that is to say the whole of mankind, to be the agent of his redemptive work, the role of Jesus is an ambivalent one. On the one hand, in Jesus' life the whole mystery of God's plan has been brought to light, his work is performed once for ever and needs no correction or supplementation. On the other hand, however, Jesus' work is to be brought to the knowledge of all men, and in that sense his earthly work is an incipient one, which will not come to its conclusion until the whole of mankind has been effectively confronted with him. Thus the history of the Church, which seems to be a purely human affair, is in fact the manifestation of the power and the grace of Christ. Apart from the influence he exerts constantly upon it, it would never be able to accomplish what it actually does. Hence, salvation cannot be found in a flight away from history, as is the case, for instance, in Neo-Platonic mysticism, or in modern existentialism. The Christ in whom we believe is not confined to the earthly life of Jesus. In and through the life of Jesus he discloses his purpose and he continues to do so in the history of the Church. Not everything that takes place in the life of the Church manifests the operation of Christ. But enlightened by the Gospels we are able to discern him at work in his changed shape of today's Church.

History has often been understood as the work of individuals who brought their superiority of power or skill to bear upon other people who had not otherwise been related to them. It does not require too much sagacity to notice the fundamental error implied in such a view. Historical activity takes place in an historical field; that is to say, it presupposes a community with definite characteristics and aspirations. The historical agents are people who belong to the field and manage by means of their specific qualities or power to occupy the centre of the field. The result is a reciprocal relationship of agents, who attempt to modify the nature or direction of the field, on the one hand, and the people of the field, who adjust their thoughts and/or institutions to the new direction their leaders are aiming at. This pattern of the historical field is found in holy history as well as in secular history. The work of Jesus was rooted in post-exilic Judaism, and it became effective in history, when the early followers of Jesus translated his intentions into the reality of the Church.

In recent times, excessive emphasis has been laid upon the disquieting role which history plays in the life of the Church. On the one hand it is held that since he was an historical figure, Jesus, too, must have been a mere man and for that very reason could not be assigned a capital role in our redemption. Salvation, it is contended, is accessible only through timeless metaphysical truths. What saves us would then be our religion, that is to say the psychological or noetic aspect of our ultimate concern. On the other hand, it is emphasized that redemption is an event yet one which in order to be effective must be a purely divine work. Notwithstanding his human appearance, Jesus must be thought of as a purely heavenly being, and his presence in history must, as in the Roman Catholic Church, be conceived of as taking place in an act of transubstantiation. These views are not just fine points of purely academic discussion. What we think of Christ has a direct and far reaching bearing upon our conduct, that is to say the manner in which our faith becomes articulate. The former view, in which the salvation is located in the human mind, implies the conviction that goodness conceived of as self-perfection can be realized by the individual's efforts and that it is in everybody's reach. Moral goodness is the same everywhere, though people may not always be able fully to realize that fact. The latter view is interested in a divine act of salvation, the fruit of which may be received without any further ado as an everlasting and unchanging treasure. The Christian's only task consists in urging his unbelieving fellow men to mind their redemption, too.

Over against those extremes, it must be emphasized first of all that the unique place which man occupies in the universe, puts the responsibility for historical life and civilization on the shoulders of all men. Hence the individual is not free to decide whether or not he will take part in it. He is a parasite who exploits the efforts of others, if he refuses to co-operate with them. Furthermore, since man is chosen by God in the wholeness of his existence all men are in principle responsible for all aspects of human life and civilization, even though each one according to his stance and ability may give preference to a specific aspect.

Beyond this general commission, the Church has realized the presence of the risen Lord as the principal source of its dynamic. Just as Jesus' life and ministry manifested God's saving will operating through historical events, so the Church is the historical continuation of that divine plan. The divine will uses human lives and wills as his agencies. For that end, man is dependent on the divine initiative with which he identifies himself by faith. Unless we behold the history of the Old Covenant and the historical work of Jesus as witnessing to God's

CHRISTIAN ETHICS

redemptive activity, there could be no faith. By opening himself up to God's redemptive will man is made capable of serving as God's instrument. The miracles of followers whom Jesus had attracted by proclaiming God's redemptive will were the most striking evidence of what God is able to accomplish through his elect. Jesus addressed himself to the actual historical situation in which the people he had called did live. Jesus makes plain that the proof of genuine faith is to be found in the fact that people accept their historical situation as willed by God. Thereby that situation is transformed in a divinely offered opportunity for man spontaneously and obediently to promote God's cause in this world.

Practically, that means first of all this. Since God makes himself known in a given situation, we should assume that it is his will that by faith we should come to terms with that situation and render it meaningful. Whether it be an adverse or a lucky situation, it is not to be evaluated in an egotistic way. For it is God who wants thereby to accomplish something in this world and thus in the lives of other people no less than in ours. Where practical interests prevail, we are very likely to envisage a speedy result of our action. As a consequence we are tempted to be careless in the choice of our means, provided only they promise early returns. Conversely, if we contemplate our action as a contribution to the coming of God's Kingdom, we have to mind Jesus' teaching. Whatever we do by faith is like a grain of seed which we entrust to the soil. It will germinate, grow up and bear fruit at the time that in the context of God's cosmic plan is deemed to be appropriate. Hence patience and long suffering on our part are required. It may be a long while until we are able to notice what results our life and deeds have had in other people's lives. Sometimes we may not even be privileged to notice results. In other instances, we may be surprised by the speed with which the results are rendered visible. There is, however, no Christian life that is devoid of evidences to the effect that faith is always bearing fruit.

In general it can be seen how God uses temporal succession for his purposes. In order to strengthen and clarify our faith, God reminds us of the great and marvellous things he has performed in our own past life and that of Christianity. God keeps up the continuity in time notwithstanding the discontinuity caused by the finite duration and the death of individuals. Yet he has seen to it that through parents, teachers and friends our faith would not be a haphazard event with a precarious basis, but rather would stand firmly on the continuous witness of the Church.

Since history is in constant flux yet brings forth works which last and survive their maker, we are confronted with the problem of authority. The issue is particularly bewildering in the Church, when God himself is seen at work in history. The historical process bring forth works, yet it is also the sphere of constant change, disintegration and death. The classicists will contend that certain works in art, social order or metaphysical insight are so perfect that they defy historical change. They are considered to be of a timeless or eternal value, and thus will never be surpassed. The relativists, on the other hand, will contend that in order to live a true life it is necessary always to live in the present moment. The past, it is held, would not have yielded to the present if it had been good enough to last. Whereas the classicists will invoke the permanent authority of the Bible, the tradition or the denominational confessions of faith, the relativists will ascribe no binding authority to them. Either view is unsatisfactory and has never been able to get consistent currency in the Church. Their basic weakness lies in their overlooking the telic character of history.

When we say that the saving will of God is the dynamic of history we do not simply mean that God has made history in order to enable time to imply change. Nor may we say that his relation to history is one in which he would interfere from time to time in a world which by itself were non-historical. In that case history would be the manifestation of God in a world which had nothing to do with God. As can be learned most conspicuously from Karl Barth's theology, history would thereby be the medium through which eternity is made perceptible in time, yet at the same time, history would be galvanized. Rather than a process, history would be a proving ground on which the heavenly bombs were dropped whenever it pleased God.

In fact, history discloses God as using the changeability of time as the means by which the goal God has set for this world may be both intimated and promoted. Thus the inquiry into the historicity of an event, necessary as it is, nevertheless does not reveal its meaning. The latter depends on the degree of clarity with which the event is capable of laying bare its intrinsic dynamic and the aim toward which it is directed. The historical-critical investigation of the Bible has so often gone awry because it was believed that matters of authority could be settled by discovering the earliest or the latest stage in a process, for instance, by ascertaining the pre- or post-exilic origin of a Biblical passage, or the earliest pre-synoptic document.

It was rather in the light of their illuminating and saving work that the chosen people has composed and read the Bible.

Thus, Christianity has seen in the person and ministry of Jesus the clearest revelation of man's nature and destiny. Of course, the men who described it, could use the psychological and literary resources at their disposal. In that sense, the New Testament is a document of its age. But the authors of the New Testament books leave no doubt about the fact that the Jesus whom they described, made such a radical impact upon their lives that they had to describe his ministry as the turning point of the spiritual history of mankind. The implication of these facts is obvious. The significance of Jesus remains ultimate throughout the centuries. Yet each generation of the Church is confronted and challenged afresh by the witness borne by the primitive Church to Christ. Interesting as that witness is in its applicability for the first generation of the Church, new ages must relate the work of Jesus to their own conditions and problems. If the Gospel were a theorem, its classical significance might be demonstrated by its uniqueness, that is to say, the inability of subsequent generations to refute it. As a decisive event, the ministry of Jesus proves its lasting significance rather by the unchanging impact it makes upon the lives of people and the radical change it calls forth in them.

What makes the New Testament, and the Gospels in particular, relevant for our time is not their character as historical documents but rather the testimony they bear to the encounter their writers had with Jesus and the effect that encounter had upon their lives. The way they report their story and the manner in which they group their material may seem to be unhistorical from the viewpoint of the modern historian. Few of the sayings of Jesus may have been preserved in their original form, and notwithstanding the effects of Form Criticism it may be impossible to reconstruct them. Likewise, it is very likely that the leaders of the early Church interpreted the significance of Jesus in terms of the Old Testament which Jesus himself may not have used. What has given to the Gospel their permanent authority is the genuineness of their witness which has been reconfirmed by the successive experiences of Christianity. The fact is not without interest that the Bible itself does not provide a proof of its authority, and that all the attempts to demonstrate it by means of theological arguments have proved to be unsatisfactory. It is through the effects that its content has upon the hearts and minds of its readers that it offers convincing evidence of its revelatory function. It is by the uninterrupted chain of believing testimony that the Bible asserts its authority in spite of the perennial attempts to depose it.

94

2. *Eschatology and Ethics*

Since God has a purpose in creating this world, the past is not understood by Christianity as something that was once real yet exists no
longer. Nor is the future understood in an indefinite sense simply as all
that is not yet in existence yet may happen. Rather the awareness of
the dynamic and purposiveness of God's will has brought about an
entirely new and unique experience of the time process. In it the emphasis falls upon the present moment. Man is to live with God, not with
mere ideas of God and his relation to time. Nor would a life of mere
recollections or of dreams of the things to come be considered a genuine
life. Christianity is primarily a religion of actuality and activity. This
contention seems to be contradicted by the authoritative place that the
Bible occupies in Christianity. Does that not mean that what God has
done in the past is of the utmost importance for us? The answer must
be categorically, No. The apparent dilemma has been called forth by
wrongly applying the scheme of physical or planetary time to religion.
For in personal experience, and especially in the life of faith, the present
moment is not a non-extensive point by which the past is separated
from the future. In human experience, the present is the totality of facts
my consciousness is capable of embracing simultaneously with the
awareness of myself. That awareness implies the past inasmuch as it
continues to operate in me. For while events themselves are annihilated
as time goes on, the effects the past has produced in the people concerned are not wiped out as time goes on but rather contribute to the
dynamic of their 'field'. That is the case even when those events are
not remembered or when people were unaware of them. No less characteristic of human time is its anticipating tendency. Man is a being
who is conscious of the fact that his life has consequences. While in that
respect, too, the goal may not be known or not specially intended, our
mind nevertheless has a directionality by which we are aware that the
present moment is not a terminus. Rather I am now preparing for a
goal ahead of me which will be conditioned by what I am in this
moment.

If the connection in which I stand with the past and the future were
merely a mental act of remembrance or hope, time would not have any
significance for religion or ethics, because it would lack objective reality.
What we call time would in fact be a mere succession of incoherent
events which would drop into the abyss of nothingness right after they
had occurred. Likewise the future would be a hypothetical reality only.
In their use of time, men and animals would not differ. Animals, too,

are endowed with the ability to remember past events and to associate present facts with their consequences. What raises man above the animal in their relation to time is man's awareness of the purpose God carries out in time. The past is not a dead nothingness but rather that portion of God's purpose which has already been executed, and the future is that portion that is still to come into being. Thus the future is not the mere succession of the past. Rather it is conditioned by the past. It will be what alone on this basis it is able to be. Yet being the final phase of God's purpose and not the mere outcome of the past, the future will comprise elements of novelty. It will not be a simple repetition or mutation of the past. Likewise, the past is not a merely incidental agglomeration of events. It is that which is essential for the preparation of the future. As a result of the divine purpose, the past can never be lost. It becomes an integral part of the time process. Hence the historical character of the Bible is not a disadvantage; on the contrary, it reminds us of that past apart from which we would never be what we are by faith.

The experience of temporal existence explains the interest which the Christian religion takes both in the history of the events by which it was brought into existence and in eschatology. The former is usually called holy history or redemptive history. It comprises the events recorded in the Bible and the effects which the ministry of Christ had upon the genesis and growth of the Christian religion. By 'eschatology', in turn, or the science of the last things, we designate the sum total of the views the Church entertains concerning the final goal toward which the time process is moving. Our life of faith rests on the assurance that it did not originate by chance or an intrinsic process in the self. Rather it has been prepared in the past by God's redemptive activity, above all by the events recorded in the Bible. At the same time, our future is not to be conceived of as a mere 'not yet'. Rather it is a process that is geared towards a condition in which we and all creatures will be in full harmony because brought together by God. In that way God's wisdom and glory will be manifested without being marred by the forces of evil. By thus extending into the past and future, the Biblical faith has overcome the cyclical view of the ancient Hebrew calendar and espoused an historico-telic outlook. A similar scheme underlies the modern concept of evolution. As a matter of fact, that concept owes its origin to a secularization of Christian eschatology. Yet in both its idealistic and its materialistic interpretations the time process is envisaged as a mere actualization of a potential reality. Jesus, in following the prophetic vision, has emphasized that through the divine purpose novel elements are introduced into the time process. Things which were not in existence and could not come into existence by an intrinsic development or mutation, enter history whenever new aspects of God's redemptive work are apprehended by faith and thus given an opportunity to influence historical life effectively. The powers of evil will be curbed and eventually be broken. Thus the whole world will be transformed from a self-assertive to a God-centred existence.

The bewildering infinity of the universe, and the perplexing quantity and multiplicity of things from which people tried to withdraw into the finitude of a cyclical view of time, will no longer be dreaded when people notice that the whole universe is integrated in the process of redemption.

In order adequately to deal with the ethical implications of the time process, it is necessary to make a clear distinction between eschatology and apocalypticism. The latter considers the time process as a mere succession of periods, whose length and specific contribution have been fixed by God from eternity. Hence, there will be a process through which the believers will pass unscathed. Yet it will come to pass with a necessity that precludes any interference or meaningful participation on the part of man or any other creature. Rather it is held that, in his inscrutable will, God divided mankind into two groups. He has chosen some to inherit the eternal glory, whereas the rest is bypassed. Such thinking was widespread in post-exilic Judaism and is not uncommon today. Eschatology, conversely, interprets the dynamic of the time process as the manifestation of God's creative will, and especially of the power of the risen Christ. His purpose comes to light when he calls people and engenders faith in them. Apart from that human participation, Christ's historical work would not only be imperceptible; it would not even be possible. Unlike apocalypticism, eschatology does not contend to possess a timetable of history and its end. It is satisfied to know what the goal will be like, and the pattern of experience of typical events in holy history.

The eschatological outlook confronts us with a momentous dilemma. We are sure that in pursuing it God is undoubtedly reaching his goal. How then is the eschatological process related to our own aims and wishes and plans? The simplest answer seems to be a clear-cut division: let God do his own work and let us stick to ours. That is the solution adopted, for instance, by Dispensationalism. But it is an unsatisfactory answer, because it implies that human activity, though performed irrespective of God's will, is considered pleasing to him. Equally in-acceptable is the idea that God is at work in man's heart calling forth a desire to establish God's Kingdom. The trouble with such a view is that it compels us to postulate two kinds of moral goodness, one consist-ing of an attitude of the heart, and another one aiming at an effective practical life. The Lutheran doctrine of the two kingdoms is an instruc-tive illustration. No less objectionable is the modern contention that God is a synonym of change. The *status quo* would be the sphere which God has abandoned, while attacks on it and revolutionary movements would indicate, where he is at work. All these approaches are typical of humanism. Goodness is identified with what is in man by nature. The real resolution of the dilemma is found in our knowledge of the nature of the eschatological process as it is foreshadowed in holy history and above all in the ministry of Jesus. While it is quite legitimate for us to adopt plans and programmes aiming at practical ends, the way to our goal must be in conformity with God's redemptive work.

For that end, humility is required, that is to say, willingness com-pletely to subordinate our goals to God's and to trust that his way of dealing with us is utterly superior to our wisdom and plotting. Such humility is not easily adopted for we do not know what God is planning for, and with, us. Nevertheless, we may be confident that he is directing us to a goal that will eventually appear satisfactory to us. The perplexity into which God may lead us at times, will become tolerable, however, if it is accompanied by our willingness to curb our self-will. We learn that attitude especially by means of prayer in which we implore divine guidance. To those who trust in him God is ready to grant light con-cerning his work. The resolution of the dilemma is further facilitated by the fact that in the portrait of Jesus as prescribed in the Gospels we have the description of a human life which was entirely in agreement with the plan of God. That picture of Jesus is not so much meant to be imitated, for we lack his specific commission. Rather, through describing the obstacles he encountered and the new way in which he met and overcame them, the evangelists intend to give us some glimpses of the nature of the eschatological process. Hence, it should be obvious that the New Testament eschatology is not so much interested in the descrip-tion of the future as such. Rather the evangelists intend to draw atten-tion to the divine dynamic as it is at work in the time process and its teleology. That experience shows that we have no innate knowledge of true goodness. Apart from faith, moral goodness is merely understood as the opposite of wrongness. Faith requires that we admit the limitation of our knowledge and be ready to be taught by the Gospel. Doing so is a lifelong process, because we are constantly in peril of relapsing into the delusion that we possessed that natural knowledge.

Thus, Christian faith is aware of a strand in human history in which the purpose of God manifests itself in a particularly clear way. All the attempts to identify holy history with history in general have ended in confusion. People will ascribe to a present or future situation absolute significance – as is done by Tillich or in the Marxist view of history – or they will lose the redemptive significance of Christ in the relativity of history. Jesus will appear to them as just one of the great examples of genuine life.

By singling out holy history and its continuation in eschatology we do not contest the fact that God's purpose is at work in all temporal processes. We should emphasize on the contrary that holy history is unduly limited when it is understood merely as a succession of historical events, for instance, from Abraham to Jesus. By 'holy history' we must understand the activity of the Son of God as he carries out in time the Father's redemptive plan beginning with the creation of this world. But except for holy history the distinction between good and evil is almost impossible to make, because goodness is but the shunning of wrongness. But the eye of faith discerns the operation of the law of equalization at work in all history outside holy history. Every discovery, every step forward in history will be used for evil no less than for good purposes, so that no real progress is possible. From the moral viewpoint all history moves in a twilight.

By faith we realize how God overcomes that tantalizing law by providing evidence that unambiguous goodness is possible here on earth. Consequently, faith is not an unfounded optimism by which we disregard the presence of the forces of evil; on the contrary, the Christian knows that they are so powerful that human effort alone will never suffice to triumph over them. By faith, we may nevertheless acquiesce in the ways in which God carries out his plan. His means and procedures appear to us as strange as they appeared to Job. But in the light of his past activities, ground is given us for hope. We have no reason or right to question his wisdom or his power. Hope is therefore an essential aspect of faith. Hope is not the belief that our wishes and desires will be fulfilled, but rather the assurance that both the time process as a whole as also our own life will reach a truly meaningful goal. Christian hope is more than the expectation that this world will always remain in existence. There is, of course, the confidence that God will keep in existence what he had brought into being, because effacing this world would be an admission of its essential imperfection. Christian hope anticipates not merely deliverance from the present evils of life, but also and above all a change of things for better. Christians may confidently hope that by their efforts some lasting progress will be accomplished in this world. The energy with which the Western world has engaged in scientific research and technological advance, finds its explanation in the confidence of faith. The difficulty the nations of Africa and the Far East have in appropriating western civilization lies in the lack of a religious basis that would enable them to embrace the spirit of that civilization.

Finally, Christian hope differs basically from belief in evolution, as that idea was conceived by Hegel, Darwin, Huxley, or Marx – for instance, that in the course of the millennia new and higher species have come into existence can hardly be denied. But the new species cannot be considered as improved and revised editions of their antecedent species. Novel phases reached were not brought about by the intrinsic vitality or energy of existent individuals. The earliest and most primitive organisms are already well-adapted to prevailing living conditions. Palaeontology has shown conclusively that the origin of a new species does not take place in a process of gradual transformation but rather by a jump. As Bergson has intimated and Teilhard de Chardin has pointed out, the leap forward presupposes a directive energy by which the transformation of a whole species is determined. Such discontinuity of the movement to the future is found in history, too. Christian hope does not reckon with a gradual improvement of conditions or attitudes nor is it discouraged when evil conditions prevail for a long while. A change for better will take place suddenly and unexpectedly. Likewise, though the mighty forces of evil may play their cruel game with us, we have no reason to fear that eventually they will come out on top. What God intends to accomplish through us may not come to light during our lifetime. Yet there are so many other Christian lives which bear witness to his Providence that we can be assured that our life of faith, too, is truly meaningful. In particular the course of holy history discloses the power of the impotent. From a purely historical basis it seems to be absurd to expect that God's cause will triumph without military or financial support put by the Church at his disposal. Yet the Bible and the historical evidence of the Church abound with instances in which the martyr, the monk, the simple layman saw their cause vindicated in spite of powerful opposition. Nor is that opportunity confined to a few outstanding individuals. God uses all those who yield themselves to his service, and the triumph of his cause is accomplished by the Church in its totality.

C. Historical Decision

In turn, the unforeseen and unforeseeable course of history and the very actuality of holy history are apt to teach us that to make history is beyond man's power. At an opportune moment, man is able to initiate a new historical process, but he is not in control of the energies thereby released nor of the development that will ensue from his initial action. The trust he puts in his own judgement or power and his freedom of of action notwithstanding, the historical energies will sooner or later overpower his work. Yet, in spite of Sartre, historical action is not doomed to be absurd. It is man's privilege to act as God's agent and to use the historical institutions for the ends for which God has destined them. By doing so he can be certain that he is contributing to a work that notwithstanding its constant modifications will be an everlasting one, namely the establishment of God's royal power on earth.

Equally important is the willingness to accept whatever new historical features came to light especially in church history. By nature man has a conservative tendency. He wants to preserve forever what at a certain moment of history had proved to be the right thing to do. But since God is intent to bring about his goal, new features will inevitably come to light. That does not mean that we shall crave all the time for what is newest or what would appeal to 'modern man'. Thereby we would simply cater to people's instability. What we mean is best illustrated by the history of the Reformation. Luther realized that through him a new aspect of the work of the Holy Spirit was demanding recognition. The novelty of that discovery was frightening yet also imperative. In spite of its novelty it appeared to be tolerable to Luther because it proved to be consonant with what God's Spirit had accomplished in earlier phases of the history of Christianity. Rome was morally free to say that the revelation granted to the reformers suited a certain type of man yet not all of them. Thus it would have accepted Protestantism as a manifestation of Christianity, without espousing it. There lies the element of truth of situation ethics. A certain conduct may be chosen as being suitable for us but it cannot, in spite of Kant, be used as a general moral principle. Thus we must be willing to grant others the right to choose different courses of action. The Holy Spirit stands for diversity in unity.

In this connection, one more question remains. How do we know in a given situation, what is the right thing to do ? Herodotus held that from the errors and follies of past generations people might learn how to escape them. But it became obvious that historical situations do not repeat themselves. Circumstances, resources and people's character are never the same. Killing a tyrant, for instance, may give a new start to a political commonwealth in one case, while it is the beginning of political disintegration in another instance. Moreover, quite apart from most people's reluctance to learn from the past, the pragmatism of Herodotus' approach made his book unfit for ethical purposes. In modern times, there is a tendency to believe that the movement that criticizes the *status quo* in the most radical way or advocates the revolutionary overthrow of the social order, should be supported because the renewing spirit of God is held to manifest itself through it. It is true that eschatology underscores the difference between prevailing conditions and God's final goal. But that does not mean that such discrepancy may be identified with the contrast of the *status quo* and the aspirations of a dissatisfied and restive social group. Not every change comes from God. The Devil, too, is very busy in history.

What makes Christian activity relevant is not in the first place, what we do, but rather the spirit in which we act. Our conscience will tell us what goal we should aim at and what attitude we should take towards the persons involved in a given situation. Where these two factors are at work, whatever we do will help to continue God's work in history, and when we act in such a way, our conscience will tell us when we have erred or harmed our fellow men. It will also move us to seek pardon and to offer retribution.

Unless priority is given to the voice of conscience, our decision will be guided by the course and weight of our interests, our place in the historical field, the degree of insight and practical experience we possess and half a dozen or more factors in addition. Since these factors will influence Christian action, too, one should never expect uniformity of Christian life. Nor do we have a right to suspect the sincerity of fellow Christians on no better ground than that their manner or course of action aims at a different result from ours.

6 Redemption

A. The Human Predicament

As has been shown, man's life is dependent on his createdness and creatureliness. Our ethical outlook and goal have been fixed by the place which has been assigned to man in the universe. Yet even within his sphere man is not altogether his own master. First of all, he is destined to participate in the execution of God's plan. He finds himself determined by his unchanging and unchangeable human nature, by the limits which inescapable cosmic determinants impose upon his will and mode of action, and above all by the fact that life in this world is harassed and debased by the operation of powers of evil in this world. There is no escape from them, and while man may attempt in various ways to adjust his life to their operation, the human predicament is not thereby substantially altered. Notwithstanding the many evidences of goodness found in this world, the human situation would be hopeless but for God's redemptive activity. For not only does the co-ordination of the cosmic determinants elude our comprehension – the ways of life and destiny appear largely irrational or absurd to us – man's life is also constantly threatened and weakened by all kinds of corroding and disintegrating influences. As a result, human life is not only not fully satisfactory, but also will never by itself give us true satisfaction. On this fact at least all the great religions of the world are agreed. It is true that this conviction is not shared by all those who call themselves Christians. There are probably not a few in our days who think that everything is fairly well with man and this world. At least they think that whatever conditions are still unsatisfactory will eventually take care of themselves or can be remedied by man's efforts. Actually that is not a Christian outlook but rather the fatalism of the well-to-do Western man. Far from being realistic, it is an expression of wishful thinking. People of this persuasion fail to heed their own shortcomings and the harm they inflict upon other people. They also overlook the undescribable misery in which hundreds of millions of people are living today. Above all they do not realize that their acquiescence in, and complacency with, the prevailing conditions give the strongest and most effective obstacle to a real improvement of the human predicament The reason why so many of our contemporaries entertain such shallow optimism, is probably in the first place to be found in the stubbornness and callousness by means of which mankind tries to brave the innumerable multitude of evils. A further and more profound reason lies in man's deep-seated reluctance to countenance the fact that even the satisfaction of biological appetites reaches into the very depth of human existence.

Such an outlook might be tolerable if man were nothing more than a species of the mammal family. However, his destination manifests itself in his inability to forget his human nature. There is the permanent and inescapable urge to be something specifically different from, and superior to, the rest of the animal realm and to recognize his dependence on a transcendental reality. In that dependence lies the possibility to be truly human. When the individual refuses to move in that direction and to actualize his destination, he remains an empty shell and his existence is doomed to utter futility. He may hide that fate before himself, but he will not thereby escape the pathetic consequences of his refusal. Since individual selfhood is specifically destined for the execution of God's ultimate purpose, it will not be destroyed by death. But what is in store for unredeemed sinfulness is the everlasting pain of utter uselessness.

Paradoxically, modern unbelief and self-complacency are contradicting themselves. Such individuals are anxious to tell themselves that they are self-sufficient entities. Yet, being rational creatures, they are not able fully to acquiesce in their condition. Such a man feels the irresistible urge to strive after truth and to be successful in whatever he does. Such experience does not suffice to establish an existential relation with God. However, our sense of self-transcendence points to the fact that man is not an end in himself. Rather, the quest of truth and of successful action goes on in him for the totality of his life. Whether or not the individual is aware of that self-contradiction, it stirs him up and gives him from time to time an inexplicable sentiment of misery and self-pity that means that no man is able fully to be reconciled with this predicament. The other great religions are also aware of this fact. Yet while they seek its cause in the conditions in which man has to live, for instance in suffering, delusion or fate, the Christian religion goes to the very root of the problem. The fault lies within ourselves. The insufficiencies, disappointments and evils of this world reflect exactly the state of things which unbelief wants to enjoy, viz. a world without a God who controls it and establishes its intrinsic order as also a harmonious relationship between man and the universe. Unbelief is contempt of God.

Thus, the Christian religion makes man's unbelief the focus of the mystery of redemption. Already in the Old Testament God makes manifest to the Israelites that in spite of man's unbelief he is willing to help him to reach his final destination.

B. God's Work

1. *The Divine Kindness*

What, from the human viewpoint, seems to be a hopeless predicament, in that man is a stranger in the universe, becomes a new reality, because God takes the initiative in man's redemption. In the person and work of Jesus, God finally discloses the secret of his redemptive purpose. God himself has made the existence of a sinless man possible and endows him with the gift of engendering a new life of faith in other people. Since the reason for man's predicament lies in his selfhood, a change could not be effected by a divine act in which the new possibility were simply bestowed upon him as an extraneous gift. Rather, God offers remission of sins and a new life on condition of repentance and faith on man's part. Man must believe that God is in earnest in sending Jesus, the prototype of true manhood.

The human problem would but partially be solved, however, if redemption were confined to the remission of sin and the response of faith. These are indispensable prerequisites of our final destination. Yet the fact that they concern us in our selfhood must not induce us to consider the remission of our sins a purely abstract transaction going on in God's mind. Notwithstanding the necessity to distinguish between self and biological life, salvation concerns the individual in the totality of this life here on earth. It is our role in the universe which as a result of our sins is in jeopardy. That our whole life is affected by God's redemptive work is conspicuously indicated by the central place that Jesus assigns to his healing ministry. How seriously God is interested in restoring the health of this world becomes manifest in the self-healing ability of all living creatures, as well as in the fact that long before the coming of Christ God had endowed men with the gift of healing.

Nevertheless, wholesome as these manifestations of God's healing will are, their effects are but temporary ones. Man's principal ill is his inability by his own strength and effort to deliver himself from his sinfulness. Faith opens our eyes to the fact that the historical existence of Christ alone gives us hope for a true life free of sin. Except for his resurrection we would never believe that such a change was possible and could be a permanent one. That God himself is at work in Jesus, and that Christ is not merely a great teacher or a saint, is evidenced by the results which faith has in our life. In faith a complete annihilation of our self-will takes place, and with Christ we attune our will to God's purpose. The ensuing change is radical. The individual is granted an entirely new outlook in life and a new motivation of his actions. Whereas it was natural for us to consider deliverance from the evils of this world our supreme good, Christian faith seeks power to transform them into occasions of blessing and tools of the Spirit, even as the Christian has been transformed by the Resurrection of Christ. By faith, the individual is capable of co-operating with God in the execution of his saving plan. No matter how fragmentarily and imperfectly man's faith may manifest itself in his life, it is rendered effective because it is united with the power and wisdom of God. As a creature, it is his privilege to take part in a divine work. He does so not in a mental process only, as in Platonism, but rather through his biological and historical existence as a citizen of the earth. Whereas apart from Christ, our life is doomed to utter futility, our life is rendered by faith into an indispensable and indestructible factor in the establishment of Christ's power over this world.

2. *Consequences*

Redemption denotes first of all a radical change in the self. In the rationalistic philosophy which was inaugurated by Descartes and reached its climax in the idealistic systems of the nineteenth century, such change was deemed to be impossible. The ego was defined as the unchangeable agent of spontaneous rational actions in the individual, and thus the ego was supposed to be the same reason in all men irrespective of the circumstances in which it was found. Redemption was therefore held to be unnecessary, since as a rational being man was believed to be truly human. That unchangeability of the ego was challenged, however, by psychoanalysis and other schools of modern psychology. According to them, the ego may be deflected from its natural course by adverse or unfavourable influences and thus may malfunction. However, the therapist, or the patient himself, may set it straight again. In those systems of psychology, no distinction is made between the self and individuality. Consequently, the ego's problem consists merely in adjusting itself to the circumstances in which it has to live. No redemption is needed in that case, either, since the therapist is able so to manipulate the ego that it will finally live in harmony with its environment. Yet such view completely overlooks the fundamental difference between adjustment to one's environment, on the one hand, and the problem of redemption on the other. Faith is pre-occupied with man's relation to his final destination. While the therapeutic value of modern psychology should not be minimized, it nevertheless tends to render people insensitive to their dignity and basic need.

As long as it is not experienced, redemption must seem to be the most unbelievable event in human life, for it denotes a change so fundamental of the nature of the ego that it seems to entail a loss of identity. Does not the New Testament speak of 'dying to oneself'? It would be unbelievable indeed if it meant a change of substance, as it is held in Theosophy, for instance. Yet the change which takes place in our redemption is not one from human to divine nature. Rather is it the transition from a disconnected relationship of the self with God to its reactivation. Since in his sinfulness man has willingly cut off that bond, its restoration is beyond man's power and abilities. Man is entirely unable to redeem himself. For even when he is utterly dissatisfied with himself, it is in the light of what he would like to be rather than in the light of his divine destination that he rejects what he is like. It is therefore in retrospect only that we are able to measure the gravity of our disregard for God and the preciousness of the new outlook of our self which we receive through faith. It cannot be denied, of course, that outside Christianity, too, individuals are capable of moral reform and ethical grandeur.

However, here we encounter also the subtle delusion of idealism which since the days of Schleiermacher has frequently been substituted for the newness of life that comes from Christ. How many people there are in our days who make a stand for social welfare and justice yet do not realize that what matters ultimately in human life is concern for other people's need rather than our moral goodness! Their mind will not tolerate the disorder or the injustice implied in the actual conditions. What matters for them is the good conscience they have. Yet the goal which they pursue is an abstract social order rather than a harmonious fellowship of people. Yet that loving concern for the fellow man is a gift which God alone can grant to those who heed his will by faith. Faith seeks in the first place what is helpful to people in their actual situation, while new forms of social life are a secondary concern only.

Furthermore, our redemption manifests the futility of life lived in disregard of God. Life is an arduous business even for the well-to-do and the successful people. Yet we are unable to enjoy forever the fruits of our strain and toil. Its benefits are for the moment only, yet our whole life is in vain in the perspective of the time process. The future would look different if I and my work were non-existent. But would it be better or worse for that? Things look entirely different, however, in the perspective of faith. Through Christ, we are incorporated into a divine plan. We have been chosen for its execution and thus our existence is necessary. No matter how large or small our contribution may be, it adds something to the process and thus brings the final goal into closer proximity. What happens in the life of faith is more than merely a new programme that is set before the individual. The relationship with God is re-established, and thus the spiritual energy needed for the work of obedience and love is rendered possible.

The modern belief that human life is capable of realizing that goal by itself and apart from divine help rests upon a dangerous delusion. It is true to say, of course, that man cannot be aware of himself without realizing at the same time that his existence in this world makes no real sense unless it is related to a reality surpassing both selfhood and nature. Yet Jaspers notwithstanding, that reality is not only not given but also cannot be known. As Pascal has so cogently stated, there is no straight logical road that would lead from unbelief or secularism to the God of the Bible. In a world whose paganism has undergone for centuries the seething criticisms of Christianity, a return to any form of pre-Christian religion has become inacceptable. Modern man may treat power, money or pleasure as supreme values and he may even find happiness in doing so. Yet he deludes himself, for his sense of self-transcendence demands a higher allegiance. He is no longer to assign them a truly religious function and ultimate significance. Hence his moral life vacillates between pessimistic cynicism and an irrational belief in his innate goodness. Leading philosophers have admitted man's moral weakness. H. Cohen and other neo-Kantians have pointed out that human goodness is never more than an approximation to the Absolute or God. Since the latter is infinitely different from us, all progress in approximation will never substantially diminish that distance. However, according to the idealistic view, man is not to be blamed for this failure because he was born with such weakness. Consequently, all that might be demanded of man would be, as suggested by Lessing, the never-ending striving for goodness. To the Christian this will appear to be a subterfuge. For as he is, man does not even want to attain to the Absolute goal

because he is afraid lest by succeeding to do so he should lose his freedom. To the idealistic outlook moral cynicism comes very easily. But
the idealist sees the cause of man's moral failure in a psychological fact,
viz. the relative superiority which man's passion and emotions have
over his will. Thus, man should never strive for higher stakes than his
abilities allow. Why is it that Christianity is so unwilling to acquiesce
in man's weakness and imperfection? The reason lies in the fact that
apart from a divine redemption, human life is utterly meaningless.
When we emphasize the fact that in God's good world we are constantly
assailed by forces of evil, we do not complain that they harm us and
render our life miserable, as is argued by Schopenhauer, E. von Hartmann, and other philosophers of pessimism. Rather it is that on account
of their deceptiveness, these forces confirm men in their unbelief. At
times, evils will challenge us by obstructing our way of action. Thereby
they arouse our opposition and thus create in us the conviction that by
our own strength and resources we are able successfully to cope with
them. That appearance makes us think that, in order to assert ourselves
in the universe and to master life, we do not need any support from
beyond ourselves. In other instances people are dumbfounded by the
overwhelming menace of evil. We hold that even if God existed, he
would not have strength enough to curb it. 'If there were a God,'
people will argue, 'such and such a misfortune would never have
befallen us.' So general and so clever are the uses of the powers of evil,
that it is next to impossible for man, apart from faith, to discern their
deception.

So enormous is their deceitfulness that even religion fails to lay its lies
bare. This can be seen most frightfully in the fact that the very leaders
and guardians of the Jewish religion brought Jesus to death in good
faith. Hence the redemptive work of God is not to be understood as a
method of providing and increasing mankind's happiness, but rather,
as is evidenced especially in the work of Christ, it conveys deliverance
from an otherwise hopeless bondage. God's redemptive purpose is also
misinterpreted when understood as an effort to promote moral goodness. Rather he wants to make us aware of his ability and determination
to move this universe on to the goal for which he had created it. Truly
moral life cannot be realized where God's will is disregarded. It is
possible only where recognition of God's power and wisdom and trust
in his saving purpose have taken root. Such a complete change in our
self does not materialize until Christ is owned as the only one through
whose help our predicament can be radically improved and this world

be rendered truly harmonious. Redemption is a process, not a momentary event. It took its decisive turn in the ministry of Jesus and it goes on in his risen life until it has been completed in his Parousia. Thus the believer's life offers a paradoxical aspect. His self has been set free; thus he is able to live in the truth. Yet the world in which he lives is still under the sway of the forces of evil. As a result, the believer has to ward off all the time the temptations caused by the deceitful nature of this world. He has the satisfaction, however, that through his militant attitude he is able in his field of action to overcome the powers of evil. Through the believer's faith, God's rule is expanded in this world. In that progress the life of Christ is shared by us. Seemingly, all people are alike, irrespective of faith or unbelief. In fact, however, we have been imparted the divine power which reigns over all things.

C. The Covenants

What happens in our redemption is often described in the Bible as a covenant. The metaphor designates a contractual relationship in which the mightier one of two partners stipulates the obligations which the other partner has to respect. In turn, the initiator of the covenant assures his partner that he has the partner's best interests in mind. By the correlation of promise and obligation, the covenant differs fundamentally from a treaty that is concluded by partners of equal powers. The metaphoric term, covenant, describes quite appropriately the specific nature of the relationship between man and God that is actualized through redemption, and especially its moral aspect.

By faith, the individual realizes that his natural aspiration after complete freedom makes no sense in this world. Not only is his will hemmed in by cosmic determinants, it is also and above all limited by the existence of a creator who is in full control of all creatures. Rather than being ends in themselves, all creatures are destined to be used for the execution of the purpose God has with this world. That divine 'plan' determines the objective of man's obligation. He exists in order to serve as God's agent. That function explains the otherwise bewildering character of the Old Testament commandments. Where the aim of moral goodness is interpreted in our anthropocentric way, for instance, as growing in goodness or as becoming happy, many of the Old Testament directives seem to lack moral bearing in the strict sense. Protestant theologians have therefore taught that the ritual prescriptions of the Old Testament had been abrogated and the strictly moral ones alone were valid. But when and through whom did such abrogation take place? And if a portion of the Old Testament legislation had been annulled, who is to decide what is still valid? Are the Old Testament directives dealing with marriage, slavery or taxation still valid, although they are not dealing with ritual?

In such kind of argumentation, the real point is missed. For the Old Testament states clearly and beyond doubt that as members of the Covenant believers are to hallow or glorify the name of God or to praise their Creator. For that purpose the Law was given. By the uniformity of their conduct the believers are to manifest the fact that they belong together as God's people. They may not claim the right to espouse a self-sufficient individualistic existence. Yet notwithstanding the fact that the Old Testament Law was enacted as a national law, their obligations are not meant in the first place to serve the material and social interests of the nation. Rather by keeping the Law under all circumstances, the nation was to extol the glory of Yahveh. Thus understood, it was not the specific content of a commandment that mattered but rather its function of training people in their allegiance to God. In order to enjoin that loyalty, Jesus, far from abrogating the ritual law, emphasized that its observance made sense only when it was related to the final purpose of God. Thus practices commanded by the Law may be replaced by others through which God's cause would seem to be better served. Hence following Jesus' example we may reinterpret the Biblical injunctions in a new way, provided that thereby God's goal will be more adequately pursued.

By relating moral life to the Covenant, we acknowledge the fundamental difference between practical or natural necessities and moral obligations. In the former group we find actions which are necessary for man because the cosmic determinants demand compliance, if man is not to be crushed by nature. In the latter group, actions are demanded because man lives in a world in which God carries out his saving purpose. That such oughtness should be interpreted as resting in a divine Law is essential for our understanding of redemption. Though we attain to a meaningful place in this world on no other ground but that God of his own accord offers us the opportunity for it, the moral obligation reminds us that God does not act in the manner of a mechanical fate. The demanding character of the moral obligation compels the individual to the recognition that true life is not a cosmic good that man may pick up or leave. It is only within the conditions that God lays down in his redemptive activity that it may be found.

The counterpart of covenantal obligation is covenantal assurance of a permanent divine design. If our experience of redemption were a momentary and subjective one only, it could hardly form the basis of a permanent moral obligation. On the one hand we might have misunderstood its meaning, on the other he might change his mind. By the idea of the Covenant we express our conviction that what God does to us in the experience of redemption is part of his comprehensive plan. Thus, we can be sure that he will not go back on it. Despite the hostility which the universe shows toward man, and the many dangers that surround him in this life, man should entertain no doubts but that God will keep mankind in existence and will amply provide for its needs. Likewise it is God himself who persuades us to believe that he will keep his promise of life everlasting, notwithstanding our moral weakness and relapses into unbelief. Israel saw the evidence of that divine purpose in their preservation as God's chosen people. That was still an anthropocentric view, however. The ministry of Jesus brought the confirmation that God is pure subject (I am 'I am' Exod. 3:14) and that he wanted to impart unpampered life to the whole of mankind. This goal Christianity sees guaranteed – as God calls forth faith without discrimination and in spite of the weakness found in the Church. Christ not only raises to himself witnesses of God's gracious work of redemption, through the power of his Spirit as it manifests itself through Scripture, sacraments and the fellowship of faith; he also prevents the forces of evil from destroying God's work. While God's final goal has not yet been reached, the Church is confident that through the permanent activity of the Spirit of Life, God's objective will eventually be reached. For it is now within Christianity's reach to transform all men into children of God, that is to say, into people who are willing to be the agents for the execution of his world-wide purpose. That hope implies the assurance that moral goodness, understood as fear of, and reverence for, God, is to triumph over meanness and wickedness in this world.

In turn, the telic character of this world confirms our conviction that the obligation which God has placed upon us is no arbitrary demand, but rather makes sense in an otherwise perplexing world – for instance, as means of discipline and unquestioning obedience. Certainly, from a pragmatist viewpoint, many moral ideals are unrealistic, including Christian morality. The moral indifference of nature is obvious. Moral goodness will not be honoured by it. Even saintliness will not save a person from the long agony of cancer, for instance. Likewise, since the Christian is not concerned with the preservation of the present conditions but rather with the realization of God's final goal, he may encounter strong opposition on the part of 'realists'. In that case, it will be easy to oppress Christian proclamation and action by means of political, economic or social pressure. But the very oppression lays bare the low motives of the oppressor. Thereby his downfall is sealed and the eventual victory of God's cause is guaranteed. By disregarding God's will the transgressor brings about his own defeat; whereas the Christian who disavows his right to assert himself, even though that decision may entail suffering, will discover that God defends his cause. Conversely, the often heard contention that good may come out of evil, rests on a superficial view of the facts. Of course, by the use of force or revolution, for instance, living conditions or the political order may be altered and the well-being of a section of the nation may be temporarily improved. But in the long run, bad means will engender new evils and disorder. Of course, true goodness is provoked by the presence of evil to remove it. But no credit is to be given to evil. It is in spite of it that the intrinsic energy of goodness is moved to act.

7 The Challenge of the Word

A. The Word
1. *Word and Revelation*

The central problem of ethical life lies in the fact that all men feel the moral urge and are unable to eradicate it, yet may, nevertheless, constantly disregard its prompting. If the moral consciousness were an expression of the individual's personal aspirations or of human nature in general, why would the individual not always act accordingly? In turn, if the moral voice speaks from outside the self, why does the individual self identify himself with it? Would not Freud and his disciples be closest to the truth in arguing that the moral standards with which the individual has grown up represent in reality the social order through which the ruling social group attains to a maximum of satisfaction or power. The mature ego would therefore be right in liberating himself from such authoritarian ethics and choose his own way of conduct. In order to understand the moral phenomenon, a clear distinction has to be made between the 'must' of biological, psychological, or social necessities, on the one hand, and the 'ought' of the moral obligation, on the other. The moral urge demands unconditional acceptance, whereas the quest for happiness or a well functioning order of social life may be subordinated to other goals. In deadly danger, for instance, some people may prefer life to happiness, or revolution to the preservation of the *status quo*.

It is different with the moral life. It may seem to be difficult or dangerous to realize its values, yet their validity is a permanent one, and its obligations are valid in all circumstances. Moral standards do not lose their value when disregarded by some and considered too rigorous by others; nor can they be abrogated as political laws can. Unlike the physical and chemical laws by which the life of our body is determined, the moral urge addresses itself to our mind and demands a reasonable acceptance. There are obviously but two ways open in order to explain that phenomenon. The moral standards may be rooted in the nature of the human mind, or in the will of God. The former explanation has been adopted in the idealistic and pantheistic systems of philosophy and in existentialism. Yet as Kant has rightly pointed out, such an approach is unsatisfactory, because all it yields is a purely formal notion of goodness, whereas what matters in moral experience is a cogent reason why specific goods are to be realized. Conversely, the theistic approach conceives of moral life as an experience in which man is confronted by an absolute will. That experience may be explained in two ways. God may be conceived as a legislator, who prescribes what actions are to be performed by man, or as a dynamic pervading the universe. Conformity with it will result in blessing, whereas opposition or disregard will mean ruin. In the Christian religion, both modes of thinking are found, and obviously they are regarded as compatible. The former is more directly related to God as Creator, whereas the latter one starts from his function as Redeemer. Yet in his dealings with man he never acts in one capacity only.

Christian knowledge of God is experienced as being based upon revelation, that is to say, upon insights that are, as it were, thrust upon the human mind. Though they appear in the human mind as self-evident, they cannot be explained as the result of human ratiocination, and their validity cannot be proven. Rather, they are received by the human mind as the adequate implementation of the self's yearning for a meaningful human life. Christianity accepts them as manifestations of God's desire to be known by man. Since they address themselves to man's rational will, the Bible designates them appropriately 'Word' of God as distinct from theophanies or apparitions of a deity. The subject matter of Biblical revelation is the relationship of God and man, where-as in non-Biblical religions revelations are understood as disclosure of cosmic or heavenly secrets. Through revelation, mankind is made aware of its being God's people and God as 'our God', both relations seen in the context of this world, not as abstract substances only. In the latter respect, God is unknowable, because as Creator, that is, as source and origin of this world, he differs absolutely from man and this world. He can only be referred to in terms of a 'negative theology'. The fact that in our religion we express God's revelation by means of rational statements has given rise to the mistaken idea that God is using human language in order to communicate with man. Actually, it is done in and through this world, or more exactly through the unchanging order and the teleological dynamic of this world. As a result, man expressed his apprehension of God's revelation by means of images and symbols, myths and religious rites, taboos and sacred use of 'natural' objects long before he used conceptual language in religion. Of course, there is a divine plan behind the development in which man learned to use verbal expression in response to God's revelation. But it must be kept in mind that the Biblical revelation has a factual basis in the signs of God's purpose that he gives in nature and history, especially in holy history. The so-called 'natural theology', like modern man's search for God in nature, contains an element of truth in looking for the disclosure of the divine in the concrete things and movements of this world. But, as can be seen clearly in Tillich's philosophy, they base their truth on what man thinks about nature rather than on God's self-disclosure. They contend to find the divine meaning in the nature of things rather than in the ultimate goal which they serve. Thus theology emphasizes the fact that God cannot be known directly. Rather our knowledge of God is founded upon the way in which God uses certain constellations in this world to arouse people's interest. Thus all our knowledge of God is an indirect one, namely through the effect these revelations have upon our mind.

In the fact that in that self-disclosure God takes the initiative, and that through the self-evident character of his revelation he leaves man no choice in the matters revealed, we see the proof of a purpose he wants to realize.

2. *Modes and Stages of Revelation*

Revelation is God's self-disclosure, yet what God makes known to man is not so much his nature. Rather he imparts knowledge of the relation in which he stands to man. God's ontic supremacy, which is an *a priori* datum, manifests itself in his creating and redeeming man. Since the subject matter of revelation is a relationship, it also implies man's identity. He is made for God's sake and therefore both ultimately determined by God and under obligation to him. Because he reveals himself through the medium of this world, God appears as the source of cosmic unity and order as well as the origin of the cosmic determinants and the telic character of the universe. Its determinants are ultimates rooted in the divine will to create.

Since revelation deals with man's predicament in general, not with individuals as such, revelation is destined for the whole of mankind. Yet on account of its purposive character it is not given from the outset in its final shape. There is a 'history' of revelation, as can be learned from the diversity of religions. Its course is conditioned by intellectual, cultural, social, and historical factors, but also by the flexibility, mobility and imaginative ability of people's mentality. Ultimately, however, the process is determined by God's plan of salvation. There is no religion except on a revelatory basis. Yet, in like manner, as in the process of acculturation in general the lower form yields eventually to the higher one, so in the history of religions. The higher religions such as Hinduism, Buddhism, Confucianism, Islam, Judaism and Christianity claim all supreme rank for themselves respectively. Their rivalry will go on in history, and according to the width or comprehensiveness of their spiritual vision, the directness and clarity of their conceptual understanding of each one respectively and the strict concentration on specifically religious issues, one or the other may for some while advance or fall behind. But Christianity sees in the history of religions a divine selection at work. Consequently, mankind possesses in the person and work of Jesus the most comprehensive and most profound manifestation of God's purpose, and thus of mankind's role in the universe. In this light we have to look at at the corresponding history of ethics, too.

The historical character of revelation should not be interpreted as though in its earlier stages God were less close to man than in the higher ones. The God who himself is the same all the time is always to be known of all men. But man must learn to understand the function he is to perform within the history of redemption. Since the goal to be reached is so far removed from what man is originally like, it is but gradually disclosed to man in the divine pedagogy. God reveals his goal in a factual way, namely, through the dynamic of the world process and historical events by which man's predicament and the outcome of his life are decisively affected. In accordance with the finite nature of man that which concerns the whole of mankind comes to light through particular facts such as holy wells and mountains, or historical events such as the history of Israel or the ministry of Jesus. Their universal significance is manifested by the serial character of those historical events, in which the selective procedure of revelation can be seen. In the specific significance which these particular events have for the people concerned, it is possible to discern the pattern of God's redemptive work in general. Religious knowledge is therefore experiential rather than conceptual. However, there can be no direct experience of God by himself as mysticism contends, nor of God in his creative, redemptive or life-giving activities. We are aware of God only through the effects which his 'work' has upon this world, for instance, its order and harmony, its teleological structure, unity and permanency. The specific difference between religious and ordinary experience is indicated by the fact that originally God's work is apprehended by means of symbols and mental images rather than by words. Of these representations, as has been shown especially by C. G. Jung, the individual may not be aware. Nevertheless, they guide and direct his thoughts and actions. In the course of history, they are replaced, however, by notions and propositions. Religious life will then be largely transacted on the verbal basis and assume a rational character. As a result, new religious experiences, for instance those of the prophets of Israel, could be communicated directly through articulate speech. Yet though identical words may be used, religious speech differs, nevertheless, from that of daily life by the fact that it points beyond its logical function to the underlying experience and finally to their divine origin. Consequently, religious terminology narrows down the meaning of words. They are used as referring to situations and processes that are related to man's salvation. Notwithstanding the fact that Jacob, Moses or Jesus are normal human beings, what is reported of them is not meant to contribute to the psychology or physiology of the human race. The Bible refers to them merely on account of the role they play in the execution of God's saving plan. For the same reason, terms like justice, love, grace and many others have, when employed in the Bible, a very specific and circumscribed meaning. That use has its compensation in the fact that religious language reaches into a depth of meaning never attained to by its secular usage.

The Ten Commandments, and the Biblical imperatives in general, the Beatitudes or the Resurrection of Jesus, for instance, are grossly misunderstood, when detached from their place in God's redemptive activity. The valuable contribution that the idealistic philosophy of Kant, Fichte and Hegel in Germany and of Bradley and A. E. Taylor in Great Britain has made to the analysis of moral life is marred, nevertheless, by their neglect of the connection in which ethics stands to holy history.

Over against those erroneous views this must be said. Revelation is to be understood as God's disclosure of himself or of his purpose, it must be conceived of as a homogeneous continuous process rather than an anthology of moral wisdom, from which one selects what one likes best. The various commandments and ethical goods found in the Bible must be interpreted as specific aspects of that process. The moral legislation of the Old Testament cannot simply be dismissed as obsolete. Since revelation is addressed to man, it may be safely assumed that man's mind is capable of apprehending and comprehending it sufficiently for the purpose for which it has been disclosed. We may arrange the ethical passages of the Bible in chronological order. But we have no right simply to discard the earlier stages as being 'primitive', or to embrace only the final development as valid for us. We may be unable fully to understand the exact role which a passage plays in the context of God's will. But the patient student will eventually discover that they are sufficiently intelligible to make us sure of our place in God's dealing with this world. Speech is not only a means of communication from intellect to intellect but also from will to will. Thus the verbal character of revelation, as it confronts us, must not be considered an absolute impediment for God, as agnostic philosophy holds. Notwithstanding the difficulties which the philosopher encounters in his attempts to define God by means of concepts, the language of the Bible proves to be adequate for the knowledge of God's purpose and man's destination.

B. Redemption and Service

In Lutheran theology, revelation has been treated under the two headings of Law and Gospel. There is some justification for such a division, yet it is obvious that thereby an inappropriate theological theory was applied to the interpretation of revelation. Law and Gospel were treated as two successive stages in the life of the believer. They were incompatible with each other, the Law characterizing the unregenerate state of man, and the Gospel his regeneration. Both were sent by God. The unbeliever was under the Law, while the believer was free of it. The result of such static juxtaposition was either an antinomian view of Christian conduct. It was entirely left to the discretion of the believer what he was to do. The alternative was to postulate in an unrealistic manner that regeneration would automatically bring forth sanctification and a conduct agreeable to God. Attempts to introduce the notion of a moral use of the Law (*tertius usus legis*) were practically useful yet of doubtful theological validity. The way in which thereby Christian mores and natural law were blended, was an admission of perplexity rather than a theological solution. A more consistent view was adopted by Calvin. He held that in recognition of his redemption from eternal damnation the believer would be led to a life of humility, patience, self-denial, and self-discipline. In this way the Christian life was brought into close and organic relationship with God's work of redemption. It might be objected, nevertheless, that with such an understanding of the faith, the Christian's life in this world would be but a preparation for the life after death.

For the right understanding of Christian life one should rather start from two equally important facts. One is that man is equipped with a moral conscience which impels him to manifest his humanity by acting morally in this world. The other is that the work of salvation is a process that takes place in the history of mankind. Under the impulse of the Holy Spirit it goes on indefinitely until God's goal has been reached. As an historical process redemption demands for its explanation a positive function of man in this world. By these two factors man is placed under a twofold obligation. Man's redemption is not to be conceived of as a divine act that takes hold of man apart from his will. Rather, God's Word comes to the believer as an offer that must be accepted spontaneously. Accepted it must be, and that not for a moment only, as though faith were confined to the act of conversion. As God remains the ultimate determinant of our life, so trust in his saving will and his saving power no less than love of his ways and confidence in his justice must permanently and necessarily be implied in faith. That attitude is the very opposite of the sinful disregard of God. Yet by such acceptance it is not only man's nature that is changed, since his sins are forgiven, but also his place and stance in the universe. As a result of his faith, man is incorporated into the process of holy history. He is no longer free to do what he pleases, but rather is under obligation to live in accordance with his new function. Faith must imply the willingness to become God's agent and servant in this world. That willingness manifests itself in the fact that his conscience is orientated toward God's final goal. The moral faculty is found in Christians as in non-Christians and continues to operate during the Christian's whole life. It may therefore safely be assumed that it is included in God's purpose. God chooses his people in order that through them as God's helpers and servants, God's plan with this world may be brought to its consummation. The ontic superiority or lordship of God determines not only our religious life, but also our basic moral attitude. Consequently, the imperative character of the moral urge cannot be interpreted in terms of moral autonomy, as was held by Kant and the idealist philosophers. God never acts without a goal in mind. When he places the Christian under obligation he does not act as a tyrant who finds pleasure in making people feel his superior power while not caring for their needs and problems. His demands are related to the condition in which man and the universe find themselves. Our world is filled with insufficiency, weaknesses and evils. Yet, in spite of the unique position which man occupies as a moral subject and as a recipient of divine revelation, man is not separated from all other creatures. Rather, through the forgiveness of his sinfulness and the assistance of the Holy Spirit, he holds a privileged position in this world. The Christian is enabled to contribute to the improvement of the human lot and to the transformation of this world. For the Christian, moral goodness is not an end in itself. Yet in spite of serving these ends, moral goodness is contingent upon an unconditional demand. For the goal, the moral goal which the Christian pursues, has been set to him by God. It is not a self-chosen and egotistic end. That such is the case is fully and effectively manifested in and through the ministry of Jesus, especially through his miracles and his exemplary life. Over against such egotistic view, Jesus taught his disciples that true life was one that followed God's example. As God was anxious to satisfy the needs of all his creatures, so man also was to serve his fellow man.

As a result of such a message, human goodness was seen in an entirely new perspective. Man was not so much called upon to rid himself of his moral faults or to make efforts to avoid wrongdoings. Likewise, Jesus was amazingly little concerned with making people morally good. Unlike the Greek philosophers, virtue was not an end in itself for Jesus. Rather, people were to subordinate their self-centred efforts and self-love to the pursuit of the interest and well-being of other people. Man was to realize above all that he was by the will of God related to other people for whose deficiencies and exigencies he had to care. For such conduct Jesus not only set an example. By calling people into his company he also stimulated his disciples and followers to embrace the same way of life. As he did not recoil from adversities, so he encouraged them to endure hardship and suffering for God's sake.

Following a Hellenistic pattern, revelation was already in the ancient Church contrasted with reason. The former was interpreted as a divine communication, whereas the latter was understood as a natural human ability by means of which man would acquire knowledge of the 'natural' things. But thereby the original meaning of revelation as used in biblical religion was blurred and distorted. The distinction itself was a good and wholesome one, yet the difference lies in the field of ontology rather than that of epistemology. The biblical writers discerned the marvel of human nature in two facts. First, man alone of all the creatures has a rational mind and thus is capable of thinking conceptually. Yet that ability would be of no avail, unless the world in which we live could be apprehended by man's intellect. Hypothetically, the incongruity between man's noëtic faculty and the nature of things could be so wide as to preclude all knowledge of non-subjective reality. Neither the existence of man's mind nor the knowability of the universe is a matter of course. On the contrary, their congruity is best understood as a special divine arrangement.

Philosophical epistemology is inclined to regard conceptual thinking and the possibility of a knowledge of truth as the result of human spontaneity. Yet man's intellect has a purely instrumental function. Unless the things of this world presented their knowable aspect to man, our scope of knowledge would be confined to ourselves. Apart from the *a priori* pattern of reason, it would be impossible to recognize particular facts as being specimens of a genus or species, or to apprehend the truthfulness of a statement. Revelation and reason belong together as joint manifestations of God's intention to be known in and through his work. Revelation is not a special faculty, but rather differs from reason ontically. Whereas the things of this world disclose themselves in their createdness and creatureliness, God discloses himself as the author and source of all reality. Their difference creates no insoluble problem. We must only keep in mind that there is no way by which the knowledge of the nature or existence of God may be inferred rationally from our knowledge of created things. According to their ontic relationship, it is the recognition of God by which the nature and function of the creatures are determined. As a divine endowment, our cognitive faculty has a twofold function. It is destined to make us aware of our relationship to God, and thus to render it a personal one. At the same time, it is to enable man to overcome the deceptive appearance of things. Thereby man is given a chance to live a truly human life and to engage in the pursuit of truth. Some people resent the idea of being confronted with it, because they fear its deadly effect. They think it intolerable to see themselves and their fellow men as they actually are. Yet while the aspect of our shortcomings, deficiencies and faults may badly shock us, there is no reason why it should frighten us or drive us to despair. On the contrary, since such insight comes from the God who offers us redemption, the aspect of what we actually are makes us marvel about the unthinkable width of God's kindness and longsuffering. It is therefore with amazement, gratitude and pride that Christians employ their reason and look boldly forward to the full disclosure of the truth.

In conclusion, this may be said. Through God's revelation we are able to gauge the wisdom of Creation by which the existence and continuity of this world have been rendered possible. Apart from revelation this world must appear perplexing and incomprehensible. The Word of God engenders in us feelings of awe, amazement and reverence, and this the more so, since God's wisdom has to assert itself against the

THE CHALLENGE OF THE WORD

forces of chaos and destruction. Yet, joyfully we perceive that the Creator has made provision for the needs of all his creatures. Through God's revelation we are also made aware of the mystery of redemption and transformation of a world which otherwise seems to remain eternally the same. Mere gratitude for the advantages and goods we enjoy would be an utterly inadequate response. For the revelation discloses an omnipotent Lord. Nor would the goodness of self-restraint be sufficient. In the light of revelation we notice the futility and guilt of our own self-assertion. No other road is left to a meaningful life except presenting ourselves for God's service. Judaism had already discovered that serving God can be implemented in three different ways, namely, through worship, testimony, and obedient service. None of these may stand by itself. Although in the course of history the emphasis has been distributed variously, yet, except for consideration of those three aspects, Christian life would degenerate into callous religiosity, enlightened self-love or haughty self-righteousness, devoid of concern for the plight of the rest of the biosphere. Conversely, it is in our worship, for instance, that we become aware of the true nature of God's lordship and thus of the unconditional character of his demand. Likewise it is only in that context that the real nature of our obligation is recognized. The life of faith is not recommendable only, because Christianity has proved in an unique way, to be able to improve man's condition in this world, nor is it to be confounded with practical necessities, for instance, that of adjusting our lives to the demands of the technological age. Rather, it is the intrinsic truth of God's work that obligates us to respond to it adequately because through the activities of faith we realize that we are made for the truth.

C. Revelation and Bible

While constantly working upon man's will and mind, God reveals himself to man only indirectly, namely, through the medium of this world in nature and in human life. The ability to discern the divine purpose within this world is found in a few outstanding 'men of God' or prophets only. The majority of people have to be guided by spiritual leaders, who will explain to them what divine work is going on in holy history and in their hearts. This phenomenon explains the important and indispensable role of the Bible. The Bible is both a record of revelations which have been addressed to the Chosen People through divine messengers, and a witness of holy history. New revelations are connected with earlier ones and reinterpreted in the light of the later ones. Thus, the Biblical books form a progressing series in which nothing becomes obsolete. Though no portion of mankind has been entirely left without the perception of divine manifestation, those people, nevertheless, are grossly mistaken who hold that without the Biblical witness they are able to probe the depth of God's plan with mankind and this world. Contemporary new religions, for instance, Western Zen Buddhism or Steiner's Anthroposophy, should warn us. Their propagators usually substitute cosmological and anthropological speculations for the work of the divine Providence. As record of past revelations the Bible rightly occupies a position of authority in Christianity. However, its usefulness for ethics depends on the correct understanding of its literature. First of all, since the Bible is the record of a process, namely, God's dealing with the universe in Creation and Redemption, single passages must be interpreted in the context of the whole process rather than in a detached way. God does not demand of us to espouse this or that kind of action, because it is good by itself, but rather because it will be good when executed in connection with his purpose. There is no contradiction, for instance, between the prohibition to commit murder in the context of private relations on the one hand, and the infliction of capital punishment for serious crimes, on the other.

Secondly, the commandments of Jesus are frequently misinterpreted. The injunctions given in the Sermon on the Mount, for instance, are meant to be respected by all men. They are not mere counsels of meritorious living, as the Roman Catholic Church holds. But they are not general moral principles, either. They are rather given to indicate the goal for which man is destined and which he must pursue, no matter how closely he actually advances toward that goal. In other words, they are not given for the mere purpose of making people aware of their sinfulness, but rather, notwithstanding their rigorism, they are to encourage people seriously to envisage the true life for which they are destined. Third, there is a problem of style occurring both in the prophets and the teachings of Jesus. Admonitions like 'cut off your hand', 'pull out your eye' are meant to indicate the radical seriousness of the divine demand. All attempts to bring God's demand down to the level of what the average person is willing to do are contrary to the will of God. God's demands are not impossible, not even for the common man, yet they require a measure of self-denial, of which we would like to be dispensed. Finally the fact should be kept in mind that the Bible is the book of the Church. Though a great deal of it may be understood by any serious reader, its depth will be hidden from those who are not in a position to be initiated by experienced Christians. The Bible has remained a living book as distinct from purely historical documents, because it has been searched and interpreted from generation to generation, and that interpretative wisdom is a living power in the historical development of the Church. While rejecting the Catholic view of Tradition, by which it is placed on a level with Scripture, Protestantism has nevertheless availed itself of tradition in the subsidiary role of collective Biblical exegesis.

Bringing the Bible up to date is an important and necessary task. But that goal will not be reached by ignoring the exegetical tradition of the past and reading modern problems into the text. Rather we shall be best served by relating our contemporary problems to the process of holy history as described and at work in the Bible.

Part Three: The Ethical Action

8 Faith

A. Nature of Faith

Christian life originates when a person to whom the Christian message has been announced not only approves of its truthfulness but also gives it his assent and eventually identifies himself with its subject matter. Yet that message not only discloses to him the fact that his actual life fails to be worthwhile. It also offers him a new stance in this world and, implied in it, the possibility and opportunity of living a life that is truly relevant. For notwithstanding Bultmann and his followers the Christian message is presented not as a mere anthropology but as a divine offer of redemption. By convincing the hearer of its intrinsic truthfulness, the message proves its divine origin. The individual sees man in general, and himself in particular, as destined for God's sake in this world. That process reaches its apex when the individual is moved to identify himself with man's divine destination and is grateful to God for being deigned to such a destination notwithstanding his sinfulness. It is this state of self-consciousness that in the New Testament is most frequently called 'faith'. The individual realizes that his existence really makes sense in God's sight.

That level of faith is what Augustine has in mind in his famous statement: 'All I want to know is God's relation to my soul, and nothing else.' But in Jesus' eyes, that is only the beginning and the weak phase of the inner faith. For the God with whom the individual identifies himself is the Creator of the universe, and the God who has sent Jesus in order to establish his kingly rule over this world. Far from being called upon to withdraw into the recesses of the divine substance, the individual is enjoined to understand his vocation in the light of his knowledge of the cosmos; faith is to be an intelligent self-consciousness. Perhaps even more important, yet also more tantalizing, is the realization that man's destination implies the necessity to accept the course of events in this world as willed by God. As God's servant man must not only be willing to do what is right, but also be persuaded that God's dealing with this world and our life is the best possible way, even when it is contrary to our hopes and wishes. Implied therein is the conviction that our life of faith is subjected to a divine testing and education, by means of which God wants us both to overcome our natural fear of earthly evils and to learn the ways of service. In that process we never are fully successful. It would be an error, though, to speak of fickleness. People have the faith by which they identify themselves with the Christian message. But for lack of experience they are prone to think that God's power and love of his elect has its limits. The genesis of faith is a process that seems to originate spontaneously in man. No wonder that Feuerbach, Marx, Comte and Freud tried to explain it as an artificial superstructure of man's passions, emotions and desires. The experience of faith repudiates and refutes such explanation, however, on the basis of the radical change in man's self-consciousness and the new opportunities and abilities thereby acquired. Faith is the evidence that God is redemptively at work in man. His rebellious disregard of God is forgiven.

The practice of Christian life is conditioned by two factors. Old habits and moral evaluations of our pre-Christian or extra-Christian life will linger on. On account of the weakness of our faith we try to rationalize them, persuading ourselves that our inability to get rid of them is evidence that they are compatible with God's will. Yet at the same time we feel the urge to adjust our way of action to our destination as God's servants. While for practical reasons it may be advisable to treat Christian ethics separately, it must be kept in mind that in the Christian life the standards of action can never be severed from the way in which faith visualizes the conditions under which our faith acts.

The life of faith is destined to be in accordance with God's work in creation and redemption. Thus it is to be lived within the framework of holy history, that is to say, that sector of human existence whose direction and dynamic have been so convincingly illumined by the ministry of Jesus. The radical commandments found in the Sermon on the Mount, Rom. 12 or Rev. 1–3, make little sense when regarded as having their validity in themselves, that is to say, for no other ground than being written in the Bible. For in spite of their inspired origin they might be as obsolete as the legislation of the Old Testament. That predicament is entirely changed when they are comprehended as expressions of the way of life laid out in the ministry of Jesus. In that case they indicate the direction in which Christian life is to move and the power by which it is set in motion. Thus they describe a process rather than a goal to be reached by all, as is held by moral legalism.

As awareness of the place which man as a person occupies in God's saving plan, faith manifests itself in the individual's life both as one's dominant and comprehensive outlook in the noëtic sphere. By it the perspective is determined in which we perceive all reality. At the same time, faith is the dominant attitude which as Christians we take in the volitional sphere towards reality. The attitude is concerned with the significance things have for the realization of God's redemptive plan. It determines the manner in which we deal with other people and the world in which we live. The two factors together make us realize that there can be no Christian life in isolation. The individual who realizes that God uses him as his agent and servant cannot be unaware of the fact that he is but one out of many people whom God has thus chosen for that same purpose. They do not co-exist as self-contained monads. Rather, it is through their interrelation that their faith is rendered effective. Their communion in worship and practical work stimulates, encourages and illumines them. That does not require that all Christian activity should be a collective one. Neverthless, it is from the common life in the Christian community that the individual direction is motivated and conditioned for personal action.

The transforming power of faith is manifested in the specific difference of the morality of Christian life. Since Christians and non-Christian live together in the same community, it is not surprising that they both should start from the same conditions and work for the solution of the same problems. Yet in our time particularly, when Christians consort with non-Christians for the solution of social and international questions, the fact is often overlooked that the Christian sees things in a different perspective. While his fellow worker is primarily concerned with material ills, the Christian is anxious to bring about a fellowship of faith and love. Likewise the Christian attitude will exclude the use of means by which others are harmed, or which in the long run may work to the detriment of the community. Thus differentiation is a process that goes on in the life of the individual Christian as well as in in the Church as a whole. It results from the very nature of faith. Failure to make the distinction will prevent those for whose benefit we work to receive the superior goods which God has entrusted to his people, for instance, material help without gratitude, charity without responsibility.

The faculty of the Ego, by which we are prompted to accept the Christian message, is conscience. That faculty itself is found in all men. It is a determinant of selfhood by which we are constrained to distinguish between values and attitudes which are in agreement with personal life, and those which are not. Its operation may be experienced as insight, admonition or accusation. Conscience is a formal faculty which parallels the noëtic faculty by which truth and falsehood are to be distinguished. There is a development of conscience which goes on in the history of religion. Since not all individuals and nations live on the same level of experience and since their historical experiences differ widely, there is a great diversity of opinion concerning right and wrong or useful and harmful for the growth of selfhood. The person who wants to follow but the dictates of his conscience is therefore in danger either of identifying his conscience with his wishes and desires, or naïvely to accept the ethos of his group as imperative. While a man's conscience will enable him to discern the higher from the lower good, provided that he seeks for the truth, we cannot follow G. E. Moore, or the ethical intuitionists, who are satisfied with the self-evidence of ethical insight. By reminding us that ethical values are valid apart from man's will, conscience urges us also to look out for the basis on which they rest. We would betray our conscience if we interpreted the multiplicity of its manifestation in a relativistic way. Plausible values have to be tested in the light of God's revealed plan. While even in that area there are differences of experience, the values so arrived at will nevertheless prove to be compatible with each other when scrutinized in the light of revelation.

Faith, as the determination of the self to let God do his work in our hearts, entails a change of our cosmic position. A person either believes or does not believe. As a mental process, however, faith is a radical decision which has power, and it grows as it is practised, no matter how weak and timid it may be originally. Of course, Christians are aware of temptations. We may enter into situations in and through which the powers of evil attempt to turn us away from the manifestations of God's kindness. Yielding to temptations will therefore temporarily block the growth of faith. Yet the 'inner faith' will not thereby be completely destroyed. Conversely, through repetition, the right actions will form a mental habit. The growth of faith will not proceed with equal speed and result in all individuals. The Word is like a seed planted in the individual. In some people it may produce amazing results already in early age and almost immediately after faith has taken root in them. That is not the general rule, however. There may be even cases in which faith notwithstanding an evil habit will not disappear or where in a difficult or dangerous situation we succumb to fear, melancholy or despair. That is not an indication that God has abandoned us. Rather, our seemingly hopeless plight is in fact evidence of a divine education. If change does not immediately occur, it may be because we are still too one-sidedly interested in our own well-being or our perfection or unwilling to be taught by God. The growth of faith is not a purely mental process. By living in the truth of God, faith apprehends the redemptive power of God. As we believe in Christ, we are made, as it were, members of his Body. What people see in us is not merely our religion, but also the image of Christ as it determines our faith. Thus, God's people is a power of illumination and transformation in this world.

B. Modes of Inner Faith

1. *Perspective*

What has been designated as 'faith of the heart' or 'inner faith' is an aspect of selfhood. Faith has two modes of manifesting itself, namely, outlook or vision, and attitudes. The outlook is formed by a segment of self-consciousness. Though not thinking conceptually, the self is aware of itself as co-existing with, and related to, a non-subjective reality. Through experience, man is enabled to form a number of ideas or images of the structure of the relationship in which he stands with the non-subjective reality. These ideas of man's actions and thoughts are guided in agreement with the nature of the individual's field of action.

Christian vision discerns a dynamic reality which makes for an equilibrium and order in this world. That is not a static condition, however, but rather it is the result of a conflict between harmonizing and disturbing tendencies in which God asserts himself as upholding the cosmic order. Christian theology describes it as a fight between God as a personal being and forces of evil or satanic powers. In spite of the objections raised against the idea of a personal God, the history of human thought shows clearly and convincingly its functional superiority over such ideas as 'being', 'energy', or value employed for the characterization of the source of reality. The Christian view of God rests on facts like the self-disclosure of reality and the care it takes of all that exists, and that nothing that exists is capable of bringing itself into existence or to keep itself in it. Faith conceives therefore of the originator of this world in analogy with the relation of the human mind and its productions. God is thought of not only as having power and wisdom to create this universe and to keep it under his control, but also as a being which is concerned with the well-being of its creatures.

Faith visualizes this world as a reliable one, whose order is solid and unshakeable. Although forces of evil are everywhere at work within it,

God is able and willing to repress them. Since he has given ample and convincing evidences of our election, faith carries with it the assurance that God will bring us to the goal for which he has destined us. Serving him makes sense because his cosmic plan does not change. Though he works in this world he is no part of it. Thus, faith watches for the signs of the advancing extension of his purpose. In all of its phases it demands that we think of employing the means and methods which are best fitted for appropriate use in a new situation.

2. *Attitudes*

In agreement with this specific outlook of faith one notices the attitudes Christianity takes toward reality. The Christian message presents itself as good news. The outstanding place that is therein assigned to man, and the cosmic teleology are reasons for joy and hope. In the Resurrection of Christ God has given proof of his ability to control and annihilate the anti-teleogical forces in this world. By allowing the destruction of the 'Son of Man', God has also shown that his unlimited love for man does not recoil from self-sacrifice. Thus, the joy of faith is not discouraged by the adverse circumstances of life nor by the realization of our unworthiness. For since God has taken the initiative in our redemption, he makes us certain that he will not abandon us again.

Next there is gratitude. Though we live in a world in which life is endangered all the time by irrational and harmful forces, we owe it to God that we are still alive and not crushed by this world's evils. Above all we could be ignorant of the ultimate meaning of life unless he had disclosed it to us. There would be no possibility to attain to a worthwhile stance in the universe except for the unmerited kindness by which his redemptive work transforms us. True enough, man is capable of creating remarkable values in the arts and sciences, in political organization and technology. But they are all based upon the abilities and resources which God has put at our disposal. While all these things take place in nature and history, they cannot be ascribed to an intention of particular things or the laws of nature. God's work in this world is therefore apprehended with reverence. By making a distinction between heaven and earth, the Bible is not so much concerned with an ontological distinction, but rather with an axiological one. God's work cannot be accepted as a matter of course nor be compared with what man does. For there is nothing of our weaknesses, error, egocentricity, or wrongdoing to be found in what God does. That the Holy One should deal with this unholy world in a beneficent manner fills our hearts with amazement and admiration, and we feel that whatever he has brought into existence should not be used except for the end for which he has destined it.

Obedience is another attitude of faith. As the Creator, God is the Lord of this world. He does not share his sovereignty with anybody else, least of all with man. Thus, nobody has a right to pursue goals which are not related to the goal which God has set for mankind. Nor are we to choose ways of action which are not conducive to the realization of God's cause. Yet man is not humiliated by such obedience. For thereby he is enabled to act as God's servant for the redemptive transformation of this world. Unlike moral legalism, however, which grudgingly yields to the inescapable authority of impersonal commandments, the Christian obedience takes delight in our privilege of co-operating with God for the benefit of this world. The means by which man performs his task have been put at his disposal by God and are not his property. That fact induces him to handle them faithfully and with care. Similarly, the people whom he encounters do not incidentally cross his path. They are sent to him by God and thus belong to his assignment. No matter whether or not he happens to like them, he has to take an interest in their well-being. Fear of God is another attitude of faith. The continued existence of the universe requires order and a God of order. Disturbance of, or rebellion against, that order will therefore be the undoing of those who attempt it. In the history of mankind that consequence manifests itself as divine judgment. No matter how powerful an individual or a nation may be, they will not be able in the long run to maintain themselves if they act contrary to God's will. Even Christianity is not exempt from it, although in its case the judgement will not lead to total annihilation but rather to the test of suffering. Faith is therefore far removed from the cheap and blasphemous belief that God is love, and that consequently my sins are forgiven, no matter what I do. On the contrary, while God's plan realizes itself steadily, empires and cultures collapse successively, and though the individual self is indestructible, its fate may be eternal futility. Fear of God should not prevent us from enjoying God's world but it should guard us against levity and spiritual security. We have good reason for praying; let us not perish in temptation. For we are aware of the dreadful results of disregarding God's will.

In turn, though sometimes this world looks so chaotic or behaves so callously that one is tempted to think there is no God; faith is confident that the Creator has not abandoned this world. On the contrary, in the life of Jesus and all that has followed since, God has given ample evidence that he continues to carry out his beneficent plan so that we may trust his promises, power and wisdom. He remains faithful, even when we have spurned his demands and harmed his work. Trust in his redemptive will in turn makes us patient and tolerant with the shortcomings and faults of the people with whom we have to deal. Likewise, trust in God will engender longsuffering when adversity seems to have no end. In many cases God will tarry with his help because he deems it necessary that in the general interest our personal wishes should not, or not yet, be granted. In that connection it will be well to remember that faith demands humility. The very fact that man is so highly privileged among all the creatures easily prompts us to forget that except for God's kindness we would not stand where we are. We have to realize that by ourselves we are nothing and do not contribute anything lasting to human history. Only as we enter into relationship with God and acknowledge that we are made for the benefit of others, do we receive strength and find an adequate forum for relevant activity. As Jesus pointed out to the Pharisees, pride tends to vitiate the best in religion. Humility is the opposite of the belief that man is able to discover all the secrets of the universe unaided, and which holds that what he does not know does not exist. Nor does humility presume that man is capable in his own wisdom and strength to render this world perfect. Last, but not least, love is to be mentioned. This is God's good world. He made it for the benefit of all his creatures. While at a given moment we may be overwhelmed by the plenitude of evils noticeable, the picture changes completely when we see this world in process and as moving towards its final goal. We dishonour God if we fail to see his world in a positive perspective. This world is God's domain, however. Not a single piece in it may be counted ours except as his gift. We are but his administrators or employees. It would be too bad if we would use the goods of this world greedily or with disdain. Rather, not only God himself but all things in this world deserve our love because they are necessary for the attainment of God's final purpose. Love as the Bible understands it is not sentimental, however, even when it manifests itself as compassion. Sentimental love takes delight in one's own emotions; love is concerned with other people's needs. It is an attitude of appreciation coupled with a sense of responsibility. We do not truly love God's creatures if all we seek thereby is our satisfaction. True love originates in the awareness that as God's helpers we have been called upon to assist them and remedy their wants and shortcomings. Through love, we attempt to deal with each creature according to its nature, situation and destination. Love does not act according to a preconceived programme. Yet it does not depend on ever new commandments or directions given by God, either, as is held by the advocates of situational ethics. Rather, love seeks those in need as individual persons, and is anxious to develop the abilities required for their assistance. Unlike the Platonic *eros*, which is a desire to let another person share in what I consider valuable, Christian love is concerned with the value which the other person has in God's eyes. That this world was made 'by God through the Son' means that God loves this world and thus, through the presence of the Son, fills it with objective values. He therefore aims at their restoration, where they are beclouded or misused. By presenting himself for this work, the Son shows that he loves the Father. Christians love the way in which as creatures in this world they are aware of the Son's love of the Father. It is felt as a dynamic which aims at moulding us after the love of Christ. Thus, Jesus rightly proclaims love as the believer's supreme attitude.

From our survey it should be evident that faith is not an abstract attitude, for instance, mere trust in God's justifying grace. Of course, it is that, too. But it is far more complex. It embraces the individual in his concrete cosmic stance, this world in its diversity and the triune God in his manifold works. Faith, we might also state, is the awareness of the relationship in which people living in this world stand to God's saving will.

C. The Sufficiency of Faith

Already in Luther's days, the *sola fide* (by faith alone) had led some of his followers to an antinomian view, that is to say, to the conclusion that faith had nothing to do with ethics. Our description of the modes of faith might equally be interpreted in the same way. Yet both perspective and attitudes of faith embrace the totality of reality. More than any other religion, Christianity is a way of life. The real problem is not whether there can be a Christian faith without a corresponding activity. Rather, the question is how to avoid the traps of moralism especially in its Pharisaic understanding and the related doctrine of meritorious works. In Pharisaism as in ancient Greek ethics, people were anxious to manifest their goodness. Similarly in modern Protestantism we are often told that in order to be considered a follower of Christ, a person must engage in specific social or political activities, or in general, that a person should not be admitted to the Church unless his moral life would exhibit his earnestness. The underlying philosophy may be stated like this: 'We (or all men) have a moral disposition. Yet life fails to make sense until that disposition is activated. In turn, where that is the case, the individual is in communion with God.' The Roman Catholic doctrine differs in two respects from secular ethics. It is held that the moral disposition is not a congenital endowment. Meritorious works require the aid of infused grace to be obtained from the Church. The reformers rejected either view. The former would be a denial of man's innate sinfulness and would make the individual his own redeemer. The attitude which is truly in keeping with man's nature is the desire to be substantially better than we are. The Catholic view is in danger of ascribing to the work of Christ a merely preliminary role in man's redemption. Almost inevitably the emphasis will fall upon the aid of the Church and the zeal of the believers living within the Church.

The antinomian view is also inconsistent. It assumes that God, though he is the Creator of this world, is in his redemptive work one-sidedly concerned with man's incorporeal self only. As a result, the practical activities of man take place in a neutral world which has nothing to do with God. The antinomians, nevertheless, had a good excuse. If man's redemption depended exclusively on Christ's past and completed work, how could we ascribe a religious significance to moral life? The answer is this. According to Anselm, whom Luther had followed, redemption is to be interpreted in terms of a juridical transaction, that is to say, as claims and forfeitures resulting from a contract. Such a view presupposes a purely static relationship of God and man. That there is a world which God has made, and in which man has to live, are incidental facts which do not affect the position of the judge and the defendant. Likewise, the chronological date of the work of the mediator is irrelevant. In Anselm's theory, it might have taken place right after Adam's fall.

Things look quite different when one follows the New Testament which treats redemption in the light of a divine purpose. The historical work of Christ is then a decisive event in the career of the Son of God. Through it, the conditions are created by which man is enabled to assume the assignment in this world for which he was created. Faith then has a twofold function. First of all, man is thereby enabled to live in the divine truth. He sees himself as related to God, namely as his servant. Yet he is also aware of himself as one who had disregarded his destination. At the same time, through that revealed image of his man is rendered willing to act in this world in agreement with God's redemptive plan. In that process, God takes the initiative, yet man would, nevertheless, be unable to live in the truth unless he responded to God by faith. Through these two factors of recognition of our stance and our determination to serve God's sake in this world, man has received redemption. He is fit for the execution of the task for which God made him. Thus faith includes both the recognition that we are under obligation to serve God in our life, as also that we are prepared to deploy zeal and look for the most appropriate means by which to execute God's will.

In what way, and to what extent, however, the believer will act in agreement with his assigned role does not depend on the determination of his self only. It is also conditioned by numerous personal and environmental factors, which, to say the least, are not under his control. For that reason, God does not consider us responsible for the imperfect or lukewarm manner in which we carry out our obligation, provided only we do not lose sight of the goal for which we are destined. We may transgress God's demand, either by our own faith through indifference, defiance or overpowering passions. Yet other transgressions occur against our will through the pressure of circumstances. We are privileged however to repent of our misdeeds and thus to re-assert our faith. By feeling sorry for them and by seeking to overcome the factors which made us fail, we return into the light of the truth which we had obscured by our wrongdoings and omissions. Thus we are not saved by our good deeds but by believing in God's redemptive kindness. Yet faith engenders activity that is in accordance with God's will. Where that is experienced, we realize that the Holy Spirit is working in our lives. What matters more than anything else in human life is not what we do and how much we do. What gives life its ultimate and decisive value is our willingness and fitness to serve God. The significance of our actions does not depend on what special effect we intend thereby, but rather on the use God makes of them.

This statement is not to be understood, however, as meaning that the life of faith belongs to a sphere of existence which has nothing to do with the world in which we live our daily life. The acts of faith are performed in the context of universal interrelatedness and as expressions of one's being a specimen of the human species. Each of our actions has its effect upon the universe. There is a difference, however, according to whether the underlying attitude is one of faith or of disregard of God's plan. Whenever we act by faith, we thereby bring to light the true form of mankind, that is to say, what man is destined to be in this world. The degree to which that form is manifested through our action, will determine the intensity and speed of historical life. Nothing that happens in this world is ever lost. Its contribution is to the making of the future. Particular actions and historical events by themselves will condition the circumstances in which things take place. But the determinative factor in history is faith. Wherever the will of God is ignored, the form of mankind will be distorted or hampered. Faith, in turn, restores its direction and energy. Thus it is on faith that the success of history depends. The intrinsic feebleness of unbelief can be seen in the fact that its deeds have a temporary effect only. Their influence may last for a considerably long while, as for instance that of Mesopotamian or Graeco-Roman civilization. But finally they must give way to new conditions as Neolithic civilization to that of the Bronze Age, or alchemy to modern science.

9 The Moral Life

A. Origin

Moral life is a form of human self-determination. We distinguish it from religious life, rational thinking and valuation. But as the self is indivisible, so is its self-determination. Its various forms interpenetrate each other. In our days the radical isolation of ethics from faith has led to serious confusion and pathetic misunderstanding of human life because conduct is an essential feature of the Christian religion. It was therefore necessary in our study to deal at some length with the religious component of moral life too. That procedure had the advantage of bringing to light a number of ethical aspects which are usually neglected in the modern treatment of ethics.

When asking how Christian morality originated, we are not interested in the historical beginnings of Christian ethics. Even if we were able to tell with certainty what contributions were made to primitive Christian ethics by Judaism, Hellenism, Jesus and the Early Church, the historical facts would not settle the problem of validity. Our problem is originally a sociological one; namely, what are the circumstances in which our moral conviction as Christians is formed? In a general way it may be said that our moral life has its roots in the Christian community, primarily in the family as the smallest of the units by which the congregation is formed. In like manner, the new convert to Christianity derives his idea of Christian moral life from the mores and orders of the congregation. Especially in the modern Protestant churches, not much such ethical instruction is given, except that certain contemporary problems will emphatically be brought to the convert's attention; for instance, alcoholism, racial equality, or urban renewal. But he will soon realize that there are things which Christians do not do or at least are not supposed to do, as for instance robbing banks, propagating revolutions, giving public offence, or publicly contradicting the minister. This Christian ethos is not so much taught as rather observed by common consent.

It is easy to discern a certain utilitarianism behind that ethos, yet underlying there is the conviction that certain things are good or evil by themselves. In the case of church mores, the collective attitude of the members of the congregation is considered as guaranteeing that God is pleased with such conduct. Such conviction would not be possible unless man had a moral conscience, by which he was enabled validly to distinguish the right from the wrong. In the Catholic Church, most lay members will find the reason for the validity of moral actions in the fact that they have been commanded by God or the Church. Differently Protestantism has on the whole enjoined its adherents to seek the reasons for which God has given such commandments. We may assume with the Intuitionists that there are basic ethical values which are self-evident, for instance, the sanctity of life, the obligatory character of contracts and oaths, the necessity of veracity, or the constitutive role which the family holds in the body politic. Yet even in such instances a distinction has to be made between the intuited values, on the one hand, and the manner in which we implement them on the other. For instance, does the sanctity of life cover all animals and plants, too? Are there exceptions, for instance capital punishment, war, surgical operations? It should be obvious that conscience or ethical intuition are not sufficient to form the basis for independent moral thinking and action. The movement from general ideas to concrete standards cannot be accomplished by means of casuistry, that is to say a purely logical procedure, through which the attempt is made clearly to discern all that is implied in the idea, and what is definitely excluded. Rather one has to be guided by the notion of a goal to be reached. While practical usefulness is a legitimate goal, it must be subordinated, nevertheless, to God's goal with man. The problem may be conceived of as a three-cornered relationship, embracing ourselves as Christians, God, and this world with man in its centre. According to the order in which the three factors are placed to each other, faith manifests itself as religion or as moral life. In the former case we are concerned with apprehending God through the relationship in which we stand to the cosmic reality. In the latter case we see the divine will realized through the attitude which we take towards this world in our own conscience. Thereby we recognize as our special duty to promote the goal for which God has destined his creatures.

B. God and Moral Life

The relation between God and moral life is conceived of in most philosophical ethics as a merely logical one. Either one postulates a supreme reality or value in order to endow the moral standards with absolute

validity or one infers moral imperatives as resulting from the ontological
kinship of man and the divine. Faith interprets the moral life as a direct
manifestation of the divine. That we should take the moral standards
seriously is God's work in us. By speaking in this context of God as the
Creator of this world we want to state that the existence of the universe
as a material world and man's existence within it are not the result of a
necessity under which God found himself. Rather he wanted to have
an unlimited material world in order to manifest his power, wisdom and
generosity. Likewise, the fact that man is not a pure spirit, but rather a
being with a material body living in this material world, points to the
divine determination that man should seek the meaning of his life in
being a citizen of this world. Yet no less important is the fact that man
is equipped with a mind far superior to anything found in animals.
That condition must be understood as so willed by God. A truly human
life may not therefore be lived in neglect of that equipment. The trinitarian view of God implies that God did not create this world and man,
and then leave them to themselves. The Son is the expression of the love
which God has for this world. It manifests itself in the love which the
Son has for the Father, that is to say, the fact that this world, with man
in the midst of it, is permanently related to God and aims at an increasingly chosen relationship with him. Yet it is not, as in Plato, a participation in the divine substance. Man remains for all time a creature.
Rather through the Son, man is participating in the cosmic work of
God as his servant. Thus man finds in the privilege of his destination at
the same time his obligation. The God we serve is not an entity outside
ourselves. From the Creation on, Son and Spirit are at work with him
in this world and thus finally in man, too. Their presence in the
universe is not as obvious in inorganic matter as it is in man. Their
cosmic work agrees with the degree of receptivity of their substratum.
In inorganic matter the presence of the Spirit is recognized in his moving power, and that of the Son in the willingness of inorganic matter to
be subservient to the development of life. Son and Spirit are no less at
work in the lower than in the higher levels of evolution. Man's service
embraces therefore a cosmic field of action, and his obligation consists
in bringing to light the wholeness of earthly existence.

Human life would be frustrated, however, if in the way of idealism
the final goal were but a human wish, or according to nominalism a
divine demand, for the fulfilment of which man lacked the strength or
the resources. As Paul in particular has pointed out, man's existence
would then be a miserable one. For, being aware of his superiority over

the other organisms, he would nevertheless thereby be confined to taking care only of his own material needs. Goethe was certainly mistaken when he proclaimed that science and art would suffice to render human life useful and worthwhile. Quite significantly at the end of *Faust* II he has the heavenly love condescending to the man who relied on the sufficiency of his restlessness as a seeker. For by himself man has merely the longing for a better life. Yet he lacks the ability to render it real.

The assurance that God is willing to let man reach his destination we have in Jesus. In him, the love of the Son becomes a redemptive reality. The Son identifies himself with the human race by taking upon himself the conditions of human life, including the enmity of men and death. Through the ministry of Jesus, man is reminded that he must not look at what he is by and in himself. Rather by taking the initiative, God indicates that he is prepared to enable man to reach his destination. That life should have come into being in this world, is by no means as 'natural', as most biologists are inclined to assume. It is quite obvious that the biosphere is an infinitesimal portion of the universe. There is no reason, either, why material existence should ever be supplemented by life. Its existence in this world is to be understood as willed by God. Life is the manifestation of the Spirit of God in this world. It indicates that the universe did not come into existence by way of emanation as held by the Gnostics, Neoplatonists and Hegel. That theory entails the untenable consequence that this world partakes of divine nature. It is the vitality of the Creator which is brought to light in the phenomenon of earthly life. In his operation, the Spirit is correlated with the Son. His aiming at full union with the Father appears in the Spirit's activity as a succession of stages of life from the virus to the human mind, especially its spiritual unrest. Son and Spirit co-operate in a progressive transformation of this world. Material stuff becomes organic matter, objects of nature are made into tools, sense perceptions are changed into concepts and finally, by means of faith, the truth of the Incarnation transforms a sinful Ego into a child of God.

Thus the quest for goodness is not futile. But the power by which the goal may be attained cannot be released except when people are willing to use it in accordance with the truth. Just as the virus perishes unless it 'feeds' on congenial material, and just as notions are misleading or false, unless they are in agreement with the nature and condition of the things designated, so moral life can be truly realized only when we envisage our true relationship to the universe and our fellow men in the light of that model that Jesus has left us.

C. Moral Objective

The moral consciousness of the Christian is rooted in his understanding of himself, as it is formed by his encounter with God's self-disclosure. Under its impact, he realizes that he is not what he is destined to be, and that his moral efforts, no matter how lofty and arduous they may be, are in no way fit to alter his predicament. More than ever, the Christian feels the absolute obligation to actualize moral values. Nevertheless his life is assailed by the evils of this world, and above all by death. Thereby the fruits of man's moral efforts are brought to naught. The futility of moral striving explains the central place which the Resurrection of Christ occupies in the Christian life. For in it, and in it alone, do we possess the assurance that the realization of a successful life is not exclusively left to man's efforts. The universal threat to the meaning of life is not warded off by seeking pleasure, success or excellency. True, none of those goals is valueless or detestable. Nevertheless, unless seen in the wider frame of reference espoused by faith, they fail to provide true satisfaction.

The Christian has no reason to look down on utilitariansim or idealism. They will be disappointing however, when practised in an egotistic way. They provide real meaning only when their objective is pursued in the service of God, and in consideration of the legitimate interests of our fellow men.

By itself the limited scope of morality has no ethical implication. It is a tragic fact, but, at least from a purely practical viewpoint, not man's fault. Yet in the light of Christ's death and resurrection one notices that our sinful disregard of God's will is the reason why no hope may be entertained concerning our ability eventually to change our plight by our own efforts. For no matter how high a level our mental life may be capable of reaching, they will be marred by our disregard of God. Pathetically enough, it is the very grandeur of our achievements that increases the belief in our self-sufficiency.

The remedy is offered to man through the Gospel in the life and resurrection of Jesus. But how is the goal to be reached? It cannot be done by simply coupling moral and religious life. We have to recognize the comprehensive nature of God's purpose. While we have a right to pursue our personal interests, we must do so in the service of God's purpose. God is concerned with the wellbeing of the whole universe as created by him. Thus, not only individualistic aims fall short of making our activities relevant for God's plan, but also those anthropocentric views, according to which ethics should be occupied with interpersonal or interhuman relations only. Since God's redemptive work aims at incorporating the cosmic forces into the harmony of the universe, Christian ethics has a serious stake in the transformation of nature, too. Neither the technical mastery of nature nor its use for healing and pleasure are purely secular matters, that is to say, morally neutral.

Some philosophers wanted to replace the idea of the 'new' world which God has in mind, by an abstract value, for instance goodness, holiness or harmony. But we land in a perplexity, if with Kant and his followers we contend that such goods are absolutely necessary for no other reason than that we are persons equipped with a moral sense. For that is begging the questions, Are we not also able to disregard our conscience? Are we by acting so to a lesser degree ourselves than by acting morally? Kant laid himself open to the criticism, when yielding to experience he admitted the presence of radical evil in man. Inconsistently, he did not allow that fact to be of any consequence for man's self-evaluation or the understanding of the universe. By artificially separating moral reason from desires and wishes, passions and emotions, the idealists contradict the mental reality. Moral decisions are as much and as directly accompanied by emotions as are the immoral ones. Hence one cannot ascribe ethical actions to reason and evil deeds to the emotions as did the ancient Greek philosophers. Naturalism holds its own over against the idealist position in insisting that the general suppression of passions and emotions is utterly unjustified both from the moral viewpoint and also from that of mental health. Yet both idealism and naturalism fail as a result of their anthropocentric and practically egotistic outlook. Do not their advocates live in a world not made by them, and do they not avail themselves of the services of their fellow men? Yet they want to act as though there were no obligation incumbent upon them to care for the rest of the world.

Unlike the realm of extrahuman nature, disturbances in the human sphere do not regulate themselves automatically. Far from leading to a harmonious social order, J. S. Mill's utilitarianism, for instance, has resulted in increasing the distance of the have-nots from the haves. That fact, in turn, is breeding a revolutionary climate in large parts of the globe. Yet most people ignore the consequences of their own activity except for the narrow circle of their families, business partners or colleagues. That is the reason why it is so important to see moral problems in a cosmic perspective.

The Christian's service is devoted to the whole of God's creation. This objective may be understood in two different ways, however. In the one, which is frequently encountered among Catholic theologians, the purpose of Christian life is held to be the acquisition of a place in the heavenly abode. Understood consistently, life here on earth is significant merely as an opportunity by means of good work to become worthy of eternal bliss. That existence is supposed to consist in the contemplation of the beauty and order of a redeemed universe. As to the activities which life in this world requires, the ethical interest is of a purely negative character. In the common daily life, it is morally important to refrain from transgressing the commandments given by God and the Church. Of real importance, however, are the supernaturally good deeds. Those are actions which are done apart from practical necessity and which exhibit special zeal for God or require a special effort of the will. For they are committed in order to overcome the resistance of the flesh. Their motive is the individual's desire to participate in the eternal bliss. In turn, such works committed with the assistance of supernatural grace are meritorious, that is to say, they give the individual a rightful claim to heavenly life.

To such view Protestantism objects that it grades this world to a mere subsidiary of heaven and reduces man's earthly life to a mere episode that makes one wonder why God created this material world at all and whether it was by mistake that he placed man into this world. Undoubtedly it makes more sense to think of this world as being intrinsically meaningful on account of its temporal existence. Thereby, the universe is given a chance to grow steadily toward the goal God had in mind in making it. It starts in an existence in which it seems to be entirely left to itself and thus totally inarticulate and passive. It moves on, however, to a stage in which the Creator's power, wisdom and love will be fully manifested. That development takes place in co-ordinated and spontaneous movement. Implied in such a view is the fact that everything in this world by what it happens to be is destined to be used for the attainment of the ultimate goal. The Christian is privileged because he is able to contribute deliberately and constructively to that process of cosmic transformation. He will do so precisely by the things he must necessarily do in order to live a human life. But he will not be driven by the necessities of nature and the pressure of social institutions. His work is performed as a free service rendered to God. The Christian is not constrained by the demands of the moment but rather his work is built upon the foundations God has laid in the past.

To adopt this perspective of life and act accordingly is not possible except when by faith man accepts the helps that God offers to him.

Hence it is not man who offers his services to God as God's peer or a kind of ally. Rather, it is God who 'hires' and challenges us to carry out his plan.

Our task points in two directions. Man is to become better fit for his task, and the impediments that this world puts in his path are to be overcome. Yet the two aspects of man's assignment must not be separated. Some teachers of ethics are onesidedly concerned with the improvement of earthly conditions and techniques beginning with agriculture and husbandry and climaxing in devotional preoccupations. With equal one-sidedness, the other group is busy with perfecting man's inner life. Yet there is no sense in asking, 'What is prior, being or acting?' The task is indivisible because it is God who sets the goal before us.

Man's task may therefore be defined as follows. Man is to learn so to put himself at the disposal of God that through man with the aid of God the power of the forces of evil in this world may be broken or used for constructive purposes. Thus, the goodness of God's creation will come fully and unimpededly to the fore.

D. Revelation and Ethics

In revealing himself through the medium of this world, God makes man aware of the fact that as the Creator he takes completely care of this world. He keeps it in existence and in motion, he preserves its equilibrium and harmony, and he provides sufficiencies for all living creatures. All these functions are implied in the existence of this world and are performed by themselves, that is to say, irrespective of anything done by man or any other creature. The universe, by its existence and equilibrium, is the evidence of God's universal grace. The world would be what it is apart from man's existence and would go on unchanged even if the human race were completely extinct. What then is the significance of man's ethical activities? Some will confine it to the improvement of social life or to mental hygiene. Unlike the cosmos which offers him hospitality, and whose eternal order has been worshipped and admired by man for ages, man himself, it is said, is an inordinate being and endowed with a murderous instinct. As a result he renders himself miserable and a victim of his uncontrolled passions, and by his hostility disturbs and dissolves the social order. Thus, for his own sake he has to curb his self will. Thus understood, moral life would be nothing but enlightened self-love.

Yet, such interpretation is not only too narrow, because it ignores man's relationship to the non-human realm of the biosphere. It also ignores the unconditional character of the voice of conscience. In turn, however, the Kantian contention that the moral good had to be realized for its mere goodness may suffice for a general description of morality. But hidden in it is already the understanding that goodness serves a superior purpose. Not only in primitive religion, but also in Pharisaic Judaism and in the Catholic notion of meritorious works the end of moral goodness consists in the satisfaction of one's needs or wishes. Such view has been rejected by Jesus and Paul and with special emphasis again by the reformers. For it implies a relationship of God and man, in which God is held to be under obligation to reward man for his goodness. Such an argument would hold good only if by means of his morality man would add to this world what God was not capable of performing, whereas, in fact, the ability to act morally is a gift imparted to man by his Creator. This objection is particularly cogent when man's sinfulness is taken into consideration. Conversely, one must never lose sight of the remarkable and numerous fruits of the Christian life. Surveying the history of the last two millennia one can but marvel about the change that has been wrought by Christianity. Hundreds of millions have contributed to a new understanding of this world and man's place in it, but also to the well-being of their fellow men on the basis of a new understanding of political and social life. Thus, it cannot be denied that Christian life produces visible effects in this world.

Noteworthy, however, as these accomplishments are, they would not suffice to make the Christian life a moral obligation. Quite apart from the historical problem, whether or not those changes could be ascribed entirely and exclusively to Christianity – race, economic factors and climatic reasons, for instance, have also been mentioned – such a pragmatic view could at the best present the Christian life as a recommendable way. It would, however, leave open entirely different options, especially in the eyes of those who feel the necessity to adjust modern man's conduct to the requirements of a technological age. Of course, such an outlook debases moral life to mere effectiveness. The value of life is thereby measured by the influence technological progress has upon human life and man's mastery of his cosmic environment.

The argument from revelation starts from the fact that in his self, man finds the desire to assert himself as a human being in this world. Man is looking for a way of life that will make his existence permanently meaningful. Irrespective of whether or not he believes in individual immortality he wants so to live that he may be sure things would be different, if he had not lived or had lived a different life, and that it matters for this world or the course of history that he lives his specific life.

It is such self-consciousness that is encountered by God's revelation. By its inescapable character and authority it shows man that his expectation is basically true. Man has a permanent destination in this world. But over against the optimistic belief that he is by nature on the road to such a goal, the Biblical revelation makes him also aware that as a result of the trust he puts in his own strength and goodness he disturbs the cosmic order, and, since the latter asserts itself eventually, he chooses a road to futility. In turn, however, the fact that the truth comes to him and discloses the nature of his predicament, he is made certain that God is concerned with him. Not only will his past in its nefarious and destructive character be neutralized as he recognizes the wrongness of his natural outlook, but also and above all is he offered the alternative of a life in which he acts as God's servant. In that life of faith the possibility is granted by God who takes the initiative in revealing and offering it to man, while the execution is left to the believer. Here lies the secret of the moral obligation. Man is aware of it in his own mind, but it is not the expression of his own desire but rather is accepted by him through faith as revelation confronts him as the only meaningful implementation of the awareness of his destination. There is no outward pressure or compulsion that moves him to accept the divine offer. He is overwhelmed by its intrinsic truth. Furthermore, he must acknowledge the fact that there is no alternative to the divine offer. As the futility of his natural life is rooted in his disregard of God, so the true life is the one which God puts at man's disposal. Finally, as self-disclosure of the Creator's work, revelation makes known man's place in nature. Primitive man's religion concerns almost exclusively his relation to his environment. The Biblical view of creation, however, relates man to the whole universe.

E. God's People

We started in this chapter from the fact that moral consciousness originates in the fellowship of the congregation. Though the Christian life demands the spontaneous participation and the responsibility of the individual Christian, our faith would not be what it is except for its collective nature. Human life will not develop outside of collective fellowship and actions. Robinson Crusoe would not have been able to continue a truly human existence except for the relics of home civilization that he had salvaged and the recollections of human life he brought with him to his island. As the experience of castaways shows, their inability to manufacture all the tools and to know all the techniques required even on a primitive level of civilized life lowers those unfortunate people soon to a subhuman level. Christian ethics deals therefore with the collective obligation under which the Church stands as it realizes its divine calling.

The response to the Church's vocation is not made with equal intensity by all its members. With extremely rare exceptions, a congregation is composed of two groups. One is formed by a few members who enjoy a spontaneous spiritual life and who thus keep the congregation in motion. The other group, formed by the majority of members, is more or less conservative and static. Such duality is not to be judged a symptom of degeneration or decay of spiritual life. Already Jesus used to differentiate methods and perspective according to whether he was speaking to the Twelve or to the 'crowds' or the 'many'. 'Progressives' are inclined to look down upon that group as spiritually dead, with little reason, however. While the fact cannot be denied that sometimes the Church is joined by people for purposes of social prestige, the majority of church members are sincere in their belief in God's redemptive work. Yet they find it hard to engage too widely and too intensely in a fight against the political and social evils around them. They are afraid of the people who are active in the exploitation of those evils. Nevertheless they are in agreement with those who advocate changes in Church life.

In the majority section of the Church, the moral consciousness manifests itself as a common ethos and church mores. Both of them are fairly stable and change but seldom and slowly, an indication of the conservative nature of that group. Conversely, in the leader group one will find diversity and the ability quickly to adapt themselves to new conditions, that is to say, symptoms of personal experience.

When the two groups are treated as independent units, the impression may be created of a divided church. But the fact that the two groups may differ in their theology or pursue different goals must not conceal their unity and interrelation. Similarly their differences must not be interpreted as though one was alive and the other one was practically dead.

The picture of the Church is at times confusing. The Church is the place at which the Spirit is at work in the interchange between its members. It is mainly the 'conservative' group, for instance, which donates the funds by means of which the projects of the 'Progressives' are financed. The health of the Church is dangerously impaired, however, when one of those groups refuses to co-operate with the other one instead of lovingly to engage, as far as possible, in common enterprises. It is God who differently endowed them with spiritual gifts, who brought about their differences. The superior group is constantly reminded by its co-existence with the majority that its great temptation is an aristocratic exclusiveness, whereas they are destined through their special insights to enlighten the common crowd. For the Gospel is to be proclaimed to all the people. The common people, in turn, are encouraged by their association with the spiritual leaders to overcome a defeatist attitude. Their fellowship with the 'upper' group is a promise that where human strength fails, divine support is still available.

A distinction must also be made between spiritual leaders and 'activists' in the Church, although it may be difficult for the sociologist to keep them asunder. Not every man who wants to set the Church on fire is driven by the Holy Spirit. In view of the almost unlimited freedom which many churches grant to their members, it is quite possible that to some people the church will appear an apt forum on which to discuss pet ideas of theirs, though they have no spiritual bearing.

The duality of church life must be kept in mind when we want to know what the Christian moral life is like. Obviously, it would be mistaken to identify it with either group. It is the interrelation between the two groups by which churches and denominations are enabled to hold together and form units. It is in the willingness of the majority to be inspired and led by its spiritual leaders, and in turn in the sense of responsibility which the leaders feel for the majority that we find the roots of their moral consciousness. Their agreement is not to be found in a 'golden mean' either. The spiritual teachers will point out the incipient and immature nature of the majority view. The latter, in turn, will recoil from the apparent lack of realism of the Progressives. The description of the Christian moral consciousness must therefore be concerned with what is meant by their interrelation. The fact that the conservatives are able to make a legitimate claim for their church membership will prevent the Church from overcharging the common Christian with excessive demands. The existence of the leader group, on the other hand, will warn the Church against acquiescing complacently in mediocrity.

F. Work and Rest

The Greek philosophers hotly debated the question whether the ethical life was one of action or of contemplation, and the schoolmen of the Middle Ages took up the problem again, mainly in view of the various objectives that the different monastic orders had set to themselves. In modern times the problem made its reappearance on a higher level. People scrutinized the relationship of 'Being or Action'. It would seem, however, that the real problem is most adequately stated in the Biblical contradistinction of Work and Rest.

Mankind lives in a world in which the things needed for the sustenance of life are available only when people make an effort to acquire them. It is a general law that the higher the level of life of an individual, the wider the range within which he can assert himself. Yet the effort required to maintain himself on that level must also be proportionately harder. Thus, man is the working animal *par excellence*. He is not only *homo faber*, that is, the toolmaker, but also *ens cogitans*, a creature who must think hard in order to live a truly human life. The fact has been emphasized instinctively in the Biblical religion. The ratio of one holiday after six days of work indicates that the demand which life in this world makes on man's will and toil is an exacting one. In turn, however, the fact that each week has a holiday witnesses to God's kindness. The bounties of this world are so abundant, and man has been so adequately equipped by God, that by means of six days of work he is able to provide enough sustenance for seven days for himself and his family. In turn, by resting for one day of each week, man will be able to restore his body and mind sufficiently to continue his work on the same scale at the beginning of the subsequent week. This is one of the points on which the privileged position of man is manifested. Animals have no holiday. They must work day in day out without a break in order to keep themselves alive.

As the story of man's expulsion from the Garden shows, the necessity to work is a curse laid upon man. Without industry and strenuous effort he would be unable to live a truly human life. Nevertheless the ability to work is not itself a curse; rather it is a privilege granted to man. While no animal has to toil in the manner man must, man in turn is enabled by means of work constantly to create new goods and to develop new techniques. That he does, not merely by tilling the soil and domesticating cattle, but also in the areas of art, technology, administration and security. Thus, man is in a position through his work to assist God in the work of Creation. He thereby transforms availability into usefulness, amorphous material into works of art, irrational materiality into rational concepts and ideas. Finally man renders himself able to work without physical toil, yet with considerable mental effort in administering and co-ordinating services in training others for useful work, or in healing physical, mental and social evils. Thereby, he lays the foundation for the divine work of redemption. Though the necessity to work is a divine penalty, yet it is not meant to render man miserable. It is a divine measure of education destined to prepare man for the voluntary service of God.

In view of such universal significance of work, even the person who is not under pressure to work for a living is under obligation to be busy for God's sake, and to contribute to the multiplication of earthly goods. It is for that reason that in the family and the congregation we train our children to render services to other people. We pity those who are so oppressed by the toil or unpleasant character of their work that they look forward to their retirement only. Experience shows that as a result of such an outlook old age gets dull and meaningless. But no less to be pitied is the man who is the slave of work and refuses to relax. Even if he does not meet a premature death from overstrain, he will deprive himself of the joy of family life and friendship and the enjoyment of God's good gifts. Yet work requires rest as its counterweight.

In the Biblical religion, the Sabbath has a twofold function. It is both a day of rest and also a day of worship and sanctification. Hence rest is more than inactivity. When in the Creation story God is said to have rested on the seventh day, or when the risen Lord is described as sitting on God's right hand, the idea is not one of idleness and retirement from activity, but rather one of sanctification as contrasted with being engaged in making things. Man's destination is not fulfilled when he increases the supply of material goods. As they were made in this world and from the materials of this world, so they are to be used for God's cause. Thus, practical life and religion are not to be treated as two independent spheres of life. By the kindness of God rather than by his own strength man has been enabled to transform nature. Accordingly, these goods are not only to be enjoyed, they are to be used in a way which conforms to God's redemptive purpose. The order of the week is of great help in that respect. The dire necessity to work results eventually in man's being absorbed by the daily task. We need the hours of rest in order to recover the awareness that there is a God who has made us for his final goal.

In our activistic age the opposite is more likely to happen. Our obsession with doing things as a form of self-assertiveness is carried over to the day of rest. Even in the Sunday we seem to be unable to relax and get into a state of receptivity. What is probably worse, opportunities to engage in a new work seem to be so attractive that modern man jumps at them without reflecting on the final goal thereby to be reached. Lack of meditation is responsible for the restlessness by which we hurry in our church life from the discussion of one problem or the execution of one project to another without ever taking time out to bring the former to a satisfactory solution. That the Early Church should have chosen the first day of the week as their regular holiday has not altered the character and symbolism of the week. The features of rest and sanctification were transferred from the Sabbath to the Sunday. As a new element, the first day of the week was connected with the Resurrection of Jesus, and thus symbolized the new life that originated in the rest of the preceding night.

As a day of recreation and sanctification, the institution of the seventh day serves to remind the Church also of the receptive character of faith. What matters in the celebration of the Sunday is not the strictness with which we refrain from manual work and 'worldly pleasures' but rather the rhythm it constitutes. True human life requires God's revelation and spiritual gifts no less than man's toil. The Sunday service, while not indispensable for salvation, is nevertheless of high usefulness. The man who contends that he is able to meet God on Sunday morning at the golf course or in his backyard will in all probability be preoccupied with everything else save the work of the Spirit. The self-scrutiny in which he intended to engage will soon be diverted by the loud noises of the media of mass communication, or the leisurely chat with like-minded neighbours. The benefit of having this extra day each week can hardly be overrated. Social reformers around the beginning of this century worried about the spiritual dangers of mechanical work in the factories. Naïvely they suggested that the worker should give his imagination free rein to explore the origin of his materials and the destination of the goods manufactured. To do so was hardly feasible then and it has become impossible today. The modern tempo of work demands fullest attention on the part not only of the factory worker, but also of the white-collar worker. Apart from the full break provided by the seventh day, the development of our inner life and even the occupation with Christian projects would encounter considerable difficulties. The value of the Sunday does not lie in its institutional character, but in the opportunity it gives us to envisage our daily life in the perspective of God's plan.

Even with a three-day work-week modern man would not become more truly human if he used his leisure time merely for rest and entertainment. The activist restlessness and the brutal worship of power, which he encounters in his work world, would quickly enslave him, because in his leisure time he did not develop counterstriking forces.

10 The Moral Dilemma

A. The Moral Aim

Kant's historical greatness lies in his discovery that the moral demand is an absolute one, because moral values possess unconditional validity. Other motives may enter into our actual decisions, thereby indicating that man is simultaneously confronted by a number of claims, all of which contend to be equally necessary. The moral rigorists have decreed that, on account of the absoluteness of the moral will, aesthetic or biological demands cannot be ascribed first rank. The natural feeling of man shrinks from such a position, however. Is it really necessary under all circumstances to sacrifice one's life? Does the ethical standard offer no alternative? Does the duty of veracity constrain me to disclose relevant secrets to people who will use them for criminal purposes? Such questions are sufficient to show that there must be something wrong in the way in which Kant interpreted the absoluteness of the moral standard.

The theologian will discern two flaws in Kant's reasoning. For one thing, goodness is interpreted by that great philosopher as a static entity whose realization may be performed in part or *in toto*. Furthermore, notwithstanding the transcendental nature of moral consciousness, Kant is unwilling to assign it a special ontic place. As a result of his basic epistemological scepticism he treats the voice of conscience as an appendix or epiphenomenon of the human mind. In other words, it is a self-determination of our subjectivity. The goal of moral life, thus understood, is goodness, that is to say, a quality of the Ego. Thereby Kant leaves out of consideration the fact that our moral consciousness points beyond itself. Even if we granted to Kant that the sphere of reality to which it points is not directly given for recognition, it would be necessary to go in two respects beyond the Königsberg philosopher. To start with, the sphere of reality, from which the moral standard derives its authority, must be conceived of as lying outside of and above that of sense experience. For the moral standard imparts direction to the latter. Furthermore, on account of its telic character, the moral consciousness cannot be rooted in, let alone identified with, subjectivity.

For implied in the moral consciousness is the conviction that by means of moral action the quality of this world will be essentially improved. One can hardly assume that by itself the Ego possesses that capacity.

It is true we are unable directly to describe what the result of our moral life will be, except in such general terms as 'a new heaven and a new earth', or 'eternal bliss', 'cosmic harmony', or the 'glory of God'. Nevertheless, we are enabled, in the light of God's self-disclosure, especially that given in Jesus, to lay down certain features of the goal to be reached. In broad terms it might be defined as implying full and voluntary co-operation of all human beings, a fruitful relationship of man and nature, and confident willingness on man's part to 'be guided by God's Spirit'. In recent times it has been suggested to subsume all these and other relationships under the concept of reconciliation. But reconciliation designates the end of enmity only. It does not imply the positive and constructive aspects of faith, quite apart from the fact that not all moral relationships presuppose enmity.

Above all, a conciliatory attitude would be wishful dreams only, unless we could be sure that the goal could be attained. If there were no power by which both moral action and the condition of this world were co-ordinated, the effect of moral action would be confined to changes in the individual's mind and in the social life of the group to which he belongs. Actually to effect this co-ordination is the Spirit's work. The Spirit is God's power of life as it operates in this world toward a condition in which all creatures manifest the 'glory' of God. In other words, each of them will be seen as being what it was destined to become, and thus as promoting the for-each-otherness as foundation of the cosmic process. The Spirit's work is not confined to engendering moral life.

As life-giving energy, the Spirit serves God's final goal in the whole biosphere. The new life is not the substitution of a heavenly energy in the place of our biological and mental vitality. Rather it is a relationship into which we enter by faith. Thereby the factors which account for the limited duration of 'natural' life lose their power. That is a condition of life which principally surpasses man's earlier stage of life. In it, too, the Spirit was at work as can be seen in the development of civilization. Man was enabled to have dominion over nature. As a result of faith, however, the individual is then not only capable of envisaging this world in the divine perspective. He is also able, in spite of his creatureliness, to transform it into God's Kingdom. Man is the only creature who is aware of the telic character of his life and thus capable of acting spontaneously and in self-determination. Again, man alone realizes the obligation to act accordingly. In that way, moral consciousness engenders moral action, and moral action becomes an effectual cause in this world.

Thus, the basic problem of human life is not, How is goodness possible? For through the power of the Spirit it is effectively present in this world. Rather we ask ourselves the crucial question, How may I become truly myself? In other words, What must happen if the possibility offered to me by the Spirit is to become an actual reality? That question does not mean as in Existentialism, How am I to actualize my potentialities? for my destination is no part of my natural life, not even potentially. It is an event which takes place when the Spirit confronts me. I am not able to bring it to pass by my own efforts. In turn, the fundamental question is not raised as in existentialism, by an Ego prior to, or apart from, a good conscience, but by people who by their faith have been made sure that their sins have been forgiven and that through Christ they have been called for holy work. Why then is it that the true life is such a problem for Christians?

B. Difficulties

1. *Limits of Choice*

If faith were a mere assent given to theological statements, or a mere sentiment of the presence of God or of the bliss of being saved, there would be no moral problem in the Christian life. Since the work of redemption would take place away from this world in heaven, our conduct would be a purely practical matter.

When the purpose and will of God are understood, however, as the work of the triune God in its unified diversity, the human predicament appears in a different light. For the Christian as a creature finds himself in a world in which he is to perform a task in the service of God. He finds his freedom considerably limited. He must accept his earthly life as God's gift. Yet he is unable to keep it in working condition except when he takes care of its necessities. The larger part of what we do each day is required apart from our moral determination by the demands of our body, of our job, of the rules of social fellowship and the requirements of the public order. The way in which we act, and the amount of what we accomplish, likewise are narrowly conditioned by our physical constitution and our temperament, as well as by hereditary features, education and social position. Furthermore, the effects of our actions are not in our hand except to a slight degree. We are living in a world whose uncertainty and instability are evident. That fact is most conspicuous in our mortality. Neither moment nor manner of our death are under our control. In general, a risk is connected with everything we do, and the higher the stakes, the greater the risk we run. Furthermore, since we know so little about the nature of this world and of the future, we are easily deceived by the appearance of things. In particular, their significance eludes us. What provides pleasure for a moment may prove to be harmful in the long run. The success we seek in life may eventually be our undoing. We have a right to expect satisfaction from this world. Yet being unaware of the consequences we stumble easily into its traps.

We are living in a world which God has equipped with many good things. Yet how often we overlook its incompleteness! Our intellect, for instance, is a wonderful faculty and far superior to anything found in the animal realm. Yet how frequently even great scholars indulge in the conceited belief that they have the answer for all of man's questions, and how stubbornly they refuse to accept moral advice. The road of human progress is a crooked one.

Probably the most formidable obstacle to right action is the fact that living consciously concerns but a small area of our existence. While human life is aware of itself in individual consciousness, the individual mind does not bring forth its faculties. What we call the transcendental structure of the mind is in fact the unconscious operation of the species as it works in and through the individual. Of course, a clear distinction must be made between subconscious and unconscious drives of the mind. The subliminal elements in the individual mind are the result of personal experiences. Though temporarily forgotten, they can be brought to the surface again. There may be traumatic effects which form strong obstacles to right actions because they may lead to neurotic ideas, emotions and habits. Nevertheless, they may eventually be cured. However, what operates as unconscious urge or constitution is the work of the 'form' or species of mankind. By it the course of human development is determined. Being members of the human race we must, in an inescapable manner, act in a human way. We lack, for instance, the advantages of the instinct and the vital resilience of the viruses, and we have no possibility to think or act in a superhuman way. While in mystical ecstasy or Yogi mental technique some individuals will reach higher levels of consciousness than the average person, those faculties are still modes of the human mind. Likewise, we are in a completely passive manner the tools of the Spirit. He will manifest himself in sudden upheavals and forward leaps in the history of human evolution.

That can be seen most clearly in his self-manifestation in Christianity. But as a rule, his operation cannot directly be perceived and is known only in retrospect in the changes he has called forth, by directing and intensifying a field of action. No matter what objectives man may pursue, they have eventually to fall into line with the eschatological process called forth by the Spirit. As Spengler and Toynbee have pointed out, the history of all nations follows basically the same pattern from rise to disintegration and self-destruction.

2. *Limits of Action*
Whereas the above limitations and obstacles affect mainly the mode of action, the social structure of life has a considerable bearing on the freedom of action. Outside of social institutions, the individual is unable in the long run to live a truly human life. We are members of the nation, of its economic and cultural life no less than its political one. The common organization, the common effort, the common traditions and the sharing of the social product prove to be of great help for man. Through them the race has been lifted from the animal level to that of civilization. At the same time, the individual is thereby aided in the pursuance of his various interests. In turn, however, these institutions have a coercive character. They demand a certain conformity of action and outlook on the part of all its members and they insist on compliance with the specific rules by which they function. That fact creates special problems for Christians.

Even where a church is co-extensive with the state, their aims are not identical, and the political rulers are not always animated by Christian convictions. Yet Christians as any other citizens will not be able to enjoy the benefits of social life, unless they are prepared to acknowledge the authority of those institutions. Whether or not those institutions should be labelled 'orders of Creation', as many Lutheran theologians prefer to designate them, or should be regarded as the natural offspring of human life, is a matter of perspective rather than of substance. For historically they all come into existence as the result of human effort and planning. Yet they originate with an inescapable necessity and thus must be considered as implied in the divine plan of creation. The tension between the secular and the Christian outlook must not therefore move Christians completely to withdraw from the life of the secular institutions. On the contrary, the latter are to be used as means by which the Holy Spirit carries on the education of mankind.

Christians will find themselves in a particularly difficult position, nevertheless, because these institutions have been brought into being by people who were bound by their sinful disregard of God's will. They may aim at a higher life, yet the organization of their institutions is based upon the conviction that that goal can be reached by man's own efforts. While in many instances one encounters belief in a deity by which an institution has been founded, man is regarded as being capable of executing its special task by himself. Thus, it is not surprising that, notwithstanding their educative function, such institutions as family and state, economy and civilization have but propaedeutic value in the development of mankind. In spite of Hegel, even the state cannot be regarded as the goal of history. That renders them in many cases impediments of Christian activity. We encounter here an irrationality similar to that found in the individual. Both religious and secular institutions originate in the Spirit. Yet though their ultimate goal must therefore be identical, they clash in the social reality. The reason lies in the fact that all secular institutions are power structures and thus based upon collective self-assertiveness. It is quite natural that those in power have a conservative outlook and are reluctant to give up their privileges and their specific outlook and organization. With its desire to transform this world, Christianity is felt by the members of the established institutions to be a disturbance. They will look at Christian action, for instance the work for civil rights or for peaceful co-existence of nations or economic systems as though they were revolutionary and subversive activities.

The Christian's freedom of choice and action is also limited by the fact that he has to move in an historical field. Living in history, that is to say, in a continuance that moves steadily on, is man's unique privilege as well as his burden. Unlike the rest of organisms, whose existence rests in themselves, man is enabled to venture forward in time. But history is a continuous process. We do not start it. Rather we stand on the shoulders of those who worked before us. We have to accept the conditions of the historical field as they pass it on to us, with its accumulation of experience and of material goods, with its position of power and a population devoted to it. Yet we also inherit its liabilities. Our predecessors bequeathed to us their errors, prejudices and weaknesses, their injustices and their vices.

Implied in the continuity of the historical field is the relative smallness of the contribution we are able to make to history on our part. The past that made us is infinitely mightier than what a single generation is able to accomplish. Furthermore, the goal of our field lies in an unknown future, which even the most highly organized computer is unable to unveil. No wonder that the statesmen and the nations who support them blunder so frequently and often end in disaster. But quite apart from the fact that historical activity is beset by so many risks, not much of the historical process is man's conscious work. In history people are moved mainly by irrational forces and unconscious urges. They precipitate events which they never intended to bring about. Forces of confusion and destructiveness, which manifest themselves in a nation's emotions, may thus result in wars and revolutions, persecutions or craving for world power although nobody intended them. The operation of those historical forces is the reason why so many historical actions end in failure. Successful activity is possible only in those rare cases where a constellation of historical circumstances gives to a leader room for a decision that is in agreement with the direction of the historical field.

C. The Spirit: Order in Disorder

The human predicament, as has been described above, might seem to be an absolutely chaotic one. Apparently that would facilitate our accommodation. Like the animals we might disregard its disadvantages and inconveniences completely and enjoy what good things the moment offers. Yet human life remains enigmatic on account of the fact that meaningful events take place in it, too, that people emerge in history, whose lives make a substantial contribution to history, and that we encounter novelty in it which manifests progress. Such apparent contradiction may be understood as the work of the Spirit. He operates effectively in a medium that does not aim at God's final goal. The perplexity which our predicament thus causes to us is largely our own fault, however. Since the days of the Enlightenment Western mankind has not only abrogated the notion of a devil and of demons, but also belief in the ontic reality of evil. Yet all attempts to rationalize our existence through the philosophies of rationalism, idealism, positivism or pragmatism, are but attempts to dodge the problem of evil.

Essential for Christian faith is the recognition of the duality of reality and the militant character of the Spirit. Even Christians may be misled by the appearance of the cosmic powers and consequently may attempt to adjust their life to the prevailing conditions of this world. Thus it looks at times as though there were no difference between the conduct of non-Christians and Christians. Yet, while the Christian, like the rest of mankind, may easily be in doubt as to the nature of his proximate goals, he has no doubt concerning the ultimate goal. Subsequent experience of the evil consequences of an action performed out of a mistaken perspective will bring the error to light. No matter how cleverly the cosmic forces may turn their destructive intentions, there is no wrong that will not eventually be unmasked.

As Christians, we have to live in this world and its institutions. Yet while we accept obediently their demands, our compliance differs from that of the legalist. What moves us is not the authority of the institution but rather the realization that the institution serves God's purpose. Thereby our voluntary compliance implies the claim for personal discretion. Thus, our action becomes a factor of social transformation. We try to overcome the elements of self-assertion and self-seeking which mar the non-Christian's participation in institutional life. Since we are still living in the beginning of the new aeon which Christ has ushered in, his transforming power is not yet fully manifested. We have therefore good reason to expect new and deeper spiritual insights and more radical changes in social life than what we discern at present. The equality granted to women, the abolition of slavery, the formation of a civil service devoted to the common good, and the rejection of war as an indispensable means of settling international conflicts are a few indications of the profound influence which Christians have already exerted upon the structure and orientation of social life. That radical change has not been accomplished, however, through the superior goodness of individual Christians. Rather it is through their faith that the Holy Spirit is enabled to make his power felt in human life. This does not mean that the Spirit requires the power of man's faith in order to triumph over the cosmic forces. Rather God is not willing to bring about redemption in human life, unless man is giving evidence that he desires God's support. Thus, there is no contradiction in the striking contrast between the deplorably small moral achievements of the majority of Christians, on the one hand, and the steady and effective progress of the Spirit's work, on the other. Rather it is by means of the contrast that the divine power proves its superiority in and through our human weakness. Faith implies the recognition of two basic facts. First, apart from God's redemptive work, cosmic energies are unable to bring about any substantial improvement in this world. Moreover, the fundamental contrast between God's aims and that of the cosmic forces cannot be truly apprehended except through the image of Christ. Apart from it, it is practically impossible to recognize the difference between the biological and social necessities, on the one hand, and the aim of God on the other.

Jesus saw clearly the relationship of the Spirit and human activity. Placing the Spirit in the centre and assigning to the activity of faith the role of a prerequisite he ruled out the ethics of prohibitions. Though he enjoined the authority of the Decalogue, he transformed its prohibitions into pointers to positive goods. The moral prohibition, he emphasized, is man's attempt to reach the ethical goal by means of his own efforts, namely, by refraining from things which appear to be valuable. Goodness is then seen in the individual's ability to resist the temptation to enjoy earthly goods.

The one-sided emphasis which Pietism and the subsequent revival movements laid upon the suppression of subjective wrongness and sin, has finally in our age called forth a strong development in the opposite direction. The goal of life is seen in the furtherance of the material good of individuals and social groups. Neither movement reaches the depth of the problem, however. They measure evil by the psychological or social effect. From the Christian viewpoint, however, evil is everything that tends to turn man away from allegiance to God, no matter whether it harms or furthers him materially. Failure to grasp this spiritual depth of evil has misled some into the dangerous belief that man has been called by God to rid this world from all evils. Equally erroneous is the opinion that as a mere imperfection evil will gradually disappear from this world. Evil in the spiritual perspective is something that must not be in a world made by God. Yet we hasten to add that on account of its ability to enter into God's good world, evil manifests its enormous power. There is no hope, therefore, that it might be eradicated by man's efforts or would wane on account of its intrinsic weakness.

The element of truth found in the various views of evil held by mankind is the conviction that this world will never be freed of evil unless man takes an active part in such a process. Christianity looks for an eventual triumph over evil in man's co-operation with God in the redemptive process. This is done in combining practical action with faith. Though faith will not remove the restrictions to moral choice and moral action, it prepares the way for the Spirit's redemptive work. While the scarcity of historical and practical opportunities dooms the actions of non-believers to almost complete vanity, the Holy Spirit is not hampered in the same way. The moral action of the Christian has always a spiritual consequence, which in turn brings forth actual changes in this world. Thereby the true nature of moral freedom is disclosed. Freedom is not a congenital or acquired faculty of the mind which, having it, I may use at all times at my discretion. Rather, it is a recurrent event which happens every time when the Spirit 'accepts' a Christian's faith. On account of the mediating role of faith, the spiritual consequences manifest themselves in the individual's life as the fruit of faith. Yet that result is not accomplished through the mental energy implied in his action but rather by the Spirit's willingness to use believers as his tools irrespective of their worthiness.

Jesus was not unaware of the evils of this world. On the contrary, he noticed their presence even where others did not suspect them, for instance, in one's possessions, power, vitality, or learning. But he refrained from propagating ambitious programmes of a better world. He did not join the community of Qumran, which on the eve of the destination of Jerusalem had devised a radical programme of cultic reform. Jesus realized that by adopting blueprints of the future man was trying to assume for himself what was God's prerogative. Jesus did not reject planning and he was certainly concerned with the future of the fellowship of his followers. Yet what he passed on to them was not a doctrine of the Church and its organization within the Jewish commonwealth. Rather he desired to keep awake in them the assurance that with him the redemptive power of the Son of God was at work, notwithstanding his Cross. Thus, they ought not to worry about their future. True, there was no refuge to which they might repair from the wickedness of this world. But the Spirit's power of life, which they shared with him, was in fact a fortress of God in the midst of the hostile forces of the universe.

D. Adiaphora

In ethical theory, the question has often been raised, whether all human activity is subject to moral evaluation, or, to put it differently, whether moral activity is the ultimate goal of all human life. Are there no *adiaphora*, that is to say, actions which are ethically neutral? The fact that God has provided rest for man should answer the question. As a rule we act in order to effect something in this world. Inasmuch, however, as this is God's world, not ours, it is evident that every change brought about in it is subject to God's judgement. Yet not all of our activities aim at a practical end. We may suspend our urge to engage in useful work and idle around. Since God grants us time and opportunity to rest it is permissible for man to enjoy himself and this world. God does not demand of man that his whole time and energy should be spent for the realization of practical ends. We may, with a good conscience, use our leisure time for play and sport, recreation and artistic appreciation, dancing, flirtation and erotic play, practical jokes and frolicking. There are certain limitations, however. God has not made us for rest and play only but also, and in the first place, for service. We act wrongly when we are so preoccupied with play and amusement that insufficient time is left for useful work. Likewise, we act wrongly when the things we do for our entertainment are apt to have harmful or destructive effects, for instance, excesses of eating, drinking or sport, cruelty and serious disregard of other people's dignity and honour.

There is still another viewpoint from which the problem of *adiaphora* has been raised. How far are the means for the performance of an action and its circumstances to be considered morally relevant? Is there a moral difference between my wearing today a blue suit or a grey one? Or, to go to seemingly less trivial matters, does it make ethically any difference if the President of the United States flies today to Texas and tomorrow to Puerto Rico, or if he reverses the order of his trips? In these and similar instances, there are decisions involved. Yet, the scrupulous person who wants to apply ethical standards to all the minutiae of life misunderstands the nature of the moral obligation. Moral judgements apply basically to the individual's outlook in its totality, in other words, to the significance which an action has for my stance in God's universe. Thus, the moral consciousness refers to all the actions whose intention is based upon that stance and the obligations flowing from it. A moral judgement can therefore be applied to those actions only which are intended to implement that relationship. The moral decision has a twofold aim. It is meant to fulfil the obligation which results from our stance in the universe. In other words, it is the response which the believer's heart makes to the combination of God's purpose with man's faith and his specific gifts, and the needs of those for whose benefit the action is intended. At the same time the contemplated or performed action is to serve practical ends, and it requires therefore suitable means for its execution. That suitability is not subject to moral evaluation except in a negative and derivative way. All modes or means of action that are not incompatible with the spiritual end of human life are acceptable. For the rest, the selection of suitable means and circumstances is a matter of prudence rather than of moral conscience. The ability to make such selection depends on subjective factors such as age, education, practical experience and temperament. Hence, it may be considerably at variance in different people. A person is not morally reprehensible for choosing means of action that to others will appear of little usefulness. One thinks, for instance, of the various and at times strange ways in which Christians in our days attempt to express their opposition to war.

In turn, all means which are incompatible with the spiritual goal of human life are wrong, even though they may have a highly useful function for the person who acts. One cannot say that the 'compatible' means are *adiaphora* in a strict sense. The decision to use but 'compatible' means is a moral act, and the necessity to make such a decision confronts us in every new situation. Within the limits of compatibility, however, the selection of appropriate means is then left to our free choice. It has no extra moral implications.

Thus, the same action may or may not be subject to a moral judgement. Food, for instance, presents no moral problem for a healthy person, provided only he refrains from consuming things which harm his spiritual life or his ability to serve God, and from excesses by which his physical and/or mental faculties are incapacitated. For the sick person, however, the diet prescribed by the doctor becomes a moral problem. Since one's ability to serve others may be impaired by sickness, recovery must be a moral objective. Not following the doctor's advice to abstain from certain victuals would be tantamount to spurning one's task as a human being. Thus it is not the things by themselves which have a moral value or imply a moral danger, but rather the use we we make of them in relation to a moral intention.

11 The Discipline of Faith

A. The Need for Discipline

If faith were confined to receiving divine gifts, God's redemptive work would have but incidental significance for us. For God would treat man, like rock and clay, as merely passive recipients of his donations. Yet man in a particular sense is an active creature. Of his humanity man becomes aware in and through spontaneous activity which is directed to self-chosen ends and has practical usefulness. Thus we must conceive of our relation to God as implying the recognition of the self's capability to act meaningfully. Faith may not be reduced to mere sentiments or a purely theoretical assent given to God's revelation.

Furthermore, when God bestows his benefits upon us, that is not an end in itself. His gifts are intended to serve his people as resources and opportunities for service. Spiritual strength, Biblical insights and charismatic gifts, for instance, are to be used by us for actions and activities by which the well-being of God's creatures is to be fostered. Yet though God's Spirit is at work in all men, human nature is not therefore spiritual. On the contrary, when we begin the life of faith, we still act very much as we did previously. True life would be one in which our decisions would not be influenced by pressures and urges from outside of our heart; they would give expression to one wish only, namely, to act in accordance with the purpose of God. Transition from our 'ordinary' life to the true one will require a volitional effort. Of course, everybody knows that Paul inveighed against the belief that good works would render a person acceptable to God. Yet Paul does not contradict himself when in all of his letters he gives extensive moral admonitions to the recipients. As Bonhoeffer has emphasized, Paul would offer 'cheap grace' if he taught that our conduct did not concern God, since we have been redeemed by the blood of Jesus Christ.

In view of the purposive character of God's redemptive work it would be strange if the New Testament commandments were meant to describe the beauty of the world to come, yet had no bearing upon the actual life of Jesus' followers. What Paul is opposed to is not man's striving to overcome his natural weakness. Rather, he reprehends the self-righteous belief that the true life had its origin in a congenital goodness of man, and that it could be activated by an act of man's will. The disposition for true goodness is dependent on the transforming work of the Spirit as it takes place in faith. Characteristically, Paul can describe the true life of the Christian by means of the indicative as well as the imperative mood. Through the indicative he describes the divine intentionality and dynamic operative in us through the presence of the Spirit. The assent which we give to the moral obligations is already the beginning of its execution. The imperative, in turn, serves to us as a reminder of the fact that the necessity to implement the divine gift through a volitional act, comes from God rather than from our planning.

The imperative addresses itself to the individual in his totality. The response to it must therefore consist in concrete actions rather than mere thoughts or emotions. Yet in its initial stage, our moral aspiration is hampered by an awkward and seemingly insuperable contrast. Though originally an activity of the self, faith seeks to motivate the Christian's whole will. Yet bad habits, prejudices and superficial views, with which our mind is replete, do not easily and by themselves disappear. Nevertheless, faith implies the desire to get rid of them. Thus the Christian who becomes aware of that contrast will start a process of renewal which requires the acquisition of spiritual wisdom through self-scrutiny as well as a training of the will. The process of spiritual discipline is complicated by the deceptions resulting from the ambivalence of earthly goods. The very discipline may become a temptation when it is made to flatter our vanity or to satisfy our lust for praise and recognition.

B. The Practice of Discipline

1. *Steps*

Though the life of faith is a gift of God, it has no other way of manifesting itself except through the mental, biological and social abilities and activities of man. In its methods, Christian discipline does therefore not differ essentially from any secular method of intellectual, artistic or moral training. It passes through two stages, namely, instruction and exercise. Though both activities develop more or less simultaneously, exercise always presupposes instruction. Instruction necessarily begins with listening to the Word of God, in the family circle, in self-study, or through participation in the worship and proclamation of the Church. Listening requires the willingness to give up not only the idea that man possesses spiritual wisdom by nature, but also his religious prejudices, and, if necessary, the form in which he learned the faith in his childhood. There is a further requirement more difficult to be fulfilled than the former one. We have to learn the difference between the literal and the spiritual understanding of the Bible. The Bible is the work of the Spirit, and spiritual things have to be understood spiritually. Acquiring that ability may take a long while. There is no short cut to virtual wisdom, most certainly not by so manipulating the Biblical text that it will confirm our preconceived notions. In the school of the Holy Spirit it becomes necessary constantly to change one's theological concepts because the Spirit initiates us into increasingly greater depth of meaning.

Parallel with that process of instruction goes the training of the will. There is hardly a congregation in which one does not encounter a few Christians who excel over the rest by their advanced manner of life. In his endeavour to imitiate their example the neophyte is likely to start with an outward copying of their pattern of conduct and devotion. But doing so will lead to the development of spiritual tendencies and habits and eventually a Christian character. During that process one learns patience, kindness, confidence and all the other Christian attitudes. There is no mental technique by which we would be enabled to evolve the power of the Spirit in ourselves. The Spirit 'comes' freely or rather manifests the power of his presence in us, whenever we open ourselves fully to his operation.

An important by-product of our growth of faith through moral discipline is the fact that it confronts fellow-Christians with an illustration of truly human life. The whole church is thereby strengthened and its work intensified. Negatively, a conduct that is spiritually guided will bring to light the specific character of Christian conduct and emphasize its uniqueness. Often we have to work in common with non-Christians. Yet a determined Christian attitude will indicate to them that we are pursuing a final goal unknown to them, and that we avail ourselves of a power inaccessible to them.

We also discover that at times it is wise to shun certain activities and pleasures in which our contemporaries naïvely indulge because in view of the relative weakness of our spiritual life we see in them dangerous temptations rather than gain. We find it desirable also to make our rejection visible by means of action because in an age of conformism the factual protest is more powerful than verbal denunciation. Experience will show that by adopting such an attitude life does not become sour or gloomy. God's world abounds in innumerable other good things which may be enjoyed without harming or endangering ourselves or others. We may go even a step further. No true spiritual life is possible unless the individual is willing to give up a habit or the enjoyment of a good that is especially dear to him. That principle applies particularly to goods which threaten to hamper the effectiveness of one's Christian witness. We impair the faith of those who want to join the Church when we conceal from them the fact that faith demands sacrifice to be made before its blessings can be reaped.

Moral discipline is not a method by which men are to be brought to moral perfection. The underlying intention of moral discipline lies in the determination to serve God and one's fellow men more effectively than is the case on the level of Christian mores. Yet it is also possible that, in spite of his zealous efforts, a Christian may be permanently unable to overcome blatant moral weaknesses and faults. Would he concentrate on a fight against them, he might easily become so preoccupied with them that his condition would deteriorate into a neurosis. In turn the likelihood is that by concentrating on his creative abilities, for instance, through service, his attention will be deflected from the sins which weaken him. While he may not be able fully to overcome his weaknesses, they may at least lose much of their power and attractiveness. From the way in which Jesus dealt with people we may learn that God is less interested in an all-round moral goodness than in acts of service, in spite of our faults. It should be remembered that moral discipline has primarily spiritual consequences. It will not noticeably change the intensity of one's vitality. For instance, the fact that a man is of the daring and enterprising type or of the complacent and/or conservative one does not qualify or disqualify him for participation in God's redemptive work. In either case he has to learn the difference between the secular and the spiritual outlook and to train himself for authentic service. In this connection, the role which tribulations and losses play in the process of moral discipline should be mentioned. On account of their ubiquity we are never able to escape them completely. But the Christian is capable of praising God in their presence. While we may not be strong enough to annihilate the evil factors which hurt and harm us, the power of the Spirit enables us to cope with them and to assign them a positive function in our lives. The very affliction which they cause to us is for the Christian a reminder of the divine plan. God will eventually bring their power to naught. In the meantime he shows us that divine power lies hidden in the weakness of the Christian.

The very struggle he has to fight against their seeming meaninglessness develops in him new energies fit for the service of others. Finally, since spiritual discipline engages the Ego in his totality, he has to overcome his innate sluggishness which dislikes the special effort required for service. Yet by following the promptings of the Spirit our actions may call forth the opposition of vested interests or time-honoured prejudices. Our body abhors the painful consequences of such experiences. Yet God uses such opposition to wake us up from our indifference and makes us realize that he wants and needs our service in order to execute his plan. Thus, we learn to throw away fear and abhorrence of suffering.

2. *Church Discipline*

The New Testament lays special emphasis upon the role which knowledge has in the development of faith. Man cannot trust in his sentiments, his 'moral sense', his 'conscience' or the 'inner light', to mention but a few of the names given to the inner voice active in moral life. That man feels an urge to do the right and shun what is wrong, should not be denied. But as we start to implement that urge all kinds of desires, wishes, and plans will interfere with our decision and will suggest a way of action that aims in the first place at the attainment of our own ends and the satisfaction of our own interests. This danger which ever besets us is not banished by the study of the Bible. Church history offers numerous instances of exegesis, even by great scholars, which were gross distortions of the meaning of the passage invoked. Remarkable of that temptation is the manner in which Ham's sin (Gen. 9:20–25) has been used to justify unscrupulous racialism. Similarly Mt. 16:18 was alleged to buttress the exclusive claims made by the Bishop of Rome for his position in Christianity.

For all these reasons, moral discipline requires the support which is offered by the educative and social function of the Church. Since in Protestantism the Church has been stripped of the authoritarian power which it had assumed to itself in the Middle Ages, many people do not realize how much the Church actually contributes to the development of their spiritual and moral life. We might begin with common prayer as it is practised both in the worship of the congregation and in smaller groups. Through its wealth of stated prayers and the wide room it accords to personal prayer we are given to understand what is the basis of Christian service. It consists of the worship and adoration of God and a concern for the divine destination not only of our own life but also that of our fellow men. By participation in common prayer, we are made to understand on what occasions, for what objectives and in what manner we are to bring earthly concerns before God. Likewise we are thereby made aware of the manifold ways in which God is dealing with us as our Lord and Saviour. At the same time, our attention is drawn to the fact that God is not merely the ultimate source of all value but also and above all a living God. Irrespective of the notions we form of his nature, he is actively present in our midst as the origin of all reality. Therefore, his people can address him with the assurance that he will answer their prayers. As the congregation is united in common worship we realize also that our fellowship transcends its sociological setting. We would not be members of a congregation but for the fact that God's Spirit had moved our hearts and had engendered in us a common faith. The Spirit conveys to us a sense of unity not made by men. We also experience our cosmic role. We differ basically from the rest of all men as those who form the spearhead of a new mankind.

As such a community, the Church is a potent aid for true life in a world which is in its majority non-Christian and whose structure is opposed to the advance of God's work. The Christian may be certain that among fellow-members he will find willingness to listen to him when he is confused or needs counsel, as well as a spirit of brotherhood ready to give him comfort and material help. Furthermore, the Church exercises a direct influence on the moral efforts of its members through its restraining and directive activities. It is true that the Protestant churches had to realize that their concept of personal faith precluded the application of authoritarian methods of discipline, as is done in the Catholic Church. Public censure, imposition of penance, exclusion from the sacraments, may still be practised on the mission field and in small denominations. Yet, even there they prove to be incompatible with evangelic faith. More adequate and more effective is that teaching of the Church which places before its members the wide and disquieting contrast between the true life, on the one hand, and the life that we actually live, on the other. The celebration of the Lord's Supper should also serve as a potent factor in the training of our spiritual life. By means of it we are reminded of the initiative which God offers to take in the genesis and development of our spiritual life. It therefore becomes us to learn the humility of receptiveness and the mystery of self-sacrifice.

In this connection, pastoral counselling should be mentioned. It is the minister's glorious privilege by means of comfort and admonition to come to the rescue of those who struggle to live a truly human life. Unfortunately, many ministers will rob themselves of that privilege by substituting clinical psychotherapy for spiritual support. No doubt the minister has occasionally to deal with persons with mental defects or neuroses. Yet, except for slight cases, he will not find himself sufficiently trained for mental therapy. The pastor should concentrate his 'care of souls' upon the great number of members who are mentally in good health, yet need spiritual advice, comfort and guidance.

In our time, the home is no longer the shelter that it used to be. Yet, life outside the home seems to offer little opportunity for personal intercourse. It is not surprising, therefore, that the Sunday worship has become a refuge and asylum from the world. This is not altogether to be bemoaned. For many of our contemporaries will find it hard to locate another place where they are approached as persons capable of spiritual life. Radio services, it seems, are but a poor substitute for church attendance. They have to accommodate themselves too closely to the nature of the medium. It is true that the Sunday congregation is a captive audience. But the man in the pulpit is not an orator who seeks the applause of his audience. He speaks as a servant of God, who is intent on confronting his congregation with the will of God. There is still another way by which the Protestant churches have replaced the authoritarian kind of discipline. To an ever increasing extent, they encourage their members to participate in the activities of various congregational groups and associations and to support the social activities of the churches. Likewise, it is through the ecumenical work of the churches that their members have learned to overcome their parochial outlook. They think now of Christianity and of social problems in global terms.

C. The Christian Vision

The Christian discipline presupposes a long-range vision of the goal to be reached in this life. The majority of people, including many Christians, lack that vision, however. Consequently, they are not able to make real sense of life. Most of them are not aware of that deficiency because they do not care or are happy with the significance they ascribe to themselves. Yet some people are not content with life unless they see themselves related to an objective goal. By his message of the coming of God's rule, Jesus taught his contemporaries that God had destined them for such a goal. Thereby they were no longer free to dismiss the question of the ultimate significance of their existence. At the same time, however, all that they did would receive value and meaning.

The vision by which spiritual discipline is guided is described in the

New Testament under two different metaphors. Starting from the human predicament, moral discipline is conceived of as a process of growth leading to maturity. Envisaging the discipline as aiming at participation in God's work, the vision presents God as loving his creation. He wants man to share in that love.

To begin with, in spiritual growth the novice in faith is a kind of spiritual babe. He is entirely dependent on the example and instruction given by mature Christians. In the same way as our inner vitality makes our body grow, the Spirit within us is intent upon letting us grow up to spiritual maturity. Just as in physical life growth requires food, so spiritual maturity will not be reached unless a person avails himself of the spiritual nourishment provided by God. The Christian feels an inner urge to transcend himself in insight and abilities.

Growth is not mere extension, however, no mere wish to know more about God or the world in which we live. It aims at maturity. That stage has been reached when the individual has moved from dependence on teachers to independent insight, from acceptance of the Church's ethos and mores as a matter of conformism, to spiritual wisdom, that is to say, the ability to see the reason why God wants things to become what love is capable of making of them. In the centre of that vision we find the assurance that in our discipline we are conditioned by the operation of the Spirit within us. Though our discipline is practised through acts of our own will, it would not be in existence but for the stimulus it received from the Spirit. In our vision we are looking forward to a mode of existence in which we would entirely follow the stimulus of the Spirit. Longing for that goal keeps our discipline in motion.

Such spiritual freedom from human authorities is not to end in moral anarchy and arbitrariness, let alone licentiousness. The teaching of the Church is not rejected by a mature Christian but rather understood in the light of the purpose for which it was given. Conversely, spiritual maturity is not identical with moral perfection. The spiritual leaders of the Church did not conceal the fact that notwithstanding their mature insights they were unable entirely to escape temptation and sin. But their faith made them constantly to aspire for wisdom. Thus they were able to recognize sin as sin in all its disguises, and to reject it. What is even more important is the fact that 'wise' Christians will care to give leadership to the Church. They stir up the apathy and complacency of the common Christian people and make them aware of their high calling.

The second metaphor used in the New Testament to keep the discipline going is that of the coming of God's rule upon the earth. It starts with the awareness that the moral action is often rendered difficult, if not impossible, by the cosmic forces and our situation. By faith we refuse to accept that situation as irremediable. Our feeling tells us that somehow God must have means of breaking our imprisonment, that has given rise to philosophical and moral fatalism. Since our moral life must be lived here on earth and through our daily activities, we are easily dejected by the triviality of the things we do. This must not be the case. Infinitesimal as our actions may be in comparison with the vastness of the universe, they gain infinite value when seen as our part of God's work. The God who grants us the possibility to act in this world may be seen from two different viewpoints. Firstly, his work in this world manifests the love he has for his creatures. By drawing our attention to conspicuous examples of that love, he urges us to embrace all other creatures with equal love. That God should love his world in all its aspects is an irritating contention in view of all the evils found within it. As a result, we are usually inclined to confine the scope of God's love to the ministry of Jesus. What happens in the rest of the world strikes us rather as manifesting the groundless omnipotence of God. Yet let us examine a few facts. Through Creation God gives a right to exist to each and every thing in this world. Nobody has a right to deny that right to any creature. Proof is the fact that God provides whatever all the beings need for existence. God loves this world. But his love does not automatically render man happy. In order to remain in existence, they must love as he loves them. They destroy themselves when they refuse to co-operate with his plan.

The vision of God bestows a comprehensive outlook to Christian discipline. It enables the Christian to find value and meaning in everything in the realm of nature no less than in human life and history. Hence he makes us wish to love his creatures with an affection similar to God's. By bringing art and science no less than moral and religious life into being, God gives tangible expression to his love of the world. Of course, artistic activities or engineering are not thereby transformed into religious activities. Yet while this world is at present divided into different and rival departments, Christian love accomplishes the unification of the whole universe. What matters in our moral life are not the ways in which we act or the objectives we pursue, but rather the love that we bestow on God's creatures. Equipped with that vision, the believer longs for spiritual strength, which will enable him to live even when by nature he is inclined to hate and to destroy. Secondly, the vision of God is an eschatological one, that is to say it reaches to the utter confines of earthly temporal existence. It is God's will that man should live in time. That fact confronts us with the immense expanse of time and makes us thus aware of the relative shortness of the span of our lifetime. It is not surprising that realizing the problem of temporal existence great philosophers like Plato and the religions of the East should have looked for an escape into a timeless existence. Yet in Jesus God made clear that there is no real escape. The meaning of life must be sought in temporality; for time is the mode of God's dealing with this world. By proclaiming the coming of God's rule, Jesus disclosed to his disciples the urgency of the flux of time. As a process outside of God and as cosmic movement, the infinity of time is frustrating. Yet, seen as the execution of a plan, time is capable of immensely increasing the seeming insignificance of human life. By faith we participate in God's redemptive activity. We are like food that within a body is transformed into a living cell. Rightly understood, the Christian vision implies the assurance that it is God who brings about the final goal. By faith we put human achievements at God's disposal. God in turn uses us by making us agents of holy history. In that way we are in time yet God repels the destructive operation of the cosmic forces. Seen in this eschatological perspective, what then is the objective of moral discipline? One thing is certain. It cannot be a static ideal of moral perfection. God is present in every stage of the time process, in the same way and with the same strength. Thus, our moral effort has to be directed toward participation in God's work as it goes on in time and to love the world as it is at the present moment. That implies the work of Jesus, and in general the past section of holy history. Of course, one can in a certain way speak of the end or goal of the eschatological process. Implied in the divine purpose, as it goes on in the temporal process, is God's intention to make himself known through this world. But that goal lies at the end of an immensely long time process. God alone can bring it about. It cannot serve as a moral goal. Conversely when the Christian is implanted into holy history, he becomes an integral part of God's people. The contribution he makes toward the redemption of mankind, and thus for human history, does not perish but remains permanently effective.

Part Four: The Moral Order

12 Dimensions of Existence

A. Existence and Reality

Ever since the days of Jeremiah, the ancient Hebrews realized that God was dealing with the human race by treating each man in a personal way. In turn, the truly human response to God's redemptive work was to be done in a personal way. But in Christian theology and ethics the influence of rabbinical Judaism and philosophical interpretations of existence has not seldom resulted in misunderstandings in the nature and the role of the Ego. On the one hand, the self-sufficiency and creativity of the Ego was grossly exaggerated; on the other extreme, the subjective character of the ego would seem to deprive his cognitive and moral acts of all value.

The way out of the dilemma is indicated in the Bible. Creation safeguards the ontological dignity and the right of existence of all creatures. Yet existence does not isolate the individual. Existence implies interrelation. There are ontological differences of reality, but the higher degrees such as the heavenly reality, are related to all that exists. Even of God we cannot speak in a meaningful way except as dealing with this world. In turn there are no independent realms of existence. Even if the astrophysicists were right in postulating a pluralistic universe, it would be held together by the will of God. Without its comprehensive character there would be no moral obligation. It would be left to the discretion of the individual to select the way in which he would deal with others.

That is the reason why Christian ethics is concerned with man as he lives in this world rather than with a detached Ego. There is nothing in this world that is ethically irrelevant. The greatest and the smallest, the cosmic forces and the tiniest virus, may ethically concern the individual. For all of them are needed and used for the existence and development of the universe. Yet, while we have to make the wholeness of the cosmos the starting point of our moral obligation, we realize that things serve different needs of God's creation. We speak therefore of dimensions of existence. For practical purposes, human decisions will usually be made with reference to one dimension of existence because their inter-relation makes of this world a very complex, and even confusing, entity. But in view of the consequences which our actions have for other things, such simplification of outlook may have undesired and even undesirable effects, unless in our action we keep in mind its complex character. What is beneficial for the person with whom we deal may have at the same time harmful consequences for others.

The enormous progress which psychology, economic theory, socio-logy, medicine and anthropology have made in our age enable us to be more clearly aware of the nature of the social dimensions. We notice for instance the fact that political measures influence cultural and econo-mic life and affect the religious sentiments of the people concerned. The war in Vietnam, for instance, tends to discredit the honesty of American Christianity in other countries and makes the Christians there suspicious of our ecumenical aims. Likewise, political life is co-extensive with the economic, juridical and cultural activities of a nation. Thus the consequences of a political action may be felt in education and national health, too. In order to describe the complexity of the Christian life we chose therefore an arrangement by which we dealt first with our relationship with God. In its light we shall proceed to the created world, i.e., with our life in social institutions and in nature. These dimensions are not arbitrarily selected. They agree with the teleological texture of reality. Apart from our relationship to God, our life would make no sense. God's purpose prevents us from interpreting this world and human life as mere nature, yet also from neglecting the physical aspects of life. Finally emphasis is laid upon the personal character of life, yet not, as is done in Pietism, at the expense of the social institutions. The uniqueness and supremacy of the Christian way of life depends thus on two facts: existence is interpreted as relationship rather than as self-sufficiency; and man sees himself in the totality of reality as it is inter-preted from the perspective of the divine purpose of redemption.

B. The Dimensionality of Existence
1. *The Texture of Reality*
Primitive Man is aware of the fact that not only his actual deeds, but also his abilities to act, are determined by the nature of the reality in which he lives. That reality, in turn, is not confined to the existence of material things. It implies a super-material texture of reality by which man is enabled in diverse manners to act in a meaningful way. Modern philosophy makes various attempts to grasp that sphere of existence,

especially through theories of value. But with the prevalence of sub-jectivism and positivism, the mode of the structure of existence is missed. Economic and political order, moral, artistic, and religious acti-vities are interpreted as psychological, biological, or sociological pheno-mena. The specific intention underlying those activities is ignored. The detrimental results of such a view should be obvious. No distinc-tion is made between the child who splashes paint on a board, and the artist who draws a picture on his canvas; or between the cat who gives suck to her litter, and the human mother who does not give up her care for an ungrateful and disobedient child.

What distinguishes artistic, religious or moral acts from purely prac-tical ones is the fact that the former ones are executed as meaningful though they are not executed for practical usefulness. The awareness of their being meaningful presupposes some kind of intimation that they are in keeping with the texture of reality.

The world in which our life is passed is not an incidental and aimless agglomeration of things, nor is it a stagnant or static reality. Rather reality is a process. It is not mere flux, however, in which an initial impulse is worked out, as is held by Hegel or Whitehead. Rather the process is determined by the goal to be reached. The process has there-fore an historical character. The past is not worthless as in process philosophy. Rather it is essential for it that certain events should have lasting significance because indicating stages of the progress of the process on its road towards the final goal. The world process, as the Bible sees it, moves on in a multitude of dimensions. This fact, in turn, implies numerous kinds of movement and agents of motion, such as gravitation, electrical and magnetic energy, atomic energy, vitality, mental powers and so on. All these movements are operating in this world, which is God's work. They are manifestations of the purpose which God has with this world and with man. Thus the world process is not the simple summation of the various earthly and cosmic particles which exist unrelated side by side. Rather they all are held together by their common function as well as by God's purpose. Notwithstanding their diversity they form a whole. By the term 'dimension' we under-stand the specific direction in which inter-related homogeneous energies are moving. There are many dimensions, for instance, chemical affinity, gravitation, life, history. While science and philosophical reflection constantly contribute to making our conceptual knowledge of these dimensions increasingly complex, rich and profound, they have done little to elucidate their mode of existence, notwithstanding the fact that the latter is experienced by all men irrespective of their intellectual training.

The dimensions of reality are best described as dimensions of fields of energy. The fields of action may be divided into groups or categories according to the specific end for which they work. There are fields of service, manufacture, language, family, nation, communication, and so on. But, as everywhere in this world, the general or generative factor is not visible. Here on earth we find but many diverse particular specimens of the categories. Take for instance the electricians. They form clearly discernible groups, in which unskilled and skilled hands, technical teachers, merchants of special tools and materials, purveyors of electric energy and officials who supervise the work are in constant exchange. The goal they pursue is the installation, maintenance, repair and eventual improvement of electrical installations and appliances. The dynamic of that field is composed of skills, technical learning, needs, tools and materials. Within the field of electrical service, people who need the service and people who satisfy those needs are brought together into a firmly knit group, yet independent of personal friendship. The main dimension of that field is to have electrical energy used for the benefit of those unable to do themselves what is required for the use of electricity. As man comes into contact with a field of reality, he finds himself bound by its dynamic. For instance, though there are many styles in which an artist may conceive of his work, he finds himself under necessity not only to use appropriate tools and materials but also to use them in such a manner that they give expression to the form of reality or of a special object.

Likewise, each field has its specific dynamic. The drive for power, for instance, which is characteristic of the political field, differs essentially from the desire for wealth, which is found in the economic field. Failure to notice that difference is the basic error of Marx's economic materialism. That these dimensions, far from being incidental phenomena, are in God's purpose, can be seen in the fact that each field moves in a specific direction which never changes. Moral life is one of those fields. Its aim is the actualization and preservation of goodness. As with other categories, the moral field has many subdivisions. Though there have been and will be all kinds of divergent views on what constitutes good, there nevertheless is complete agreement that the objective of moral life is moral goodness as distinct from the artistic or biological one. We have no detailed knowledge of the way in which the various fields of reality and their dimensions are related to each other except that all of them are rooted in God's cosmic plan. Hegel's philosophy of history presumes to know much more about them than can reasonably be ascertained. We may say confidently, however, that all of them are obviously indispensable for the attainment of this world's final goal. That fact is visible in the mutual significance which things in the various fields have for each other. In the biosphere, for instance, one will find a dense texture of ecological helpfulness and usefulness. Yet a similar kind of interrelation is also discernible between inanimate nature and the world of organisms.

We would therefore misread reality if, after the fashion of humanism we interpreted the existence of a specifically human field of action as implying a complete detachment from the rest of nature. As he gets his food from the earth, so man has in turn a special responsibility for its preservation and appropriate development. While in all likelihood the biological evolution has reached its final stage in man, the cosmic process goes on in the interrelation between mankind and nature. While interrelation may imply burdens, it is also and above all the evidence of the love God has for this world. Cut off from the rest of things, the 'nomads' would exist in a most miserable state of unchanging self-sufficiency. It is not out of their own strength that the things of this world exist for, with, through, and within each other. Unless God had endowed them with such abilities and potentialities, they would neither be in a position to enter into relationships with each other nor to do so in their specific ways. The ethical relevance of the various categories of fields lies in the fact that thereby man is enabled to become an integral portion of the universe. In that way he is given the possibility to apply his abilities not only to his own salvation. He is also in a position to co-operate effectively in the redemption of the universe.

Though each field of action has its specific function, there is considerable overlapping because the same people are agents in various fields. The electrician is probably also a father, a citizen, the member of a church, a city dweller. Each action of an individual is therefore more or less conditioned by the various fields to which he belongs, and in turn affects the equilibrium of those fields. Ethical theory has often isolated the individual from his field. If meant as a mental construct invented to bring out the distinctive character of ethical activity, such view is legitimate. But in ethical instruction it is essential to treat moral life as a comprehensive field interrelated with numerous other fields. I never act morally as a pure Ego. In turn, however, the fact that my moral life takes place in the complex texture of human social life must not be interpreted as though the moral values were the result of social life.

2. *Harmony, Chaos and Change*

Notwithstanding the limited knowledge we have concerning the interrelationship of the various dimensions of reality, we are certain of one thing. The totality of God's creatures forms an ordered universe. In spite of the manifold factors of which this world is composed, they serve to keep the equilibrium of the universe intact, and through their interrelation prevent it from disintegrating into chaos. They are also thereby fit to contribute to giving a positive meaning to the cosmic process. From the way in which God deals with man and discloses his will to him, we may infer that his ultimate aim is cosmic harmony. By that term we understand a condition in which all the creatures work voluntarily for the furtherance of the needs and interests of their fellow creatures.

Yet both in ancient philosophy and in medieval theology no clear distinction was made between order and harmony. The present order of the universe is not yet harmony, however. It is due to divine arrangement, according to which the diversity of things and dimensions would be prevented from reducing the cosmos into chaos. The self-assertion of the creatures is not by itself directed toward harmony. As a result, we find in our world a great deal of disharmony within the universal order. While the cosmic order arouses our admiration, we must never forget that it harbours also the seeds of discord and distortion. Instead of likening this world to a self-regulating organism, we should better follow the Stoic philosophers who spoke of a law, or laws, that God had imposed upon the universe. Most appropriate however is the Old Testament view according to which God has set a dam to the Sea. That means that the powers of chaos and destruction are not excluded from this world, as is held in the dualistic systems. Nevertheless, these forces are limited in strength and thus prevented from making havoc of God's Creation.

The Resurrection of Jesus is the clear and unambiguous sign that earthly reality is not destined permanently to remain in that precarious balance. Through Christ the enforced order is to be replaced by the creation of a harmony from within. The New Testament calls it a new earth and a new heaven, for it implies a radical change on the part of all creatures. They will abandon voluntarily their desire to use their self-assertion in defiance of the established cosmic order. By faith in the risen Jesus we participate in that cosmic change and thus realize that he is indeed the redeemer, not a mere example of good life. All attempts to establish ethics upon the basis of the 'natural' order of the universe are misleading, notwithstanding the elements of truth implied therein.

As long as one starts from the actual condition of this world, it is impossible to draw a clear line of demarcation between constructive and destructive factors because either of them happens to operate with the same necessity. Thus the ethics of the Law of Nature as well as those of natural realism carry self-destructive tendencies within themselves. It suffices to place side by side the unrestricted glorification of erotic love, characteristic of the 'new morality', on the one hand, and the tragic and frustrating effects of that same love as described in modern literature, on the other. If handled consistently, Christian ethics does not spurn or disregard this world. But by faith we envision as our goal this world in the light of its eventual harmony, and thus as a world to be freed of its contradictions. God brings healing to this world through the work of Christ. Thus Christian life is not a mere adjustment of a good man to a wicked world, as in Platonism. Rather through his followers, Christ transforms this world into the realm of God's sovereign rule.

The multidimensional character of human life, on the one hand, and the limited possibilities of individual existence, on the other, make for great diversity within a human group. Each of its members will move in a different direction according to his temperament, vitality, education, sex, race and other factors. That diversity accounts for the fact that, even among Christians, all do not implement their vision in the same manner. There is no harm in such diversity as long as through faith they all participate in God's redemptive work. The intention of God is frustrated, however, if and when Christians insist that, except in their specific field of action, no service can be rendered to God. The Church at large was thus rent in the Middle Ages through the conflict of papacy and empire. We notice a similar effect in our days, when political allegiance or social standing rather than the goal of Christ determines the choice of one's ethical position. No harm is to be seen in the plurality of ethical types as such. Rather the evil lies in the contention of the 'radical' that one's own type is the only one that has a claim to be adopted by the Church. In that context it makes no difference, whether the radical outlook is on the revolutionary or the conservative side. Faith demands that each type should recognize the others as walking with him in the furtherance of Christ's course. The disruptive character of ethical particularism is so difficult to combat because it has undeniable facts on its side. It cannot be denied, for instance, that money is an important lever of civilization. How easy it is to conclude that the manner in which we make money must not be considered a moral problem. Is it not the necessary means for a good end? Yet the problem is not whether Communism or capitalism is the better way of making and using money. That is a purely practical question. The fault of ethical particularism lies in its foreshortened perspective. The historical field with which one identifies oneself is treated as a final reality. Consequently, the making of money is considered an absolute, rather than a means by which man is enabled to work for the transformation of this world. It will be good to keep in mind that magnitude is a factor that dangerously influences our ethical reasoning. The greater the power of a field, the more obvious is the profit one derives from it, and the closer the temptation to associate our existence with its specific dimension.

3. Reality and Time

Things never simply 'are'. They have an inalienable and indestructible nature, or the power to preserve their quiddity. Furthermore, they do not simply exist. Existence in this world is always existence in time. The result is flexibility and changeability. Though the nature of things remains unchanged, their mode of existence, their shape and their intrinsic energy are constantly subject to change. Classical ethics treated the moral relationship as one between beings who would never change. Yet the very contrary is true. Our stance may shift from one field or dimension to another. We change our job, or circumstances have radically changed, as a result of a lost war or a revolution. There are also the vital changes from the freshness of childhood through the firmness of mature age to the increasing incapabilities of old age. Those changes will naturally condition one's outlook in life and one's attitude. All these and many other changes will certainly leave their marks on one's ethical outlook and attitude.

Secular wisdom counsels us to acquire adaptability as the most effective means to cope with change. Such advice may be useful when it is a matter of practical expediency. Since it is an adaptation of behaviour rather than of personal conscience, no ethical problem is involved. One might be tempted to say that Christian ethics is entirely unchanging and unchanged. Are not the Christian outlook and attitude directed towards the realization of God's sovereign rule in this world?

Could it be that God's purpose would ever change? Of course, some modern scholars contend that Christian ethics is and always has been a product of history and that today, too, it must follow the vicissitudes of history. Such arguments rest on an erroneous identification of the origin of moral obligation with its practical application. Of course, there is a history of Christian ethics, and it abounds in various and often quite original ideas, of which some have been deservedly dismissed, while others will make their re-appearance from time to time. The perplexity called forth by this history arises from the fact that ethics is concerned with the transformation of this world. It cannot therefore be confined to abstract principles. They must be applied to the most urgent needs of a given situation or age. That the emphasis placed upon certain practical tasks should be continued, even though the situation has changed, is probably an inevitable development given the conservative tendency of most people. In Christian ethics, that tendency is intensified through the authority of its principles. The fact should not be overlooked, however, that through the operation of the Spirit stagnation in ethics is regularly challenged by pneumatic protest. It was to be expected that, in a period of rapid social changes like ours, the Church should encourage a radical re-thinking of its ethical task, even though that might invite misconstructions and at times obvious heresies. Theologians have occasionally shown greater interest in the political or social aims which they represented than in God's aims, and some have advocated principles of action which had little do to with Christ's outlook. The demand for repeated change in Christian ethics is unavoidable. Yet those who plead and work for it must not overlook the fact that their practical applications deal with an historical situation, and as all history will be something provisional only. It is our privilege, however, to be able to say relevant things in spite of the historical character of our ethical message. By placing God's Kingdom in the centre of our efforts, we participate in his lasting work.

The determinative of God's eschatological purpose may play a decisive role in church life, however, unless its transcendent character is fully recognized. The practical aims of the Christian life will always be chosen in accordance with the social, political or cultural stance of the people concerned. The interests of the labour unionists, for instance, can never fully be reconciled with those of the directors of an industrial corporation. Likewise, in the highly developed Western world life looks different from what it is in the 'underdeveloped' countries of Africa. What needs most urgently to be done appears in a different light, according to whether people belong to the Japanese circle of culture or to that of the Western world.

In spite of such divergencies the Church is not permanently split on moral questions. Important as it is that in our Christian life we should pursue practical objectives, they have penultimate significance only. Unless God accepted our actions as means for the radical change of this world, they would share the pathetic futility of secular and 'natural' ethics. Wherever this outlook is kept alive, opposite views found within the Church can be reconciled.

13 Institutional and Personal Ethics

A. Institution and Organization

Moral consciousness is a striking manifestation of the telic character of man. In every sphere of life he aims at a higher life. The idea of man's divine destination has been understood by Jesus and the apostles as emphasizing the fact that man is not yet truly human. A very potent and precious aid for the realization of his moral aspirations is found in social institutions such as the body politic, the family, the religious community, the market and others. They are patterns or structures of collective action performed by a group. They aim at the realization and enjoyment of various kinds of specifically human goods. Their ubiquity indicates that they originate with an inescapable necessity wherever human groups live. Yet in primitive society, no clear differentiation has yet taken place. Social rules and rites serve in a comprehensive way for the satisfaction of all human needs. Yet, even in our days, no clean separation exists. The family, for instance, is a religious, biological and legal institution regulated by laws of the state. Each institution has a specific function which does not change. Yet it is interpreted in different ways in history. Irrespective of its historical form, however, those who are engaged in the specific pursuit of an institution are all supposed to tend it and cultivate its specific good. Institutions have, as it were, a life of their own. A college, for instance, is not owned by its president, nor by its trustees, its faculty or students. That fact is recognized in the charter granted to it by the government of its home state. On account of that autonomy, institutions have authority and power to take measures against recalcitrant members.

Social institutions owe their existence to the fact that man's is a telic nature. He is never satisfied with his actual condition. He feels that what he needs is not mere change of condition, as in animal life, but rather life on a higher level. When a group happens to actualize a social good, the new reality is used as the basis or goal of an institution. In doing so, the group manifests the fact that it has comprehended the necessity and significance of such good and that it is determined to give it public recognition. In outward appearance there may seem to be but little difference between a business corporation and a social institution. But the former is owned by the stockholders who may dissolve it and distribute its assets among themselves. Likewise its officers and directors are supposed to work for the personal profit of the stockholders. Conversely, an institution comes into being whenever a group encounters or re-affirms one of the dominant values of human life, such as justice, education, trade, kinship or salvation. These values assert themselves as essential aspects of man's self-understanding. Thus, they make an irrejectable demand on man's compliance. In order to operate effectively, institutions must be organized. Usually that is done by an historical group, such as a clan, a nation or an army. In organizing an institution is is given a stated form and specific authority. By doing so, the group indicates its intentions to accord to an institution and its specific good a generally recognized and permanent position. In that way the specific function of each institution is intensified and its results are multiplied. The political institution, for instance, becomes articulate by giving itself a government; economic life forms a market with a banking system and a chamber of commerce, and the cultural institution establishes schools and invites emulation by publicly exhibiting its works. An institution may be organized in many different ways, according to historical circumstances, available resources, cultural level, practical experience, size and vitality of the group and other factors. Political democracy, for instance, is by no means the same in Sweden, Britain, France and the U.S.A. It can clearly be seen what differences of religious background, historical developments and political experience have gone into their respective makings.

Social institutions have been explained by Rousseau and his followers as resulting from natural law. Over against this view, Lutheran theologians of the nineteenth century developed a theory of 'orders of Creation.' By making man, God would have placed him into a definitive pattern of collective life. That view implied the same faulty reasoning as Rousseau's. Yet, while Rousseau's hypothesis left it free to man to alter the form of social organization, the Lutheran interpretation identified the form of organization with God's will. Thereby the political status prior to the French revolution, for instance, that is to say the feudal system, was to be regarded as an unalterable requirement of true faith. While such a view proved to be untenable, the idea of orders of Creation has called forth a conservative tendency in Protestant ethics. More appropriate would be the contention that the coming into being of social institutions is not a merely sociological event. In view of their ubiquity, necessity and authority, the social institutions are best explained as a divine device. By means of it mankind is both reminded of the fact that it has not yet reached its destination, as also that it is assisted on its way. The specific form of organization, in turn, is a human work by means of which ethical compliance with an institution is adapted to a given situation, and thus rendered effective.

Consequently, social institutions are subjected to two different ethical perspectives. Function, basic value and goal of a specific institution remain in principle the same throughout human history. They are destined to assist man in becoming human. Yet since man is not yet what he is to become, inevitably the manner in which he conceives of goal and function of the institutions is tinged by his actual understanding of himself. He has therefore constantly to inquire what is the most appropriate image of man by which to measure actual institutions. In view of the long span of time which still may lie ahead of mankind, the necessity of permanent scrutiny is obvious.

The other ethical perspective concerns the relation between the good to be realized by the institution, on the one hand, and the aims and methods implied in the form of organization, on the other. Since the people who are responsible for the function of the institution are fallible beings, their view of justice, for instance, will come more closely to the satisfaction of their interests than to their moral insight. Thus, not only churches but all social organizations are constantly in need of reform.

B. The Function of Social Institutions

Asking how social institutions came into being is an otiose question, because no evidence is available. We can only say that they are absent in the animal realm yet are found wherever human beings live together. The recognition of their nature is not so much to be sought in their origin as in their function. The latter, in turn, makes its appearance especially in its intrinsic dynamic and its goal. The social institutions aim at producing and protecting the common goods of an historical group. They are concerned with those values which are essential as expressions of the specifically human character of the group, such as stability and social order, justice, peaceful exchange of merchandise or scientific knowledge. These are goods apart from which the difference between man and animal would be obliterated. Characteristically, however, these are values which the individual is unable to realize out of himself. Thus understood, social institutions are not static structures but rather social dynamisms. Whenever an institutionalized order gets galvanized, it prepares its own disintegration. For the centripetal tendency of the institution has to brace itself over against individual self-assertiveness and the conflict of personal interests among its members. Thus, within the institutionalized group a twofold struggle is normally going on. The whole group will manifest its authority and power *vis-à-vis* its members; and individual members and factions will pursue their aspirations for control of the group over against those in power. Hence the members of an institutional group are not able to occupy a neutral position. Those in favour of the *status quo* are actually supporting the ruling section of the group. In view of the fact that institutional life is to guide man in the process of humanization, yet that man has not yet reached the stage for which he is destined, institutional life may be considered a preliminary stage of holy history. In that process, God keeps man on the move. Every new vision of man's destination ushers in a new period of history.

In that process, the social institutions perform a threefold function. Firstly, they curb the individual's unruly desire for independence and keep him within limits set by specifically human goals. Then they educate the members of the group. Through insisting on respect for their basic rules, the social institutions develop and improve in their members the ability to act in accordance with their specific goods. They also succeed in familiarizing their members with the advantages implied in their specific goods. Finally they have productive function. They stimulate and encourage their members to co-operate in the realization of specifically human goods by which common life is benefited. They also enable their members to produce goods which otherwise are unobtainable, and methodically to multiply them through co-operation. The more the intrinsic rules of an institution are practised, the more efficient such a group will become. Excellency does not so much depend on congenital abilities as on the zeal and industry with which a group applies itself to the cultivation of specific goods. Ancient Israel, for instance, concentrated on religion. Hellas on rational culture, and Rome on political justice. In all social institutions the purpose of God is in conflict with the forces of evil. That fact explains the ambivalent role ascribed to them by various ethicists. In their majority, they will underscore the advantages brought about by the institutions. Yet some of them have rejected one or the other of the social institutions. The apostle Paul had already serious misgivings concerning marriage. The left-wing reformation and Hobbes, for instance, discerned in the body politic the traits of Antichrist; to some Mennonites, education implies the lure of pride and conceit, and there are sects today to whom even the Church represents a diabolic temptation to worship men rather than God. In all such instances, it may be said, however, that the faults of an historical group are wrongly ascribed to the institution as such.

Christians will gladly participate in institutional life. It is true that the historical churches to which we belong comprise but a fragment of mankind. Yet in spite of their limitations it is obvious that their dynamic aims at the common good of mankind. The theory according to which the sole value of the social institutions lies in their being a fence against sin, for instance that matrimony is to prevent sexual inchastity, is contradicted both by their productive function by which social goods are multiplied, as also by the Biblical teaching. The absence of social programmes in the message of Jesus and the apostles is not to be interpreted as evidence of social indifference. They only reject the rationalistic theory that the goal of social life is reached by means of social efforts. What renders our ethical life truly meaningful is the fact that God uses man's agreement with his will in order to render the redemption of mankind possible. Since God has assigned a special place to man, the significance of social institutions transcends their practical results. Human life is destined to serve higher ends, namely to co-operate with God in the establishment of his definitive rule over this world and to transform mankind into God's people. That is the reason why Christianity rejects all kinds of religious glorification of social institutions. It cannot consider the classless society of socialism or the Platonic republic as ends in themselves. They are, at the best, means for the spiritual transformation of mankind.

Though in their historical form manifestations of the human mind, the social institutions are willed and used by God as tools or agencies of his redemptive purpose. First of all, they serve the realization of moral order. No government, economic system, civilization, or any other social institution will be allowed permanently to remain in existence unless it is constantly willing to consider God's authority and will paramount. Furthermore, the social institutions are given power to impose sanctions upon those of their members who in a serious manner disregard or violate their rules. People do not automatically enjoy the benefits of a social institution. They must pay the price for trespassing the social order. The juvenile drop-out for instance, must realize that his self-inflicted lack of education bars him from economic opportunities. Similarly the criminal is confronted with the punitive power of the state, and so in all social organizations.

That God should disclose his judgment in particular through the vicissitudes of social life is of special importance for the development of spiritual life. In their personal fate, even Christians have difficulty in understanding the justice of God's judgment. The differences of individual destinies are so shocking because we lack a generally recognized standard by which to compare individuals. One might therefore be tempted to believe that there is no justice in the way in which God metes out the lots of men. Things are quite different with institutions because all of them rest on the same rules and pursue the same goals. Members of a social organization are therefore able to discern their share in its collective guilt. For instance, when schools are miserly financed or insufficiently equipped, the result will be a lowering of the cultural level of the whole nation.

Above all, God uses social institutions as means by which the goal of redemption, namely the transformation of mankind, is to be accomplished. While it is true that man is made for togetherness, that is not the ultimate goal. Even love will be a mere emotion, unless it is related to the institutions in which the lover and the loved one stand. In order to render their relation permanent, lovers must have common objective interests. In order, however, to make such fellowship truly worthwhile, the Christian aims at that common life in the service of God which the Spirit renders possible. For that end Christians treat people as made in the image of God, and the social organization as the reflection of what God does redemptively for the deliverance of mankind. While aware of their creaturely limitations, they are nevertheless mindful of God's promise that his Spirit should be bestowed upon them. With his help they are confident that they have been chosen by God to be the initiators and leaders of the new mankind. It is through them that spiritual light and energy will be infused into the people around them. Christianity has discovered the mystery of social life. The social institutions are symbols of the true life. They indicate that man, and man alone, is privileged to share in God's cosmic work. What is infinite and simultaneous in God is mirrored within the scope of creatureliness in man's handling of the social institutions. The view is occasionally held that faith may be practised in private life only, never in the public life of the institutions. The contrary is true. God pours his Spirit into the hearts of certain individuals and thus renders them able to overcome prejudices of their contemporaries and to accept new spiritual visions. Through the inspiration of such people, slavery has been outlawed, women have become man's equals, political administration has been transformed from exploitation and embezzlement to public service, not to mention numerous minor reforms. That success gives us hope that in the course of time God will bring that process to a successful end, in which his will alone will rule over man.

C. Personal Life

1. *Christian Equality*

In modern Protestant theology the subject of ethics is usually divided into individual or personal ethics, and social ethics. That would be a consistent procedure, if ethics were to be understood in terms of commandments or principles.

In that perspective, the moral Ego would lead an existence independent of both this world and its own concrete existence. In that case it makes sense to ask the question how the Ego's moral conviction should be applied to the various spheres of reality. Things are quite different when not only the Ego but also concrete existence and this world are held together by the fact that God has brought all of them into existence as a unified world. The legalistic approach leads to abstract social programmes, whereas the condition of the people involved is, at the best, taken care of but incidentally. Jesus and the New Testament writers, however, are interested in the predicament of people. They were not unaware of, or indifferent concerning, the fact that the people to whom they address their communication lived in institutionalized groups, viz. the Jewish people, under Roman dominion, proud of their Temple, taught by theologians of the Scriptures and suffering under an economic depression. Likewise, Jesus and his apostles did not deal with other people as though they were 'mere men' or 'moral personalities', or an abstract 'I' related to an abstract 'Thou'. Rather it was essential for them to meet their contemporaries in a common Jewish environment of the first century A.D.

Of course, there is an element of truth in the distinction between personal and institutional ethics. An organized institution is composed of human individuals, and its group life is kept in motion both by an intrinsic dynamic of the collectivity, and by the way in which its members participate in its activity. Sociologically the distinction between private and public life is a valid one; yet it concerns merely the situation in which people meet, not the ethical nature of their relationship. Even in our most intimate relations, we are conditioned by the institutional character of the group to which we belong.

Within the group, all members are expected to comply with its rules and to aspire for its goal. The group has power to enjoin the necessity of co-operation on the part of the members or at least their majority. Christians accept that obligation for themselves. They may not agree with the particular aim of the historical group to which they belong. Nevertheless, they realize that the social institutions or systems are valuable because they curb the impact of the forces of evil, and protect and develop the goods which are indispensable for human life. Christians assume therefore responsibility for the well-functioning of their group. To them, it is the place which God has assigned to them for service. Thus they comply voluntarily with its demands, notwithstanding disagreements concerning goals and methods. Yet the primary concern which is on their heart is with the common good of the social institution. They are more interested in justice over against injustice than in advocating a certain philosophy of law, for instance.

Since Christianity sees the social institutions as pointing beyond their sociological function toward the purpose of the Creator, the Christian attitude implies an element of transcendence. On the most general level, Christians will go beyond merely conforming with the existing order in a purely passive way. They will consider themselves responsible for the common good of their group, and will be moved by the Spirit to come to the assistance of those who are unable fully to take care of themselves, yet for whom the social order fails to make special provisions. Among them are the invalids, the indigent, the lonely, the unwanted, the feeble minded and many others. They are moved so not because they believe in the equality of all men. Rather they realize that by their deficiencies and ills these people are prevented from living a truly human life. Thus, they try to restore them to participation in the social fellowship.

We cannot therefore agree with Tillich, who wants to take the equal dignity of all men as the starting point of Christian ethics. Christian love would then secure to each man an equal share in the social goods. That is an utterly unrealistic view. The fact is thereby overlooked that God's world is not a world of equality, but rather of diversity and differentiation, and in which the lots are distributed according to divine wisdom rather than according to merit or distributive justice. If there is any equality, it is not of dignity but of the shame of sinfulness. What moves Christians to feel compassion with the helpless, and in general with the deficiencies of human life, is participation in the commiseration God shows for those people. Taking into consideration the permanent inequality of people has not served as a quietive in Christian life. Rather it has stimulated Christians to seek out the chances they have, to use their material and spiritual resources for the benefit of others. In that ability they discovered a criterion of truly human life. It is true to say that in the history of Christianity, attempts have not been lacking to transform Christianity into a social or socialistic organization, in which an equal share of happiness would be guaranteed to all its members. Yet without exception they have all failed. In turn, however, the Christian congregation has survived and is certain to survive into all future, not as a social monstrosity or a museum piece, but rather as the salt and light of the world, or, in Wilfred Monod's beautiful phrase, as the 'fellowship of those who love in the service of those who suffer'.

In turn, a shortsighted vision of Christian ethics might reach the conclusion that Christianity treated this world like a hospital which was trying to keep its patients indefinitely. Of course, Christian ethics is primarily concerned with people rather than with social organizations. In that respect it differs fundamentally from such movements as National Socialism and Communism, whose leaders are prepared to sacrifice any number of people if only the ultimate goal could be fostered thereby. Christianity is convinced that it is up to God rather than to man to bring about the final consummation. Yet it is no less convinced that the goal of history cannot be reached, until people have understood that it is necessary for their own sake to come to the rescue of human suffering. Through the very inequality they have to learn to identify themselves with mankind in its actual condition. The fact that the remedial activity of Christianity has been adopted in our days by most governments and that even Communism should vie with the churches in feeding the hungry, building hospitals and schools and promoting hygiene is proof of the value of such activities. There remains the fundamental difference, however, that the secular institutions treat as an end what to Christianity is an opportunity for humanizing people. One further step of Christian 'transcendence' is found in practising forgiveness. The representatives of social institutions are aiming at excellency yet are also aware of the disturbing influence of the forces of evil. As a matter of self-preservation the institutional ethos tends to be harsh on those who do not comply with the social rules, no matter whether they fail by their own fault or for mere weakness or lack of experience. While Christianity does not approve of those failures, it is inclined to take a positive attitude towards the transgressor. Instead of censuring or punishing him, it tries to make him understand that the common good as well as his own interest require co-operation with the institutions. Many Christians will seldom be in a position to contribute more to another person's life except through humanitarian help. There are some, however, who have been enlightened and strengthened by the Spirit. They will consider the greatest need in the life of their fellow men their being ignorant of God's kindness and lacking of spiritual life. By means of witness, example and instruction, they will act as leaders towards the higher life. They do not intend to alienate them from activity in their social group, but rather will teach them in a new manner to make full use of the spiritual opportunities implied in their social stance, namely, to become servants of the divine purpose of redemption.

2. *The Power of the Charismas*

The 'spiritual' Christian is like the spoonful of salt by which the meal is seasoned, or like a small lamp kindled in a dark room. Quantitatively he may appear insignificant, because he has but little power or influence in comparison with other members of the group. Nevertheless it is through the Luthers and Calvins, the John Knoxes and George Foxes, the Martin Luther Kings and Pope John XXXIIIs, yet also through hundreds of 'smaller' saints, that the spiritual climate of a whole age is transformed and its direction changed. Their spiritual ingenuity lies in their ability to discern in the institutional life possibilities of a further advance towards the realization of God's purpose in the historical life of mankind. These men and women differ from the 'average' Christian in one important respect, because they are privileged to experience the Spirit of God as operating in themselves. By way of contrast they consider the most serious deficiency in man's life his lack of a genuine relationship to God. Of course, the material, mental and social ills of mankind are not matters of indifference to them. Nevertheless, they will point out that all such help may eventually prove to be an obstacle to man's final destination. People may get accustomed to thinking that governmental power, social organization, science, or economic affluence are safe means by which to solve all of man's problems and needs. Such views lie behind the 'godless gospel'. Social relief becomes a substitute for the Gospel to the non-Christian world. The churches, too, offer economic programmes and technical know-how. Fortunately, however, God raises from time to time people who remind the Church that it must rely on the grace, power and wisdom of God, if mankind is ever to become God's people.

The temptation that assails the charismatic Christian stems from his loneliness which is caused by the rare incidence and the ontic superiority of the spiritual gifts. Thereby the charismatic has been lifted up so high above the other members of the Church that he may feel unable to communicate his vision to them. Yet, his gift has been imparted to the 'man of God' for the benefit of others. That is the reason why the spiritual leaders of the Church have accepted their mission as a meaningful commission. They have proclaimed their new vision and verities in the assurance that the God who sent them would open a door to their message, though apparently all the world misunderstood them. Over against the Christian understanding of the task assigned to the individual in social life, modern man will be inclined to assert the tension in which he lives. Of course, there is no social institution but will limit the freedom and self-assertions of its members. That is the only way by which the common good can be realized. Furthermore, since in their organized form social institutions are governed by a relatively small portion of their members only, it is also natural that members of the governing section will formulate the rules of institutional life with special regard for their own interest. That rule applies to economic and cultural organizations no less than to the body politic. Consequently, those not belonging to the ruling section will feel their freedom unduly curbed or their interests unjustly neglected. The individual has a right to complain about injustice and arbitrary rule. Yet the basic rules and limitations of social institutions cannot be abolished or disregarded if the common interest is to be safeguarded.

Another fact is also frequently overlooked. In this world in which by God's will the ontic goodness of Creation and the forces of evil exist side by side, the goal of life cannot be seen in bringing about a perfect world or perfect people. Rather it consists in being mindful of the purpose of God as it pervades this world. Truly, human life would be impossible if there were no social institutions or no necessity to live and work in them. Notwithstanding the limitations and shortcomings of its historical life, mankind is enabled to move on towards its destination. That is accomplished through personal life, especially through faith. By the latter man is enabled to discover the opportunities to grow beyond his actual conditions towards humanitarian relations with other people and eventually towards the acquisition of spiritual power. On that basis genuine humanity is rendered possible by God. By incorporating believers into the life of the risen Christ, he intensifies and expands their limited spiritual abilities infinitely.

14 Religion and Morality

A. The Realism of Faith

In the preceding chapters, the close relationship of Christian ethics and revelation has been emphasized. The question not yet answered in this: Undoubtedly there is a 'natural' knowledge of man's moral obligation. Does revelation add anything to that recognition? The answer must be No, as far as the substance of the law is concerned. All over the world, people are concerned with the protection of property, life, authority, family and so on. But in his debates with the scribes, Jesus will stress the fact that revelation discloses the ultimate purpose which is to be served by the moral obligations. There is no agreement in 'natural ethics' as to the degree to which that protection of the moral good should go.

At first sight, revelation, too, seems to be of little help. For as the Creator, that is to say, as source and origin of this world, God is not directly given to human knowledge. Are we able to proceed beyond Kant who tells us that by the idea of God we should designate the supreme determinant of reality? How is it possible to proceed from that idea of pure transcendence to social life? Idealist philosophers see no special problem here. In their view man is to be guided by ideals, that is, by the ever widening extension of actual goodness, as reached by man at the present moment. While that goal remains ever elusive in spite of man's moral efforts, it can, nevertheless, be conceived of as being analogous to what we have accomplished, or at least aspire for. While such method is of considerable practical usefulness, we cannot follow the philosophers, who will equate that ideal value with the divine or God.

In Christian ethics, great weight is given to the fact that in this world, God's work is constantly interfered with by forces of evil. Consequently, the picture we receive of this world cannot be considered the analogy of God's redemptive work. All earthly data provide but a distorted image of God's actual operation. Nevertheless, in the life of faith the confusion and perplexity is overcome. For in the changes which God calls forth in human history, it is possible to notice the trend of his activity. While in the awareness of faith, too, God is not directly given, his work is perceived symbolically. We are rendered conscious of events which, while taking place in this world, differ from it substantially as a result of the decisive changes they bring about in mankind.

Since God pursues a purpose in history, he cannot be conceived of as object, concept or cause, as we do with the subjects of practical activity or science. He must be apprehended as the one who cares for us, that is to say, as a telic reality.

As a result, we are not able to grasp God adequately and comprehensively by just one kind of mental activity. It is essential for the life of faith that God is not only apprehended as the origin of the supreme value, but also as the one who calls forth decisive changes in our earthly predicament. Consequently, faith approaches God in two different modes or movements, namely, religion and morality. While both attitudes are dealing with the same God, they do so in different ways. In the moral act, man surrenders his will to that of God. In religion, man is anxious to experience the goods by means of which God brings about man's redemption.

In the ancient religions of the *polis* or the Empire that duality is absent, because it was believed that God was directly given in the existence of the body politic. As a result, worship of the gods, stated feasts and divinely given laws were part of the social order just as sowing and harvesting ceremonies. Though similar phenomena are encountered in the religion of ancient Israel, theirs have a different meaning. The Jewish festivals, at least in historical time, are not primarily part of the social order. Rather they are destined to remember the great deeds which God had wrought in Israel's past history, and in which he had given evidence of Israel's election. That interpretation is stressed in Christianity. The Sabbath-Sunday, for instance, ceases to be a social institution. The community celebrates on it the redemptive work of Christ and God's triumph over death and the cosmic forces. That is an indication that the social order, though instituted by God, is no end in itself but rather transcends itself and points from an earthly event to the activity of God. It has become the God-given opportunity to let his transforming power become articulate in this world.

Consequently, in response to what God is doing redemptively in Christianity we find both the concern with the social order and also religion. Neither of them can function appropriately without the other. Hence they are not just in juxtaposition, so that they might alternate. Rather theirs is a dialectical relationship. Thus alone is it possible to safeguard the specific function of both of them in a correlation. The numerous attempts that since the days of the Enlightenment have been made to reduce Christian faith to mere morality have invariably not only neglected considerable sections of the Bible but also have eventually lost sight of God himself. As a result, they have ended in a shallow utilitarian or hedonistic kind of ethics. Yet 'mere religion', for instance mysticism, is also in danger. It leads to a withdrawal from this world and will end in indifference concerning the events and people in our environment. Through the dialectical relationship of religion and morality, Christian activity receives an historical foundation in holy history, the specific nature of which is characteristically expressed by the idea of the Covenant.

B. The Covenant

1. *Nature of the Covenant*

For the life of ancient Israel the idea of the Covenant had a threefold significance. First of all they were thereby reminded of the fact that in the redemption of mankind God takes the initiative. Both the chosen people and the revealed law, far from being eternal, had originated at a certain moment of history and served to give meaning to history. Notwithstanding his efforts, man would not be capable of finding true meaning in life but for the fact that God pursued a purpose with mankind in this world. Furthermore, the giving of the Law on Mount Sinai stressed the fact that the origin of the moral order was found in God rather than in man or nature, notwithstanding the psychological and sociological elements which have gone into its making. Finally, the Israelites realized that it was God who wanted man to be permanently related to his Creator. In the Covenantal relationship, God is dealing with mankind through the medium of an historical group. Individuals are incidentally addressed by God in the Old Testament yet as members of the chosen people, not as though they were self-contained beings.

The goal of the Covenant is described in a number of different ways, for instance, as justification, life everlasting, salvation or entering God's Kingdom. Phrases like 'entering the Kingdom' indicated that believers are destined actually to participate in the power which God wields over this world. Yet Jesus makes also clear that the life of faith is a process rather than a momentary event whose drastic consequences are to last forever. The Christian may not notice an immediate change occurring in his life, once he has embraced faith. He may be sure, however, that the seminal nature of his faith makes a real impact upon this world. Significantly, nevertheless, the emphasis does not fall upon moral perfection. The believer's power lies in the fact that he is privileged to serve as God's tool of redemption. Especially he has been granted the ability to transform the religious outlook and attitude of people.

The goods of the Covenant have been distributed to all of its members equally, yet God has laid down the rules for participation in his Covenant. In Judaism it was held that the prerequisite was found in strict observance of God's law. Already the prophets had fought that view, however, because it would disagree with the divine initiative and the holiness of the Law. Paul stated the problem afresh, though, in terms of rabbinical theology, namely as Justification by Faith. Thereby Paul laid bare the essential features of covenantal fellowship with God. Human life, the apostle points out, is never satisfactory from the viewpoint of the moral order. For what God demands is holiness, that is recognition of God's transcendence rather than moral perfection. It will be found however that even the most moral people will time and again yield to the temptation of disregarding God's work in the universe. Complying with the moral order, Paul goes on, cannot be the ultimate destination which God has set for man. For then God would be subject to the moral order or the Law which is his work, in a way similar to the Greek Gods who were subject to *Diké*. Rather, God sets himself as a goal for man in his prevenient kindness and superior power as is most clearly disclosed in the ministry of Christ.

Hence faith is not so much the assent given to doctrines concerning God or to moral commandments given by God – they are secondary manifestations of faith – but rather the attitude in which the self is prepared to let God do his redemptive work in one's heart. The first step in faith is not the resolve to act more morally than one has done in the past, but rather the sorrow of repentance for not having acknowledged God in his divinity. There is no inner contradiction between God's disclosing himself as supreme value, on the one hand, and his revelation through the Law and the many Biblical commandments, on the other, or between God's love or grace and his justice. By revealing his demanding will, God indicates that contact with him cannot be established on man's terms. The glib way in which modern writers talk about union with God makes no sense. It is but wishful thinking. In turn, however, love is the most appropriate term by which we may describe God's willingness to bring man into harmonious relation with his Creator. The divine call as well as the divine demand as they are seen in the Covenant express but the two sides of the same redemptive work of God. Yet Christian ethics cannot be reduced to a single principle, be it justice or love. They are to be understood in their interrelation in God's creator will.

For Christian faith it is essential that it should be described as taking place within the framework of the Covenant, or, as more recently it has been customary, in its relation to holy or Biblical history. To view the Christian predicament in the perspective of holy history was a helpful device used by theologians in rebuttal of those exegetical critics who failed to notice the specific nature of Biblical history. As a result, they reduced the Gospel to a report merely of incidental events, like the rest of secular history. By way of contrast, the term 'holy history' would designate a series of temporal events held together and guided by a divine purpose. Nevertheless, for the characterization of the Christian life, it seems to be advisable to employ the notion of the Covenant, because it expresses in the most appropriate way the functions of religion and morality.

The image of a Covenant calls to the mind a relationship of two partners who join voluntarily for the common realization of a mutually agreed and desirable good. Within the scheme of holy history, as also in Anselm's theory, redemption is a divine work in which the individual believer occupies an entirely passive role. Yet the Covenant implies the divine initiative as well as man's obligation to act, notwithstanding his inability to find a truly meaningful life apart from God's initiative. Nevertheless, the Covenant respects man's freedom to accept or reject the divine offer of redemption. Reformed theology has rightly postulated that beyond the historical covenants made with Noah, Abraham, Moses and Jesus, one has to go back to an Adamic covenant. All human life is destined for fellowship with, and redemption through, God. The distinction of a covenant of works and a covenant of grace, however, was a misunderstanding of the nature of the Covenant. The 'new Covenant' concluded in Jesus, should not be interpreted as being in contrast with the old covenant. The specific function of the renewed covenant consists rather in underscoring the universal scope of the one Covenant, and God's love of man.

Those who approach ethics from a philosophical angle may be inclined to see in the idea of the Covenant an unnecessary encumbrance. They will probably object that moral action can sufficiently be explained as originating in man's determination to improve himself or this world, and in his conviction that Destiny or cosmic causality has enabled him so to act. But it was precisely from such a basis that Hitler and Mussolini launched their reign of tyranny and brutal extermination, and for which the Soviets claim the right ruthlessly to oppress all dissent by force. We overlook easily the fact, however, that the same temptation lurks in all secular systems of ethics. Relating our actions to the Covenants we notice that an order of urgency must be observed in the choice of our plans and objectives.

The human heart is so prone to justify and glorify its own desires and interests that we are almost inevitably led astray in our moral thinking, unless we are guided by factors outside and above ourselves. The idea of the Covenant reminds us that God himself takes the initiative in our moral life and offers a guiding hand. Through the Covenant he also discloses the purposive character of his dealing with his people. The way in which he selects his agents and direct his people's life and actions presents a clear criterion by which to discern self-centred from God-given enthusiasm and self-seeking stubbornness from unrestricted obedience. The effectiveness of our witness depends no less on the clarity with which we are thereby enabled to show why we move in the right direction, and on the true ground of goodness, than on the things we do.

2. *Duality of Faith*

By faith we are connected with a God who carries out his plan in history rather than with a mere divine substance. Nevertheless, what makes the events of holy history relevant to us is not the fact that they have taken place as is so frequently surmised in historical critical theology. We stress it because it is the way in which we are rendered sure of God's concern for us.

Thus understood, Christian experience runs on two parallel lines. Through religion, man seeks to envisage his life in this world as governed by God's kindness and directed towards a harmonious relationship with him. The 'God for me' perspective of religion is supplemented, however, by the 'me for God' perspective of the moral order. To religion the stress lies on the fact that the world in which we live is God's world, made by him and effectively directed towards its spiritual transformation. Notwithstanding the shortcomings, chaotic tendencies and evil forces found in this world, the universe is not destined to run down to complete disintegration and not even to an unending continuation of its actual condition. Rather it is held together by the redemptive love of God. Thus, we have the assurance that it makes full sense, even though we may not yet be able to discern its final goal. Such trust and assurance is supported by the way in which God has manifested himself in holy history. Thus, the religious attitude is truly meaningful irrespective of our moral achievements.

Nevertheless, the divine initiative manifested in the Covenant was misunderstood by those theologians who held that it did not matter what man accomplished in this world. Rather, God has a purpose for this world, and in particular people living in it. Thus, man's concern for the moral order is no less essential than religion. In view of the fact, however, that the two spheres of life require two different perspectives, the parallelism of religion and social concern is not a mere appearance. In the centre of religion, for instance, we find trust in, and love of, God, whereas in the moral sphere we encounter obedience. Likewise repentance in the moral sphere is concerned with particular wrongs I have committed or evils I have caused as a result of omission. Repentance in religion is concerned with the disregard of God's will in general, not with the circumstances in which an action of mine took place. Trust in God, similarly, in the field of religion is the confidence that God will not abandon me in the presence of earthly evils. In the practical field, trust is the assurance that working for the moral order is not futile. It will make its impact upon this world, because it is performed in agreement with the direction that God has assigned to the universe.

Since this duality of religion and morality seems to be irrational, theologians have usually over-emphasized either of them at the expense of the other. Yet we are unable to bring about a full synthesis. We have to envisage the work of God as the ground and foundation of our existence as well as the goal of our practical life. The only true synthesis is found in the life of the God-Man, for whom everything he did was directly related to God's final goal, and therefore considered worthwhile doing. Of the Christian it must be stated that he is holy because by God's grace he is engaged in his service, irrespective of his moral achievements or his piety.

C. Participation in the Covenant
1. *Worship*
The Covenant has often been interpreted as a particular event of past history, on the strength of which Christians were urged to behave accordingly. In fact, however, the Covenant is a process, by means of which God's unceasing and unchanging purpose concerning mankind is manifested. In various historical acts its reality and power have been

disclosed, and its meaning has been increasingly illumined. Yet through the Covenant we stand in the same direct relationship to God as did Moses or Jesus. The God in whom we believe is not a deity who acted once merely in order to retire then into inactivity. He is a 'living God', and the privileges of the Covenant are destined to be enjoyed by all coming generations no less than those of the past.

We participate in the Covenant mainly in two ways, namely, through worship and prayer. One might be inclined to add also the study of the Bible, church instruction and perhaps also church discipline as other independent modes of participation. However, strictly speaking, those activities have merely instrumental functions in a relationship in which we are directly confronted with God. Though our knowledge of God is but an indirect one, our experience of his work is based upon direct confrontation with his work. The covenant is a relationship in which God is dealing with mankind through the agency of his chosen people. Thus there is no room left in religion for a purely private contact with God as is claimed by religious individualism and Christian existentialism.

Worship is a collective activity in which the Church through priests and ministers reminds the worshippers of the fact that God is seeking man. In turn the congregation expresses its desire fully to live in the Covenant relationship and to experience the blessings implied in that relationship. In recent attempts to adjust the Church to the technological age, the fact is usually overlooked that not withstanding its sociological features the significance of the Church lies in its being the symbol of the Covenant. The leading role which ministers and priests play in the Church is not derived from their academic training. Rather the latter is the means by which those to whom such roles have been assigned are enabled efficiently to perform their office. By symbolizing the Covenant, the leaders in worship are not speaking and acting in a personal way and on their own authority. But the ecclesiastical offices are not grounded in the congregation, either. For the latter represents the human partner in the Covenant relationship. Through the leader in worship, the congregation is reminded of the fact that God wants them to be his people as he is their Lord who cares for their wellbeing.

In gathering for public worship, the congregation expects to be reminded and assured that they are not helplessly left to the mercy of the cosmic powers. They want to be strengthened in their belief that God is with them and on their side. Calling the minister a 'teaching elder' is, to say the least, dangerously misleading. For the congregation does not assemble in the first place in order to learn what is written in the Bible or thought by theologians; they are able to read it by themselves. Rather laymen are anxious to be influenced through the mouth of their leader, what bearing the content of the Bible has upon their salvation. In turn, through common prayer, the confession of sins, the recitation of the creeds and the singing of hymns and chants, the congregation gives expression to their certainty to belong to the covenantal fellowship and its blessings. By itself, there is not a single part of the public worship that does not have its secular counterpart. Yet the congregation gathers in the assurance that whatever goes on in its worship is directly related to their redemption. Thereby, the worship of the Church obtains a specific and unique colouring.

2. *Private Devotions*

Private devotions are useful and edifying, providing they do no cut the worshipper off from the congregation, but rather are the continuation of the common worship. Whatever I learn of God through the Bible is spiritually significant and helpful if and when it is received in the same attitude of receptivness and openness that in the public worship symbolizes our role in the Covenant. Increasing our familiarity with the contents of the Bible for mere information is certainly not worthless. For the depth and width of God's message cannot be fully apprehended except when we instruct ourselves by studying the Scriptures. Yet, our reading of the Bible must be coupled with the desire to learn more about the spiritual implications of the Covenant and our place in it. The Church's educational effort should move in the same direction. In our times, the public school aims one-sidedly at furnishing the knowledge of facts and techniques. Unfortunately, the Church deemed it necessary to pursue the same course. However, the goal of religious education consists in having good reasons why we are Christians. For answering that question, it is certainly not sufficient to know why it is that one joined this congregation rather than that, but rather why one is a member of a Christian church at all. That kind of rather vague religion is capable of being deepened and becoming articulate, as we allow the Church's proclamation to penetrate into our mind. There is no general rule for reaching that goal, nor is there any kind of devotions that would work in each case and situation. It can be stated with assurance that the desire to grow in one's religion and participation in worship are indispensable mental movements both in order to make our obedience to God articulate and to foster God's cause. Of course, what makes the Christian life relevant is the Spirit of God as he operates in a person's heart. But not only is the acceptance of God's call an indication of the effectiveness of the Spirit within us. It is also undeniable that the power of the Spirit cannot manifest itself in our hearts unless we attune our will to it. The modern tendency to treat religion as worthless or even incompatible with the Christian faith is bound inevitably to weaken both the Church and the progress of God's cause in this world.

Personal religion has to cope with difficulties and dangers which are absent from collective worship. Personal religion confronts us constantly with the question, Is what seems to me so certain and convincing in my religion really the work of God's Spirit? Though I am anxious to eliminate those subjective elements from my experience, it is its alien character that makes me try to describe it in terms of subjects with which I am familiar. Such doubts increase in proportion with the increasing magnitude of the subject experienced. Thus, it is not surprising that in our knowledge of God we are frequently and harassingly beset by religious doubts. Things are different in collective worship. There doubt is excluded. The religious group starts from the assurance that its life of worship is the very evidence of the ongoingness of the covenant relationship. The multiplicity of types of experience and their constant interchange serve to neutralize apparent contradictions.

In addition to the constant and inevitable doubts connected with personal religion, we mention the temptation of overrating one's own spiritual maturity and significance. The self-evaluation of the religious person oscillates from thinking too highly of himself on the one hand, to fits of depressive self-condemnation and despair on the other. The contact he has with the deity will elate the Christian and cause him to consider himself as superior to non-believers. Yet, the awareness of his sins will lead him to the recognition that as one who has disregarded his redeemer he is not worth anything. Yet even if I were blameless in my personal life, I would be a person who shares in the general guilt of the race. The individual must pass through these stages in order to learn that what really matters in his faith is what God thinks of him. For God alone has the standard by which the true value of a person is to be measured. Notwithstanding the dangers and limitations of personal religion, its practice is an essential incentive of faith. The greatness of God's grace and forgiveness cannot be truly evaluated unless we realize two facts. In redemption, God is concerned with each of us personally.

Furthermore, we are but instrumental in redemption. These two facts constitute the real value of our existence.

3. *Prayer*

The most potent and effective antidote against those doubts and false evaluations is prayer. For prayer makes us conscious of the fact that in faith we are not confronted by notions of our mind or by troubles reflecting our emotions, but by the reality of God's work. Prayer is not a 'dialogue with God', for then God would be on man's level. Rather, its basic result is God's encounter with man through Christ. Through the Covenant God descends to man, and man, in turn, has been lifted high above all the other creatures. He has been granted the privilege of having access to his creator, notwithstanding his unworthiness. In that encounter, God as 'God for me' enables and encourages me to bring all my needs and problems before him, while in my capacity of 'me for God' I offer myself to him for service, praise and thanksgiving. In scrutinizing ourselves, we are able to perceive that the desire to pray is the clearest indication of the Spirit's working within ourselves. In turn, such awareness will increase our joy to be able to pray, and our eagerness to engage in prayer. The efficacy of prayer is based on that encounter and man's readiness to act accordingly rather than on the rhetorical or theological qualities of our prayers. In granting prayers, God does not reward us. Rather it is his will that those who acknowledge him for what he is, shall share in his redemptive work. Thus he always imparts good gifts to those who pray, even though his gifts may not be what we wanted to receive. Prayer is not intended to remind God of the things that are on our heart as though he were ignorant of them. Rather we make thereby an effort to join our life, or a portion of it, directly with God's saving activity. Prayer is based upon our desire to detach ourselves with respect to our special concern from all utilitarian contacts in order to see it in the light of God's purpose. Doing so will assure us of God's willingness to pay attention to everything in our life that we bring before him. For that reason, nothing is too small and insignificant to be brought before God in prayer. In turn, none is so large or so difficult that it would not be comprised by his purpose. God does not need our prayers, but we need them because it is through them that our life is incorporated into the divine harmony of the universe. Thus, through prayer we are rendered cognizant of the fact that we live in a world in which human life makes sense at all. As he calls us into his Covenant, God offers us an opportunity in all conditions of life effectively to work for his cause. It is our privilege that through the prayer of intercession we may effectively influence the course of events in the numerous instances in which we lack insight, strength and resources to give practical assistance. Thus, we have good reason for thankfulness, even when the actual conditions in which we stand may be far from being happy ones. The contention that human wishes and praises are heard at all in the infinite vastness of the universe would seem to be an absurd one but for the fact that in the history of the Covenant, and especially in Christ, God had granted the proof that he cares for man. In turn, notwithstanding the apparent absurdity of prayer, man in all ages and zones has dared to present his prayers to the deity. In that phenomenon we see the evidence that it is God's Spirit who makes people pray, although their practices of prayer may be superstitious and their subjects naïve.

Prayer is the bridge by which religion and moral action are connected. By it not only the willingness is created to comply with God's demand in general over against our self-seeking desires, but also the right attitude is engendered by which we overcome the sense of strangeness which separates us from other people and God's world. Through intercession we establish an intimate contact with people and causes in their concrete situation. Prayers are no substitute for practical assistance. Yet through them we are rendered sensitive to the fact that the people for whom we feel concern have been laid upon our heart by God himself. Thus we are under divine obligation to help them, yet also have the assurance that through us God wants to accomplish his plan for them. In turn, it is obvious that apart from prayer, morality will degenerate into egotistic perfectionism or shallow utilitarianism. In either case, the moral effort will in the long run be self-destructive. Perfectionism will degenerate into self-admiration, while utilitarianism will be governed by expediency.

In Christian religion thanksgiving and praise are the supreme subjects of prayer. Of course, it is true that in all religions, including our own, religious life starts with petitions. The transition from disregard of God to a religious attitude usually takes place when we are in tight situations. No wonder that we turn to God for deliverance. Only gradually are we in a position to control the egotistic element in our religion. The prayer of petition is not evil. The Covenant relationship implies the assurance that God is prepared to come to the rescue of his people when their strength fails them. But too easily the request becomes the only concern of prayer. People act then as though God were under obligation to relieve them from all their troubles, distress or weakness. That in the midst of an insensitive and callous universe God should encourage us to come to him with our requests is far from being a matter of course. He is above all our Lord. Hence when he promises that those who seek him shall find, he wants us to know that if we are willing to serve him, all that is required for that purpose has been made available for us. We are permitted to ask for all that serves our well-being and that of others who are dear to us. Yet it is not to be requested as an end in itself, but rather as the prerequisite of the service we are ready to render to him. Prayer, and the prayer of petition in particular, must not be considered a human possibility to get hold of God. Rather through it we are offered an opportunity by which we as creatures may be united with the Creator. Prayer also reduces for us the apparent contradiction between God as mere subject and God's presence in this world to a helpful dialectic. We pray to God rather than to anything in this world, because that is the only possibility to render human existence meaningful in the world. For in prayer we heed God's transcendence. At the same time prayer is a mental act in which we are concerned with God's work rather than his ontological nature, as we move our existence and the things and people around us into the light of his purpose.

Part Five: Spheres of Ethical Life

15 The Fellow Man

A. The Institution of Neighbourhood

Of the various human relationships, two there are by which particularly intimate fellowship may be established. They are the neighbourhood and family. In an age characterized by an excessive individualism, these relationships seem to be of subordinate value only. Other people are supposed to serve mainly as objects, over against whom one has to assert oneself, or as means which should be used for self-realization. Even in ancient Israel, the commandment to love one's neighbour was not given prominence. However, by proclaiming it as a constitutive part of the Great, or fundamental, Commandment, Jesus re-interpreted the term and vastly enlarged its applicability. In Israel, neighbourhood had been discovered to be a divine institution, that is to say, a social structure that comes into existence with an inescapable necessity. New in Jesus' understanding of neighbourliness was the realization that what gave meaning and authority to the commandment was the underlying mystery of individuation. Seemingly creating a detached existence, individuality is in fact determined by the institution of mutual supplementation. Its operation is a paradox. For communication between human individuals is rendered possible by the fact that all men belong to the same species, Man. But such communication is made difficult by the fact that each individual differs from all others not only by nature and heredity but also by historical, social and geographical circumstances. These differences in turn may cause alienation, separation and even hostility. Yet, strangely enough, individuality implies also the possibility of fellowship through mutual assistance and help. Of course, no individual represents all human abilities and potentialities. No man, not even the most powerful, wealthy or good, is in a position to satisfy all the needs of a single person, let alone those of the whole mankind. Nevertheless, the individual differences are so distributed in mankind that there is a correlation between the totality of human abilities on the one hand, and the needs to be satisfied on the other.

The universal character of the institution of neighbourliness does not mean that each man is destined to relieve the wants of all other people but rather that God's plan for mankind will be fulfilled if and when each man, in his place and according to his abilities, comes to the support of others. According to Jesus, my neighbour is a human being who happens to come into contact with me, and to have needs which are not taken care of by any other person or agency, and for whose alleviation I am in a position to do something. Not only topographical conditions but also nationality, race, religion or sex may no longer be regarded as limitations of my obligation. What ties people together as neighbours is the fact that God has created all men and has set before them a common goal. The basic meaning of the commandment, as Jesus understood it, was God's intention through human agency to realize a people on the basis of the Covenant. God had so arranged the life of mankind that through the diversity of their gifts and endowments people could supplement each other and eventually would fulfil all their needs. For its central function in the development of mankind, Jesus places neighbourly love above all civil and criminal laws. He extends its validity to the anti-social, the outcast, the stranger and even the enemy. Nevertheless, neighbourly love is not understood as a vague love of mankind in general.

The element of proximity, originally present in topographical vicinity, survives in Jesus' interpretation. The neighbour is not to be sought in persons who by status or domicile live far away from us. He is to be found first of all in the 'brother', that is to say, in people living very close to us, in the same family, street or town, riding on the same train or working in the same office. Living together implies responsibility for those around us. Yet Jesus would not confine neighbourliness to the people living in proximity. The invitation he extends to the taxgatherer Levi, the example he sets forth in the story of the Good Samaritan, or the commandment to love an enemy, too, are indicative of the universal frame in which he conceives of love. In our days we act in the spirit of Jesus when we show concern also for people of other continents whose hunger or illiteracy or slave labour has been brought to our knowledge through the media of mass communication. Thus the scope of neighbourliness, while potentially unlimited, is nevertheless not Utopian. The ethical element of proximity is not to be seen in vicinity or natural relationship but rather in a mental attitude. It denotes the determination to assume responsibility for other people when able to do so. Neighbourliness will never allow any differences between myself and other people with whom I have entered into contact to erect an impediment by which I feel justified to treat them with indifference, contempt or hatred. The necessity to practise neighbourliness is not grounded in sociological or psychological data. Of course, people have soon realized that mutual aid is a matter of prudence, and that mental life is sharpened and enriched when we enter into exchange with other people. But from a prudential viewpoint, opposition to other people and inimical reaction may also be a counsel of wisdom at times. In spite of all reasons to the contrary people have always established neighbourly relations, and will most certainly continue to do so. In that fact, we see that neighbourliness is a manifestation of the divine arrangement of human relations, not a sociological device invented by man. The human side of the institution is found in the way in which the relationship is organized and interpreted. Yet, notwithstanding the fact that circumstances and environment change, the institution of neighbourhood and its goal remains the same. For its goal does not change, and thus the necessity to cope with it is an inescapable one.

By treating neighbourhood as a divine institution, Jesus rejects all kinds of moral individualism. Christian life is always a relationship between myself and my neighbour. Implied therein is a divine privilege. The neighbour has a right to claim my help. God did not make me that 'I should do what I am', but rather that with my abilities and resources I should heed my fellow man's claim.

B. The Neighbour
1. *His Position*
The manner in which Jesus interpreted the commandment of neighbourliness shows clearly that for him it was not a social rule destined to render a difficult situation tolerable and perhaps to promote happiness. By stressing its character as a divine commandment and coupling it with the demand to love God above anything else, Jesus implied that its principal purpose was to be found in a divine goal. In the last analysis, mankind is thereby to be enabled to devote itself completely to the service of God and by doing so to live a rich and meaningful life. This destination implies that the 'neighbour' is God's concern. Through our love, he is to undergo a far-reaching change of his predicament and, consequently of his personal life too. Such interpretation did not imply a criticism of the earlier understanding of the commandment. The ancient Israelites were right in seeing in the peaceful relations of farmers one approach towards the final goal set forth for man. Thus the neighbour does not simply live side by side with me. His presence challenges

me. That we should be able to live in neighbourly relations is an indication of the way in which God enters into our life both by providing neighbourly help and by challenging us to come to his assistance.

The commandment of neighbourliness supplements the unequal way in which God has distributed his gifts and bounties to men. Individual existence is a fragmentary one, and there is no human being who has been equipped with everything needed for a full life. No man is what he wants to be, let alone what he should be. On the contrary, in a number of respects each man falls short of what it takes to render him happy and efficient in moulding his life. We cannot agree with Liebniz, who held that everything in this world was prearranged in such a way that automatically human lives would tie in with each other in a harmonious pattern. In fact, there is obviously a minimum of order and co-operation found in mankind. Rather there is enmity and lack of regard for each other, and thus the deployment of human life is obstructed. Yet God has granted each individual an inalienable claim for assistance, a fact of which everybody is aware, though such claim is frequently ignored or its right questioned. Christian faith sees that claim within the context of the Covenant, and hence recognizes its right without restriction. The legitimacy of that claim is based on the abundance of goods found in this world, of which at present a great deal goes to waste. Yet love of one's fellow man does not require riches. A friendly word, a smile, a little gift – that is to say, things which have but a small practical or material value – are nevertheless sufficient to make other people realize that someone cares for them, and that their life is not meaningless. For that reason no one should be discouraged by the fact that for his need no truly powerful or experienced helper is in sight. Yet too frequently we overlook the evidence of other people's kindness, because we want powerful or expensive help.

Acts of neighbourly love have to be performed within a social setting. As a result, people may lose sight of the spiritual goal of their action and develop, instead, a sense of superiority or may look down on the recipient of their aid with a certain disdain. That is the reason why Jesus admonishes his disciples that they let not the right hand know what the left hand does. They must in no way measure their deeds, that is to say, refrain from all kinds of comparison. The goodness of their action lies in their willingness to mind the divine call as it comes through their neighbour, and in the gratitude with which they recognize the privilege of contributing to the attainment of God's goal.

As Jesus sees it in the light of brotherly love, human life rests upon the basis of general mutuality. He who receives, may not be able to repay to him who helped him. But whatever kindness he receives is meant to remind him of his ability in turn to assist others in their specific needs. Of course, such view differs fundamentally from the ancient *do ut des* principle ('I'll give you something in the expectation that you'll do the same for me'). While he must recognize the general validity of mutuality, the fellow man is not to feel an obligation of reciprocity towards his helper.

Viewed in the context of the Covenant, neighbourliness is not meant to render people happy, if by happiness we understand the satisfaction of our wishes. Man's destination is not to be seen in the fulfilment of his desires, but rather in the realization of the divine goal. Happiness and destination are not exclusive of each other but priority is to be assigned to man's ability to work in the service of God. If that goal is rightly understood, a feeling of satisfaction will ensue. The value of neighbourliness is therefore conditioned not only by our knowledge of God's demand. He for whose benefit we perform our action will not be able truly to appreciate the value of the service rendered to him unless he is aware of the end to which it is related. That effect does not require that he should know the Biblical commandment. But the result will depend on the nature of our action. Is he able to notice that it is performed without any egotism and for his supreme good, namely, the awareness of God's kindness at work in mankind?

2. *Neighbourly Love*

a. ITS NATURE

Notwitstanding the simple language in which it is couched, the understanding of the Great Commandment presents unexpected difficulties. First of all there is the semantic problem. The English verb 'to love' and the corresponding norm prove to be rather vague. 'Love' may designate all kinds of sympathy, desire and lust, none of which corresponds exactly with the Hebrew verb *ahab* and the corresponding Greek verb *agapan*. Both verbs denote an association in which a person identifies himself with the purpose or plans of another person, or with the end for which a good is used (e.g., to love mammon, Matt. 6:24). Moreover, the English word expresses the desirability of the object loved whereas in the Hebrew the recognition of its worth stands in the foreground. Finally, the English word connotes the subject's desire to possess or control the object loved, whereas in the Hebrew it is the wish or need of the object loved which determines the direction in which my action is to move.

On top of the semantic problem we find the exegetical one. The Old Testament injunction was meant to stress the complete reciprocity of services implied in the topographical neighbourhood. By combining the two commandments of love, Jesus indicates that the interest of neighbourly love does not lie in the social field, but rather in the purpose that God pursues with mankind. While the commandment was originally destined to curb people's natural egotism, its meaning has now been transformed into a positive task executed in God's service. That one is ready to live as God's servant will manifest itself in one's willingness to care for the well-being of one's fellow men no less than for oneself.

Characteristic of Christian love is that it does not ask how difficult its task is or how propitious the circumstances are for carrying out the task. Christian history abounds with examples of such daring love; think, for instance, of George Müller and his orphanage in Bristol or of Hudson Taylor and the work of the China Inland Mission. Instead of delineating in advance the extent to which it is willing to go, it simply starts its works and leaves it to the Spirit to keep one moving.

Thus understood, Christian love differs widely from Plato's idea of *eros*. *Eros* is an act of sympathy caused by the relative perfection of a person or an object. Christian love, in turn, devotes itself to a person in need. It does not ask whether or not he deserves help. Yet, if necessary, it will assist him to overcome his faults. Plato's love, however, recoils from people who do not meet the standards of high value. The problem has been seriously confused by Nygren's study, *Agapé and Eros*. The Swedish scholar has popularized in Christian ethics an unrealistic and vague usage of the term *agapé*. The student of the Bible will find that Christian love is by no means incompatible with emotions or natural love. Nevertheless, the New Morality and similar movements are even more seriously confused when identifying erotic love with Christian love. The Bible describes *agapé* or Christian neighbourliness as a personal attitude. It is interested in the fellow man as a being destined to become a child of God, that is to say, as a manifestation of God's redemptive will. Apart from faith, love is concerned with the fellow man's achievements or endowments, with his body or his mind as what they mean to me in a given situation. As the situation changes, my love is correspondingly affected. It may be inflamed to hotter fire, or it may wane and even come to an end. While neighbourly love will adjust its implementations to the fellow man's changing conditions, its changes do not affect the concern for his needs. They are aimed at effective aid only. Thus my help may consist of material help, or by acts of healing, teaching or guidance, yet also of an emotional attachment, as for instance in friendship and married life. While neighbourly love may have an emotional component, it must never be swayed by it. Its dominant feature is the concern for the fellow man's destination to become a child of God rather than the subjective sentiment of what he means to me or what I feel for him in the present moment. Jesus reminds us, for instance, that the grudge I harbour towards a person must not make me forget that God has made him my brother. That seemingly schizophrenic conduct is nevertheless meaningful because the seat of Christian love is in the self, whereas its manifestations are executed by our mind and body. Their significance depends on their objective and varies according to whether or not they are motivated by faith.

While in Christian life a good deal of neighbourliness is shown in mere conformity with the mores of the congregation, Christian love is kept alive because the Spirit moves people from time to time to deal with their fellow men in the light of God's purpose. Such people act with extraordinary power. Though all Christians recognize that the execution of God's plan requires a complete surrender of our abilities and resources for the service of God, too frequently we recoil from giving to our fellow man more than a portion of our abundance. Deutero-Isaiah had already pointed out, however, that the secret of neighbourliness lies in its ability and willingness to sacrifice oneself for a fellow man's destination. Jesus interpreted that mystery by telling his disciples that such sacrifice does not necessarily consist in the giving of one's life.

b. THE GOAL

We have to give some evidence of the fact that we take the divine commandment seriously. In that connection Jesus speaks of 'pulling out one's eye' or 'cutting off one's hand'. In other words, by an act of self-limitation we give up the use of a good, preferably one that is dear to us or that has a natural usefulness for us, if and when it proves to be an obstacle to our intention to help a fellow man. As a means of self-discipline this can be done in many different ways, for instance in giving up the use of liquor or tobacco or the possibility of married life, or in espousing frugality of life, or in engaging in voluntary relief work. Such activities and abstentions may not directly aid people who are in need. Nevertheless, they have a spiritual function within the Church. By them an example is set for fellow Christians. They are thereby persuaded that many goods which we consider necessary and indispensable, may without loss be dispensed with. The practical value of such actions lies in the fact that through discipline we gather reserves which may be used for difficult cases.

Apparently the commandment of neighbourly love implies a contradiction. Its basis is the fact that all men are destined to become members of the people of the Covenant. Yet in the nature of the case such fellowship is always limited to a relatively small number of people. Not only are our resources limited so that our help is confined to a few, but it is also of the nature of personal relations that they cannot be extended to an unlimited crowd. Paradoxically, however, we are able – notwithstanding those limitations – to reach a fairly large group of people through our neighbourliness. That is so first of all because the community in which we live constantly undergoes changes in its composition so that we are confronted with new people all the time. Above all, however, our acts of faith bear witness to the power of the Spirit. While they may be performed in secret, their result and motivation are rendered widely known on account of the public character of the Church. As he proclaims neighbourly love as organically connected with love of God and as demanded by God, Jesus shows what he regards the goal of truly human life. Man is destined to participate actively in the life of the Covenant, which consists in the mutuality of for-each-otherness. Neighbourliness, though it may start as a one-sided activity, will eventually enable the needy to overcome the sense of helplessness and spiritual torpor which results from his preoccupation with his want. Through the consideration and help which he receives he will be stimulated and encouraged to return to life in mutuality.

By expanding neighbourliness from a social rule to a universal commandment, Jesus has, in the opinion of many, undermined true ethics. For he disregarded what seems to be a basic principle of ethics, namely, that receiving and obligation must be in a strictly reciprocal relationship. In fact, however, Jesus did not completely disregard that principle, though he modified it considerably. He saw the significance of neighbourliness in the divine arrangement by which God had made it possible. Hence he enjoined those whom he had healed to give thanks to God. Yet he was not unaware of the many who failed to show gratitude. It seems that he was more interested in promoting God's cause than in a rational social order based exclusively on reciprocity. Two things should be given careful consideration, however. First, Christian ethical thought is concerned with life in the community rather than with individual relations. Hence, reciprocity is not to be understood as a kind of remuneration given to one. Gratitude is due to God, who has shown the necessity of neighbourliness and by whose Spirit people are animated to act accordingly. Furthermore, on the basis of rational – that is to say, utilitarian – considerations, ethical life must inevitably be confined to a relatively small group of 'worthy' people. In his grace, God is anxious, however, to come to the rescue of all men. With such a perspective, people are to be given evidence that there is undemanding goodness, independent of, and prior to, their own goodness. That is a risky method, but it is the divine one, nevertheless. Such understanding of God's way avoids the moral indifference of universalism, yet keeps the door open for unworthy and ungodly people. This is a world in which much enmity, envy and callousness are rampant. No wonder that fear and distrust are found more frequently than gratitude. It is only through actions of neighbourly love that people can be assured that God loves man, because those who help them are willing to work in the service of his love.

The commandment of neighbourly love has often been understood as being the equivalent of the Golden Rule. Yet that principle in its traditional form is the product of practical wisdom. We are advised against harming other people, if and when they are in a position to retaliate. It is different with the positive perspective in which Jesus advises his disciples to do to other people whatever good things they would like (Mt. 7:12). With the emphasis placed upon the Christian's initiative in doing good, Jesus no longer states natural wisdom but divine strategy. Likewise, Jesus' understanding of neighbourliness has nothing in common with the ancient *Ne quid nimis*, that is, never go to extremes. For Jesus, love does not wait for the fellow man's response in order to define its scope. As he shows by giving himself into the hands of his enemy, love will go as far as the neighbour needs it. It has no limits.

Equally unsatisfactory as basis of true life is the often repeated Kantian principle that human beings must be taken seriously as persons. Of course, I am destined for personal life, and so are all human beings. Consequently, I do not derive from intercourse with other people all fruits and benefits, unless I am dealing with them on a personal fundament. Yet the principle of personality is but a basic limiting element in human relations. I have no right to treat men as mere merchandize, as was the slave in ancient Roman law, or to brutalize them as though they lacked heart and mind. But no matter how far we stress personalism, it remains a self-centred attitude. It lacks a stimulus for taking a constructive interest in the other person.

3. *Organized Aid*

The expansion of Christianity and the intrinsic strength of its idea of neighbourliness have produced numerous programmes of assistance on a global basis which are executed through private organizations, churches, and/or governmental agencies. Since the original motive and stimulus of organized aid is rooted in the Christian practice of neighbourliness, Christians have been the principal instigators and agents of such activities. Their willingness to serve those in need is not contingent on personal relations, as was the case in the pre-Christian pagan world. Rather, it rests on the existence of human want, on the one hand, and their ability to help, on the other. Nevertheless, experience has shown that when the element of direct contact between donor and recipient is completely absent, aid is apt to degenerate into bureaucratic routine whereby the people approached become mere recipients of alms. The impersonal character of relief is even more outspoken, where relief is given in the form of research projects and technological assistance. Easily, such help loses its Christian outlook and goal. A utilitarian viewpoint prevails, whereby the usefulness of the programme is limited to the alleviation of the one problem or want to which such an organization is devoted. What is worse is the demoralizing effect which such practice has on both administrator and recipients. The inevitable consequence of the enormous economic and social power, that many of the modern relief actions have, is a growing distance between the administrators and those who depend on their good will. In turn, the mechanical mode of distribution tends to stifle in the recipients the spirit of initiative and self-help and to increase their egotistic outlook. Worse, probably, is the effect organized aid has on the donor. Since he lacks not only contact with those to be helped, but frequently also adequate information about the nature of the project for which his money is solicited, the donor's giving is increasingly depersonalized. What moves him to give is social pressure rather than willingness to act in a brotherly way for people in need. This lack of contact, in turn, makes the recipient think that those who help him are exceedingly wealthy. Instead of being related in a more intimate way with the donors, he is tempted to envy them and to make immoderate requests. The 'widow's mite' disappears unnoticed in the balance sheet of the relief organization.

The fact should not be denied that in cases of nature catastrophes, revolutions and wars, when immediate relief is imperative, there is no substitute for the modern type of organized aid. Nevertheless, the tragic consequences mentioned require balancing counteraction. For that purpose the Christian communities seem to be the only agency capable of effective counteraction. There is no cogent reason why church relief should ape the methods of secular organization, when it is in a position to create its own. Since interest taken in individuals forms the basis of neighbourliness, churches will make efforts to establish them on a broad basis between donors and recipients of relief. Such means are, among others, visits of representatives to the donor churches, correspondence at large between recipients and donors, explanation of the donors' motives given to recipients. This does not mean that relief should be used as a lure to conversion. However, it offers an opportunity to bear witness to our faith. Doing so will be profitable to the recipients, even if they are repelled by other aspects of our religion. Through such witness, God becomes a reality in human life both for the recipient and the giver of help. This is of special importance with regard to problems that have grown beyond human control, as for instance, the race problem, the predicament of the under-developed nations, or dehumanization through technology. From a purely practical viewpoint, the personal involvement seems to be superfluous because it does not add to the material help given. Seen in the spiritual perspective, however, it is of greatest value. Through it the possibility of a Christian vista is created, and the way is paved from mere almsgiving to a personal interest in another person. Such attitude, in turn, will be of increasing influence upon the recipient's understanding of neighbourliness.

The ideal form of neighbourliness, because least exposed to distortion and misunderstanding, is friendship. What unites people in friendship is not the satisfaction of a material need, but rather a mutual sympathy. In that relationship, too, Jesus inaugurated a remarkable change. In antiquity, equality of rank and/or interest was considered its solid basis because it would safeguard either of them from becoming dependent on, or falling into the debt of, the other. The uniting bond would be found in the pursuit of common ends. In the friendship with his disciples, however, Jesus would show that friendship may also be established on the foundation of mutual give and take. In spite of his superiority, the master or great man is not doomed to lifelong loneliness because he has no peer. Of course, he would be unable to enjoy his superiority unless he saw in it a divine gift bestowed upon him for the benefit of others. In turn, the common people, though lacking creativity, are nevertheless granted the privilege of friendly intercourse with the genius or the generous benefactor without being humiliated by his greatness, provided only that out of gratitude and appreciation they accept his gift. By his example, Jesus disclosed the secret of all true friendship. It is so valuable because through it the spiritual experience of the mature Christian is communicated effectively to those for whom Christianity is a mere convention or who are beginners in the new life.

C. Realization of Neighbourliness

1. *The Claim of the Fellow Man*

An entirely new aspect of neighbourliness was brought to light when Jesus showed that the needy man has a right to claim the support of his fellow men. Charity was understood in antiquity as an act of generosity, in which the donor would act in complete independence and the recipient had to regard himself as lucky if somebody else took an interest in his need. Nobody was under moral obligation to help him. By giving the commandment to love one's neighbour, God had placed the needy person on the believer's heart. By declaring all men his children, and thus destined for life under the Covenant, God had privileged the needy man to claim the assistance of his fellow members. Hence the miserly, callous or thoughtless way in which the needy are so often treated is a sinful transgression of God's saving will. In turn, the appropriate way in which the needy manifests his want and demand is by means of request rather than by violently snatching away from those who have what one thinks is needed. As Jesus taught in the parable of the Friend at Midnight, however, he has a right to make his request known time and again, even though he may thereby importune those in a position to help him. Medieval Christianity recognized the right of the beggar to ask for alms as a necessary social institution, because it offered an opportunity to perform meritorious works. Protestantism envisages poverty from a different angle. Recognition of the needy person's claim implies willingness to let him have all the opportunities we possess and to assist him in acquiring the skills and resources upon which depends our own prosperity. Under present conditions, the 'haves' will remember that it is by the Grace of God that they possess what is theirs; yet also that they will be deprived of their privilege unless they will recognize the responsibility which by the will of God they have for the needy. The needy, in turn, will realize that God himself will eventually vindicate their cause, if only they will be prepared to do his will. There is a divine judgement which takes care of the needy that trust in God.

By accepting that rule of neighbourliness, both partners will be blessed. He who gives may thereby learn to give generously and gladly, while he who is in want may be taught how richly God has already showered his benefits upon him notwithstanding his want, and how much reason he has to be grateful to God. With such an attitude he is delivered from the brink of despondency, envy, and hopelessness, which in the long run oppress the needy's mind more than does material want. In turn, he may develop initiative and solicit support. Thus he makes his way forward in spite of his small base. Max Weber has instructively shown how faith becomes instrumental in engendering active fellowship and economic development.

2. *In Quest of the Neighbour*

To Jesus' contemporaries, the question, 'Who is my neighbour?' was of utmost importance. Yet in telling the story of the Good Samaritan, Jesus made clear that they were asking the wrong question because it presupposed a permanent division of mankind. Some would be predestined by God, or destined by a freak of nature, to be my neighbours, and those were to be loved. God's commandment was not to be applied to the rest. Of course, when all men are regarded as destined to form the people of the Covenant and love of the neighbour was the law of the Covenant, the problem seems to be even more difficult. How should all of them be loved? Yet, in turn, why should some be excluded from neighbourly love though God had chosen them? For the commandment does not say, 'Love all men', but rather, 'Love your neighbour'. But how do I manage to find out my neighbour among the billions of my contemporaries? Personal sympathy, remarkable achievements, national or blood relationships are too particular and subjective to be used as criteria. The very absence of a criterion to be found in the New Testament would seem to provide the answer. For the execution of God's purpose it does not make any difference whom I love, provided only that through acts of neighbourliness I contribute to the increase of divine life in this world. We are obviously free to make our own selection among the needy people. We do not have to ask, 'Who needs our help most?' By engaging in such inquiries I might waste my time in searching while I should spend it in loving. For the same reason, it makes little difference whether I devote my love to people around me or to people in a foreign country, provided only that I am anxious to avoid all discrimination and do not run away from an obvious task in my proximity. Whenever we heed another person's need, a divine seed is planted in this world which in due time will bear fruit. What is indispensable, however, is openness to other people's needs. Since our fellow man's claim adds to our own burden, we prefer to shut our eyes and ears to his requests.

God himself seeks to overcome our dullness and callousness by confronting us from time to time with suffering, want and confusion, in order that their blatant cruelty, injustice, or apparent absurdity should arouse our compassion, indignation, or protest. While the evils involved may not surpass what goes on regularly, the circumstances in which they occur around us hurt us more than ordinarily – for instance, the suffering of a child, the death of a parent of small children, or the senseless murder of an advocate of a noble cause. Through the lessons thus thrown upon us we begin to understand the urgency of neighbourliness. The needs which are most pressing are those in which personal commitment is required, such as loneliness, despair, envy, jealousy, or distrust. The commandment to love one's neighbour as oneself would seem to frustrate one's joy of life. Is not our existence thus placed under a permanent obligation called forth by the ubiquity of evils in this world?

However, a couple of considerations will compensate such a gloomy thought. First, the obligation points to our ability. I am not doomed to be a passive onlooker of the world's evils. God has endowed his people with power to relieve a neighbour's wants. Furthermore, we, too, have a right to bring our needs and problems before others, trusting in God's promise that to those who ask will be given. For the 'good man' it is easy to overlook the blessing of request. Yet most people, by no means the aged, sick, infirm, and lonely alone, feel oppressed by a sense of worthlessness or of being superfluous, and wait for a recognition of their usefulness. By our requests we contribute to restoring their self-esteem, provided only we have enough patience with their weakness. We may be sure that God has made some people fit to meet our needs. Ideally, mankind forms a universal system of mutual giving and taking. In actual reality that is not the case, however. Nevertheless, instead of complaining about neglect and indifference, we have reason to realize how deeply we are in other people's debt. For the rest it is in our power to contribute to the improvement of our predicament. The self-righteous person, is a constant source of irritation for all those who have to deal with him. When we ask God to forgive us our shortcomings and omissions, we are willing to do the same to our fellow men, we alleviate the tensions in social life and help to bring about harmony within the people of the Covenant.

3. *Modes of Neighbourliness*

Concomitant with the tendency of modern theology to concentrate upon the psychological manifestations of faith is the attempt to define neighbourliness in psychological terms. Yet, though the ethical act takes place in the human mind, it is not its psychological structure that constitutes its specific character. As Jesus showed through example and instruction, neighbourliness receives its ethical meaning from the end thereby to be reached. In view of the numerous healings reported in the Gospels, one might conclude that he conceived of that end as integrity of body and soul. Yet Jesus' teaching leaves no doubt about the intrinsic connection between man's wholesome condition and God's redemptive purpose. People are healed in order to enable them adequately to perform the task of service for which God has destined them. In a world filled with evils, God wants us to aid the neighbour so that he may overcome those shortages and wrong attitudes by which he is prevented from living a truly human life, or is seriously impeded from reaching that goal. Hence neighbourliness implies material help no less than mental and psychic help.

Nevertheless, more important than the selection of the most appropriate means by which that goal can be reached is the clarity with which the ultimate goal is envisaged and more or less directly intimated to the fellow man. Where the ultimate goal is lost sight of, neighbourliness is bound to fail in giving lasting satisfaction. It is quite natural that with one good obtained, others are desired; yet the supreme good is the service of God for which faith prepares the Christian. In order to help the neighbour, people will focus their efforts in the first place on the removal of a particular shortage or ill and their cure by means of health services, social welfare agencies or free public education. They often fail to notice, however, that what makes life so difficult are personality problems. Others who recognize the problems may attempt to heal them by a psychotherapy that shies away from touching the very depth of the ego.

This fact is especially obvious in the race problem. The difficulty of the American negro is not in the first place one of economic equality, health or education, though their significance must not be underrated, but rather of social equality. Theoretically the abolition of slavery has conferred full equality upon him. In fact, however, the white society in which he is forced to live refuses in general to recognize him as their peer. Consequently, increased social and civil benefits are not welcomed with the enthusiasm which the white friends of the negro expect, because they do not change the inferior place which he occupies in the white society. Christianity is in a position to attack this central problem. It has an over-arching unity which can be used as the basis of a true fellowship, notwithstanding the fact that many other problems have not yet been solved. Instead of making themselves the champions of a new economic and constitutional policy, the churches will work more successfully in bringing about fellowship in Christ. In that connection the mutuality of Christian life is of great importance. True fellowship is not a gift one-sidedly offered by the white churches. It also requires readiness on the part of negro Christians to join the white fellowship from which distrust and false racial pride keeps many negroes away. This does not mean that the churches should suspend social and political activities for the benefit of social minorities. As so often in Christian life, the main problem is that of the right priority.

The ultimate task of neighbourliness is the formation of the people of God manifested in the unity of the Church. In its fellowship mankind will learn that all the good things of this world are God's gracious gifts destined to be enjoyed by all men. From the communistic Utopias that condition of the earth differs in two respects. It is built upon voluntary consent, not on political and military power, and it is a condition gradually to be realized through the operation of the Spirit, not through a collective *fiat*.

Neighbourliness requires compassion. The effectiveness of what I do for another person depends to a large extent on my willingness to recognize his want as a real evil which makes me feel sorry for him and desirous to see him rid of it. It may even happen that I see his real need more clearly than he does, so that I have to tell him what is implied in his predicament. Compassion is tender. It does not hurt a fellow man unnecessarily by drawing his attention to his faults. Yet it does not spare him by pretending not to notice his faults, for without knowledge of ourselves we are unable to serve others in a useful way.

Yet in disclosing to him his shortcomings and errors, compassion will keep one from assuming an attitude of superiority. For he is not to imitate the counsellor, but rather to learn through him what keeps him from entering into that full fellowship for which he is destined. Compassion is able to give the sufferer genuine comfort, because it gives him the assurance that there is another person who is willing to share his burdens. In antiquity philosophers would advise the sufferer to seek in himself the power to master his pain, just as though by becoming insensitive to one's suffering its cause had been removed. Likewise, Buddhism teaches him to forget himself and this world, as though a merely mental reality were more real than that of experience. Neighbourliness will take one's privations most seriously. They are an indication that God is displeased with the present outlook and attitude of man. That is a harsh truth, of course, yet it becomes tolerable when the compassion of neighbourly love is experienced. Such compassion, which wants to help, differs basically from sentimental pity. Pity is an egotistic emotion. Through it an onlooker expresses his feeling that there is no hope of improvement for the suffering person, because the onlooker is unwilling to help and presumes that other people will share his outlook.

Are there any intrinsic limitations of neighbourly love? Are we really supposed to love the Hitlers, Attilas and Neros? Can you shoot at the enemy soldier and yet love him? What about the rapist, the murderer, the pimp? Can we love them in the same way as we love our parents, friends or co-religionists? Would that not encourage crime and seriously harm the law-abiding people? Such objection would be justified, if neighbourly love meant condoning crime. The legal system, as will be seen, has not been abrogated by Christ. It has its legitimate place in human society. But Christianity has also learned that the criminal, the outcast and the social outsider are no less in need of neighbourly concern than the 'good' people. The prison chaplaincy, for instance, is a service we owe to the prison inmates. Likewise, though not all criminals will be reformed, we have to confront them with the guilt of their deeds yet also with the possibility of divine pardon. Moreover, since he, too, is destined for membership in God's people, we have to offer to the ex-convict a real chance to begin a new life by encouraging him and giving him material support. Summarizing, we would say that we must never allow our social and political institutions to deprive us of our privilege and obligation to love our fellow men without discrimination. Outward circumstances may limit that privilege to intercessory prayer. Its subject matter would not be the request that God should prosper our enemies and oppressors in their wickedness or anti-social attitude, but rather that God should grant them an effective confrontation with his Gospel.

16 The Body Politic

A. The Purpose of Political Institutions

Of all the social institutions, none makes itself more constantly and oppressively felt than governmental order, and none else seems to be more indispensable. No wonder that all over the world it is held in a peculiar way to be related to God.

Lutheran theologians of the nineteenth century considered the social institutions, and in particular political order, as implied in the very creation of man (*Schöpfungsordnungen*, ordinances of Creation). That interpretation is helpful, provided only that it does not mean that the institutions came into existence immediately as the world, or man, originated. In a teleological understanding of man, it would mean that at a given moment of history the political order was necessarily bound to make its appearance, because from his very beginning man was endowed with the disposition and the organs for a rational order of life. The operation of a divine purpose then would be seen in the fact that social institutions were found all over the world, and that in spite of numerous attempts to abolish one or the other of them, they remained indestructibly in existence. In turn, attempts to explain those institutions as the result of incidental historical actions, for instance, a social contract (Rousseau) or usurpation of power by anti-social elements (Marx) are refuted by the impossibility to abrogate them. The fact that there was a pre-institutional epoch of history preceding the institutional age, is not proof that man is able to get along permanently without social institutions. Rather it proves the historical teleological character of mankind, which it took him a long time to attain and which distinguishes him from the animals.

The circumstances under which political bodies take their origin do not explain why there is government. Paradoxically, government and subjects are correlated. Thus one may find that governments exploit their subjects, yet never go to the point of exterminating them completely, for the well-being of the ruler depends on the good will and co-operation of the citizens. As a pattern of common life which comes into existence with an intrinsic necessity and which determines its own goal, the body politic may therefore be said to derive its function from God while it comes into historical existence as this or that state or nation through human efforts and planning. The divine factor lies in the institutional structure of political life which is everywhere the same, while the human factor is responsible for the diversity of governmental forms and policies.

In the Bible, the body politic is considered an organization in which divine authority has been delegated to the king. As a result, political power is able to serve constructive ends notwithstanding the egotism, injustice and lust for power of those in power and their people. Through the governments, the purpose which God has with mankind is directed, enforced and in part executed. While that representation is symbolized in the person of the king of Israel, all governments of the world participate more or less directly in it. Speaking of political life, Jesus lays special stress on four points: (1) In this world, political government is necessary and its legitimacy is to be acknowledged by all men. (2) In a world of sin and evils, political government has been assigned the task of curbing human anarchy, and thereby it promotes the common good of the citizens. The rulers are therefore to be obeyed and served. (3) Political organizations have a temporary function in the history of mankind. Eventually, their delegated power will be replaced by the direct exercise of God's rule in the 'coming' of his Kingdom. All people will then be willing to act in agreement with the impulses received from the Spirit. (4) The goal of that development will be the reign of the Son of Man, that is to say, an epoch in which mankind has reached complete selfhood as God's servant. This means that Jesus sees political life as taking place within an eschatological process whose teleological dynamic is the result of God's redemptive purpose. With such views Christianity rejects a naïve optimism, according to which the human desire for improved living conditions will eventually and probably soon be fulfilled, because human planning and technology will overcome the injustice and the egotism inherent in the body politic. Yet neither does the Church share the pessimistic views entertained by Lord Acton or Jakob Burckhardt, who denied that the state had any value because political power was an instrument of moral corruption. Since God himself inaugurated the eschatological process, positive achievements are to be expected from the body politic participating in it. Yet Karl Marx entertained a fallacious hope when he expected that with the proletarian revolution the foundation would be laid for a social order that would dispense with the coercive power of the state. Human efforts alone will not be able to prevail against stupidity, crime, corruption, greed and lust for power. Secular eschatology, as proclaimed, for instance, by Ernst Bloch, is a massive self-delusion.

Following St. Augustine, Christian theology has usually taken a rather gloomy view of political power, until the Enlightenment and idealism brought about a shift into the opposite direction. Both attitudes are unsatisfactory, however. The older one neglects the positive element in the body politic, namely, the promotion of justice and the common good. The recent view, in turn, overlooks the dangers inherent in politics, especially the unscrupulous pursuit of power, the suppression of freedom, economic exploitation and unreasonable warfare. Yet Hobbes' *Leviathan* no less than Hegel's rational dialectic are one-sided exaggerations. The body politic is neither Anti-Christ nor the supreme good of mankind. Its function is a provisional one while it serves God's purpose; it is not redemptive. Through the agency of government, God shields mankind against its self-destructive tendencies.

B. Government

1. *The Form of Government*

Students of history have always liked to look back to those outstanding rulers of the past whose reign seemed to be the Golden Age. Yet the provisional role assigned to political life forbids us to identify any exercise or form of government with the ideal order. In Greek philosophy, especially that of Plato, it was held that the well-being of the body politic depended on the right form of government and consequently on the right distribution of power. That principle has prevailed in political theory right down to our time, where the conflict between dictatorship and democracy seems to be the principal issue of constitutional theory. The Biblical writers, however, never shared that belief. To them, divine calling evidenced by spiritual power and justice was the criterion of the true ruler.

A radical change of political thought occured in the eighteenth century, when the Enlightenment taught the equality of all men. Thereby the *volonté générale*, or democratic government by public acclaim, and thus through, or on behalf of, the people, would seem to be the only reasonable form of government. With the exception of small groups, there seems to be consensus among Christians today to the effect that the form of government is at the best a secondary issue. What really matters is a government's concern for justice and the common good. Likewise, the freedom of the church does not depend on a special form of government. Democracies, like the USA and France, have outlawed any connection between religion and political life, while in some of the modern dictatorships, the Church enjoys complete freedom.

2. The Nature of Government

The Body Politic is an institution which is based upon the correlation of ruling power, on the one hand, and the allegiance and co-operation of the citizens on the other. Both of them pursue the common good of the nation on the basis, and for the realization, of justice occupied within the body politic. As an articulated collectivity the body politic offers the possibility and opportunity of performing many tasks which individuals are unable to accomplish. Such definition would apply to other institutions, too. The specific feature of the body politic lies in the fact that power is used for the pursuit of justice and the common good. From a purely pragmatic viewpoint, the principal characteristic of government is its sovereign power. For without it, it would not be in a position to perform its basic functions of justice, order and national responsibility. Yet in the teleological perspective those functions are paramount, because apart from them the exercise of power would degenerate into oppression or robbery. For ethical purposes, it matters less to inquire from which factor we should start than that the correlation of power and functions were kept in mind. The ancient Hebrews learned their political theory from the way God was dealing with them as his chosen people. Jesus enlarged that outlook by drawing his followers' attention to the manner in which God was exercising his sovereignty over the whole of mankind.

a. POWER

Right down to the present day political power is considered a divine gift. Opinions differ, however, as to the seat which power occupies within the body politic. Was it given to the rulers alone, so that their subjects had passively to accept their reign? Or was that power granted to the whole nation so that the government would represent the nation in its totality? The Christian view too considers political power a divine gift. God has established a correlation between his people and himself by which he is established as their sovereign Lord, while his subjects are endowed with the ability to serve him. The Covenant which God had made with the chosen people is the archetype of political organization and the symbol of the body politic. Just as God is in the first place concerned with the establishment of justice in his people, so each political commonwealth is to be ruled in justice. For that purpose the government has the right to levy taxes, to require support in warfare, to enforce compliance with the laws, to establish order and to foster the common interest of its members. In order to work in that direction, a nation must be free and sovereign and have a territory of its own, because thus alone is it able as a collectivity to co-operate with God as its partner. In turn, however, sovereignty and freedom are not ends in themselves. Nations exist as patterns of collective life, because through them God's redemptive work is to be fostered. For that end they have their laws. The Old Testament emphasizes the divine origin of Israel's legislation in order to indicate that nations are under God's moral order and judgement.

The divine origin of the political institution implies that the government has a right to enforce the co-operation of the citizens in its endeavour to act as God's representative. Yet power and authority ought to be sought in the nation rather than in the government or the ruling group. The theocentric view of political power as held by the Church was radically challenged when in the eighteenth century the idea of democracy was advocated as the necessary consequence of 'natural law'. Political power, it was held, is seated in the nature and reason of individual men. Political action had to be performed by the total population or in its name. The element of power in political life was accordingly to be the power of reason; and force was to be employed in the hypothetically rare cases when an appeal to reason proved to be insufficient to bring about compliance with the existing law.

The Bible treats the power of enforcement as an integral element of the body politic as constituted by God, for instance by decreeing capital punishment as the penalty of a number of crimes. The divine origin of that power is seen in its wholesome effects. In the course of the centuries the repressive power of the government has bridled the anarchic and brutal instincts and destructive urges in man. That would not have been the case, however, if political power were merely a manifestation of brutal force. Its effectiveness lies in two facts: it is used for the maintenance and restoration of justice; and it operates constructively for the realization of the common good. That such ends should be aspired for constitutes the basic paradox of political life. The body politic, both in its rulers and members, forms an association of sinful men. The rulers cannot therefore be expected to use their power in a blameless way. Yet the use of their power is tolerable only when they acknowledge that, as a divine gift, it is to be employed for God's sake. The idea of the absolute power of the monarch, for instance, which resulted from a misunderstanding of the Reformation doctrine of the two kingdoms of God, had to make room for a constitutional government. That change implied that the power granted to the ruler had to be used for the benefit of the nation, too. Likewise, the purpose of democracy must not be interpreted as weakening of governmental power. Those in power must have the right to use their power to the fullest, yet it must be done in the exercise of their office. Democratic supervision misunderstands its function when it tries to control the government rather than advising it. Governments misuse their power also when they aim at world dominion or total victory, that is to say, power over areas which are God's prerogative. Such desires entail their immediate judgement. The result is blurred judgement and choice of unreasonable means. Though it is an exaggeration to say that power as such has a corrupting effect, it is certain that the craving for unlimited power has such results, hence it cannot be said that in political life we are confronted by the alternative of power politics, on the one hand, and the self-realization of goodness, on the other, as was held by Anabaptists and Quakers, and more recently by Tolstoy. While the political ends are not the ultimate goal which God has designed for mankind, they are destined by him to be indispensable means for the preparation of God's final goal.

In the political thought of the eighteenth century, the intrinsic limitation of political power was expressed through the idea of inalienable human rights. Their advocates held that those who combat the state as the embodiment of power, overlook not only the protection given to them by the body politic, but also the furtherance they receive from the government's concern for the common good in establishing and maintaining civil order. To disregard them would make a ruler unworthy of his office. Yet the very fact that in different times and in different countries various rights were proclaimed as inalienable ones should be taken as an indication that they, those basic rights, are not grounded in 'natural law' or the existence of man. It is true that any system of laws must be rooted in a few basic principles or rights, by which limits are set to all the laws passed or to be enacted. The choice of such principles depends on historical circumstances and is not the same in all nations. That is the reason why the UN Declaration of Human Rights is given various interpretations, and why some countries are wary to adopt it.

b. JUSTICE

The noblest, yet the most delicate, function of governments is the actualization of justice. This has to be done for people who by nature are unruly and prone to do what they like, and it is to be done in a world, whose goods and bounties are in no direct way designated for specific individuals or groups of people. Nor is there any unambiguous criterion by which justice could be measured. The ancient principle *Suum cuique* (Let everybody have as much as is due to him) presupposes a material principle, in order to ascertain how much and what is due to everybody. No such material principle of universal applicability exists, however. Thus, it is the responsibility of the government in the given circumstances to decide what the right relationship of its obligation or contribution on the one hand, and the rights and privileges of the law-abiding citizens or the punishment of the lawbreaker on the other, shall be. This will be done by enacting laws and establishing judicatories as well as by a system of governmental services.

The difficulty in making justice prevail in the juridical sphere and the administration lies not only in the solid and thorough sense of justice and the measure of wisdom required, but also in the ever shifting dynamic of the power structure of the body politic. Those in power will want to arrange a political order which will in the first place safeguard their own power and interests. In turn, since those not in power will strive to come to power, governments and majority parties will join forces to curb the legal rights and civil privileges of the opposition.

The purpose of the penal law is the protection of the social and economic order and its members against those who endanger it. The main purpose of legal punishment is to express a nation's strong disapproval of a violation of rights which the ruling group or class regards as vital for its well-being. Other functions of the law, for instance deferment, education or prevention of recurrence, are subordinate to the basic purpose. While the kind of penalty and its severity may differ considerably between capitalistic and communistic countries, for instance, they have inevitably this in common, that they serve not only the common good but also class interests. In this context, capital punishment occupies a conspicuous place, because it has an irrevocable and irremediable effect. Envisaged in the light of moral condemnation of crime, capital punishment points to the fact that a nation considers certain crimes, for instance unprovoked and premeditated murder, an especially severe breach of its social texture as well as the sanctity of the law. Of course, penal laws by themselves are no deterrents of crime.

Their effectiveness depends on the social esteem in which they are held. Crime that remains unpunished, or whose severity is minimized invites repetition. Hence the further existence of the perpetrator can no longer be tolerated. His deed shakes the very foundation of the body politic. It seems that, by advocating the abrogation of the death penalty, people are more interested in the well-being of the criminal than in the wrong done to his victim and the social order of the nation.

It would be Utopian to look all over the world for the same system of legislation or taxation. There is no harm in such diversity. It simply shows that God's redemptive purpose is carried out through all kinds of different people. That is a comforting fact, for it implies that the judgements of the human codes are no ultimate verdicts. All of them will be revised eventually in God's final judgement. Nevertheless, it is by means of the positive law that the political order serves the plans of God. By enacting laws a nation pledges itself to stay in the service of the goal which God has set forth for mankind. Though laws may be very primitive or partial or unnecessarily harsh, they are to be preferred to anarchy and lawlessness. Law is the general way in which weak and sinful men give expression to their awareness of a cosmic order or a divine will that rules the world. The intrinsic discrepancy of God and man is the explanation why all human laws and their enforcement are bound to be compromises. Yet it is also true that in the use of the law, human and divine will are united. Hence laws are symptoms of an attitude by which people recognize an absolute order.

The sanctity of the law lies in the general intention for which it is given, namely, to tie the nation's existence to the cosmic order. Its sanctity will not be destroyed or lost when people enact an unjust or foolish law nor by the fact that inconsiderate or vicious people pass false judgement. Yet a purely formalistic law like Roman Law, for instance, is apt to discredit the sanctity of the law because it is more interested in goods than in people. Likewise, on account of the moral limitations of the people concerned, the judge must have discretionary power to apply the law to the situation and the condition of the defendant.

Much of the work of the government is determined by precedent, tradition and routine. Yet, from time to time, a country is confronted with problems which concern its very existence: for instance, an economic crisis, a constitutional dispute, or the possibility of war. Such problems require ethical decisions which by the nature of the case cannot be based on a plebiscite. The decision has to be left to the government. It is not by chance that in Biblical parlance both God and the

Messiah are called King. The constitutional history of Israel shows that it is not so much a question of title or form of government that is emphasized by that designation. Rather, it is the necessity to place the ultimate ethical decision for the future of a nation into the hands of responsible persons and ultimately those of the King, the President or the Prime Minister. In such a situation the head of the government may seek other expert advice. But the ultimate decision is an ethical one which he has to take personally and for which he alone has to give account. The greatness and the difficulty of his office lies in the circumstance that in the absence of a written law he has to decide what in a given situation is demanded by justice and the common good of his and other nations.

c. COLLECTIVE INTEREST

Sagacious analysts of political life such as Macchiavelli, Hobbes or Nietzsche reached the conclusion that it is a struggle for power conducted by individuals. In fact, however, political life is considerably more preoccupied with the intrinsic dynamics of the body politic as a collectivity than with the pursuit of personal interests. That must be so because the ruler who neglects the well-being of the nation undermines his own position and risks the loss of his office. The body politic is formed by the interrelation between the government and the nation plus country. It must be a very shortsighted ruler who is not aware of the fact that the success of his reign depends on the territorial integrity of his country and its prosperity. No nation can exist without a territory of its own, for it is the living space of the nation. It furnishes the possibility of growing food, of mining raw materials, and of engaging in economic exchange. Likewise, it is the nation that through its work is able to raise the taxes by which the ruler is enabled to act politically.

The primary concern of a government cannot be with individual citizens as such, but rather with the country as a whole and thus with national institutions and agencies. For instance, the government has to take care of the establishment of an educational organization covering the whole country, while it must not necessarily hire all teachers or assume direct responsibility for the teaching of all the young people. Likewise the government must decide in what manner oil deposits or minerals are to be mined and traded. But the actual drilling of oil wells and the financing of mining corporations may be left to individuals. In turn, however, the citizen's loyalty implies his willingness to work for the common good of his country not only by way of the ballot and correspondence with his representative, but also by keeping the laws and paying his taxes, and by refraining from using his privileges to the detriment of others.

The principle of Concern for the Collective Interests may be implemented and executed in various ways, depending on political ideas, historical traditions, available resources or social and international conditions. Except for the realization of justice, the common interest may widely differ in scope. In some countries education and cultural affairs are regarded as the national government's responsibility. Under communism, economic life is also included. In other nations the task of government is confined to jurisdiction. Likewise there is no agreement as to the share which the government and the people respectively should assume in national life. The liberal political school, for instance, believes that the natural goodness of man, if only left unhampered, will eventually bring about an ideal order of things. It would therefore limit government interference to a minimum. Others, on the contrary, feel that the life of the nation is terribly beset by greed, lust for power, corruptibility and stupidity. In the interest of the nation it is held by them to be necessary to contain private activities and to run most of social, economic and cultural life by a wise and honest leadership (Mao). Communism shares that distrust yet sees its root in capitalistic privileges rather than in human nature. We must be content with the general readiness of the politician not to be entirely forgetful of the common good. According to historical circumstances, one or another political principle will prove to be most useful. There may be situations in which the nation would disintegrate if it were not held together by the firm and energetic will of the government. In other situations when political apathy of the nation threatens its position in international life, a liberation and liberalization of political life, and a shift of responsibility may offer a new lease on life to a stagnant nation.

In general, there is no concept or form of government that would be specifically Christian. The purely formal characteristics of sovereignty, concern for justice, and for the common good are recognized by Christians and non-Christians alike. Though specifically Christian aims may be realized in a nation, the idea of a 'Christian state' is Utopian, for those in power will invariably implement those aims in terms of expediency and personal interest. The influence which Christians exercise in political life, as in the social institutions, is not the result of organizational measures. Christianity works because it takes place within the eschatological process. While it is in men's power to change the actual structure of a political order, they are unable to give permanency to any form or structure of government. Yet God's judgement will see to it that the excesses of political life will eventually be curbed. Christians are therefore more interested in good government than in the results of power politics. It is naïve to believe that the ideologies of today's big powers will remain permanently the main issue of international politics. For those images of the global role of the big powers lack a metaphysical basis. They are but mirrorings of wishful thinking. We do not know what this world will be like in A.D. 2200, but it is certain that it will be quite different from now.

C. Christians in Political Life

1. *Active Participation*

What then is the Christian to do in view of the ubiquitous and powerful role which egotism and disregard of God's will play in political life? By the example of his life, Jesus has shown that the answer cannot consist in complete withdrawal from political life. Wherever that way was chosen, as in monasticism, for instance, it was regarded by Christianity as an exceptional practice. Monastic life was to serve as a reminder to the Church that it was in danger of such an involvement in the affairs of secular life that the divine goal of history would be lost sight of. Though Protestantism rejected monasticism, it could not overlook the dilemma. In its midst, groups such as the Anabaptists, Mennonites, Quakers and Jehovah's Witnesses renewed that warning and kept the protest alive. As a result, Protestantism has learned to take a dialectical attitude towards political life. Political power is obviously the most efficient means of securing the supplies which are essential for the common good. Church leaders have therefore frequently striven for political influence and put themselves at the disposal of the rulers.

Participation in political life cannot be regarded as unethical by itself. Political life is man's prerogative. Animals may associate and act as groups. But they have no laws and are unable to make decisions. Thus, political life offers to human beings an unique opportunity for taking part in the realization of God's redemptive purpose. This is especially true of the constructive, educative and protective functions of the body politic. As can be seen in the work of the prophets and of Jesus and the apostles, the body politic creates the conditions in which the saving work of God can and will be carried out effectively. The power of the government prevents the enemies of the Gospel from thwarting the work of faith. For that reason, Christianity has stressed its conviction that Christians are under obligation to be loyal citizens, notwithstanding the fact that those in power are fallible human beings and far from being sinless. Christian allegiance is more than political conformism. It implies the willingness to respect the laws as intended by the lawgiver rather than looking for loopholes fit to serve one's own interests. Christians are also understood to be people who practise the 'better' righteousness. They heed spontaneously the common good, unlike those who regard the laws of the country as an intolerable imposition.

2. *The Christian Reservation*

Christians are not only aware of the shortcomings and the sinfulness of those engaged in political activities; they know that politicians may be tempted to condone crime and vice when it serves their interests. Christians also realize that the highest goods obtainable through politics, viz. justice and the common weal of the nation, can never be the supreme good of human life. Though Christian life takes place within the framework of the nation, it aims at the remission of sin and the life of the Spirit. Those goods cannot be attained by means of politics. Thus Christians will participate in the life of the nation, yet in a detached way. They will consider it their privilege to decide how far they will support a political system or action. Such an attitude entails at times considerable difficulties. It demands of the Christian to be the critic and judge of his own party or government, or even to engage in opposition to them. Yet while he is in disagreement with certain measures taken by them, he does not want to stand completely outside. We may feel unable, for instance, to support an act of legislation, or a war which our government wages against another country. But we do not give up allegiance to our country. Since we have to live in a sinful world and are aware of our own sins, it is impossible for the Christian to disentangle himself from the perplexing conditions in which he lives. While his faith enables him to visualize a world completely under Christ's control, it is not by his own actions, but rather by Christ himself that such an order of things will be brought about.

Nevertheless, those are grossly mistaken who pretend that in actual life there is no difference between Christian and non-Christian activties. Their ethical outlook points into opposite directions. The Christian detachment prevents the Church, for instance, from identifying itself with the body politic, even when the Church is part of the establishment. Furthermore, teaching witness and political criticism on the part of the Church set the Christian life conspicuously and effectively apart from the secular attitude. Since political life is a practical activity, governments will hardly be impressed by the presentation of political theories, even though they are backed by church assemblies. The only way in which the Christian attitude may assert itself in cases of disagreement is by means of public protest and, if necessary, by means of non-cooperation. In most instances, such protest will be more effective when it becomes articulate as a movement. Inasmuch as many politicians and businessmen in the Western world are members of the Church, they are not to be blamed for engaging in expedient activities. What may render them reprehensible is failure to recognize the conflict of motives in which they may find themselves. For it is by blurring the issues that they are rendered unfit for the Christian goal. Where Christians realize their inner conflicts, they form, notwithstanding their shortcomings, a kind of third column above the conflicting secular forces. By the presence of such clear-eyed and frank witnesses the body politic is prevented from losing entirely sight of its humanizing function. In turn, even though not many Christians may assume such an active role in public life, their orientation directs the nation beyond an affirmation or defence of the *status quo*. Yet their interest does not lie in gaining a position of power, nor is its goal mere progress; rather it strives for a higher level of human existence.

Against this interpretation of the Christian attitude towards politics, it has been objected that the coercive power of the government is incompatible with neighbourly love. Yet while in outward appearance there may be little difference in this use of force between a police action taken against rioters and a hold-up, their goals are completely at variance. The government employs its repressive power in the interest of the law and in the pursuit of justice and order. Since, in that respect, governments are in the service of God's redemptive plan, Christians pray for those in power. We do not ask God that he should make them prosper in their pursuit of ends on which we may disagree, but rather that he should keep them willing to fulfil their providential task honestly. God should make all of them, our government no less than the foreign ones, instruments of his justice and peace.

Christianity will interpret its task in political life in a twofold way. It will recognize the privileged position which governments hold in God's world. Government is able to lift man above animal existence so that reason is capable of reigning in him. Yet Christians also notice the precarious foundation on which governmental authority rests. God has entrusted the office of judge, and thus the power of life and death, to beings who are not only subject to misunderstanding and error, but may also be inclined to disregard God's will. Thereby they will lose sight of the very goal for which government was instituted. Seeing the instability of all kinds of government, Christians may strengthen the political structure by seeking political office or participating actively in the work of political parties. While, like the rest of the citizens, Christians will agree or disagree on special programmes, legislation or administrative measures, they will insist on responsible action and will make clear that theirs is responsibility to God. Thereby the body politic is made aware of the direction in which it is to move. Conversely, however, Christians will refuse to comply with laws and governmental orders when compliance would imply a betrayal of what Christianity considers the ultimate goal of the body politic. That is not a subversive attitude; Christians are prepared to accept the authority of the government in its quest of justice and order. They will therefore submit to the penalty for their 'disobedience'. In the case of conscientious objection to military service they will be ready to perform non-military work that is beneficial to the nation. They will refuse, however, to admit that their attitude, which is based upon the will of God, is morally wrong.

D. Burning Issues

1. *Revolution*

Of issues which vex modern Christianity's attitude towards political life, we single out three which are of a particularly perplexing character, namely revolution, warfare and internationalism. By 'revolution' we understand the violent removal of a government in order to terminate a régime of intolerable injustice, under which a substantial section of the nation suffers. Whereas the political law provides standards of justice for individuals and particularly groups within the nation, there is no law that states what justice should be like in the intrinsic dynamic of the nation. Thus the only way by which a substantial section of the nation may try to get redress for unjust suffering is by way of a violent uprising.

What justifies a revolution and distinguishes it from a *coup d'état* or *Putsch* is their motivation. The instigators of a *coup d'état* want mainly to occupy the seats of political power. The revolutionary conspirators intend to bring about a radical improvement of political and/or social conditions because they deem the existing order and government to incorporate intolerable injustice. In ecumenical circles, there has been recently talk about a 'Christian revolution'. It seems, however, that the advocates of the 'Christian revolution' use ambiguous language. For the Western world, the term would designate a radical rethinking, reorganizing and reorientating of traditional Christianity. Applied to the world outside NATO, however, the 'Christian revolution' is meant to be a political revolution. A subtle distinction is introduced, however, between political revolutions that are man-made and therefore reprehensible, whereas others were made by God. The latter ones would make it a moral obligation for Christians to participate actively in them. Yet, what criterion is there upon which such a distinction could be based? One is afraid, lest underlying such a distinction, one would find ultimately purely subjective approval of a revolutionary movement.

The genuinely moral issue lies in a different sphere. It is God himself who provides the political institution as a necessary means of humanization. He does so notwithstanding the fact that the body politic has a power structure. Revolutions, like wars, are instances of extreme use of political power. God accepts them as means for the execution of his plans, provided that those engaged therein intend to further thereby justice and the common good as they understand them. The right to stage a revolution is rooted in man's divinely granted privilege to bring about and foster justice in this world. Its necessity is to be found in the operation of the powers of evil by whom established justice is at times perverted into injustice.

From the Christian viewpoint, one thing is certain. Christians may not ignore the challenge of those who lay bare the injustice of our age. A mere defence of the *status quo* would be evidence of callousness. But there is no Christian revolution. There is only a Christian revolutionary dilemma. Christians may join a revolutionary movement, yet are under no moral obligation so to do. Of course, a revolution is the quickest and most comprehensive way to tackle social evils. But there is no revolution which does not inflict great harm to those previously in power and to their supporters but also to many innocent people. That result is a doubly tragic one because no revolution will ever bring about permanent improvements. Valuable as is the humanization which can be brought about by means of political action, there is one fact that may not be overlooked. The accumulation of power has always undesirable consequences in the lives of those in power as well as of their subjects. As an alternative, Christians have sought the remedy of social injustice in works of charity, patience and trust in the gradual victory of God's redemptive work. Yet they face a painful alternative. The changes brought about by the eschatological process appear only slowly, and the amount of relief that Christian charity offers is extremely limited. There is some comfort, of course, in the thought that the fruits of neighbourliness are permanent ones while revolutionary changes succumb to conservative tendencies which may breed new kinds of injustice. Nevertheless, we cannot deny the fact that, in spite of peaceful methods, such suffering and need goes uncared for. Thus no matter which alternative Christians select, they will always have reason for regretting their inability to create a perfect new order in this age. In turn, Christians have no right to disavow a government brought to power by a revolution. In Eastern Europe Christians, with few exceptions, refused to identify themselves with Communism. But they had to realize that behind the revolution there was a real desire to bring greater social justice and brighter living conditions to the lower classes than those which were granted under the capitalistic system.

2. *War*

The body politic has the power to press people into military service and thus to force them, when the occasion comes, to kill those whom the government considers the enemies of the nation. Yet ever since the days of the early Church, Christians have wondered whether so to do was compatible with God's redemptive will. Certainly waging war is the quickest and simplest way to settle an international conflict, at least temporarily. But it is also true to say that wars never really solve a problem. On the contrary, they breed new wars. War is inevitable in a mankind which has not yet overcome the power of sin. God's disapproval of mankind's sin is manifest in his unwillingness to deliver mankind from the recurrence of wars. The fact that most people hate war in no way prevents the actual outbreak of military conflicts. Yet the possibility to wage war lures the mighty nations into self-destruction as can be learned from the history of all the military empires. This self-destruction is an historical device by means of which God prevents the big nations from completely destroying this world wantonly, and from suppressing the diversity of nationalities. The twofold function which war serves in God's plans is not to be understood as a Hegelian dialectic, in which out of an antithetical relationship a new and higher good is brought into existence. War rather serves to show that, as Lord of history, God is not only the giver of good gifts, but also its judge. God makes clear to us that no issue is permanently settled through the use of power, and wars, far from being able to end all wars, are the seedbed

243

of new disagreements and conflicts. Furthermore, wars are fought in the hope that, through victory, a nation might be able to reap greater advantages from another group than would be possible by peaceful means. Yet that hope is fallacious. While from a purely economic viewpoint it may happen that the booty gained is higher than the financial cost of a campaign, history shows that the loot is quickly squandered, to say nothing of the irreplaceable loss of lives, the horrors inflicted upon the civilian population and the dreadful demoralization resulting from the suspension of social controls. Christians and non-Christians are agreed in our days that there is no reason for the glorification of war. Yet as one should expect, all the attempts to limit or prevent wars by political measures, such as the Geneva Convention or the United Nations, prove to be ineffectual because they leave the power basis of the countries concerned untouched. Likewise, political pacifism, that is to say, the effort to withhold nations from warfare by means of persuasion or non-aggression pacts, proves to be futile. Though in our days people are fully aware of the horrors and folly of war, for many even more attractive and desirable is still the satisfaction that politicians and soldiers derive from the exhibition of valour, the lure of adventure, the brilliance of national honour and the possibility to subdue the enemy and make him feel his inferiority. There is no bridge of understanding from the hawks to the doves, since either of them is appealing to political and psychological facts, yet neither fact has absolute character. Are there moral reasons which could outweigh the psychological arguments?

Jesus did not leave a special word dealing with warfare. But he understood the commandment 'Thou shalt not kill' from God's regard for human life and fellowship, whereas in the Old Testament it was an ordinance of the civil code. Why is it that a human being should menace at all his fellow man's life? Jesus saw clearly that the root of war, as of murder, lies in the individual's heart. The individual overrates his own significance and exaggerates the wrong done to him. Hence he is unwilling to forgive and to be forgiven. This undue self-esteem poisons even the most intimate relations within the family. Nevertheless, we try to repress our desire to avenge ourselves within the family, yet, except we overcome it, that repression will create a mentality of hatefulness which from time to time erupts as political controversy, social unrest, racial conflicts and even as war. Christians contribute to the purification of the national and international atmosphere by means of 'meekness'. They consider their relationship to others as a precious divine gift and show their gratitude by means of services rendered to them. Christianity rejects war like all discord, because men are made to live with and for each other. Realizing that quarrels and conflicts may have their roots in both disputants, they are prepared to ask the other party for forgiveness and to pardon them in turn. Christians stand in the midst of the eschatological process rather than at the end. They have no promise of establishing universal peace. Yet by trying not to be embittered by the wrong they suffer, they are preparing this world for acceptance of reconciliation. This may seem to be a long road towards international peace, yet it is the only effective one. By living peacefully with others and by working for mutual understanding both in their neighbourhood and in their nation, Christians can do a lot in order to reduce the incidence of war. In our days conscientious objection to military service is considered by young men of draft age as a repellent to war because it is a conspicuous protest. For making such protest articulate, conscientious objectors deserve the full support of the churches. But it is a mere act of witness, not a political action. Therein lies also its weakness. It is a protest, reminding the nation that war ought not to be treated as a matter of course. Yet the C.O.s protest lacks the constructive energy by which the war-making tendency is overcome. But conscientious objection is obviously the very limit to which the Christian attitude towards war is able to go. As such, it is superior to other forms of anti-bellicism. Objecting to the use of certain weapons, for instance nuclear weapons or Napalm, as means of warfare, makes little sense. The deadly effect of massed non-nuclear or conventional weapons will probably demand as many victims and devastate a country as thoroughly as A-bombs. Similarly, nothing is gained by the distinction of just and unjust wars. Even if there were wars in which one party had a clean record, while the other one were all wicked, the ordinary citizen would lack the evidence by which to settle the issue. As in the case of revolution, the Christian must bear the burden of an insoluble moral dilemma. For that reason, his protest will be credible and effective only when it is coupled with work for reconciliation and co-operation for God's goal.

3. *International Relations*
It is of the nature of political bodies to aim at independence. In the exercise of their power they aspire for sovereignty, and hence for economic self-sufficiency or autarchy. But peaceful expansion is impossible, since political frontiers have become stationary. In turn, the rapid increase of population and the enormous progress of modern civilization

have rendered economic exchange and political co-operation necessary. Isolationism has become a practical impossibility. The result is a growing tension between national self-assertion and global interrelations. What are Christians to do in such a situation? In the history of Christianity, the churches have until recently been co-extensive with the various nations, and thus have often been the champions of blazing nationalism. Yet no matter what other ends the earth may serve in God's plan, one thing is certain – this world in which we live is made for the benefit of mankind. From its understanding of Creation, Christianity takes seriously the unity of the human race, notwithstanding the fact that it is diversified into numerous races and nations. There is a marvellous correlation of mankind and the earth. The latter is wide enough to provide living space, food, and ample resources for technical production. Even more amazing is the fact that a common pattern of cultural development is found all over the earth, and that there has been from the beginning a tense exchange of economic goods, techniques and ideas. Yet considerable are also the differences of nationality and of living opportunity on the surface of this globe. No wonder that people of one country often look in envy upon the conditions of other nations and try to get a share of their territory and its population. Thus one discerns in mankind a strange co-existence of cohesive and divisive tendencies. It is obvious that harmonious relationships would be in the general interest. But in the confusing diversity of living conditions, where do we discern the criteria of justice and common interest?

The historical principle, for instance, is artificial. Why should a nation be entitled to reoccupy a territory today, though its ancestors had not lived there perhaps for a millennium or more? Can the fact be completely ignored that nations and countries undergo changes, often momentous ones, in the course of history?

Equally unrealistic would be a partition of the habitable earth on a purely statistical basis, whereby equal territory would be distributed. Fertility, climate, geographical accessibility, mineral deposits would be additional factors to be taken into consideration. Yet their true nature would become manifest through use and research only. It would be necessary to redistribute the land periodically with consequences more disturbing even than the shifts of territory resulting at present from warfare and peace treaties. Not much hope can be set on the federative principle, either. Theoretically a federation of all nations on the basis of the *status quo*, yet with the possibility of regular periodical revision, would seem to be an ideal solution. But in practice it would endow a world government with a neutral army large and powerful enough to quell rebellions and to enforce the changes decreed by it. Yet, in that case, world government would be at the mercy of the generals.

What is Christianity able to do in such a situation? Its basic task will be to manifest the unity which mankind has in Christ. That task is rendered especially arduous by the fact that Christians, too, must be citizens of a country, and that their country makes high claims on their loyalty. Thus, they find it hard to believe that God originated the diversity of nations in order that they should live with and for each other. In the secular sphere itself, love of one's country has been replaced by nationalism, accentuating the fragmentation of the modern world.

It is not by chance that the ecumenical movement and the World Council of Churches should have come into being at a time when the secular bonds of international life began to disintegrate. Thereby Christianity expresses its conviction that the unity of our world cannot rest upon the mere desirability of international co-operation. Rather it is the redemptive will of Christ by which the centrifugal tendencies of modern mankind are prevented from atomizing the race.

The historical significance of the World Council does not so much lie in what it does – for practically all its activities are paralleled by other secular organizations – but rather in its motivation. The WCC reminds the whole world of the fact that the only power that is able to re-unite mankind is the power of a divine saviour. His work is not confined to denominations and churches. There is a kind of subterranean Christianity, too. The social aims of Communism and other secular organizations have been borrowed from Christ and bear witness to his healing power. Even the new 'secular religions' are but an imitation of Christianity, notwithstanding that they deny his power and even his existence. Thus the ecumenical movement is a challenge both to the affiliated churches and denominations, as also to the secular world. Practically useful as the merger of denominations and other organizational activities may be, they are of secondary significance. What really matters is the fact that the WCC symbolizes the exclusive lordship of Christ and the inability of secular forces to remedy this world. The ecumenical movement discloses the fact that modern Christianity is aware of Christ's presence as he works redemptively in this world. That implies a spiritual understanding of unity in diversity, and diversity in unity over against uniformity. Through the WCC the example of that unity is set before the nations and countries of the world. It is the only basis on which the inequality of historical conditions can be transformed into fruitful co-operation. The WCC is not the millennium, on the contrary. Without fervent prayer for Christ's ongoing work of illumination and encouragement, it might easily become saltless. But its presence is a sign given to this world that the unity of nations is possible and not a mere dream.

17 Economic Life

A. Significance

Like political activity, economic life is a characteristic feature of human life which has no parallels in animals. If man wants to assert himself over against nature instead of simply adjusting himself to its indifference and hardships, if he wants to live a life by which the effort of living is rewarded, he has no choice left. He must engage in economic activities. Compared with animal life, man's relation to nature is an unfavourable one. While like animals man needs food, shelter and security, they are not directly available to him. Physically, man is not too well equipped for the satisfaction of his needs. Economic activity is the way in which man uses his mental abilities and specific skills as powerful means to create goods which nature denies to him. Economic life is a social institution. It exists independent of individual wishes as a necessity rooted in the relationship in which mankind in general stands to nature. By means of economic activities man is able to create for himself a new dimension of reality in the cosmos and to become the lord of nature. Unlike the bounties of nature, whose quantity and quality primitive man has to accept as nature provides them, economic goods may not only be increased in volume without limit, but are also capable of qualitative improvement. Thus they are an important source of happiness. Their production and distribution have, therefore, a mighty influence upon the way people live their lives, and so does their lack or loss.

For the Christian, this view of economic life must be related to man's destination. The modern tendency to consider the value and meaning of economic life in the constant growth of the GNP (Gross National Product) is dangerously wrong. It fails to take into consideration the consequences which such increase has on the lives of the people concerned. Rightly have sociologists pointed out that the mere augmentation of production has a high price and that it does not automatically further the wellbeing of producer and receiver. The introduction of new goods creates new problems, too. Enlarging a road system, for instance, poses serious problems of maintenance, safety, finances and health.

Above all, economy is not an end in itself. Its purpose is to make the abundance of useful goods so available to mankind that the whole race will be benefited thereby and fostered on its way to its final destination. Not everything that has been produced, or may be produced, will serve the best natural interest of man, let alone his spiritual development. Thus man has to learn through the economic process, which activities and their products are worthwhile, and which ones are harmful to the human race in its totality as well as to the individuals directly thereby affected. Since the effective manufacture and distribution of economic goods requires collective activity, economic life impresses its mark visibly on the social structure groups too. Hence the discussion of economic ethics cannot be confined to the economic process in the purely technical sense. It must constantly deal with its effects, too. Above all, we must keep in mind that the creativity displayed in economic life is, and is not, to be regarded as man's natural equipment. It is so inasmuch as it is found in all healthy humans; it is not so inasmuch as it is not found in the pre-human organic world and cannot be explained as man's own creation.

Economic life is a complex process. Merely manufacturing things or engaging in activities are not sufficient for economic life. A number of other factors are required. Most important among them are the availability of raw material, permanent settlements, legal order, a generally recognized system of economic equivalences, and a market. From the fact that in each phase of economic life people are engaged, numerous ethical problems are implied in the economic process. That there should be such ethical problems is evidence of the Spirit, who works in that specific way in man. Therein lies the supreme dignity of economic life.

While single individuals are able to manufacture goods for their own use, their work has no economic significance, unless and until they join a community in which they trade. Even so, however, their economic activities rest on a precarious foundation, except when such community is co-extensive with an established political commonwealth. The latter guarantees the peace by which the economic transactions and goods are effectively protected against wanton interference.

B. Factors of Economic Life

1. *Labour*

Work is the indispensable basis of economic life. While nature is the rich source of the materials required for economic life, it does not provide many of its bounties ready for human use and consumption.

In turn, man is the only creature to whom has been imparted the ability to transform the objects of nature in order to adjust them to his plans and wishes. In his primitive age, man was almost as much determined by nature as the other animals. He differed from them, however, by his aspiration to improve nature. Man does not share the happiness of the animals which are prepared to accept circumstances and living conditions for what they are. Man is a restless creature, because he is never willing to be content with what things are like. Thus, he uses his ability to work in order to liberate himself from his dependence on nature. He transforms nature into the work of his hands.

In turn, successful operation in economic life requires a task force composed of people who have the necessary skill for the production of the goods needed or desired, and who are willing to accept employment and to co-operate with their fellow-workers. Not every individual is capable of working. But the necessity to work is incumbent upon mankind as a whole and is best served by a division of labour according to specific skills. There is no hope that the necessity to work will ever disappear. While it may be possible to reduce the working time of industrial production, there is hardly danger that the work week will be reduced to five or ten hours. Not only the ever-increasing population of the earth and the general desire for improved living conditions will make further demands on production; the growing volume of manufactured goods and their distribution will also demand a rapid increase in additional services for maintenance and repair.

Work implies effort and toil, in order to adjust man's condition to his wishes. For nature is rather reluctant directly to provide for the sustenance of human life. Minding the inescapable necessity of work, modern man declines to ascribe a value to work in itself. Employers and employees alike rather take a utilitarian or hedonistic view of work. They treat it as a potential means by which, through making money, happiness or power will be obtained. Of course, man has a right to aspire for satisfaction in life. Yet in these popular views work has no more value in itself. Such an outlook is found to have detrimental consequences. In the majority of lives, work takes up a substantial part of the waking day. If no satisfaction can be found in performing the work, that is to say, if people do not put their self in their work, they have to look for meaning to be found in their leisure time. As a result, they will seek satisfaction in their pastimes and hobbies, for instance in the bar room, in sport, TV, or simply in idleness and boredom. Yet, by doing so, they will gradually lose their selfhood.

Quite different is the Christian view. The facts are not denied that work requires effort and may be burdensome, yet also that through work the means for the preservation and enjoyment of life may be acquired. The toilsome character of work is emphasized. It is God's will that sinful men should labour hard in order to reap his work's fruit. No hope is left that in this world man will ever be delivered from the necessity of work. Yet, its compensation lies in the fact that God himself is an active God. Therein lies the dignity of work. To share in God's activity is man's privilege.

The monotony of specialized industrial work makes it difficult for modern working people to recognize their dignity, yet man excels over all other creatures by the fact that he has creativity. It is his privilege to bring things into being which were non-existent, and to him is imparted the prerogative incessantly to increase the volume of goods in his world and to better their quality. Whereas the ability to create new philosophical ideas or to produce works of art is confined to a relatively small number of ingenious men, everybody is capable of participating in the production of economic goods. That dignity is imparted to man, both for his own benefit and for the common good.

Realizing that fact, the Christian will work conscientiously and thereby promote the growth of his specific abilities. Moreover, through the regularity and discipline of such activity his moral character may be strengthened, especially his dependability, purposiveness and willingness to co-operate within the economic community. The wholesome consequences of such moral development will equally be experienced by the community as a whole.

The Christian view of work has been misunderstood by those who hold that man was destined to lead a playful life without work and that it was in consequence of his sin that he was compelled to work. Labour is not meant to render life miserable for man as a kind of Sisyphus task, which, in spite of its strain, produces no useful results. It is destined to benefit the human race, and it continues to do so even though by sin it is rendered toilsome. The ability to work is the means by which God enables mankind to support itself in a world in which nature provides but reluctantly and sparingly what the race needs. On account of that social function, all people capable of working are under moral obligation to engage actively in work. Since the economic community is coextensive with the body politic and overlaps with the areas of culture and civilization, the obligation to work may be discharged through activities which are not strictly speaking economical ones but which contribute to the well-being of the economic community, for instance administration, teaching or research, even the protection of the national security, entrusted to the police and the armed forces.

Since work is destined for the sustenance of mankind, Christianity insists that adequate remuneration should be granted for all work done. In figuring out what would be adequate, not only the quantity and quality of the worker's achievement is to be kept in view, but also his needs as a member of the community, for instance, the number of his children, his age and experience. Christianity has no standard method by which adequate remuneration is to be ascertained, nor can it boast of having a principle by which profits should be shared between employer and employees. What adequate remuneration is like will be the ever varying outcome of negotiations between the parties concerned. Christianity insists on fairness, however, that is to say on a mentality of mutual responsibility and readiness to avoid whatever would seriously harm either party.

Work is not primarily a means by which individuals earn money, but rather a social function for the benefit of mankind. Consequently, in cases of emergency, all capable of work are called upon to give assistance without compensation. As a social institution, economic life is destined to benefit all the members of a social group. That fact, in turn, obligates all people capable of performing work to be ready to participate in the economic process. The loafer must not expect the group to support him. Is there also a right to work? Not every worker will appear acceptable to every employer. But the economic organization or the government must see to it that no man be excluded from gainful employment for merely non-economic personal reasons, for instance on grounds of race, sex or religion. There are situations, however, where for economic reasons full employment of the whole labour force is not feasible, because the market is clogged or dispirited. The social function of the market demands that under such conditions provisions should be made for the sustenance of the unemployed and their families. Marx was wrong, however, in contending that unemployment was devised intentionally by the capitalists in order to have a reserve army of cheap labour at their disposal. A brisk market entails good wages for all workers.

Economic development in the communist countries has shown that even in a socialistic state, economic activities must be governed by considerations of rentability. In eastern Europe, full employment is accomplished only by means of low wages and standards of living. Mao was right in telling his followers that, in such circumstances, love of poverty is a desirable virtue. In turn, Christianity throws also doubt on the wisdom of the social views embodied in the modern welfare state. Receiving public assistance without corresponding work is demoralizing both for the recipient and his environment. While in all countries there is no place for millions on the labour market, an infinity of public and social needs go begging that might be satisfied by the unemployed. The economic community disintegrates unless it is a community at work.

Keeping that perspective in mind is doubly necessary in our age, when by the Grace of God work affords a prosperous life rather than mere subsistence in the Western world. Symptomatic for that development is the steady lowering of the contractual length of the working week. The right use of leisure time has become an immense and frightening problem. The utilitarian concept of work, which sees in it but a source of income, fails to answer that problem. For fun and entertainment prove to be boring when pursued as one's only pastime. Christian faith points to the unlimited opportunities for service and self-education for which the length of leisure time offers unexpected opportunities. Once one moves in that direction, one discovers with amazement that ever-new possibilities turn up.

2. *Property*

It is obvious that nobody would ever have engaged in work destined for the use of others if he were able to take away with impunity the fruits of his fellow man's labour by means of robbery, theft or fraud. Economic activity presupposes the willingness of the body politic to protect the rights of those engaged therein. Most important of those rights is property. There is a number of sources of property, for instance by manufacture, purchase, occupancy, donation and heredity. Yet they all have this in common: that within the economic community an object owned may not be taken away from the owner except by his consent. In that respect there is no difference between private and corporate property, including national property.

Quite frequently the question has been raised whether or not property had a metaphysical basis. Those who plead for a purely human, and incidental, origin will point to the various ways in which the notion of property developed in primitive mankind. The fact that in many places property was conceived of as standing under the special protection of the deities, or even as divine property lent to an individual, indicates the awareness that the very existence of property is far from being a matter of course. As a matter of principle it must be stated that the manner in which mankind has become aware of the usefulness of a notion has no bearing upon its authority. Property is one of the determinants of the economic process. Though abolishing, at least theoretically, all private property, even Communism sticks tenaciously to the ownership of the state, and it has decreed heavy penalties for disregard or violation of the common property rights. Apart from property, the economic process would not convey the satisfaction which man is destined to enjoy. The fact that the ancient Hebrews had the commandment 'Thou shalt not steal' in their code of divinely promulgated laws shows that they had good reason to believe that property was an integral element of the economic institution. By means of it mankind was to be given the prerequisite of the condition for which it was destined. Man's development toward full manhood cannot be reached except on the firm basis of property rights.

In order to develop his specific features, man had to detach himself from nature, whose goods may be picked up by whoever takes the trouble to will them and to take them. Yet while nobody is responsible for nature's production, property enables people to assume personal responsibility for the manufacture, storage, preservation and use of the goods owned. That is true of the collective property of the communistic countries no less than for private property in any economic system. Such responsibility implies, however, recognition of the communal character of economic life. That important aspect is overlooked by economic liberalism, in which it is held that my property rights entitle me to any use I like to make of my goods, including their complete destruction. The opposite is true. My property rights are limited. By the fact that the body politic guarantees, though it does not create, property rights, it has the right to decree that no use should be made of my property which would disregard or harm the interests of the economic community. The fact, for instance, that I own a forest does not give me the right to burn it down.

We conclude. That there is property and that it is a social institution is a determinant of human life divinely set forth. But the legal form in which property exists is left to be decided by the community. The moral discipline implied in the administration is not dependent on private property, as used to be the official teaching of the Catholic Church. The moral obligation to make the right use of property is incumbent upon a penniless administrator of public property no less than to people with assets totalling millions of pounds.

Also to be considered is the fact that property rights are under a two-fold limitation. Since property as an integral element of economic life is guaranteed by the body politic, the latter may curb personal property rights, if and when such measure is demanded in the interest of the economic community. There is no way of telling in advance the limit to which this prerogative of the body politic may be extended, except that the owner's personal rights may not be completely wiped out. For he, too, is a member of the economic community. From the moral viewpoint, Christians recognize that as a divine gift, property may not be used for purposes which are nocuous or fatal to the material and moral well-being of other people. Positively, property is one of the means by which we are enabled to come to the succour of the needy.

As all earthly goods, property is ambivalent. It provides security against natural and political calamities, especially in a monetary economy, in which practically all goods may be changed for money, and where money may buy practically all conceivable goods. In turn, however, it is that very usefulness of property by which people are tempted anxiously to stick to their property to the detriment not only of personal relations but also of faith. The miser and the greedy are inclined to put their ultimate trust in their property, rather than in God.

The principle of diversity which presides over everything in this world, manifests itself in the economic community in the fact that poverty and wealth are found side by side. There is no even distribution of the goods of life. From a purely formalistic understanding of justice, a redistribution of all the wealth on earth has been demanded. Nothing permanent would be accomplished thereby. The thrifty would keep their share in their safe, while drifters would squander it immediately. Thus, new inequality would soon be the inevitable result. Christianity will emphasize that one's social responsibility increases with the growing volume of property, as also the concomitant danger of using one's economic power in an egotistic manner. The size of a corporation, for instance, may easily reach the point at which it is able to dictate wages and prices and to become a potent factor in politics, irrespective of the interests of the community. While a certain amount of economic inequality is a healthy condition of the community because it acts as an incentive to competition and to improvement, the point may be reached at which monopolistic or quasi-monopolistic power results in oppression of competitors and exploitation of the economic weakness of the consumer. This tendency toward increasing accumulation of economic power characterizes the economy of the Western world in industry, commerce and banking. In such cases the power structure of the economic community will manifest itself in labour unrest or consumer strikes and eventually in drastic legislation or revolutionary upheavals. The desire of the community to restore a complete equilibrium will never be fully and permanently fulfilled. Complete control of the economy by the body politic will lead to wastefulness and stagnation, while unlimited freedom will encourage a return to the former intolerable conditions.

Various attempts that have been made in modern times to stabilize the economic development, for instance through heavy taxation of high income or state ownership of the means of production have shown that the task surpasses political wisdom. The basic problem is not that of discovering a rational kind of economic organization, but rather of curbing and taming the motives which lead to the egotistic use of economic power.

In many parts of the world, voluntary poverty has been adopted as the most effective antidote. Yet, while complete detachment from earthly goods may be a healthy medicine by which people are enabled to concentrate on spiritual wisdom, it is no solution. As Jesus and Gautama Buddha themselves, so their followers were not willing to starve. They relied on the charity and hospitality of people who continued to live in the economic world. Yet, though voluntary poverty is no panacea, it implies an important insight. The ability to multiply the volume of economic production has led modern man to an obsession with property. He wants to possess many economic goods, simply because they are available and improve his status, yet without regard for their intrinsic value and for no ulterior reason. While in the age of Puritanism Christianity had to fight the lure of luxury, in our age it is the temptation of indiscriminate spending. Thereby modern man renders himself miserable. He concentrates on making money and finds his satisfaction in the things money can buy. Christianity does not consider property an evil in itself and does not restrain people from participation in economic life. But it insists on the priority of the spiritual outlook. Economic goods are to be enjoyed and to be used for good ends. They are not to be allowed to control us. As all spheres of this world, so the economic institution lacks in itself the resources to keep it under control. Unless man has his foothold in faith, the economic goods will get control of him. This is true not only of the wealthy people. The poor man, too, may get so preoccupied with his economic predicament that he loses sight of all the other spheres of life.

3. *Money*

Though a relatively recent feature in economic life, money has proved to be of extreme usefulness. As a means of exchange, it has delivered the economy from the narrow limitations and cumbersome methods of direct exchange through barter. By being simple, rational, easily divisible, convertible and mobile, it has enabled finance, trade and industry to form a closely knit system over the whole earth. It acts as a potent stimulus to new production and the expansion of commerce, and as a convenient and relatively secure means for saving and peacefully accumulating economic goods. By stimulating the production and distribution of economic goods, money has brought about a rapid increase of wealth, and for that process there is obviously no limit.

Money's marvellous usefulness is coupled, however, with serious dangers. The economic stimulation made possible through money is dependent on large capitals. As a result the gulf between the wealthy people and the rest of the population grows constantly wider. Thereby the rich are not only alienated from the mass of the non-rich, but the latter group feels envy and greed, and desires to acquire the goods of the wealthy by means of crime or revolution. Furthermore, in its accumulation, money has become a potent public power that according to circumstances operates as an ally or rival of political and military power and exercises an enormous influence upon the destinies of the modern nations. Least noticed, yet in many respects most dangerous, is the fact that through the use of money many goods of the community which by nature are not economic ones, such as places of scenic beauty, works of art, and even social prestige or love, may be bought by money. Thus, money has not only become a source of social and international friction, but also of dehumanization. Christianity has not concluded that on account of those unpleasant developments man should forgo the use of money. Not only is its practical usefulness undeniable, but it is also an evidence of the providential care which God takes of man. By enabling man to discover money as a means of economic exchange, God confirms man's instinctive awareness that he is destined to rule over nature.

However, through the actual use that man makes of money, the community is seriously endangered. Experience shows that financial measures and social relief are unfit to bridge the gulf by which the rich and the poor are separated. The bitterness and hatred continue to keep them asunder. Equally pathetic is the fact that the process of dehumanization, which has been occasioned by the use of money, cannot be remedied by money. Lavish contributions to universities, museums and theatres are not suitable to deliver them from their curse by which they have become economic goods. Once money has been transformed from a tool by which to rule nature to an instrument of dominion over other people, man is a slave of money, and no amount of it will deliver him from his servitude.

That man should have deviated from the course for which money was destined, so Christianity holds, is due to assigning to money the supreme place in life or to placing wealth on the same level as divine gifts. The distortions of modern capitalism are rooted in the attempt of medieval devotion to buy God's pardon and favour. The remedy cannot be found in abolishing money as a means of economic exchange. Many such attempts have been made, yet all have ended in economic disintegration or a return to the money system. Christianity has discovered two ways by which to preclude servitude to money. First, the divine gifts promised to man, such as pardon, new life and power of the Spirit, are supreme and must necessarily reduce economic goods to a secondary place. Because those gifts cannot be bought, man, by aspiring after them, is constantly confronted with the necessity to decide whether or not a good available should be treated as an economic good. In addition, the communal character of God's redemptive gifts has opened our eyes to the fact that money can, and must not only, be used for commercial and financial purposes, but also as a very potent means by which to establish and improve human relationships. Imported as an unsolicited gift, it helps to win the friendship of people. Money has offered us the possibility to bring swiftly and effectively the right kind of relief needed, to the ends of the world. Thus it has become an extremely useful means of giving expression to our concern for our fellow man.

From the Old Testament law of tithing, Christianity has learned that money is an effective means by which our care for God's people may be given expression. What matters is not the exact amount of ten per cent donated for ecclesiastical and social purposes, but rather the willingness in a tangible way to acknowledge the fact that material goods are destined in the first place to serve for the furtherance of spiritual ends. To do so requires spiritual insight, because its extreme usefulness gives the powers of deception, lawlessness and crime an opportunity to make wrong uses appear commendable or legitimate. In truth, however, money is the divine gift, by which man is enabled to transform the objects of nature into evidences of love. It is not money as such that has such beneficial effect; on the contrary, money, in a clandestine manner, attempts to deceive man and make him its slave. Rather it is God who has made man capable of inventing money as a means by which effectively to transform the raw materials of nature into economic goods. He is the same God who through his Spirit enables man to use economic goods as a means by which to establish personal fellowship.

4. *The Market*

Modern economy presupposes a free market in order to operate effectively. That freedom applies to production, distribution and consumption of economic goods and a credit system at the disposal of the members of the economic community. The modern market manifests the true nature of the economic community. It is not a hazardous agglomeration of people, but rather a system in which various technical and commercial functions are intimately interrelated. Unlike the premonetary system of economy in which equivalent goods were exchanged on the basis of desirability, the free market is characterized by the intention to derive a profit by taking part in it. The life of the market was thoroughly revolutionized by the invention of the machine and its industrial use. As long as economic goods had to be manufactured, the volume of economic output was strictly limited by the availability of skilled workers and of easily accessible raw materials. With the machine, production and sale of economic goods were enabled infinitely to expand. Hand in hand with the rapid augmentation of economic goods, the possibility to make profits equally increased. Accordingly, the number of rich people is proportionately considerably greater today than it was, say, two hundred years ago. As the volume of available goods increases, the general prosperity of the economic community concerned would also increase. It has been said that the modern standard of living of the upper middle class by far surpasses what kings might have enjoyed in the Middle Ages.

Nevertheless, the modern development of the market has two heavy inconveniences. In order to keep profits high, it is necessary to produce at low cost, because competition does not allow one to raise prices for finished goods indefinitely. Such policy is possible because the lowest classes all over the world lack the goods, the capital and the power of labour unions to enter into a successful contest with their employers. The relative gains of the producers and distributors of economic goods will be increased when the number of those who share in them is kept low. For this reason, the owners of goods will try by means of advertising to persuade the middle class to employ their income for the purchase of consumer goods rather than invest it in capital goods. In the Middle Ages the customer dominated the market because, as a rule, the production of goods did not surpass the actual demand. In the modern economy enormous quantities are produced in the hope that the public can be convinced that they need the whole supply.

The other inconvenience of the free market is the constant fear of losses. Quite apart from the market, economic goods are elusive. They may be stolen, fraudulently obtained, embezzled, lost or squandered. Yet the market has also, in addition, the possibility of intrinsic deterioration by means of crises. The weak point of the free market is the institution of credit, that is to say, the lending of money for future production of what seems to be a useful economic enterprise. Production in the market economy is meant for a potential army of customers. But goods available may not be sold because the public does not like them or does not need them, or because, in a war, vast quantities of military and civilian goods are destroyed rather than used economically. As a result there is a lack of capital, and thus the national economy is impeded from functioning normally. Various devices have been tried out or suggested. Most vicious, though quite popular, is inflation. By a steady yet relatively small annual devaluation of the currency it is hoped to neutralize the consequences of unsound fiscal policy. Quite apart from the fact that finally a slow inflation turns into a galloping one, inflation is a process by which those directly engaged in production and commerce are enabled to get rich at the expense of those who invest in savings accounts or life insurance.

Christianity understands the intrinsic contradictions of the market as willed by God. The possibility of making profits is an indication of God's kindness. God is generous; he has not doomed man to live on a subsistence minimum. Rather he has been placed in a world which promises to reward his toil by increasing returns. Since the cause is to be sought in God's will rather than in a 'natural' development, it implies his promise that in all realms of reality mankind is constantly to be enriched. This would not only apply to economic geniuses and to cultural achievements, but also to the spiritual enrichment of the Church. In turn, the possibility of losses is to remind us that economic goods are not an essential element of human life. God imparts them and takes them away in order to remind us that it is he who takes care of us.

The productivity of the market has rendered many people obsessed with a craving for wealth and a desire to get rich quickly. Consequently, moral considerations are easily set aside, when they would preclude or diminish the chance of making big money. Family life is often disrupted, because husband and wife neglect the children, since the mother works, though without economic necessity. Christian faith implies contentment and gratitude for what one has. There is no reason why Christians should shun the market, but they are not obsessed with the desire to make money at any cost. They are aware that the market is a part of the economic community. It would not function except for the constant co-operation of its members. Profits, which the individual makes, are destined by God for the benefit of the whole community, no less than for one's own prosperity. Hence paying taxes is a natural implication of participation in the market.

18 Civilization

A. The Institution

1. *World and Spirit*

By civilization we understand all the practices and conditions of social life by which man's theoretical preoccupation with nature finds outward expression. There is a fashion in our days by which civilization and culture are radically separated. Yet, both are products of the human mind; they differ merely by the direction of their attention. Civilization is interested in practical usefulness, whereas culture looks out for meaning. Both, however, have the same subject matter. In civilization we are confronted with a baffling paradox. We are and are not the authors of our mental life. Language, for instance, is the medium of communication and understanding. That phenomenon is evidence that the activities of the individual mind are manifestations of a collective agency; on lower levels the same phenomenon is found. Organic life is both a form by which animals are determined as specimens of a species and a spontaneous activity. All mental acts of man imply strict regard for truth and meaning. Yet they are not standards which the individual has set to himself. Rather, they determine all mental activity in an inescapable way. In that fact, faith discovers a divine arrangement. Civilization is a social institution willed and determined in its nature by God. It is God's Spirit himself who is at work in civilization. He both manifests and realizes thereby his purpose. However, we also see that in civilization growth may be stunned, plans thwarted, lives destroyed, and people harmed. Such interference on the part of hostile forces is evidence that civilization is not purely spiritual and may not be held to form the highest level of human existence. An entirely different and superior level has been reached in the fact that the Risen Jesus is willing to share his spiritual life with his followers.

The co-existence of the two levels of human existence, one rational and one spiritual, explains the seemingly contradictory attitude Christians adopt towards civilization. They are not in a position to neglect civilization without disavowing God's work of Creation. But equally unacceptable is the idealistic view in which faith is interpreted as a product of the human mind and thus merely an aspect of culture. A mere juxtaposition would not be feasible, either, because it would constitute an unreconciled contradiction.

2. *Towards a Christian Civilization*

If I understand him correctly, Richard H. Niebuhr has stated the case in the most satisfactory way. He holds that a Christian has first to realize that faith is not a cultural activity. It is basically concerned with a non-worldly reality, namely redemption, rather than with values. In turn, culture may never claim to be a bridge from natural to supernatural life or religion. Once the fundamental difference between faith and civilization has been realized, however, the value of civilization as an instrument of faith can be acknowledged. Civilization may be enlisted by faith in order to project mental experience into the outside world and to endow its presentation with clarity, depth and tangible authority. Seen in that perspective, it is even legitimate to speak of religious culture. Of course, culture can never be used as a substitute for religion. For instance, the use of glossolalia, modern music, or dance in public worship are no equivalents of spiritual content. Conversely, however, civilization is enriched and deepened, when associated with religion. But nothing could be further away from truth than the modern contention that western civilization had a messianic mission and was able to save the rest of the world. It is true to say that through its civilization the West has been enabled to harness the forces of nature, yet at the exorbitant price of seriously dehumanizing and depersonalizing the population of the western hemisphere. Worst of all, its achievements have engendered in the people of the West a sense of racial superiority, as though the white man alone were worthy to create that civilization. Such outlook antagonized three-quarters of the world. Yet hypocritically we pretend not to see any reason for such resentment. The enormous power and the immense possibilities of action which modern civilization imparts to man manifest to the eyes of faith God's wisdom and the love he has for man. God has lifted him thereby infinitely above all animals. Yet civilization is ambivalent. It may and will be used for constructive, yet also for destructive purposes. The larger man's abilities and powers grow, the more the peril of misuse increases, and the more horrible are the instruments of mass destruction. Likewise, the media of mass communication have granted to some people and corporations the possibility to pervert and confuse the minds and hearts of people on an extremely large scale. The same civilization which has so excessively augmented man's power has also immolated human grandeur to success. In all the fields of human activity moral and spiritual judgment is frequently surrendered to a spirit of violence, cleverness, greed and ambition.

In such circumstances the Spirit cannot manifest himself in a steady movement of progressive evolution. His work is temporarily stopped and distorted by different cosmic forces. It is also retarded by the fact that the average Christian has not fully experienced the power of the Spirit. Hence he is afraid of new developments and is inclined to support the *status quo*. On account of the ambivalence of civilization Christianity has proceeded soberly by selecting and testing those elements which appeared to be useful or usable for its mission and by eliminating those which seemed to be incompatible with its goal. Since that testing goes on constantly in the Church today, Christians are no longer bound by the selections made by Jewish Christians or Paul in the New Testament age or by the Reformers. While the basic principles do not change, their implementation is a new one in each new cycle of civilization. Such selections take time. There is no immediate agreement on them. It is not surprising therefore that particularly in the initial stage of transition to another culture people should go to extremes, some espousing excessively rigorous attitudes against the onrush of new developments while others lean towards complacency.

In that way, the Church will gradually impress its mark upon contemporary civilization. That happened simultaneously in Byzantium and ancient Western Europe, and again when the Reformation was brought to various countries of Europe. The genesis and flowering of a Protestant culture has often been misrepresented. Historians like Harnack and Troeltsch would place one-sidedly all emphasis upon the development of Christian thought. We still lack a comprehensive study of the interrelation of piety and culture in Protestant history. People fail therefore to realize that the post-Protestant existentialists are in fact the going-to-seed of Protestant culture. In its *aggiornamento*, even the Catholic church attempts to follow the Protestant example of coming to terms with modern culture. In that process in which a Protestant culture has come into being, Protestantism has refused to follow Hegel's or Marx's contention that the Spirit is aiming at a kind of civilization whose pattern would be but the logical development of present conditions. Very consistently, theologians like Pannenberg, Moltmann and Jüngel emphasize the futuristic tendency of history but refuse to identify the goal with a set of historical conditions. Protestant culture reflects the unrest of the human heart. Man is unable and unwilling to be satisfied with the accomplishments of history. Within Christianity's history there may be periods of cultural stagnation, but they will last for a time only. They are the respite which the Spirit grants to the 'weak brethren' in order to give them an opportunity of catching up with his advance. His vitality is manifested in the fact that after such standstill he is manifested in a new historical impulse.

Seen in this light, man is destined to be enriched by civilization, provided that he is willing to keep it under spiritual control. When Jesus says, 'Collect yourselves treasures in heaven' (Matt. 6:19), he does not advise us to withdraw from this world and disregard civilization. Rather, he bids us to admire its spiritual origin, and to employ it inasmuch as it is a manifestation of the Spirit, and for the ends God has in mind with it. That is to say, the Christian cannot ascribe finality to civilization. Rather, it is a means by which we are enabled to render our life and the lives of our fellow men more human and more meaningful than they had been.

B. Media of Civilization

1. *Speech*

In order to develop the ethical implications of the preceding discussion, we shall single out a few especially central media of cultural life. Speech is probably the most important one, for apart from the gift of language the individual mind would be extremely handicapped in communicating his thoughts to other people. The extremely primitive conditions of pre-lingual human life indicate the enormous limitations which that state imposed upon man. Speech has a twofold function. By arranging a sequel of vocal sounds in a permanent way as a word, man is able to identify and arrange his thoughts in an orderly way. The hypothesis according to which words originated in a haphazard way is refuted by the permanent use of words, their unchanging meaning and the possibility to be understood by others. The origin of language is found in the operation of God's Spirit, as a result of which man's mind has a structure corresponding to that of the other beings. Or perhaps we might say that by means of language man gives expression to the significance which this world and its component parts have for us. Both in that correspondence of word and meaning, and in the communicability of thoughts by means of words, we encounter manifestations of the for-each-otherness that by God's will characterizes all created things. Speech is not merely given to us in order to make statements concerning facts, as Wittgenstein held, nor is it simply coupled with an emotive faculty (Ayer). By speaking to another person, I make him realize that I know something that is relevant for him and that I care to make him aware of that fact. It is obvious that man could not by an act of his will endow speech with the ability to communicate. Rather the conative volitional element implied in speech must be understood as being rooted in human existence. The mystery of speech lies in the fact that in addition to addressing itself to other people's intellect and emotions, speech goes as word of consolation, admonition, confidence or love directly to the other person's heart. It is through speech that the most intimate relations of human beings are established.

Like all things of this world, speech, too, is exposed to forces of deterioration. The philologist, for instance, is inclined to narrow down the usefulness of speech by identifying words with definitions. Originally words are symbols. It is the original function of speech to make articulate the significance which a fact in this world has for myself as a human being. That means that what is directly given of the fact is to be understood as a guide post to all that is contained therein and may be discovered; the grammarian sticks to the original meaning of the word. It is easy to see how detrimental an effect such understanding will have upon the interpretation of poetry and religion, whose form of presentation implies an invitation to try to probe the depth of its meaning. The ever-changing understanding of the Bible bears witness to these facts.

Being based on the for-each-otherness of the creatures, speech must satisfy four demands. The first one is veracity. According to Jesus, that is the very essence of speech, and promises and informations should not need any confirmation of their truthfulness, for instance, by means of an oath. Using speech to conceal something or to mislead somebody is a perversion of the very function of speech. Then there is condescendence. It is as a human being that I am able to know things and to talk about them. My partner has the same qualifications. I deny our common humanhood when I talk to him as though I were superior to him, because I know what he does not know. To do so is the temptation of the scholar and the expert, except when talking to their peers, and often also that of the pastor. Truth is the manifestation of the Spirit, rather than the creation of man's mind. Hence, truth is to be communicated to all men and requires the humility of a servant. Thirdly, speech is given us for the communication of things that are relevant. The origin of speech is probably to be thought of as the awareness of God's work in the operation of the self. The terseness of the Biblical style is a model of speech that mentions nothing irrelevant. The Bible warns frequently against loquacity and unnecessary words. Finally, as a means by which the Spirit enables men to become truly human, speech is meant to be helpful. There are many things I know which do not profit my neighbour. Love will therefore keep away from him what might harm or hurt him, or tell it in such a way that he will at the same time be encouraged, strengthened or comforted.

The multiplicity of languages and dialects reminds us of the intrinsic difficulty of comprehension. Speech is superior to sense perception, because it enables us to pass on to others relations, attitudes and structures in addition to the appearance of the things perceived. But in the absence of immediate verification, speech is subject to error and misunderstanding. Verbal communication requires therefore a special effort in order to make oneself understood and to understand. The possibility to translate from one language into any other is an indication that the Spirit uses speech as a means to manifest the unity of mankind. In turn, the multiplicity of languages discloses the tendency of the individual and the ethnic group to assert themselves as a self-contained entity. Thus, mutual understanding presupposes not only the belief that mankind is in the first place a spiritual unity, but also the willingness to learn wisdom from the various literatures of mankind.

We are living in a period in which propaganda and the media of mass communication have done great harm to speech. We hear and read so much what is not only of little or no value to us, but is half true or outright lie. It is used as a cloak for commercial or political interests. Those who spread the news try to persuade us to follow their lead. As a result, no attempt is made any more to grasp the depth underlying the words. ('The medium is the message!'). No wonder that the churches are occupied with the historical facts found in the Bible or social demands derived from it, while little is still done to understand and communicate the mysteries of faith, whose medium is the word.

MacLuhan concludes that, as a consequence of mass communication, speech has completely lost its ability to communicate. Its function, he contends, had been taken over by visual presentation, and the person in front of the TV set would have no choice but to make up his own mind in order to ascertain what the meaning of the things seen should be. If that were true, we would have entered an age of sheer subjectivism. Actually, however, the pictorial presentation including the documentaries is slanted. In appealing to the onlooker it suggests: 'This is the true life, and these are the things that matter in this world.' This effect may be achieved in those who attend to no other communication. Yet since these media appeal to people's emotions and imagination rather than to their self, their effect can be counter-balanced by true speech, and in particular by the Christian message. Biblical religion is especially closely related to speech. The very fact that the Spirit engenders speech is evidence of the fact that God is not only a God who acts but also a God who speaks or who wants to be known in a way that makes communication possible. All true knowledge implies awareness of the meaning of the things known, that is to say, the significance they have for the work of the Spirit. It makes good sense to distinguish natural knowledge from revelation. Revelation is the recognition of the significance which an earthly fact has for the attainment of man's ultimate goal. Such insights will be expressed by means of the language used normally by its recipient. In that respect, the Bible is historically conditioned literature. But the value of an insight does not depend on the date when it was first apprehended but rather on its intrinsic truthfulness, that is to say, its ability to point to significant facts in this world. It is both naïve and inconsistent to reject the Bible or the writings of Plato or Confucius for no better reason than that they were composed prior to our birth. The historical form in which they are written is rather to be considered a challenge to discover the meaningful fact that led to their discovery. The literary form of statements does not tell us whether or not it is a true insight or a mere opinion. The latter gets eventually obsolete. The former may be in need of a more adequate form of expression for a new age yet leads us to unchanging realities.

2. *Art*

Cultural life assumes basically two forms corresponding to the higher interests of man, namely, art and science. The former aims at giving tangible shape to the meaning of this world, whereas the latter is concerned with its practical usefulness. Both of them provide security for man, science by increasing his dominion over nature, and art by setting his mind temporarily free from preoccupation with the demands and dangers of life. The basic objective of art is praise, and the means by which it gives expression to it is form. Historically, art has its origin in religion. Not everything in this world appears to be praiseworthy to the common man. The artist points out values by which things are rendered relevant to the human race. By giving artistic form rather than imitating nature, the artist indicates that the significance he ascribes to his subject is a possibility implied in nature rather than an actual reality. While the world of art is not as real as that of practical experience, it imparts to it a splendour that makes it worth living. The artistic form discloses the structure of reality which may be conceived as proportion, harmony, movement or contrast. The work of art is born out of a vision which comes to the artist in an unsolicited way as a gift of the Spirit. Thereby he is enabled to associate full meaning with the things of this world.

In view of that origin, it would hardly be correct to say that art has nothing to do with ethics. But the fundamental problem is not whether or not the artist should strictly adhere to the code of bourgeois ethics. On account of the charismatic character of his visions the artist will find his standards of conduct in himself. By the principle *l'art pour l'art* the modern artist expresses his refusal to confine art to utilitarian purposes. Likewise it was a necessary act of liberation when, in contrast with classicism and idealism, the 'naturalists' contended that the artistic value of a work of art did not depend on its subject matter. The artist's vision may be applied to the whole world of human experience. The moral problem of art originates in the fact that the operation of the artist is animated by the desire to bring his work eventually to the attention of the public. What he wants to show is not in the first place his accomplished craftsmanship. Rather he wants to use the latter in order to emphasize the relevancy of his subject. By endowing his subject with an artistic form, he indicates that he is convinced that it deserves to exist.

Here begins the artist's moral responsibility. Though conceived in the solitude of the study, the work of art has a public function. The artist wants to share his creation with the public, and hence publishes or exhibits it or has it publicly performed. The reason for that desire is not basically to be found in personal ambition or a subjective craving for recognition. The Spirit from whom the artist receives his vision, addresses himself to the artist as individual yet discloses to him as a member of the human race the things that are relevant for mankind as a whole. Art is never a merely private affair of the artist. In transforming his original vision into a concrete poem or statue or sonata, he must always keep his potential public in mind. The excessive subjectivism of some modern painters, for instance, reduces their works to the level of private documents. Their form of presentation is not fit to confront the reader or onlooker with relevant things.

By presenting his work to the public, the artist acknowledges that he identifies himself with his subject or rather with the perspective in which he has presented his subject. He is not to be reprehended for dealing with crime, vice, or the physiology of the human body, including sex. Obviously they, too, are integral parts of human life. But the artist misuses his gift when he approves of, or glorifies, actions and attitudes by which social life is harmed or perverted, and crimes or vices are presented as being the normal human conduct. The Christian artist, too, will not shun such subjects, but in his perspective their tragic aspect, their futility or inner contradiction, their wretchedness, ugliness or superficiality will be brought to light. Mauriac is certainly right when he argues that saintliness is no suitable subject for literature. The 'literary' lives of Jesus either are poor literature, or fail to bring out the real grandeur of Jesus. Only through the saint's fight against sin or the wickedness of his environment is it possible to present the saint's life as being relevant for the reader.

Publishers, clergymen and judges have recently hotly debated the question of obscenity in literature and films. That the artist should be attracted by the subject of sex is hardly surprising in view of the universality of sex and the role it plays in many people's life. It seems to be absurd that a detailed description of sexual activities should be judged obscene when encountered in a work of art, but should be classified as useful information when found in a scientific or popular work on sexual practices. The problem is not quite as simple, however, as it appears at first sight. All depends on the author's intention. Does he confine his description of sexual details to the characterization of the role which the mystery of sex plays in the lives of his people? Since concentration on the essentials is a criterion of good penmanship, does the artist intend by the insertion of otherwise unnecessary details to cater to the reader's desire for sexual emotion? Books and pictures of that kind are obscene, and, when exclusively devoted to that end, are pornography.

Like everything in this world, art is ambivalent. It serves to lift man's mind above the necessity of work into a realm of unencumbered pleasure. From the actual, yet unsatisfactory, reality of this world art has the power to create a truly meaningful, though merely possible, world. As a 'hidden persuader', the artist is able by means of the artistic form to appeal directly to the heart of his public. He avoids thereby the detour which the argumentative presentation of philosophy and theology must take. Christianity has therefore made ample use of religious art. It should be stated, however, that the modern suggestion to hand the whole common worship over to dancers, jazz musicians and actors overlooks an important fact. Faith needs the assurance that our lives are guided by a reality that determines and transcends not only our own existence, but also the universe in which we live. Art as the manifestation of the truly possible stands in between our earthly condition and the work of God. It lacks therefore the assurance of actual redemption, apart from which our lives make no real sense. For that reason, art may legitimately be used as an aid to public worship, yet not as its substance or centre.

In the process of humanization, the Spirit uses art as the means by which people learn to make a clear distinction between usefulness and meaning. However, art does not bring forth meaning; it only points out the possibilities of meaning without ever giving the assurance that the possible meaning will be realized. No wonder that philosophers held that art was concerned with mere appearance and thus deceptive. It is hardly strange that the ancient Israelites used art merely for religious purposes, that is to say in a field whose significance had been ascertained in holy history.

Many people are tempted to equate artistic appearance and reality. Consequently, they fail to distinguish between reality and art. Worst are the pathological cases in which people have so completely identified themselves with artistic reality that, like Pirandello's Henry IV, they are unable to adjust themselves to actual reality. Idealism is also prone to such a delusion. People may become so enamoured of the image of a better future which their imagination effects in their mind that they take it for granted that with an intrinsic necessity the image will eventually come true. Such an attitude will turn them away from their responsibility for the future.

3. *Science and Technology*

Finally we mention science as a medium of civilization. We are using the term in that broad sense in which it was used in the philosophy of antiquity and the Middle Ages. We do not limit its use to the natural sciences as is so often done in modern times. It rather denotes the totality of verified and verifiable knowledge, as it has been gathered methodically and critically.

Modern scholarship and Christian faith are agreed that science is necessary, yet do so for different reasons. Scholars are perturbed by the fact that this world observes a cool neutrality, and often hostility, towards man. They hope by means of science to establish control of this world, and thus to prevent it from unexpectedly interfering with human life. Science then is the effective means of man's self-assertion. Christian faith considers science a means of recognizing the conditions under which life has to be lived in this world. Thus it prevents the Christian from entertaining erroneous views of the condition under which he lives. Underlying these differences one encounters divergent ethical views. The modern scholar holds that man is the creator of his noetic faculty and that by means of intensive training and carefully devised instruments he is capable of eventually deciphering all the riddles of this world. Thus, even granted the incipient or incomplete character of our present knowledge, man would have a right to regard himself lord of this world. That position would entitle him to use the things of this world according to his discretion. The criterion of truth is seen in the amount of power that science enables man to derive from a subject. The special slant thus given to science would imply that the question of the existence of God is irrelevant. Science is supposed to have rendered him superfluous.

To Christianity, this utilitarian positivism appears both superficial and presumptuous. The meaning of all things would then lie in their usefulness for man. To this attitude, Christian faith objects sternly. While through science, man is able to control the things of this earth, he is not the owner of the universe, for he did not make it. He has no right to use the earthly things according to his discretion. They are to be employed in accordance with God's redemptive purpose. Furthermore, one has to be careful in speaking of the creativity of the human mind. The paradox of knowledge consists in the fact that knowledge and truth are born out of ignorance and blindness, or rather that they are engendered in man through the activity of the Spirit. The primary task of knowledge is not to be seen in reaching agreement among the different and often divergent views which various people hold concerning a subject, but above all to eliminate one's subjective prejudices which enter into the making of knowledge and to see it in its relation to God's purpose. Christian faith humbly admits that human existence does not explain the meaning of man or of the universe, unless it is envisaged in its relation to God's goal.

The modern scholar, who is so critical and meticulous when he investigates particular entities, usually changes his attitude when it is a question of general forms and determinants. In order to prove to himself the sufficiency of his mind he will unscrupulously resort to subjective opinions and unproven hypotheses. The Christian's attitude is the very

273

opposite. Realizing that in his thinking the Spirit of God is at work, he will not only make an effort to free that knowledge from its subjective conditions but also keep in mind the ontic limitations of his knowledge. While he has the evidence that God is dealing with him all the time, the Christian realizes that he is not able to know more of God than God deigns to disclose to him. He will not try to prescribe to God what he ought to be and to do, nor tell him what eventually he will be like if he heeds the philosopher's advice. Seen in the right light, science is a way to humanization. It makes people aware of the inexhaustible supply of goods found in this world and it makes people wonder why God has chosen man as the recipient of so much knowledge.

Technology is the application of modern natural science to practical problems. Through the invention of machines and the harnessing of the energies of nature, the narrow limits of man's possibilities have been removed, and mankind is now capable of increasing its productivity without measure. The result has been a substantial improvement of the living conditions of millions of people. The limitations of space and time have been greatly reduced, the food supply has been augmented beyond all expectations, and many dangers and hazards to health and happiness have been successfully repelled. In that development we notice the Spirit at work preparing mankind for its task of dominion over nature. But the improvement which technology has brought with it has been outweighed by the use made of it. The increase in productivity has not only augmented the powers of landowners, businessmen, industrialists and bankers. Their amazing control of natural resources has also led to wasteful, thoughtless and reckless methods of exploitation. Contamination of our rivers and lakes, air pollution, overcrowding of cities, shortage of recreational areas, depletion of forests, oil wells and mineral deposits, constant increase of noise are the pathetic witnesses of such attitudes. The contemporary situation is worsened by the ambition of the scientist and the greed of the manufacturer which put machines and drugs on the market prior to a careful and extensive test of the reliability and safety of their merchandise. The incidence of accidents has vastly grown. The development of big cities has cut off from nature the majority of their population, and the greater rentability of large industrial plants and stores influence economic life in a direction in which the rich are getting richer and the poor poorer. The worst consequence which the rise of technology has brought with it is the mechanization of man. His daily life is to such an extent conditioned by clocks, electric switches, cars, radio and TV that little room is left for personal life. Concomitantly, modern man is more and more alienated from contact with nature. As in the field of science, an historical process, for which no one in particular is responsible and which no man has planned, has taken control over the lives of man. The point has been reached in our days where man is but the servant of the machines which he has built. It is to be feared lest this dehumanization should go on with increasing speed, because it is extremely profitable for the small minority of those who own and exploit the natural resources and control the manufacture of goods and their distribution. The support of so many millions depends on employment in the various branches of technology. It is not surprising therefore that people should fear that any radical change in the methods of manufacture and distribution could impair their living conditions. Except for rare and limited cases of civic self-help action there is little hope that technology itself will start a reverse movement. Even communism, which in theory is so keenly interested in the well-being of man in economic life, has succumbed to the demands of industrialization and the ambitious planning of the technocrats. Yet man is made for personal fellowship, and his health depends on contact with nature. It may be possible for a while to deprive him of such relationship, but it will not be feasible to destroy his longing for a worthwhile life. Christianity is able to offer a lead in that movement. People enjoy a deep-going fellowship in the Church because what unites them is God, the supreme determinant of their life. Likewise, their reverence for life is not only based upon the conservationist's joy derived from untouched wilderness areas; it is in the first place rooted in the respect for the work of God who has made this world. Spoiling nature is disregard of God's will. Thus, through the presence of a believing remnant, mankind will always be kept aware of the perversity of the style of life into which it has been lured by the detrimental and suicidal course which modern technology has taken. The future of mankind will hardly be a return to primeval simplicity. The advantages derived from technology are too momentous ever to be abandoned completely by mankind. But faith will insist that the technological civilization must remain under man's control and be used for the benefit of all men.

19 The Social Order

A. Loneliness and Social Group

The more the individual becomes aware of himself, the more confused and unsatisfactory his situation seems to be. He finds himself determined by institutions which confront him with the basic goods of human existence. But the social institutions do not care for what he feels or aspires after. He sees in them the proof of man's superiority in this world, for no animal has to do with justice, economic prosperity or religion. But in the confrontation with those institutions he is not himself. As a legislator or a businessman he is but a subject of the institution, differing from others merely as the occupant of a numerical place. His selfhood is given even less attention by nature which gives him an opportunity to live. No matter how enthusiastically he may enjoy its sublime beauty or admire its mysterious order, nature shows no special interest in him. It is concerned, so it seems to him, with the species rather than with the individual specimen.

No wonder, therefore, that Sartre and others are telling us that being a person is a distinction for which a high price is to be paid. Personal existence, they contend, is absurd and in conflict with itself, being selfhood for which there is no use in the universe. Still others will point out the ambivalence of individuality. Being self-contained, the individual seems to have his full meaning in himself. But on account of this self-sufficiency, other people seem to be barred from imparting anything essential to him. Thus, he would be doomed to permanent solitude, the more so because other individuals might not need anything from him. On that basis, it is no wonder that modern man bemoans his loneliness. The tragedy of modern individualism lies in the fact that the individual robs himself of love and friendship, the two goods which would render his lot tolerable. As a result of his self-centred attitude, he is unable to make love. What he calls love is an emotion produced by the presence of another person. It comes to an end when he or the other individual declines to make further use of it.

Over against these interesting, yet highly speculative, views, Christianity, in alliance with common sense, points out that man is not in the first place made in order to be something, but rather in order to act and to accomplish things. Yet that goal cannot be reached in individual isolation. It is as a human being, not as an individual, that a man is able to live a meaningful life. That can be done only by participation in the life of a social group. Two kinds of concrete fellowships are at man's disposal, namely societies and social groups. The former kind serves an end, for which the aggregation of people is but a means by which to intensify the effort. Such are, for instance, the Red Cross, social and political pressure groups, or the shareholders of a corporation. There is only one requirement for membership, namely the willingness actively to support the specific end for which the society came into being. Usually the only demand made on the individual is payment of dues or signing a petition. Quite different are the social groups whose end lies in themselves. Their aim is to give and promote personal contact among its members. Membership in them is dependent on one's personal conditions for the specific kind of fellowship of that group. Such kind of association is found in neighbourhoods, professional associations, the personnel of a business firm, or service clubs. Nations, citizenries and, at least in the sociological perspective, the Church are also to be counted as social groups. They all have this in common, that their activities serve to make articulate their members' sense of belonging together. They are not meant to be part of a comprehensive social reform. It is by participating in the activity of such social groups that the individual succeeds in overcoming his feeling of solitude. That man is destined for such social life can be seen in the fact that he has the gift of speech by which he is capable of apprehending and expressing the basic values cultivated by the social institutions. Membership in these groups is in a constant flux. Young people grow into adulthood; people move to a new location or change their place of occupation, or are promoted to a higher level.

In seeking admission to a social group people look for three things, namely, belonging, recognition, and communion. Unlike the societies in which membership depends exclusively on the individual's free choice, the social groups make admittance dependent on their own choice and decision. The principle requirement is the individual's ability and willingness to co-operate harmoniously with the other members of the group. The individual recognizes that to be accepted by the group is a privilege that makes him the peer of all the other members, and that, in dealing with people outside, he shares the reputation of the group. An American, for instance, who travels abroad, is treated preferentially not on account of his personal merits, but on account of his US citizenship. A person's honour does not rest primarily on things that he does, but rather on his group's conviction that whatever he does is for the benefit of his group. In turn, acceptance by a social group imparts full meaning to his life. The impact which an individual is able to make upon history is bound to be infinitesimally small in view of the immense duration of history. Within the life of the group, however, success and failure, co-operation and opposition are easily recognized, and notwithstanding their relatively small significance are integrated in the ongoing course of history. Perhaps even more important is the group experience itself. In a social group, the accomplishments of each member go to the credit of the group. Conversely, the individual shares the honour and reputation of his group, even when no remarkable deed has been achieved by him personally. The valour of our soldiers or the inventions of a fellow citizen make me proud to be a member of my nation. Thus, acceptance results in a marked increase of one's joy of living.

In the process of humanization, the social groups play a decisive role. Purely private relations which rest on friendship and love remain basic to a man's desire for a truly human life. But they rest on an emotional foundation and therefore do not pursue a firm and steady course. Love is the mother of virtue and of crime, and friendship has inspired heroes and gangsters alike. The social groups do not depend on emotions, and therefore they function continually and steadily. Above all, they, too, are a prerequisite of a truly human life. Of course, the humanistic view, according to which work in a group renders a person truly human, is an optimistic exaggeration. A mere glimpse of the political and cultural life of our days suffices to recognize the confusion in which the nations of the world find themselves. The ultimate significance of a social group depends on the spirit by which it is animated, which may be the Spirit of God or the spirit of anarchy, rebellion, and sin. In turn, however, faith would not be able to manifest its power except for the possibility offered by the existence of social groups.

The value of the social groups lies in translating their basic aspirations into practical realities such as parliaments, universities, banks or artists' studios. Absolute ideas are changed here into the activities of daily life. The small talk of neighbours or citizens may appear banal and trivial when compared with the lofty concepts of the guardians of social institutions. Nevertheless, they are the way in which the directions given by the institutions affect and mould the lives of the people. The interest which a neighbourhood groups takes in the cleanness, neatness and embellishment of its area, the respect for each other's property, and the willingness to accommodate each other by means of baby-sitting and assisting in an emergency may seem to be insignificant in comparison with the events in foreign politics or labour and management conflicts. But by forming the pattern of life in many thousands of communities, these small social units form the basis on which the order, security and stability of a country rests.

The increasing specialization, not only in the theoretical sciences but also in practical activities, operates as a factor by which communication becomes difficult. But in the practical co-operation within the group, a way is found back to common conversation and action. Most people are members of more than one social group. In that way an overlapping of interests and activities is accomplished by which not only national life is enriched and deepened, but also international co-operation is rendered possible.

Attempts have been made to explain the origin of social groups as resulting from the individual's inability by himself to master his destiny when confronted with the forces of nature, and the powers of history. But not only is it recognized that the feeling of need never suffices to bring about its fulfilment; it is also obvious that belonging and recognition, which the individual seeks in the social group, are not directly related with biological needs. More plausible is the belief that the existence of social groups is part of the divine plan of humanization as the concluding phases of biological evolution. A comparison of secular social groups with the Church discloses a common pattern of association. It is therefore safe to assume an intrinsic teleological relation between secular and spiritual groups. As life in the groups is required to implement faith, so in turn the Church has to supplement the secular groups. Their objective is the cultivation and conservation of relevant goods. The existence of the Church points to the fact that none of the goods considered relevant by the secular groups may be considered ultimate. The mere desire to live a meaningful life does not render the life in the secular groups a full life. Furthermore, historical and geographical factors will influence the life of social groups. That explains the differences in the outlook and aspirations of the representatives of the same group. Accordingly, faith, too, will be implemented in different ways. In their practical orientation, Presbyterians in Scotland, for instance, will be in the first place Scots like the rest of their nation, whereas Reformed people in Holland will share the national outlook and attitude of the Dutch. The result will not be relativism, however, because by faith action within the group is directed towards the common supreme good, namely, the establishment of God's Kingdom. In many Christian lives, the result will be a dichotomy until faith succeeds in asserting its priority.

Finally, a word should be said about the role of personality images. Since the social group intends to realize goals which are considered relevant for its well-being, the members of the group are looked upon primarily from the viewpoint of usefulness they have for the life of the group. Likewise the individual member will think of himself in terms of his ability to be of service to the group rather than in the light of actual behaviour and performance. Fanatics of individualism have assailed the use of personality images as hypocrisy. It is true, of course, that by means of propaganda the image of a politician or a movie star may be built up out of all proportion. Nevertheless, an image lacking a foundation in facts will eventually blow up. In turn, however, the images formed in the social group are meant to express the potential usefulness which the individual has for the group. As agencies for the realization of absolute values, all social groups believe they have a clear view of their worth and usefulness, and its members share in its prestige. A US senator, for instance, is accorded the honour of his office even prior to, and independent of, his actual achievements. Social status in general is founded upon the assumption that, having been accepted as a member of a group, an individual is capable of adequately contributing to the activity of his group. This procedure applies to the fellowship of faith too. Paul and John in particular are fond of characterizing the Christian life as one of being in Christ, or of being branches or members of Christ. They want to say that in God's eyes the significance of our life does not depend on our actual behaviour and performance but rather on the fact that Christ has accepted us as members of his body. Hence, what we actually do is but the more or less incomplete way in which we translate the urge of Christ's Spirit into social reality.

A person who sees himself 'as he is', that is to say, apart from the significance he has for the life of his group, will inevitably be driven to shame, condemnation of himself and despair. In turn, the image which the group forms of us is apt to stimulate our initiative and to give us courage to change our life, notwithstanding the obvious difficulty of doing so. By relating our individual existence to Christ, the true man, through the image of 'being in Christ', the Church makes us aware of the abilities and possibilities we possess. My true dignity may be hidden from the eyes of other people. Yet, though they may misunderstand, humiliate and slander me – and perhaps for good reasons – they are not able to discourage me. I know that my true life is that of a child of God.

B. The Outsider

Theoretically each individual should be a member of a social group because he is unable to grow into true manhood except through the interrelation of people within a social group. In fact, however, one encounters individuals living without real participation in the life of of social groups. Of them there are two types, namely, the outcast and the 'radical'. There is hardly a social group which will accept or tolerate all those who desire or need its fellowship. Some are forcibly excluded on account of their unwillingness or inability to conform to the standards of fellowship of their group, for instance, the prisoner, the inmate of a mental asylum, or the leper. Others find it difficult or impossible to be accepted, especially members of racial minorities, or, as in Hinduism, the untouchables. Experience shows that being cut off from intercourse with social groups not only impedes the growth of truly human qualities, but tends gradually to dehumanize the outcast. In some cases, especially that of racial minorities, new social groups have sprung into being. But even when such a minority is able to grow into a self-sufficient cultural and social group, its growth is stunted by resentment felt against the majority group.

On account of the harmful consequences which severance from the majority group has for the people concerned, Christians will make efforts to let them participate in the fellowship of their social group, just as Jesus did with tax-gatherers, Samaritans, prostitutes and non-Jews. In our days it must be kept in mind, however, that the granting of full civil rights and making available the services of welfare agencies, valuable as they are, do not affect the basic problem. As long as they are refused acceptance by the majority group, the outsiders will – rightly – consider all other measures mere evidence of the refusal to terminate the outcast status. In turn, however, there is little hope for speedy solutions, because Christians are themselves a minority in the national majority. All they are able to do in the present situation is that, in addition to stating the task, they are willing themselves to initiate contact with outsiders. They have the promise that doing so will be a light in the darkness of social prejudice. In turn, the one outside has to realize that he will not be granted full status in the social group while clinging to an anti-social attitude or resentment towards the majority group.

Different is the condition of the radical, for instance, the individualist, the anarchist, the nihilist or the hippy. Seemingly, all these people are in protest against the social group. However, the fact that they associate with their equals is enlightening. They acknowledge the fundamental role of guiding human ideas. What they object to is the way in which justice, beauty, wisdom, communion or religion are implemented in the extant social groups. In view of the conservative tendency of those groups, the absoluteness of those ideas is being blurred and obscured. In order to emphasize their aspirations, the radicals feel a compulsion to present them as the opposite of what the majority has established as guiding moral standards. It is obvious that such outlook will lead to gross exaggerations and eccentricities, but no less obvious is the observation that criticizing the excesses of radicals is used by the majority as a pretext to leave everything unchanged.

The radical may seem to be a highly undesirable type of man because he does not only challenge the majority's long established belief in the truthfulness of its standards, but also is apt to disturb its peace and order. But he plays a providential role in human history. By being a nuisance he acts as God's gadfly, who reminds the social group that the conditions on which its standards were based had vanished. Thereby, he makes plain the ever recurring necessity of change. In most instances the remedies recommended by the radical will prove to be Utopian and impracticable. Nevertheless, they point to a fundamental weakness which, if left unheeded, will end in collapse or violent change of the establishment. Usually there is little hope of persuading the radical that his extremism is irrational and practically worthless. Being enamoured of his charismatic state, he will fanatically stick to it. But the uselessness of engaging in dialogue with him does not justify ignoring his challenge.

C. Social Imbalance

In contrast with the amazing and universal order that we notice in the cosmos, human life is conspicuous for its disturbing tendencies by which social groups are at times brought to the brink of chaos. It is easy to discover the reason for that condition. The human mind is in no way commensurate with the enormous task of knowing the world in which we live. To the uncertainty called forth by error and ignorance, to the retardation and failures attributable to stupidity, laziness and carelessness, one has to add the consequences of sin, namely, the stubborn refusal to acknowledge the truth when it confronts us, because it is not our truth. All these factors have their repercussions in the social groups, especially in the operation of its power structure. This is due to the fact that they pursue a goal that is relevant. Consequently decisions have to be taken concerning the means and methods by which that goal is to be attained. Since there are individual differences, often of considerable latitude, among the members, and since decision-making, in order to be practical, must be limited to a relatively small number of people, frictions and conflicts are inevitable, even in the most homogeneous and harmonious groups. One is the conflict between conservatives and reformers. In national life, for instance, those in power will be in favour of preserving the *status quo*, while closing their eyes to the inherent evils that continuation of the actual conditions may bring to a minority group or a new generation. Similarly the routine methods of the bureaucracy may be wasteful and uneconomical. In such a situation, Christians will be mindful of the common good and recommend appropriate changes.

In turn, radical members of the group, often supported by the younger generation, may be more than critical of existing conditions and will insist on comprehensive and deep-going reforms. In view of the confusion and the cost of such measures, Christians will inquire into the necessity of such changes and the alleged advantages of the proposed goals. In our age people are too easily inclined to be more interested in change for change's sake than in real improvement. Even in the presence of manifest evils, Christians will ask whether full use has been made of the resources available and their feasibility. One thinks of the amazing results which the self-help programme of the Urban League has produced in negro higher education. One wonders whether the difficulties by which so many foreign aid programmes are beset in Africa and Asia are due to failure fully to exploit the native resources. The Bible states emphatically that, in making man, God equipped him with all that is necessary for his development. While the help that comes from fellow men is certainly included in those resources, nevertheless it is such a precious and naturally limited good that we have no right to count upon it as long as we have not yet made full use of our personal resources. Our foreign aid programmes in Africa and Asia have so often backfired and brought so small returns, because we strengthened the native's feeling of impotence. Certainly the 'developed' nations have an obligation to help the underdeveloped ones. But the wisdom with which that aid will be used, and the success of those relief actions, will depend on the degree of educating them to practise self-help.

Another type of friction will develop in social groups from the struggle for leadership. Frequently, it is simply lust for power that makes a man seek the top place in a nation. Here again Christians will emphasize the priority to be given to the common interest. Their support will go to the man who is most likely to serve the well-being of the nation. Experience shows that this qualification for public office is not always found in candidates who are members of a church or denomination, while they may be encountered in persons who have no church affiliation.

Open conflicts arise mainly in the fight of labour and management, in the rivalry of political parties and in international disputes. The use of power may lead to the destruction of life and property on a large scale. It is obvious that in a sinful mankind violent methods will commend themselves because through the defeat of one party the dispute is terminated temporarily. Peaceful solutions, such as obligatory mediation, have been recommended. Yet thus far neither appropriate laws nor competent judges have been available. The reason why the laws suggested have proved to be ineffective is not to be seen in the inability of the legislators, but rather in the tendency of the parties to have their power treated as a factor in their favour. The losses resulting from such conflicts must therefore be counted as the penalty for people's unwillingness to find a mode of reconciliation. A head of state or a president of a labour union, who happens to be a Christian, will make an effort to avoid an open conflict. If and when one breaks out, he will try to reach a peaceful settlement. But he will not be able to preclude aggression or provocation from the other side. The advice that he should surrender his cause to the other side without offering resistance is hardly practicable, because in such a case his nation or union would hardly follow him.

By resorting to open conflict, people are putting the decision into God's hands. They will experience then that God is not always with the largest battalions, yet also that victory cannot be interpreted as God's approval. Rather, God's justice may be seen in the fact that to either side he offers an opportunity to use a war as a means by which the contestants may judge their cause in the light of the common good. The very uncertainty of the issue is to remind them that the well-being of a social group does not depend on victory, but rather on justice. Power conflicts are seldom confined to the two opponents – as a rule they affect also third parties. A lay-off, for instance, may influence the whole national economy. The outcome of a strike may affect the consumer, because it entails higher prices. An industry which presses the government so hard for protection that tariffs are raised may wreak a catastrophe upon the economy of another country whose exports competed with the protected industry.

For the Church to take sides in a political controversy would not only be unwise, but also morally wrong. For in all likelihood there are Christians engaged on either side. Hence, one-sided statements of the majority would imply a denial of the minority's ability or competence to judge the issue in a Christian way. The service which the Church is called upon to render to a political body consists rather in stating the direction in which a Christian solution should be sought. By assuming the function of political decision-making, the Church weakens and harms itself. For thereby it dooms the minority to inactivity in the Church, and, as a result of its one-sided position, it must share responsibility for the possible excesses of the group whose interests it sponsors.

The case is different with individual Christians. Tolstoy and others have contended that, on account of its inherent power conflicts, political activity is incompatible with Christian love. To this the conscientious Christian politician will reply that it is love for his fellow citizens that moves him to work for a just and socially minded legislation and for the use of government funds through which such legislation will be implemented. In the pursuit of that goal, a clash of powers and interests is unavoidable. But the Christian will see to it that the Church, in which he stands together with members of the opposite party, should not be disrupted. In a world of power conflicts the supreme task of the Church consists in demonstrating its unity. With those members whom the legislators have forgotten, Christians will demonstrate their solidarity by means of material assistance and support of appropriate legislation. Likewise, where the race question and civil rights legislation for coloured people have split the denomination, Christians will plead with the dissenting brethren to join in the search for unity. As long as the Churches are divided on that issue or any other one, they have neither competence nor strength to tell secular groups that they should be concerned with unity. We should not delude ourselves. The unity demanded of the Church is unity in the Spirit, rather than merely organizational unity.

Closely related to this problem is that of equality. Both ancient philosophers, who held that all men were equal as rational beings, and the Apostles, who proclaimed that all men were equal as God's children, were far from deducing social or political consequences from such equality. They were rather convinced that in the social group remarkable differences were encountered. But the philosophy of the Enlightenment taught that potentially all men were equal, that the actual differences were but incidental, and that all men had equal rights and could make equal claims on the nation. In the economic sphere, however, colossal differences remained. However, Marx, Engels and Lasalle asserted that those in privileged economic positions had succeeded in obtaining their advantages by criminally exploiting their fellow men, all of whom had originally possessed the same status. Yet even Communism has not been able to ignore the differences of skills, education and experience, or the various degrees of significance which different people have for the life of the nation. Obviously the well-being of the nation is best served when the greatest possible number of its citizens receive the best education fit for them, and when all of them are given employment and the job for which their training has prepared them.

By establishing schools open to those who want to learn, Christianity has shown special interest in education, and it supports states and municipalities in their endeavour to make education as universal as possible. It is not unaware, however, of the basic differences between learning and creativity, especially in the arts and sciences. Above all it will emphasize that social usefulness is in the first place dependent on people's moral attitude and their spiritual gift. Where these endowments are ignored, social life degenerates into routine and bureaucratic self-complacency.

In conclusion, two things should be stated. Christian life is lived in a world of conflict and controversy. There is no hope that that condition will cease completely. Yet Christian life and especially its reconciling work is not for that reason doomed to futility. In a world of struggle, Christianity creates oases of peace and love. While they are constantly threatened from the outside, they are at the same time signs and symbols of what true life is meant to be. They refute the claim of those who consider fighting and use of violence essential for human progress. On the contrary, it is in keeping with the lessons of history to say that, through Christ's presence and work in this world, willingness to make peace and avoid conflict has been increased. The inward relations which faith establishes among persons, prove to be more effective than the outward stimuli which cause conflicts and discord.

The second point concerns the danger of procrastination. Since people are so easily tempted to start a quarrel, it is no wonder that even Christians are discouraged in a conflict situation. They give up all attempts to keep peace and to work for reconciliation. Allegedly they hope that conditions will be more propitious at a later moment. Characteristically, however, Jesus counselled his followers to postpone everything else and to try above all to be reconciled. Of course, in some instances, tempers will cool down after a while. But even so the resentment and the bitterness which are called forth by the conflict will not be forgotten. Rather they will poison the relationship of the people concerned and render an accord more difficult than it would have been when the quarrel started. In a conflict situation, contextual ethics would probably reason that right and wrong on either side should be weighed and the solution sought on a middle line. From the viewpoint of faith, it is the termination of the conflict that matters, whether I am right or not. What moves me to seek an accord is Christ himself who urges me. If I do not yield to his urge, when the conflict arises, what right do I have to hope that he will repeat it at the time I consider opportune?

20 The Family

A. The Structure of Family Life

1. *The Benefits of the Institution*

The institution of the family has come under heavy criticism during the past decades. Yet to judge from the number of marriages, that criticism does seem to lack convincing power. According to the critics, the family is a relic of our animal ancestry. But features such as mutual affection, parental authority, the home, extended care for the offspring and their education, language, the common procurement of food, the creation of family property, life-long duration, mutual aid and the awareness of the continuity of generations, are unique phenomena in the human family and preclude direct derivation from animal conditions. Since those features are found all over the world and their basic forms are everywhere the same, it would seem to justify the assumption that the family is a kind of social association that reflects the needs and abilities of human nature. The family may therefore be considered an institution willed by God and serving the ends he has with mankind. According to the New Testament, the family mirrors the relationship in which God stands to mankind. The Church has therefore in turn considered itself the true family of God on earth.

Though families normally live within larger social organisms, each family considers itself an autonomous entity which watches jealously over its privacy. It wants to regulate its internal affairs in complete independence and resents all attempts to interfere with its life. On account of the numerous ways in which the family has organized itself in the course of history, any ethical view must start from its basic features. Confusion will inevitably result when a given historical form of family life, for instance the type found now in the American, English or German middle class, is treated as normative standard. The ethics of the family must be seen in a dual perspective. We have to describe the advantages which the institution of marriage offers to its members, and then to study the demands of God implied in the gifts of family life. Fundamental in that vision is the awareness that the family is a whole. Within it one finds different functions: husband and wife, parents and children, brothers and sisters, young and old. Yet all of them are indispensable for the well-being of the whole family. Thus there is no room for a preferred position. The authority of the head of the family is considered as a special gift, namely, the ability to work in a responsible way for the benefit of the whole family. Likewise the mother has the privilege of taking care of the biological continuity of the family. Each member of the family makes his specific contribution for the benefit of the family's good. What distinguishes the Christian family from the natural family is the awareness that it is through the Spirit's operation that the work of the various members brings about a harmonious relationship.

The family is held together by a special kind of affection. Its members are aware of the necessity to stay and live together for better and for worse. Family love is typically different from erotic and sexual love. It has its roots in a sense of belonging together. The normal family mood is one of friendship, and the harmony of the family circle explains why it is that more gaity and joy is usually found within it than outside of it. Whatever one member does affects all the members of the family. They exchange their daily experiences, share their joys and sorrows, try to support each other in their work, and foster the harmony of their common life. Family life has its frictions and quarrels, too, but, as a rule, they are of limited duration. The necessity to live together makes its members willing to be reconciled with each other. There is danger, of course, that reconciliation should not be a genuine result of love, forgiveness and co-operativeness, but merely an act of giving in on account of the necessity of living together. The suppression of resentment, bitterness and hatred will eventually generate nervous troubles and even neuroses, or it will be acted out outside of the family, for instance in vandalism, brutality or bellicosity. The attitudes leading to religious persecution, class warfare, social strife and wars have a powerful root in the family. They result from a lack of true love in family relations. The attempt to get rid of those social plagues apart from a change of personal attitudes is therefore a vain and Utopian enterprise. In turn, family love is the cradle of public order and unity.

Another outstanding feature of the family is parental authority. The family would not be able to act in a meaningful manner unless the interrelation of its members were held together by a directive will. Parental authority may be misused. Nevertheless, it is not an usurpation of power on the part of the parents, but rather an indication of the teleological structure of this world and human life. As it is born, the babe is not an independent and self-supporting entity, but rather a member in a chain of generations. His course of life is determined by the family into which he is born. To act with authority is an inherent right of parenthood. To take that right away from the parents is tantamount to depriving parenthood of its supreme privilege. For parenthood is not confined to the biological fact of giving life to a child; it is also a relationship of persons to a potential person. As such it implies the special responsibility parents have for the education of their children. Some would hold that the child should not be given religious instruction until it were able to make his own choice. Such argument overlooks the fact that human life cannot be lived except in the continuity of the generations. Each generation afresh receives its initial stimulus and outlook in life from the parental generation. No man is in a position to mould his life entirely by himself and in complete disregard of tradition. Parental authority is restricted in its prerogatives. In the Christian view the parental authority is destined to foster the child's development as a potential person. That gives the father the right to demand obedience on the part of his children and to chastise them. Through the exercise of parental authority, the family is rendered into a centre of discipline and order. Regularity in the daily routine and the assignment of regular tasks to the children will prove to be highly effective. Its rationale is mutual service. In turn, the autonomy of the family guarantees a certain amount of freedom to its members. The normal appeal which the family makes is a request for voluntary co-operation.

Since parental authority is directed towards personal growth, the child is increasingly less dependent on his parents and must learn to make his own decisions. He has a right to re-think what he has been taught and to decide personally what the future course of his life should be like.

The home is the prerequisite of family life. Though the family is a part of the social group, it demands privacy for itself. While economically and politically the family remains dependent on the group, tribe, or nation, its internal life is self-contained. The intimacy in which its members are united is inaccessible to outsiders. It is not surprising, therefore, that family life disintegrates when two or more families are compelled to share the same room or when their dwelling place may not be shut off from other people's gaze. Russian Communism was initially inclined to see in the intimacy and seclusion of the family a remnant of capitalism that had to be abrogated. Families were forcibly joined lest they would have privacy, even in sexual relations. Likewise, children were to be brought up in government homes and withdrawn from parental authority. Yet experience soon taught the disadvantages and dangers of these measures. As they grew up, the children would be vexed by a sense of emptiness and a lack of initiative and planning because they had no place to which they belonged. Conversely, the home gives to the individual a sense of belonging and stability, because it offers him a shelter to which he may take his troubles and fears whenever he is hurt or harmed by the outside world.

The home is more than the room, apartment, or house in which the family lives. Otherwise, in our age of excessive mobility, an infinite number of people would never be able to have a sense of being at home. What makes a dwelling place a home is in the first place the determination of the people who inhabit it to be by themselves, so that – without their permission – it would not be open to other people. Selection or at least personal arrangement of the furniture and the decoration of the room are indications of the longing for a home. Common interest and effort in its maintenance, neatness and beautification contribute substantially to transforming the utilitarian character of the dwelling into an implement of personal life. Failure so to do is one reason for the drabness and ugliness of slums, and it explains in turn the unrest and dissatisfaction of the inhabitants.

Education is one of the basic gifts that the family imparts to its members. Long before formal education in the school begins, the family performs an educative function. Its results or failures will lastingly influence the children's and the parents' life. Within the family, the little child acquires the first elements of behaviour, mores, speech, normal skill, social graces, evaluation of people and things, the basic structure of social life, and understanding of itself as well as the zeal to accomplish things and the joy over these achievements. An important educative factor in family life is the common work done by its members for their benefit and pleasure. Likewise the report on their outside activities and experiences. For the development of the child's character, of greatest importance is the assistance which, in an unsolicited way, members of the family give each other. Equally effective is the close scrutiny with which the family watches and appraises the behaviour and accomplishments of its members. No outsider will dare do it with such frankness and sympathy. In that way the foundations are laid of personal life and the understanding of its reciprocal nature. The parents who fail to take this educative task seriously not only hamper the further progress of the child; they also impair their own development as persons because they do not learn to assume responsibility for an assigned task when it is the most natural opportunity in their lives so to do. Many parents seem to think that their educational obligation has reached its end when they send their children to school. Yet the possibilities of the school are limited, especially in our days. What is of even greater consequence, its function is mainly utilitarian. Only incidentally the teacher of today will appeal to the child as an incipient personality. Thus the child's growth into personal life is principally dependent on the example set by the rest of the family and the help they give him for his development. The beneficial results of family life are rooted in the fact that it implies a system of order by which many of the details of life are regulated. It is able to discharge that function in a satisfactory way, because normally its order is preserved by voluntary compliance. In turn, that voluntary nature is its weak point. Family life is disturbed whenever a member refuses to comply, yet also when the family, especially the parents, do not insist on its observance. Permissiveness, apart from this order, makes a tyrant of the youngster and makes it hard for him to find his place in life once he leaves the bosom of the family. Yet, mere insistence on parental authority will also fail to educate the child, unless the parents have rendered their home a place of order.

2. *Christianizing the Family*

The institution of the family was in existence long before the Jewish and Christian religions made their appearance. Yet, like other social institutions, the understanding and organization of the family have noticeably profited from the contact with those religions. The Christian family marks a step forward in the evolution of the human race. Characteristic of the Bible is the view that God's relationship to mankind is that of a father to his children, whereby the emphasis falls upon his patient care for his children and his educative purpose. This new vista led in turn to the idea of the Church as God's family. Thereby, the human family, in turn, was seen in a new perspective. The Church as a religious association became the model of the human family. Thus, instead of being a sociological phenomenon, the family was looked upon as the medium through which God brings the natural qualities of man to fruition. Within the history of redemption the family is thus both a divine gift and a challenge to its members. As God's present, we admire its simplicity and appropriateness, and we give thanks for its blessings. By calling himself our Father and by granting us the privilege to address him as such, God discloses both his condescension and the sublime goal of family life. The family is destined to be the basic form of human fellowship in its various aspects. Through the family institution, the possibility of a truly human life is offered to mankind. The Christian family is composed of ordinary people and is not dependent on a specific form of organization. Its members differ from the rest of mankind, however, by the fact that they make an effort to combine the natural potentialities of family life with the vision of a divine purpose and the trust in the power of the Spirit.

The Christian family is not an ideal organization which has already reached its goal. Rather it is engaged in a process of transforming itself. The social history of the Christian family offers therefore a confusing picture. Its organization has assumed different shapes in different countries and ages. Yet one also notices in its history a constant deepening of its spiritual self-understanding. The history of the family, like all social institutions, is a paradoxical story. Its form of organization and its interpretation are subject to historical changes, and thus are in perpetual need of rethinking and of adopting new forms of organization. Yet, on account of the fact that God uses it in order to realize his purpose with mankind, all its historical forms are primarily concerned with rendering its fellowship increasingly effective and useful. The consequences of neglect are more serious than is usually assumed. The child will be in search of a beneficent substitute, and will hope to find it in premature sex, homosexuality, liquor or drugs, or will turn his frustration into vandalism. It is not necessary for people whose form of family life differs from that of Western man to give up their traditional form of family organization in order to be Christian. In the light of God's plan they may faithfully engage in the adaptation of their inherited forms to God's purpose as Western Christians have done with theirs.

Not only the form of family organization is subject to change, however. Through a Christian understanding of the family we also learn that it is not an ultimate end. True human life cannot be found in a self-contained individual; it is life in fellowship. Man's greatest need is association with other human beings. In turn, we are capable of enduring biting want and substantial losses as long as there are people willing to console and befriend us. Conversely, the most harmful danger for family life and for social life in general is the claim the media of mass communication make on our time. The harm does not lie in the first place in the immorality of some of the programmes, but rather in the fact that valuable time is wasted on programmes which have little or no worth at all. Yet the time spent on them is lost for family life. Unfortunately, the evil is increased by the fact that the isolation into which those media banish the individual condition his behaviour. He may lose his ability to enter into personal contact with others. Fellowship eventually degenerates into an impersonal exchange of the news.

Having time for each other is the prerequisite of a healthy and happy family life. That life is spoiled when the parents, or the children, spend all their leisure time away from the home, and also when both parents are wage-earners. The social reformers of the past century combated social conditions in which mothers, too, had to work in order to save their family from starvation. The tragic paradox of our age lies in the fact that mothers seek a job in order to share in the general affluence of the middle class. For the children a baby-sitter or nurse does not replace the mother. There is no substitute for her interest in, and care for, the children's needs. Some psychologists contend that the restlessness and lack of peace of many contemporaries is a symptom of their search for identity. But the hope is in vain that in discovering their identity they will find peace and satisfaction. For the 'identity' is but a new role which the individual plays. Thereby he cuts himself off from valuable fellowship and pretends not to be in need of anybody else. In fact, however, his true identity would lie in personal relationships with others. Yet, on account of the limited number of members who form a family, a warning must be sounded against the exclusive sentimentalism of the 'family spirit'. The love which in much modern ethics is described as the centre of Christian life may degenerate into a vague emotion with little ethical significance. Such a family-centred person may bear no hatred against any one in particular, yet he also lacks the determination to take people outside the family seriously and enter into fellowship with them.

The family is an economic unit. While there is room for personal property owned by each member, separately, there is also family property to be used for common purposes, e.g., furniture, appliances and food. In an age of waste it will not be easy to teach the children to make careful and considerate use of those objects and to realize that reckless and destructive use on the part of individual members harms the whole family economically. Within it, the concept of 'private property' has a limited application only. As long as somebody lives in the family communion, they expect him to use his income and resources for the family's good. The head of the home, for instance, has no right to contend that he may use the larger part of his earnings for his own benefit. In a Christian family, he and its other members will rather forego special luxuries and entertainments, when e.g. by doing so they may enable a member of the family to go through college. No wonder that, within the body politic, the Christian family forms a model of responsible and wise handling of money.

The unity of the family will remain on a utilitarian level unless it implies spiritual homogeneity. The growth of fellowship within the family is seriously hampered when some members decline participation in the family's spiritual life. In turn, the small child, though unable fully to understand its meaning, has a right to take part in the prayer life of the home. The prayer practice will eventually disclose the significance of prayer. Basic differences in religious affiliation will entail divergency in the general outlook in life. Spiritual homogeneity does not mean uniformity. It may be that as a result of Vatican II even the Catholic Church will lower the walls by which formerly partners in a mixed marriage were separated in their spiritual life. It will be true, however, that a Christian who marries a non-Christian will encounter unsurmountable obstacles when he looks for that complete personal fellowship which God offers the Christian family.

As every man knows, the unity of the family is an aim rather than an accomplished social condition. This is particularly true when changes succeed each other as rapidly as in our time. By nature and purpose, the family is the guardian of tradition, and its structure is built upon the conviction that human life is unable to grow, unless the new generation uses its privilege and avails itself of the conditions and accomplishments of preceding generations as its foundation. Yet the critical efforts of the nineteenth and twentieth centuries have abolished much of the values and the strict order of the preceding period of history. In such circumstances, the present generation demands in the first place freedom for its own experiments in living. It shows little interest in merely continuing the work of their fathers.

3. *The Crisis of the Family*
The family, including the Christian family, is now in a crisis. The old forms are in a process of disintegration while no definite new form has made its appearance yet. In that situation, the young people may realize that running away from home and perhaps joining a hippy group is in the long run a disappointing and disillusioning experience. Yet the family's insistence on a return to the tested order of family life

is futile, too. The dawn of a new solution depends on the patience and benevolence of the older generation which has to learn not to be frightened or irritated by the uncommon views and looks of the 'gangsters'. Equally important, however, will be the determination of the younger generation in freedom to choose a new order of life. Finally, both of them must keep in mind that what gives a movement lasting significance is not the novelty of its appearance. The truly new movement must be determined by its allegiance to the institutions of social life. The problem of adolescence cannot be solved by by-passing the family. Either generation will then realize that in order to preserve the unity of the family, they must refrain from absolutizing a form of family organization.

The unity of the family will not be attained by mere emotions. It depends on the will of all its members as they are engaged in the activities of the home and work for its common good. Hence within the family there is no contrast between white-collar work and blue-collar work, between menial and noble activities, between trivial and important things to be done. Whether it be a necessary task or an act of beautification, a difficult job or the mere pleasure of entertaining, makes no difference. Within the family all activities are enjoyed and voluntarily done. No reward is expected, yet all are equally appreciated. In that respect, the Christian family is the training school for Christian participation in public life. Right things are done because one enjoys serving others.

The fact cannot be denied, of course, that even in a Christian family relations are not always harmonious, nor are its members at every moment ready to co-operate. Yet the Christian family provides ever new stimuli to resume one's responsibilities, and it offers a perspective and field of action by which reconciliation and the restoration of order are facilitated. Thus there is good reason for believing that the Christian family will weather the present crisis and be able to create new forms of family life. If we are right to consider the family a divine institution of social life rather than a temporary form of living together, we may also be sure that God will not abandon his work mid-way. The present crisis of the family lays bare weaknesses of its former organization. Now to be stressed over against its authoritarian character is the co-operative nature of the members of the modern family. Likewise, children are to be trusted as persons in the making. Instead of an abrupt change of the adolescent's status from mere passivity to full independence, a gradual education and emancipation towards personal life is required.

B. Marriage

1. *Nature of Marriage*

Within the family, marriage forms the most important institutional factor. In it two persons of different sex are united with the intention to live together for the rest of their lives. The husband-wife relationship differs essentially from other relations of the two sexes, for instance, that of brother and sister, uncle and niece, or of women fighting with men for equality in public life. The spouses are kept together by a sexual attraction in which not merely nerves and circulatory processes are engaged, but rather two persons in their specific sexuality. That nature of sexual attraction becomes articulate as an erotic bond, as a feeling of inner harmony and homogeneity, as a longing for permanent fellowship, or as a desire – through contact with the other person – to discover one's own identity. However, such sensations do not form the essence of marriage. They are but the way by which nature lures people into willingness to be united in marriage. In this provisional character of the means of attraction we see the fallacy of romantic love. As the married couple will realize, no less important than the features which they have in common, and for practical purposes the most important ones, are those in which they differ. Again, most weighty among them is the differentiation of the sexes.

When the fact is fully realized, marriage is no longer understood as mere co-existence or friendly co-operation of two people. Rather both spouses aim at co-operating in such a manner that the diversities of their individualities may supplement each other. In a Christian marriage neither spouse tries to assimilate the partner to his own nature and outlook. They intend their very differences to be joined in a fruitful and meaningful union. For that paradoxical effect marriage has been treated already in primitive times as a holy institution. Its natural basis is related to a divine dynamic and goal. In their sexual relations people may ignore or deliberately overlook the fact that they are persons. Yet what moves them in their passion is not just the secretion of glands, but rather it is their very Ego that acts and experiences. Because that is so, sex is not by itself a disturbing factor, but rather a constitutive element. In turn, the specific function which sex performs in married life throws new light upon the nature of the Ego. According to existentialism and individualism the life of the Ego consists in a quest for identity. In such outlook it is assumed that the individual has everything that renders life meaningful in himself. All attempts to explain the origin and purpose of marriage in a purely naturalistic way do violence to facts implied even in the most primitive forms of marriage. Of course, sexual intercourse is possible as a purely physiological act, and it has even assumed institutional form in prostitution. But such activities do not lead to marriage. In turn, the fact that in spite of promiscuity and prostitution the institution of marriage should have been recognized may be taken as a sign that it was established by God as a determinant of human life. While the specific ways in which the institution is implemented depend on historical circumstances, the institution itself is an essential feature of human life, not encountered anywhere among animals.

In marriage, the sexual differences of the two partners serve to accentuate their individual differences. Within the family, the marriage bond indicates the possibility and desirability to overcome the strangeness by which the partners are separated and irritated. Matrimony implies the hope that a spirit of willing co-operation and harmony can be established between the spouses.

2. *Love*

One cannot speak in a meaningful way of sex in the singular without keeping in mind duality of sexes found everywhere in the organic world. The philosophers like to talk about human nature as though the differentiation of the sexes were incidental and an anatomical phenomenon only which were irrelevant metaphysically. The differences of sex are not confined however to anatomy and physiology. Their mentality and outlook in life are determined by their different physiological functions. What takes place in sexual attraction is the longing of the male sex for the female sex, not just that of two individuals for each other. Full life cannot be found in the individual; it must be sought in the individual's participation in social life. But humanism robs the image of life of its depth by ignoring three facts. Firstly, my fellow man is not an *alter ego*, in every essential respect like myself. Rather he is a stranger to me when I first meet him. Also, humanity is fully realized only in the interrelation of individuals, not in self-contained self-realization. Furthermore, that relationship is not mere co-existence. In marriage, for instance, it is a mutual give and take of persons, whose basic outlook is determined by their different sex.

By joining in marriage, Christian spouses give expression to the mystery of human existence. Masculinity is destined to be masculinity for a female and *vice versa*. The spouse has potentialities which cannot be actualized except through the other. As *semen* and *ovum* must join in order to produce a new child, so in general husband and wife must become aware of their supplementary relationship if their married life is to be truly satisfactory. Physiologically, the mutual interdependence of the sexes is a complete one. Neither sex has in that respect reason for boasting of its superiority. Since their different mentalities are conditioned by their biological functions, one can hardly speak of the mental inferiority of either sex. In this interdependence we find the deepest ground why casual sexual relations are bound to leave a feeling of unfulfilled longing.

While young people have an instinctive awareness of the interdependence of the sexes, the potentialities of their interdependence cannot be brought to light except through continued fellowhsip and exchange. The difference of the sexes is not an idea whose truth can be rationally proved. It is a dynamic fact that has to become real in daily encounter and experience. Though it has a sexual basis, its actuality covers all aspects of personal life. As an ongoing mutual challenge and response, married life continues to remain fresh and fruitful even at an age when sexual intercourse has ceased. What keeps the personal interchange among the spouses on the go is marital love. That love is the readiness never to be repelled or frightened by the partner's strangeness and to make every effort to bring the divergencies of outlook to a constructive synthesis. In a Christian marriage that dynamic is intensified by the example of God's love for man. Envisaging God's relationship to his people under the image of husband and wife, three features of a good marriage are disclosed: (i) Marriage is meant to be a permanent relationship. (ii) Its purpose is to seek one's happiness in promoting that of the spouse. (iii) Given the frailty and sinful inclination of man, married life requires the constant willingness to forgive on the part of the spouse hurt, even in the case of infidelity. In the traditional Catholic doctrine, the purpose of marriage is seen in the procreation of children. If that were the case, marriage were relevant merely as a sexual relationship, and the childless family would be devoid of meaning. The union through interdependence, in turn, conveys meaning to marriage, even when of the fire of early erotic passion a few embers only are left.

True Christian love is anxious to encourage the spouses to exchange experiences and views, their activities and projects, their grief and joy, their apprehension and hope, in such a way that the partner's condition is as relevant as one's own predicament. That is what is meant by marital union. The most amazing feature of married life may be seen in the fact that the 'happy marriage' does not require any agreement of out-look or common adoption of religious and moral assets. Its success depends on the willingness of the spouses to use their differences as occasions to enrich each other. This desire to exist for the partner and through him engenders the will to stay permanently together.

3. *Permanency*

The weakness of the 'New Morality' lies in its resignation and moral defeatism. It starts from the assumption that whatever is sought in the partner is the satisfaction of one's own sexual and erotic desire. The partner is therefore merely the occasion by which to reach that goal. No wonder that sexual experience, even when enjoyed, frequently leaves the partners empty. Attempts subsequently to seek compensation in liquor or drugs will prove to be of little avail. What is even worse in the modern freedom which allows to choose an unlimited number of sexual partners, is the resulting loss of one's ability to develop true love. True love realizes that the partner is not merely a body with sexual organs and sexual sensitivity, but rather a person whose special needs I have to discover and whose special gifts I must learn to appreciate. With such an aim, marriage is not a mere reciprocal exchange; rather, it is a permanent one. The religious ceremony's special value lies in the fact that the relation in which marriage stands to God's will is unmis-takably pronounced therein. The Church proclaims to the couple and their company that marriage is a special blessing which God grants to mankind, as also that its wealth and depth will not be discovered except by faith. By God's will, marriage has a twofold function. In it we find the clearest and most articulate expression of the pattern which underlies all human fellowship. Mankind does not reach its goal in a uniformity, as Plato and all totalitarian politicans and rationalistic philosophers hold. Rather, mankind is to find its unity in a daring exchange of their different gifts and a loving endurance of their weak-nesses and faults. At the same time the institution of marriage symbolizes the nature of God's redemptive work. Though we are not divine, God is prepared to let us share in his work, and in turn, he is willing to come to our succour in all our needs and shortcomings. Incompleteness is the characteristic of everything in this world. Yet marriage symbolizes that through the reciprocity neither partner wants to receive the equivalent of what he has donated, but rather rejoices in the opportunity of enriching the spouse. It is that conscious concern for the partner that prevents the infatuation in which the individual loses sight of himself.

In the area of sex and marriage more than in any other field of Christian ethics, the practice of the Catholic confessional has led to a tragic shift. Attention has turned from the goal to be reached by faith to the things to be shunned by the believer.

Whereas in other spheres of ethics the Reformation has vigorously restored the positive perspective, in the field of sex and marriage the medieval outlook to a large extent has survived. Our age is just beginning to restore the right attitude. It manifests itself especially as reverence, love and fidelity. Over against naturalism, by which sex is but one of the several human instincts and hence of no special significance, faith treats sex as a most valuable divine gift enabling us to experience in our existence the mystery of supplementary co-existence. The high esteem in which women are held in Christianity indicates how poor life is where that reverence is lacking. On that new basis, personal love is possible. The spouse is not considered a mere cause of pleasureable sensations, but as one's greatest treasure and hence worthy of one's constant care. That attitude is closely related to purity. Sexual purity stands in contrast with obscenity. The latter is an attitude which devaluates sex by treating it as something dirty to be enjoyed in secret only, yet that is doubly enjoyed when dragged into the semi-public atmosphere of the smoker or the bar-room or found in magazines or books not destined for the general public, and thus exposed to derision. Purity is opposed to any derogatory treatment of sex. It is not shielded for the mere reason that it is natural, for natural things may be perverted and become indecent, but rather on account of the end which it serves in God's plan. Purity does not abhor a humorous reference to sex, but it discerns even in its weaknesses and clumsy handling evidences of its basic value.

Fidelity, finally, is the attitude which I owe to the partner through whom the unique role which the other sex has for my own life was revealed to me. Ideally that role would be performed by one's first partner. Yet in the casual and thoughtless way in which today many people enter into their first sexual encounter or contract marriage the first partner may often fail to play that role. It may be that only later in life, or in a second marriage, sex becomes truly meaningful for a couple. Not until and unless that stage has been reached will they be able to realize the exclusive and permanent function of their union. Thus experience plays a decisive role in the genesis and cultivation of the sexual attitudes. Prior to personal experience, the ethical attitude is a matter of mores and hence subject to questioning on the part of the adolescent. Sexual experience discloses the facts upon which the sexual mores are established, and thus will be the means by which the value of sex is personally apprehended. Yet that may often mean that it was by a faulty action that the individual received his initiation. That explains why the life of Christianity is an aspiration for goodness rather than its full achievement.

One further question. What is the basis of marriage? As a social institution, it rests on the determination of the couple to grant full reciprocity of life to each other in an exclusive way. From a secular viewpoint, a common-law marriage is as valid as one solemnized in a church. Seen in a religious perspective, however, marriage is the way in which two people give outward expression to their belief that by the kindness of God they are destined to attain a joint existence. For God has so arranged the life of his creatures that two imperfect and fragmentary beings are enabled to join in a functioning whole.

If the oneness of husband and wife were accomplished by their own efforts alone, we might agree with Kierkegaard that the risk in choosing the right partner was so enormous that it was inadvisable to take it. The real risk in marriage does not lie in the difficulty of choosing the right partner, although that is a problem. Yet that is merely a reason why hasty and uncritical selection of a partner should be avoided. The real problem is to be seen in the sinfulness of man. Jesus told his disciples that it was not enough to shun adultery, fornication and promiscuity. Since sin is the self's wrong attitude towards God, even moral determination and the marriage bond will not suffice to keep the marital relationship unbroken. God has to be requested to purify the spouses' minds.

By establishing marriage as an essential institution of human life, God has sanctified sex. Marriage is not to be regarded as a secure haven that protects the people concerned from incontinence. The will to have sexual fellowship is a constitutive element of marital union. Consequently, no Christian should look contemptuously or self-righteously down upon people who openly practise immorality. The Christian answer to infidelity is not an immediate demand for divorce. On the part of the lapsed partner, it will require confession of his wrong and request for pardon. The wronged spouse, on the other hand, must realize that he or she married a sinful person rather than an angel. He must be willing to forgive and to make a strong effort fully to re-establish mutual relationships. In the way it rejoins the opposites, marriage both actualizes that union and symbolizes the need of forgiveness as a mark of truly human life.

Marriage is meant to be a lifelong association, for the possibilities inherent in the mutual relationship of the spouses are unlimited. That fact is not realized by people who plead for a limited duration of marital life. The fact should not be denied, of course, that after some while a couple may feel that what they are able to give to each other has been exhausted. The reason is not to be found in the institution of marriage, however, but rather in the fact that the couple took no interest in movements and projects going on around them, or failed to acquire friends who would work as catalysts in the couple's relationship. Those people could bring to light hitherto unexplored gifts and interests. In general, it should be said that any marital relationship which from the outset is destined only for a limited time will eventually destroy itself. The very terms of such an arrangement will render the couple unwilling seriously to confront each other in the search for union. If marriage requires permanency in order to become truly meaningful, is divorce compatible with the Christian faith? Do internal conflicts justify the severance of the marriage bond? Some churches are strictly opposed to divorce, yet consider permanent separation without the right of a new marriage a legitimate measure. Seemingly they have the authority of Jesus on their side. Divorce is logically inconsistent with marriage. For when the couple got married they intended their union to be a permanent one. Yet Jesus was not likely, contrary to his general teaching method, to enact new laws, more rigorous than those given by the scribes and the radical sects. Rather he wanted to illustrate the new life God was willing to impart to his followers. They should solve their marital problems in a positive way, rather than negatively, through divorce. Jesus wanted to stress the fact that once consummated, marriage was destined to be a life-long relationship. When, according to Matthew, Jesus allowed divorce in the case of adultery, the evangelist did not amend and mitigate a commandment of the Master. Rather he bore witness to Jesus' realism. In moral life, man does not act consistently, but rather is often prone to yield to sin. Hence there are instances in which, humanly speaking, the marriage relationship has been broken beyond repair by the fault of one of the partners. In the case of human inability to mend the broken pieces, divorce is the consistent termination of their relationship. In taking such a stand, Jesus did not condone adultery nor legitimize divorce. But a mere effort of the human will may prove not strong enough to cope effectively with the obstacles which prevent the couple from attaining the aim of true marriage.

C. Sex

1. *Sex as a Marital Tie*

As amply shown above, marriage is never exclusively a sexual relationship, especially when sex is merely understood in a physiological and psychological sense, as instinct and urge. Nevertheless sex plays a central role in it. Yet sexual life develops in the adolescent, irrespective of marriage, and continues to make itself felt in the adults. While it is possible to discipline and control it, it never ceases to remain an integral part of human life. Though repressed or inhibited, it continues to make itself felt in the individual's unconscious life. The sexual urge is accompanied by the most potent of emotions; no other sensation will yield a greater pleasure and satisfaction than that experienced in sexual intercourse.

What makes the sexual approach desirable to both sexes is not merely the exciting sensation of the bodily contact. The woman is proud and happy because she feels instinctively that she is taken seriously in her womanhood. In a similar way, the man's approach implies an element of aggressiveness, because he wants the satisfaction to be acknowledged by the woman in the subduing role of his masculinity. It is this combined experience of pleasure and of existential satisfaction which, particularly in the early stage of married life, effectively facilitates their mutual adjustment. It helps powerfully to counteract the difficulties and disappointments resulting from the spouse's otherness.

2. *Sex as Disturbance*

Sex has also irritating and disturbing effects. For instance, sexual intercourse may result in pregnancy. There is nothing in the sexual act as such that would give a forewarning of that possible effect. But in many cases, and especially in the case of the unmarried woman, it encumbers her with a heavy responsibility. Also, there is no legal obligation that would force a man to marry a woman whom he has sexually initiated. Yet if he breaks up the relationship, he leaves her the bitter feeling of having been cheated in her womanhood. In order to do justice to those painful and powerful aspects of sex, the Jewish religion severely restricted sexual intercourse to married life, surrounding it with strict prohibitions against sexual perversions, premarital intercourse and adultery. The public authorities were charged with prosecuting such transgressions. Basically the same attitude was taken by the medieval Church. However, regulation was but partially effective. Moreover, from an ethical viewpoint, it was objectionable because it limited sexual morality to outward conduct, while the personal element in sex was neglected.

It is also obvious that the Old Testament view had completely ignored the element of emotional self-transcendence and had treated sex exclusively as a means of procreation. In turn, the rising naturalism and materialism of the last two centuries suggested that sex was a purely physiological phenomenon like eating and drinking. The individual was held to have a right to indulge in sexual pleasures, provided that it was accomplished with the full consent of the partner. Since the resulting satisfaction was the rationale of sex life, the special mode by which the end was reached was of no significance, even the concept of 'sexual perversion' was to be abandoned. Insufficient physical effort, the comfort of modern life, heavy caloric intake, the social freedom enjoyed by the young girl, and the universal availability of contraceptives have rendered that 'new morality' pretty general in our days. Formerly, public opinion served to protect the young girl's chastity. In our days, those who favour sexual freedom try to make their outlook reputable by exercising strong social pressure, and will ostracize the girl who refuses to comply with their demand. Dissenters are depicted as old-fashioned and hypocritical. However, the gain in pleasure demands a high price. By treating sex as a purely physiological affair the partners deprived themselves of the existential experience of inter-dependence. Sex has become an article of mass consumption which is cheap, yet not worth much, because it is merely to bring about a bodily sensation. Pregnancy in most cases leads to abortion or early marriage. The latter seems to be the desirable alternative. Yet, on account of the immaturity of the spouses, it leads frequently to strained relations and divorce and to faulty education of the offspring. Abortion, though illegal, is obtainable with relative ease, yet it is no solution. The man tries to get rid of the undesired consequences of his deed by way of reckless disregard of the woman's lot. The woman, in turn, will punish herself by cutting off a living portion of herself. Those who bemoan and denounce the immorality of the younger generation usually overlook an important fact. Deplorable as is the modern trend, that clamouring for full erotic freedom merely reflects the moral climate in which the new generation grows up. We reap the fruits of an education which glorified freedom without responsibility. Thus there is not much hope that individual exhortation and warning or legal measures on the part of the college authorities, for instance, will bring about a real change of the situation. Only influences which **are** more powerful than public opinion will be able to accomplish a change. In an age in which the Churches themselves have widely yielded to permissiveness and subjectivism, many of the younger people will undecidedly waver between moral rejection of the sexual revolution and practical inability to resist the social pressure. The uncertainty, characteristic of the Churches' attitude toward sex, has good reasons. In emphasizing the pleasurable character of sex, the sexual revolution has laid bare an inconsistency in the traditional Christian view, understood as implying that sexual desire and delight were morally evil and a kind of diabolic perversion of the natural desire to have progeny. Psychologically, the couple's desire to have children does not by itself call forth sexual emotions; these accompany the desire to enjoy the relish implied in their union. That experience is universally found, and it in no way interferes with procreation. These facts show that sexual feeling of happiness is an integral part of human existence. Sexual emotion should be treated naturally as it was in the Old Testament, and sexual 'fun' is not by itself immoral. But people overlook so frequently the fact that a thin line divides erotic play from the earnest of sexual reality. 'Play' ends when the young man is confronted with the pregnancy of his girl, with whom he had 'played'. Enjoyment of sex has a place in married life, where it counterbalances the burden of mutual responsibility. The moral problem of sex is not to be seen in the biological fact that there are instinctive urges at work in man as well as mental life. The problem results from the metaphysical fact that man is destined for communion with God in the totality of his life. Hence people have to decide whether their sexual existence is positively or negatively related to that goal. Where young people are really in love with each other and are determined eventually to get married, premarital sexual relations will have the same inconveniences as in other extramarital relationships; but their intercourse will not have the detrimental psychological consequences, because their connection implies already a sense of mutual responsibility.

A rapid change of the present situation in sexual morality is hardly to occur. The outlook upon which the 'sexual revolution' rests serves to feed many commercial interests which are not easily defeated. This is particularly true in a civilization in which success and pleasure are worshipped as supreme deities. Except for the rare cases where the spirit of the family still moulds the young people, a real transformation will probably require a new sense of responsibility and reverence for the purpose which God has in mind with man's earthly life.

3. *Celibacy*

Another problem connected with sex is that of celibacy. Since sex is the most effective means by which God enables man to overcome the alienation of otherness, is it not necessary for all adult people to get married? The answer should definitely be No. It is true that the supplementary character of the sexes not only symbolizes the structure of all those relations in this world in which otherness is implied, but it is also the effective means by which human life is enabled to reach its destination in God's service. Yet it is not sex alone by which one learns the mystery of supplementation. Rather, when people look out for the way in which God has built this world, they may be enabled to discover the secret of that relationship. Through his faith that person may also become aware of the divine pattern of the union of opposites. Since it is faith by which the mystery of supplementation is discovered, even unmarried persons are able to comprehend and to practise fruitful co-operation with the opposite sex. In that process, sexual experience is not worthless. Through it, the individual is enabled to proceed from a dim apprehension of the mystery of the opposites to an existential comprehension. We cannot follow the Catholic view, in turn, according to which voluntary lifelong celibacy is a meritorious work. That doctrine is fraught with the fear that all sex is unclean. Yet there is no Biblical foundation for such a view. Men like Paul would choose for themselves celibacy, but not because it was morally superior to marriage. Rather they felt that the inevitable preoccupation with family problems would unfavourably affect their missionary activity. Such consideration should be supplemented, however, by the thought that in many situations marriage has intensified the blessing which Christian workers have been able to promote. The reformers have rightly emphasized that the Protestant manse set a remarkable model of family life, and it became an exceedingly valuable educative factor in the congregations. Likewise, on the mission field, the presence of a wife who shares her husband's enthusiasm and zeal has visibly increased the efficacy of his activities.

The Christian view of sex seems at first a confused one. Christianity takes sex as an integral part of human life, yet at the same time emphasizes the necessity to be fully aware of its dangers and sinful implications. Actually, the two attitudes are intrinsically connected. Because it is nature, sex is to be accepted as God's gift. Yet because it is the most powerful manifestation of our vitality, it easily prompts the individual to disregard God's will and purpose. Thus, when Jesus says in oriental metaphorical style, 'If your right eye offend you, pluck it out and cast it from you' (Matt. 5:30), he does not advocate sexual asceticism, let alone physical self-mutiliation. Rather he wants to teach his followers radically to dissociate themselves from sin. The fact that the sexual urge is an integral factor of our nature is not to be construed as a reason to condone its misuse, as we are so easily apt to do. It is true that, like hunger and thirst, sex is a natural instinct. Yet it is the use we make of our instincts that makes them morally good or evil.

In our churches one now notices a widespread defeatism concerning sexual morality. Naturalism, existentialism and situation ethics seem to dominate the Western world, and public opinion seems to be agreed that sex and loose morals are synonymous. There is no reason, however, why we should underrate the power of the Spirit as he operates through Christian example. It is well-known, for instance, that Catholic girls, with the evidence of voluntary chastity before their eyes, are on the whole remarkably stronger and more determined in resisting the temptations of 'free love' than non-Catholics. They are not ashamed and not afraid of being different. May not the deepest reason for one's defeatism lie in the fact that modern Protestantism has increasingly shifted the religious emphasis from God's redemptive work for man to what man makes of his religion for himself?

21 The Church

A. The Nature of the Church

1. *The Role of the Primitive Church*

Religion is found all over the world, and it forms a special field of social action. In it, people see themselves in relation with a reality higher and mightier than themselves. Religious worship has also a structure of its own which cannot be replaced by that of any other institution. The religious field is composed of a community and special agents who mediate between the group and that superior reality. Membership in the religious community demands initiation, dedication and worship, all of which are dependent on knowledge of that reality and its mode of operation. Such recognition is laid down in doctrines, myths and holy rites. Being based upon group experiences, these implements differ from one religious body to another. The same holds true of their respective forms of organization, and Christianity is no exception to that rule. It also manifests itself in a great diversity of churches.

All the Christian bodies are agreed, however, in their belief that they are the legitimate descendants of the original Apostolic Church. The first Christians reported that a radical change had occured in their minds. Their whole outlook in life and their attitude towards this world and fellow men appeared to them the very opposite of what they had been formerly. Reality was seen in a new light. Jesus had taught them in every thing to discern the evidence of God's sovereign power and redemptive purpose, yet also to be aware of the operation of his judgement that would block the road to a meaningful existence to those who spurned the divine initiative. This teaching, which originally had been a mere theoretical wisdom to the Disciples, became through the resurrection of Jesus a new way of action. The Apostles discovered in themselves a new spirit of fellowship by which they were all held together, and made willing to assist and support each other. That new experience enabled them convincingly and potently to bear witness to God's work in Jesus and to mediate that power to others. The resurrection of Jesus gave them the assurance that the same spirit that had been working in him, was also manifested in their lives. Subsequent generations of Christians realized that their own life of faith was of the same nature as that of the primitive Church and that the history of the apostolic Church had been passed on to them as example and standard. From time to time, and particularly when the Church was threatened by the danger of conforming with the spirit and mores of its environment, enthusiastic Christians would call it back to the condition of the primitive Church. Such reformers may occasionally have gone to extremes by demanding a strictly mechanical imitation of the ways and forms of organization of the primitive Church. Nevertheless, practical requirements have set things straight again. The Church has eventually understood those demands as appealing for recognition of the normative character of the function and structure of the original Church. Notwithstanding the constant changes which the Church has undergone in the course of history, it has recognized that it would lose its identity and betray its divine mission, if it did not learn from the primitive Church what its privileges and obligations were.

2. *The Goal of the Church*
One might be inclined to think that, as a result of the risen Christ's presence, the Church would not only automatically be kept in existence, but also be moved towards the goal which God had set forth for her. Yet the Church is formed by the correlation of Christ's redemptive will, on the one hand, and the faith of its members, on the other. Hence, while Christ is all the time willing to assist a Church, the latter may, nevertheless, stagnate, because its leaders and/or members do not care to avail themselves of the privileges and resources put at their disposal.

What then is the end for which the Church exists? It is to remind its members of the value and importance of their spiritual life, and by doing so to enable them to lead the rest of mankind to a spirit-guided existence. Subjective idealism referred to a similar goal, and was naïvely convinced that to reach that goal was a matter of course. But all that was hoped for was a state of mind which the individual expected to attain by a reasonable effort of his will and a sane understanding of his nature.

The Christian reacts naturally to the proclamation of his goal with a feeling of terror. He is aware of his limitations as a finite creature, living in a universe of numerous determinants. How will he be able in such a world to assert himself? And how is he to be able to lead others into the realm of spiritual freedom? It is hardly surprising that, thus formulated, the goal of Christian life seems to be an unattainable Utopia, even to many members of the Church. There are several factors, however, that are destined to encourage us. According to Christian belief, God, in creating the cosmos, created heaven and earth, in other words not the material universe only, but also a realm of values. Both realms do not simply co-exist. Rather the realm of goodness attracts the material world. We are living in a world which is destined to improve in quality. Likewise man, though a member of the material world, is unable to withstand that attraction. He may not desire to become good, but he cannot help feeling that he should be better, or at least better off than he actually is. Thus the work of Christ does not take place in a neutral or indifferent world. He is actualizing what more or less consciously all men are waiting for.

Of course, human existence would be doomed to futility, if man were simply confronted with the cosmic forces. The conflict would inevitably end in utter defeat. But as a member of the Church, the Christian lives in a realm in which Christ, through his spiritual power, weakens and eventually defeats the forces of evil. As he wins people for his service, he diminishes the power of the cosmic determinants. In spite of them, the Christian is not doomed to inactivity and a purely passive acceptance of this world as it is. By means of prayer he is able to incorporate himself into the divine process of cosmic transformation and thus to be lifted up above the earthly necessities. His mind shifts from terror and cowardice to confidence and courage. Even with the new perspective, the individual believer might remain a captive of his fear, except for the support he finds in the fellowship with other Christians. Not only among his contemporaries will he find friends who console and strengthen him; the records of the Church will also tell him of the marvellous examples that the great Christians of the past have left us.

Through the Church, mankind has been imparted a belief in its dignity which in its boldness no philosopher has ever dared to repeat. They may have taught that the good or wise or great man was worthy of having a glimpse of the divine, yet the large majority would die without leaving a trace of its existence. In its policy of membership, the Church expresses its belief that it is man as man that has been destined for fellowship with God. Children, strangers, members of all social classes and races are called without discrimination. By that practice the Church has made a momentous impact upon the social structure of mankind and has operated as a powerful stimulus for social justice. Though the differences of functions and abilities are not ignored, they are no longer allowed to cut any person off from the community of the believers. Yet since the common destination rests upon the gracious will of God rather than upon an ontic superiority of man, Christian belief will not altogether move in the direction of natural law which dominates modern social and political thought. The very fact that the common vocation of mankind does not necessarily result in the redemption of all men explains why Christian social ethics will always imply a differentiating factor. But the differences are not allowed to be the source of friction, humiliation or oppression. It is to be kept in mind that the Church does not regard herself as the ideal social organization. Rather it symbolizes in terms of human association the working kindness of the heavenly world. We might also say that through the Church God discloses his total purpose concerning this world, from the Creation to its consummation. Hence it is possible for the Church to participate effectively in the redemptive work of Christ, notwithstanding its manifest shortcomings and imperfections. The gifts coveted in particular are spiritual insight and power, love and compassion – that is to say, the abilities most helpful for the service the Church is to render to its actual and prospective members.

It has become customary to divide the Church's work into social service and evangelism. Such division is misleading, however, since man is not a mere compound of body and mind, but rather an integral and indivisible individual. He would be badly served if we separated the two activities. The result would be an over-emphasis placed upon one aspect of personal existence at the expense of others. Of course, there may be instances in a person's life in which, above all, he needs comfort or exhortation, or where disregard of his physical disability or sickness could be a sign of spiritual blindness. But, notwithstanding the shift in momentary perspective, the Church is always preoccupied with people in the totality of their lives. Since the Church is a community in which both divine and human energies are at work, its members are receptive as well as active. Lutheran orthodoxy has somewhat one-sidedly laid all the stress on the fact that man is unable to do anything for his salvation, and that the only way open to him consists in receiving the evidences of kindness offered by God (*sola gratia*). Puritanism, in turn, would place all emphasis upon God's commandments and man's obedience, without which there could be no salvation. All emphasis was laid upon the right and full preparation for the divine present. The reciprocal relationship between believer and God demands, however, that both sides should be stressed. There could be no redemption, unless God had taken the initiative and man were willing to receive it as a divine gift. But since man is in the service of a divine purpose, faith must itself work out in the Christian's readiness to do for God's sake whatever is in his power. Conversely, while moral obedience is the evidence of the Christian's recognition that God is dealing with him in a kind way, that obedience must, nevertheless, be seen as a God-given ability to do his will, not as the manifestation of man's natural goodness. That same principle of reciprocal relationship is applied to the actions of faith. Since the Church does not discriminate against him and is willing to help him, the beneficiary of God's grace must be ready on his part to aid others, whenever they need it and he is able to help them. In his literary campaign, Frank Laubach implemented that principle by promising people to teach them to read and write, provided that they, in turn, were willing again to teach others what they had learned. The Church expects of all its members that whatever spiritual insight and strength they have received should be passed on to others. The individual Christian is enabled to act as a Christian because he is a member of the Church. The Church provides, through the Scriptures, the orders of worship, and its stated prayers a wealth of forms which are in turn used in a personal way.

Since through the Church God carries out his redemptive work, the circumstances which lead to a person's membership in the Church have also to be considered God's work as it is initiated by his call. For the Reformers, that vocation was bound up with the individual's place in society. Thus his vocation would imply his social position as the locale of his obedience of faith. Christian service was thereby more or less confined to concern shown for one's narrow environment. Today, the Churches exist apart from the political and social order. Vocation implies therefore that any place in this world can be considered an occasion for service.

3. The Function of the Church

As God's agent of redemption, the Church cannot be satisfied with being the supreme institution of social life; it has to act accordingly. It is by its deeds rather than by its theological self-interpretation that the Church operates upon its environment. As it understands itself, the Church's principal function consists in being the visible sign of the presence of Christ in this world. Far from being dead, God manifests his life-giving power. Through its very existence as well as its activities, the Church bears witness to that power as it was disclosed in the

313

Resurrection of Jesus. Being a special body in this world, the Church indicates both the weakness of biological life, which comes inevitably to an end, and the fact that through the Spirit's power earthly life can be transformed into everlasting life. Hence the finitude of earthly existence is no reason why people should despair of their lives. The very co-existence of life and insufficiency found in the Church is a sign of hope. That such hope should be tied up with an historical organization is of special importance; it indicates that our hope cannot be established upon our natural existence as such, yet also that it is not a flight away from this world. As it has its roots in past history, so its future is to be in this world. In turn, however, the message of hope implied in the existence of the Church is not to be interpreted as a merely quantitative increase of the joy of life or an improvement of biological and social living conditions as is held in Marxism and political liberalism. The history of the Church bears witness to the power of the Spirit, through whom earthly conditions are conformed with God's redemptive goal. The historical character of the Church points to a development by which external conditions will be radically transformed, notwithstanding its organizational weaknesses and the personal shortcomings of its members. The Church's witness is carried out mainly by way of enlightenment and of healing. Christians are privileged to be the 'light of the world' and 'salt of the earth'. As she invites people to join her ranks, the Church announces to mankind that, as he is, man is not yet what he is to be like, nor is he able to overcome his insufficiency, unless he lets the Spirit do his full work in him.

Apart from the Church, man is not able truly to understand himself and the actual predicament of the universe, notwithstanding the fact that he is constantly plagued by the feeling that something is wrong with this world and himself. He is likely to find the fault with other people, circumstances, or God himself. As should be expected, man outside the Church is also ignorant of the means by which his life would become truly tolerable. The Church, living by the Spirit, is able to furnish guidance, to both its members and other social institutions. Of course, the Church has no special knowledge or ability to assume leadership of those institutions. But, over against the utilitarian outlook found in many of them, it draws attention to their ultimate destination. As an association which is not directly concerned with practical results, the Church reminds mankind of the dangers implied in their one-sided pursuit. By its very presence and message, the Church makes them aware of the self-defeating consequences of their naïve egotism. From the example of the Church they learn that by following their 'natural' trend they dry up their wells, whereas they are destined to be roads to man's development as the supreme creature.

The Church sees its function also in healing human lives. In the Christian perspective, man is not an undeveloped being to be brought to growth or an incipient being to be led to completion. Rather he is considered a sick being. He is impaired in the normal use of his abilities, or he is struck by forces by which the normal conduct of life has been rendered impossible. That is a view of life which most non-Christians do not like, the more so since most of those addressed will point to the fact that they are physically and mentally in good health. Over against that attitude, Christianity will insist that what God does through the instrumentality of the Church is not just an improvement of the human predicament, whose realization might be pleasant yet not necessary. Rather the Church points out that, without its fellowship, the so-called normal life is one which ultimately destroys its own meaning. The Christian message is not meant, however, to render man utterly unhappy. It is proclaimed as the offer of healing that disease of which possibility the patient was not aware. It is true to say that occasionally the emphasis has been laid one-sidedly upon the misery and hopelessness of the human predicament; but such excesses have never been able permanently to hold sway.

4. *The Church in the World*

What do we have especially in mind when we speak of the activities of the Church? Do we think of any particular denomination, e.g. our own church? Or of all of them? The answer will depend on our perspective. As has been stated, ours is a theological presentation rather than an historical, sociological or phenomenological one. Thus we state that the Church signifies the whole work of Jesus from the beginning of his ministry to his Resurrection and final victory. It presupposes his earthly ministry, and it will eventually be followed by the manifestation of his glory. Substantially, it does not change. It is all the time concerned with the redemption of people whose existence demands full and objective meaning, yet who are unable to bring it about themselves. What men have hoped for has come into being through the fellowship which started historically as the primitive church in Jerusalem. Seen in the light of God's purpose, the Church has never changed its nature or task and will never change them until the full triumph of Christ's successful work is manifested to the whole of mankind. It is misleading to speak of a 'new revelation' which would succeed the cue given in the work of Jesus. In the history of Christianity new aspects of his work have come to light, and new depths are opened, as happened, for instance, in the Reformation. Thus Christianity is granted an increasingly deepened understanding of God's redemptive purpose. But its subject matter remains all the time the liberation and illumination offered by Jesus.

Nevertheless, what we are aware of is not the direct vision of that redemptive process, but rather a number of denominations and churches, whose spiritual life has directly or indirectly been kindled by contact with the primitive Church, and which, in turn, pass on that life to coming generations. Thereby the Church is imbedded into historical, social and cultural life. That is the reason, for instance, why we may not simply equate the voice of the Church with the Bible. The Bible appeals to our personal understanding. A critical procedure is therefore required by which our own interpretation is tested. A subjective element is required, for the Bible addresses itself to the reader as a message, destined for him personally. Yet is our understanding compatible with the way the primitive Church of our denomination interpreted it? Our image of the Church implies both our personal understanding and also our willingness to accept the authority of the primitive Church and of our own denomination. Our notion of the Church is also formed, however, by the activities of our denomination, as it bears witness to the truthfulness of the message by which, historically, it has been held together. This fact again points to the historical consensus of the contemporary Churches with those of antiquity. Both aspects are of equal importance. The personal understanding alone would replace the church by subjectivism, as may be learned from the example of Kierkegaard and the 'negative theology' of our contemporaries. The exclusive emphasis laid upon authority would in turn deprive the Church of the life of the Spirit and reduce its activities to a rigid confessionalism or a statutory interpretation of the Bible. Thus, by speaking of the 'Church', we have in mind a mental synthesis of subjective and objective elements, grasped in a process of reformation, like a film.

B. The Work of the Church
1. The Church and the Christian
The Church has been given to us as a fellowship by which the gap between our task and our material strength is to be bridged. It is recognized in sociology that many projects which an individual is not capable of performing alone will be accompanied when undertaken by

a group of like-minded people. In turn, the religious individualist deprives himself of many opportunities to be helpful to others, because he spurns co-operation with fellow Christians. It is not in the first place the number of people by which an enterprise is rendered possible, but rather the equal direction of their wills, or their common dedication to an assignment. The more complicated the technical aspects of a problem, the greater is the importance of collaboration. The relief actions of the World Council of Churches, for instance, would not be as effective as they are, even if the sum total of all the people devoted to its relief programme were willing to act directly. Conversely, however, the efficacy of the activities undertaken by the Church depends on the spiritual strength of each of its members. Thus Church activity moves in two directions. Individual Christians experience that the Church illumines their faith and heals their spiritual defects. Simultaneously, the Church works upon other social institutions in order to make them fit tools for the execution of God's redemptive plan. In all its activities the Church works in its dual way as source of illumination and of healing power. In turn it endows its members with the ability to perform both kinds of work, though with varying emphasis.

The Church is the place at which mankind has for the first time and effectively become aware of God as working out man's complete redemption, and through its historical continuity and spiritual experience it has been able throughout the ages to guide people to the ultimate truth. The guidance thus given is not meant to be a substitute for practical knowledge. The Bible does not tell how to win a war, and the Church is not content to be able to give advice for success in business. Man must take all practical decisions by himself. The Church will teach him, however, how to work in order to serve the common good. Thus man is helped to overcome his congenital error to believe that all things have their meaning in themselves, whereas in fact they are used by God for his purpose. Hence no increase of natural science will ever teach a person what it is right to do. The answer to that question can be found only in the redemptive order of the universe. Human history is not a progress from a few truths to many truths, or from a fragmentary to a comprehensive one. Rather one is led from error to truth. While in the whole history of mankind the guiding hand of God rather than man's intellect leads man on, the basic error has not been brought to light until the proclamation of Jesus. The Church holds that truth, yet not as a static set of doctrines. Rather, by becoming witness to the redemptive significance of Jesus and the subsequent history of redemption, it stimulates people to ponder the implication which those events have for himself and other people.

Closely related to illumination is the Church's operation of consolation. Christians have to live in this world and thus are in a particular way exposed to the nefarious assaults of the forces of evil. Since Christians are so accustomed to thinking of the goodness of God, it is not surprising that in a calamitous situation they should feel perplexed and helpless. Yet the wisdom of the Church comes to their rescue. God has devious ways in which he leads his people, yet eventually brings them to the assigned goal. In this respect, the Church of today is remarkably weak, although it tries to hide that weakness behind pastoral psychology and counselling. What people need is consolation. That can be given only when he who consoles is himself certain of God's unlimited willingness to help and his ability to do so.

Since the Christian, even when sure of the forgiveness of his sins, will never be able fully to escape the power of temptation, the Church reminds him of the value and necessity of spiritual discipline and education. It is a fatal error to believe that the spiritual gift of goodness will work automatically in a Christian. The better he happens to know his own weakness in its relation to his whole character, and the more he learns to use the most appropriate methods to strengthen in himself the will to goodness, the greater will be the likelihood of his controlling his temptations. Another aspect of the Church's work is healing and relief. The individual Christian is both the recipient of these gifts and also is enjoined to practise them. Since Christianity takes man in his totality, it is obvious that all defects, both of life and property, of body and of mind, are destined to be overcome. The fight against them seems to be hopeless. The people whom we help materially may by their own fault be brought back to their original misery; the world population grows much quicker than the number of Christians ready to help. Above all, the temptations of public life and of defiance to it are so alluring that all remedies seem to be ineffectual. It would be childish if, in order to triumph over such pessimism, we should try to persuade ourselves that the natural development of mankind would be so effectively influenced by humanism or science that all needs would eventually vanish from this earth. The Church will rather point out to its members that God is redemptively at work in human history. The process is a slow one when we think of the hundred thousands or even million years that separate the birth of Jesus from the first appearance of man here upon this earth. Yet, in the light of Jesus' ministry, one is able to see the steady advancement in the history prior to Jesus, and upon that fact the Church builds its assurance that the eschatological process goes on and will eventually reach its goal.

It is therefore gratifying to see the churches emphasizing afresh the ministry of healing, not only by building hospitals and dispensaries, but lately also by means of pointing to the spiritual gift of healing. Sick people suffer not from a sick body only; they have lost a portion of their human existence. It is therefore good for them to feel the spiritual support which fellow believers give to them. Similarly, relief is not confined to material goods. Anything that we have, and are willing to share with the needy, is experienced by fellow believers as a means by which they may be restored to wholeness. All these services the Church will render to its members, in part through the professional services of ministers or fraternal acts of friendship, and in part through worship, common prayer, and the use of the Scriptures. Group activities – e.g. Alcoholics Anonymous – may prove to be most helpful, because personal problems are thereby taken care of in a personal way. The 'objective' activities have the special advantage of preventing a fixation. The individual who needs guidance, comfort or relief, will not be tempted to put his trust in the kindness of the person who is willing to help him, but rather in God's readiness to help.

2. Church and Social Life

a. THE CHURCH'S COMMISSION

While the Church has an unique character and function in dealing with its members, it is as a social institution also destined to exist in the midst of the social life of non-Christians. Its very existence adds something to the work of the other social institutions, which they do not possess by themselves, yet which proves to be essential for their well-functioning. Understood in that way, the task of the Church is not confined to proclaiming to man his sinfulness, or, existentialistically speaking, his self-alienation, but also his divine destination. The New Testament sees the Church rooted in the saving purpose which God has for his whole world. Thus the task of the Church has a positive aspect, too. The Church is to make mankind conscious of itself as God's work and thus capable of participating in the operation of God's kindness. As a result of that cosmic outlook, mankind and this world are enabled in full harmony with each other to reach their final destination. The universe is not only made by God; it also exists for him and is destined to co-operate with him. This positive view of the role of the

Church is absolutely required as counterweight against the purely negative aspect. When the radical lostness of man is one-sidedly stressed, people will believe that, by passively accepting the divine condemnation, they will be saved. Yet God is not just the prime cause of a world which, after having made it, he leaves to itself. The creatures are not treated by him as passive entities. By means of the Incarnation, he indicated that he had made this world through his Son. The work of Jesus was to be continued by the Church who acts in Christ's name, just as the human mind was chosen to transform this world according to its pattern; so Jesus told the Church to suffuse the universe with the Spirit of God. As the arm and mouth of Christ, the Church feels responsible for the salvation of all men.

Sociologically seen, the Church is but one of the basic institutions of human society. But, as a rule, the sociologists fail to notice the power of Christ that works in it, of which the Disciples were so strongly aware. As a result of that presence, the Church is not simply the spiritual function of social life. Rather it determines and transforms all aspects of social life. Conversely, where the uniqueness of the Church's spiritual function is recognized, the Church is seen to be an extraordinary institution. It transcends all other social organizations on account of the purpose which God pursues through it. Whereas the other social institutions serve to make man's present situation meaningful and tolerable, the Church prepares the complete transformation of this world.

b. THE STRANGENESS OF THE CHURCH

People take the existence of the other social institutions for granted, while the Church seems to be a stranger here on earth whose right of existence and presence in human society is rather questionable. Yet, paradoxically, it is through its 'unnatural' character that, the more man is at home in the realm of concepts, the more he separates himself from the life that surrounds him. Science makes him disregard the nature of the things which form this world. In a much deeper sense the man who believes in his lordship over this world is unwilling to use those things for the ends for which God has destined them. With increasing rapidity and avidity, he employs them exclusively as means by which to enjoy himself or to make money. Through the Church human life is very much like travelling in a trailer, or a Boy Scout who carries his tent with him. One is able to establish home, wherever one happens to be. As a result, man feels himself a stranger in this world. Far from being the measure of all things, man discovers the humiliating fact that in itself this world is incommensurable with the human mind and refuses to be assimilated to him. That sentiment of fundamental disparity is intensified in proportion with man's growing knowledge of the universe's immensity. The larger the area which science has discovered, the more unlikely is man to be able to control it. Yet the Church offers man a home in the cosmos by disclosing not only its centre, but also the goal and direction of the whole. The Church forms the dynamic centre of the world. But that 'feeling at home' in this world does not mean that the cosmos has made its peace with man and that man enjoys the harmony of earthly existence. Rather paradoxically, man is at home while on the march to a distant goal. His home marches with him all the time. The insistence on the *aggiornamento* which dominated the Second Vatican Council shows that the Catholic Church, too, understands its existence as being on the march yet ever at home. The Churches of the Reformation were conscious of the necessity to consider reformation as a perpetual process. That attitude implies the Church's assurance that man's acting upon this world makes sense, when it is done under the influence of God's Spirit. Hence it does not matter whether or not the effects of such activity are immediately visible. The Church's activity lacks that convenient yet deceptive time table by which Communists and Dispensationalists believe to be able to chart their station in the redemptive process. In view of its genuine eschatological outlook, which takes the countless millennia of God's work into consideration, the Church does not impatiently look forward for sudden changes in this world, nor does it want to overthrow its present order.

As no other institution, the Church is directly related to God's redemptive plan. It therefore considers itself the supreme institution, established by God, and it claims, therefore, spiritual authority over all worldly life. That claim does not imply – as it has occasionally been understood by the Catholic Church – that the clergy had legislative or juridical power in worldly affairs. In a similar way, mistaken Protestant denominations may like the role of a political pressure group. Rather, the Church's supremacy means that the Church is in a position to declare to earthly institutions and their members what purpose God pursues through each of them specifically and by what means that purpose may best be implemented. No one should be surprised to see that the instruction offered by the Church is resented by those outside, and such briefing may lead to conflict and even persecution, for nobody likes to have his wrongs pilloried. Such was recently the fate of the Confessing

Church under Hitler, and of the Catholic bishops in Communist Eastern Europe. In turn, of course, it may also happen that, for fear of such repercussions, a church should prefer to keep its peace. In other instances, Church leaders have been carried away by a spirit of partisanship. Such aberrations will not go on within the Church for a long while, however, because countervailing forces will soon rise from its midst.

It would be a serious error to believe that in order to avoid such excesses, the Church should confine itself to proclaiming moral attitudes or purely formal principles, while refraining from taking sides in a concrete issue. Yet though it will be necessary for the Church to address itself to actual problems, what really matters is the spiritual character of the Church's stance and statements. In a political situation, as in cultural or economic matters, the Church will serve God by approaching a given situation with the awareness that its life is fed by heavenly sources. This fact accounts for the fundamental difference of perspective which is found between the way in which the work of the Church is evaluated by sociologists and politicians, on the one hand, and the Church's self-evaluation on the other. The secular scholars find the value of the Church in the advantages it offers to the secular order and institutions in the pursuit of their specific aims. Conversely, the Church is anxious to offer them a new dimension to be added to their understanding of themselves, namely that God has destined them on their part to contribute to the remaking of a new mankind. The Church is able, for instance, to tell the government that it is cruel and a denial of human dignity to coerce men to take up arms against another nation though they are opposed to killing their fellow men. Similarly, the Church may draw the government's attention to the fact that it is a costly neglect of manpower when employment of people is based exclusively upon their intellectual capacity rather than their personal qualifications. Likewise, the Church may remind the government that inflation may be a financial development that alleviates the burden of the nation's debt; yet thereby millions of people of the middle and lower classes see their savings or their insurances and annuities dwindling, while the rich get thereby richer.

c. CHRISTIANIZING THE WORLD

It may be objected that by acting in such manner the Church would be concerned with purely secular problems. In fact, however, it is with the perversion of natural conditions that the Church is preoccupied in proclaiming the truth. It may not be able immediately to change conditions. Nevertheless its public protest will retard such activities. At the same time, the members of the Church will thereby be taught where their opportunities for action lie, and will be given a deepened understanding of the secular institutions. Of course, the Church is neither to replace the 'secular' institutions, nor to become subservient to them. Political and social life, civilization and dealing with nature have their legitimate place in the spiritual, no less than in the material, history of mankind. They are at man's disposal and are the subject matter of human history. Yet they are also used by God as the instruments through which he transforms man. The Church is simultaneously a portion of mankind's social life, yet under obligation to guide it. By themselves they lack both a clear vision of the goal for which they are destined by God, as also the strength by their own resources to reach their appointed goal. It would be Utopian, nevertheless, to strive after a 'Christian state' or a 'holy nation'. All we can hope for is that through the presence of Christians in their midst, the other institutions will eventually be enabled to carry on their specific function in the light of a Christian vision. Of course, neither theological training nor deep experiences of faith will by themselves render a person competent to give advice on the technical problems of the secular institutions. But equally unjustified is the contention that the experts in a field are the only people capable of guiding an institution. As far as it is a matter of spiritual judgement, Christians are most competent to tell whether or not a political course or a work of art are spiritually ruinous or constructive.

There is a tendency in the modern world to separate public life and civilization completely from the Church and religion. As a rebuttal of the clericalism of the Catholic Church, such attitude is natural in a mankind which pretends to have attained to maturity. There is no reason, however, why the Church should regard the situation as hopeless. Court sentences and laws concerning religion are not ultimates. If Christians see an error in them, they are entitled to make their mind known. The Church's strength does not depend on public recognition or political privileges. Rather it is strong on account of its participation in the power inherent in redemptive history and in the truthfulness of the message entrusted to it. In the last instance that power of the Church is spread through the lives and presence of Christians. As a result of their decency, justice, or charity, their environment is transformed, no matter how indifferent or hostile its stance seems to be.

If it wants to reach those outside, the Church cannot content itself with telling what ought to be done by them. It must give evidence of its own commitment by engaging in activities which are meant to transform this world. This may be done by joining a secular movement of protest or reform, e.g. the Red Cross or CORE (Congress of Racial Equality). Yet in such cases, the Churches must be careful not to compromise their spiritual goal. The Church must have the courage to show that what her allies consider their final goal is but a means, and perhaps a rather doubtful one, in the Church's eyes. In that way mankind will learn what the supreme good is like for which it is destined, and that by the operation of holy history its views of what is best are apt radically to be corrected. Feeding the hungry and clearing the slums are moral necessities, but not ultimate goals.

The Church is not free to decide whether or not it is to take an interest in the secular order; Christ himself has laid such responsibility upon it. Yet, while serving the needs of the secular order, the Church is never the servant of secular organizations. Rather is it essential for it that its services should be rendered in freedom and at the Church's discretion. In an age where all people in need turn to government and Church with their requests, it is especially important that the Church should not be moved by sentimentalism. It might lose sight of its specific function. That danger cannot be avoided, however, by making Christianity a religion of solitude, as Gogarten, for instance, suggests. While what the Church has to say should throw the secular world into a crisis, its proclamation should nevertheless consist in guidance, rather than in condemnation. Unless there is obvious evidence to the contrary, it must be assumed that all those who work in the secular orders do so *bona fide* and intend to serve the common good. Theirs is a tragic situation, however; they want to build up lasting structures, yet are inclined to hamper or harm them by using inadequate or wrong means.

C. Ecumencity

It was not carelessness when in the preceding sections we referred so frequently to the Church in the singular, notwithstanding the fact that the Church of which we speak and in which we act is the Church formed by our denomination. As we have shown there would be no Churches and denominations at all if Jesus had not worked in and upon his followers as the bearer of the Spirit. Through the formation of the World Council of Churches, Christianity has given visible expression to its belief in the basic oneness of the Church. It is safe to assume that for the majority of Christians the period of denominational rivalry, of proselytizing and of slandering, is definitely over.

The World Council of Churches gives impressive expression to the belief that Christianity is basically one, because it has one spiritual head, namely Jesus, and that notwithstanding the diversity of denominations it has but one task here on earth. It brings the message of redemption through Christ to the whole population of this globe. What is implied in the unity of the Church has not yet fully come to light. To some denominations it means a loose organization, yet far-reaching practical co-operation. Others desire a closely knit federation with interchange of ministers, members and services. Finally, the Church of Rome, which in the last years has opened itself to the ecumenical ideas and movement, contends that the primacy of the Pope and the fundamental confession of his church are essential and indispensable features of the united Church. The majority of Protestants will point out that uniform oneness is not the way in which Jesus dealt with his disciples. The formative principles of Christianity remain concealed behind the diversity of species and individuals. Even when we grant that in the Reformation human stubborness and undue criticism of the opponents were not absent, the split in the Church was unavoidable. A new approach to God was forming itself in the late Middle Ages. In the reformers that process had reached the point, where the difference between the old and the new could be stated in a clear and unambiguous manner. No wonder that the reformers were willing to preserve the administrative oneness of the Church, yet that alone, if the new movement were allowed to have its own way of worship and devotion.

It is quite natural that after several centuries, in which Protestant vitality manifested itself mainly in its ability to split up into innumeral denominations, sects and small particles, thought is given to reunion. Many Protestant entities are the result of historical incident or personal ambition. Nothing would be lost if they merged with related groups. Yet there are other denominational types, such as Lutherans, Methodists, Quakers, Anabaptists, who represent specific kinds of spiritual outlook and who play still an active and essential role within Protestantism. Their followers are not likely to give themselves up at present. Christianity would definitely be impoverished by their disappearance.

That all the denominations should disappear in a universal merger is a most unlikely event and not even desirable. The divine self-disclosure, by which the Church has come into being, will inevitably be interpreted in various ways. If one of those interpretations is accepted by the majority of the members of a denomination, that group will be tempted to contend that it is the only true understanding. Over against this, the dissenting group serves as a reminder of the fact that God's revelation, even when adequately apprehended, is never exhaustive. Thus dissent adds to the full understanding of the Christian message. Through the right of dissent, the Church is preserved from stagnating and the work of the Spirit is given free rein.

Closely related with the ecumenical movement is the missionary work of the Church. Recent events, especially the anti-colonialism which tinges the nationalism of all the younger nations, have compelled the churches radically to revise their missionary outlook and activities. Until recently, the missionary enterprise implied the desire to add congregations overseas to the sending churches. The new congregations were to be replicas of the churches at home, including their denominational orientation. That situation was bound to come to an end. The congregations on the mission field demanded to have their centre in their nationality, the more so since a sizeable number of indigenous young people had received adequate academic training. As a result, a complete change in the theology of missions and missionary practice was rendered necessary. Of course, older and younger churches are equally agreed on their right and obligation to spread the Christian message all over the world and to intensify their efforts to reach all non-Christians. But since so many indigenous Christians receive their theological training in seminaries of the western world, there is no more need for sending out missionaries of the older denominations for that purpose. The 'younger' Christians have now become the missionary arm of an united Church universal.

While the younger churches make strong efforts to overcome the particularism which denominational missions have introduced into their spiritual life, the complete transformation of the mission fields into national churches will present considerable difficulties, for the formation of such is not a merely organizational task; it requires the creation of new types of Christian faith in which the specific cultural background of each nation becomes articulate. The older churches will be confronted with an equally hard task. Formerly it was a matter of denominational pride to support one's own missionary enterprises. It is to be feared that with the disappearance of that motive the interest in evangelism abroad will decline. Yet the younger churches are found almost exclusively in the underdeveloped and undeveloped countries. Thus they are all established on a financial basis which is more than precarious. The older churches have to learn that in a very generous way they are to support the younger churches, with financial aid and technical assistance.

From the view-point of the 'older' churches, the whole development on the 'foreign field' may seem to be disquieting and even dangerous. They had taken it for granted that they were conveying the divine truth to a world of superstition and error. In the ecumenical age they have to resign themselves to the role of advisors of pupils because they are inclined to consider them as insufficiently informed on the spiritual problems encountered in their midst. In their desire to adjust their churches to the home conditions, the leaders of the younger churches may be tempted to throw out more of the universal tradition than is necessary and healthy. Yet as the history of the Eastern Orthodox Churches shows, intercourse and exchange in the World Council of Churches will gradually lead to tempering the excesses. We should be the more willing to use restraint in judging the younger churches, as we realize that in the West, too, we are engaged in a process of radical re-thinking and re-adjustment to a world in transition.

22 The Biological Order

A. Nature and Ethics

1. *Man and Biosphere*

Many philosophers would limit ethics to interpersonal relations or to the subject's intrapersonal life. The implication of such views would be that man's dealing with the non-human world was not subject to moral standards. Accordingly, man's bodily existence could be regarded merely as an obstacle to truly personal life rather than an object of moral activity. Hence people could be free to deal with the material world as they please.

The weakness of such arguments lies in the unquestionable fact that we do not know personal existence apart from the body and the world around us. Furthermore, that surrounding world cannot be brought under the Ego's control by a *coup de force*, because it represents an orderly self-supporting and self-regulating system. If not treated according to its intrinsic laws, it causes disturbance and harm in the individual's life. The interval that separates the modern man from the first origins of life is an immense one. Nevertheless, it is obvious that throughout the numerous steps of evolution the nature of life has not substantially changed. Like the micro-organisms, man belongs to the biosphere, that is to say, the area formed by the crust of the earth and the surrounding atmosphere.

That man should find himself living in the biosphere is not a contingent fact, as so many ethicists are inclined to assume. It is the result of God's creative will. Christianity has seen its belief in creation confirmed by experience. Conversely, man's existence in this world finds its explanation in man's role as guardian of life. The manufacture of the A-bomb has driven home to us the realization that it is in man's power entirely to destroy life here on earth. In turn, the space flights have demonstrated man's ability to spread earthly life to the rest of the universe. It is man's privilege to become the giver of vitality to an otherwise barren planetary world. Thus, the order of the biosphere is not one of classification or regularity only; rather, it gives expression to a divine plan. The scientist has not comprehended his task as long as he overlooks the telic character of the order of nature. Materialism notices rightly that man is an integral part of this world. In order to act meaningfully, man must deal with the objects of this world according to their specific nature and in awareness of the limits thereby set to the scope of his activities. Yet that philosophy is mistaken when it ignores the essential difference between living organisms and lifeless matter, and between the passive and contingent character of purely causal processes and spontaneous action which implies selectivity and differentiation in its contacts. In turn, there is a naturalistic philosophy which is aware of that basic distinction; yet it is unsatisfactory for ethics because it places all vital processes on the same level. Where the notion of values is introduced, as for instance by Nietzsche and Simmel, an idealistic element is inconsistently added. The outstanding position which Nietzsche accords to super-man is alien to nature as we know it. In it weak and poor, small and large are equally constitutive. Utilitarianism has rightly emphasized that moral activity must directly or remotely serve a practical end. Notwithstanding Kant, the notion of goodness as an end in itself lacks meaning. The utilitarian ethics does not ascribe ethical value to this world. Man's environment is merely to be used as a means to facilitate life or to render man happy. But what then is it that makes a person happy? The momentary sense of pleasure may prove to be deceptive; frequent consumption of sweets, for instance, may result in caries of the teeth. Moreover, my very pleasure may become the source of irritation or even hatred on the part of my neighbour. Or the exploitation of the copper deposits in North Chile is highly profitable for the international corporations engaged therein, but it hardly helps to solve the economic woes of the country. It should be evident then that what is lacking in all these approaches is the idea of a final goal to be reached or a supreme value to be realized through our actions.

2. *Bios and Ethos*

That *desideratum* is seemingly satisfied in the idea of natural law as it was developed in the ethics of Stoicism. It is held that by means of its innate goodness this world moves towards its very completion. In order to be satisfactory, life should therefore be lived in agreement with the order and movement of the cosmos. Rationally consistent as this philosophy seems to be, it has never worked. The reason should be obvious. Since the success of man's activity depends on the practicality of his actions, regard for the natural order of things is advisable. But, in view of the shortness of life, people may argue that the momentary success should be preferred to the permanent order. In that case the natural law may serve as a counsel of prudence. It lacks, however, the authority of a moral obligation. Furthermore, the appeal of the natural law is based upon the assumption that human life itself is but part of nature. But that is a doubtful assumption. Does the universe really care what happens to the individual? In view of the short-comings of all types of philosophical ethics, Christianity's claim to go to the very bottom of the problem deserves careful attention. Belief in a divine creation secures an objective value to this world and destines nature as the God-given means for man's development. The eschatological hope, set in a renewed world, ties man permanently together with nature. Man's dominion of nature is not a temporary device for this life only; it serves God's ultimate purpose.

There are two outstanding features of the Christian attitude towards nature. First, the ancient dichotomy of body and mind has to be recognized as a fatal error. Thereby the development of mental life and the use of nature's goods were completely separated. Such duality is incompatible with the fact that this world in its totality is the work of the same creator. All things found therein must therefore be correlated. Second, man's dealing with this world must be related to an ultimate goal in which man and nature are united in a harmonious relationship. As a result of that arrangement, the special role which man performs in the universe is permanently safeguarded. Of all the creatures of this world, man alone is able to make decisions and to act with a view to the future. From the fact that there is a world in existence, we infer that, as they are, all things are willed by God and will be used by him for the attainment of his final goal. Hence in order to be in agreement with God's purpose, ethical action must satisfy two requirements. The ethical action must meet the practical requirements of the moment, yet it must also be orientated towards God's final goal. In turn, no particularly grand or outstanding deeds are necessary in order to render life meaningful. It suffices to do one's daily work in the family and on the job. Then we may have the assurance that God is arranging whatever we do and whatever surrounds us for the attainment of our final destination. Nature is never the mere sum total of what is seen around us. All things are aiming at the consummation of God's world.

Yet the fact must not be overlooked that it is as a creature of God, not as a divine being, that man plays his role in this world. As a creature man shares in a particularly outspoken way the self-assertiveness of all the creatures. His divine destination does not spare him outbursts of passion in which his instincts and desires break loose, irrespective of his destination. That happens in Christian life, too. Yet the Christian becomes aware of the fact that such conduct is unbecoming to him. It is a special kindness of God if a person is enabled by the Spirit to keep his passions under complete control. Though human life is not altogether one of passions, there seems to be a certain rhythm in which passions and the life of the mind alternate in human conduct. It is evidence of God's kindness that in spite of such inadequacy he is using man for his redemptive plan. Paradoxically, it is man in his limitations and weaknesses who is used by God for the execution of his saving purpose. Thus, in his co-operation with God, the Christian occupies a unique position within nature. Though particular things may harm us and give us the impression of nature's callousness, yet nature as a whole, as Saint Francis described so beautifully, is the messenger of God's redemptive love.

B. Human Life

1. *Life and Death*

Christianity has developed a real love of life, not of mere biological vitality, but rather of the power which stems from unconscious depths and enables man to act meaningfully and creatively. Thus he brings things into being which did not exist previously, yet which, once manufactured, will enrich human life. Unlike animals, which are but consumers, man is primarily a maker (*homo faber*). The Christian enthusiasm for life is tempered, nevertheless, by a sober realism which is aware of the precarious position of human life, threatened as it is by infirmity, disease, insanity and death. Of all earthly evils, death seems to be the worst one. For through death, man loses not only in an irrevocable way that he has and has accomplished, but also and above all himself. That human life implies an inner contradiction has been recognized in many religions in which people entertain the hope of a new life after death. What is the use of all the toil of life, if eventually that life is terminated for good? Even if it should be true that my sacrifices and labours have fostered the interests of my country, even if it could be said of a great man that he had radically changed the historical position of his nation; if death is an absolute end, what will I know of the consequences of my deeds? Perhaps even greater strength lies in the argument of those who have at one time or another enjoyed genuine happiness or satisfaction. If such conditions are possible, why do they not last forever? Why is it that through such transitory delights man is made to be permanently unhappy?

The ancient religions were not able to answer those questions. When they referred to the return of spring after winter, or to the tree which would grow new leaves in lieu of those shed in the fall, they were employing symbols. Yet the symbols failed to be adequate, for even a child knows that all individual plants and animals will perish some day and will never come to light again. Recognizing that man, too, is a part of nature, Christianity has been wary to use nature symbolism as a means by which to render mortality meaningful. Nevertheless, Christianity has defied the futility of death. That man, though called upon to live in communion with the living God, should die seems to be absurd. The reason of that fate, as seen by Christianity, lies in man's disregard of God. Though destined to have his biological life transformed into spiritual and everlasting life, man prefers to live by himself. Just as in the biological process of evolution, animal life had reached a new level in *homo sapiens*, so again by the Resurrection of Jesus people were made aware of the new level of Spiritual life into which mankind had entered. Yet, eventually all who believe in Christ will be transformed by his spiritual energy. It far transcends all physical and mental energies. However, the life of the Spirit is not to be understood as a mere heightening and intensification of the biological life. Rather, it is the ability through the instrumentality of the biological forces to apprehend the true sprititual character of human existence. The imparting of the new life is not meant to be an end in itself. Though the bodies of those who receive the life of the Spirit will die like the rest of mankind, their Egos will not perish. By means of a renewed mankind, the whole universe will be filled with some kind of new life.

Apart from belief in Christ, man cannot hope for a new and heavenly existence. It is in this earthly life that the Ego receives the transformation of his life. This new life which is at work in the believers is the cause of their ability to engender the same kind of life in others. That life is the evidence that such existence is possible and at work in this world. This view implies that in the 'life to come' the individual will not lose his memories or self-consciousness.

Except for passing aberrations, the Christian emphasis has been on life rather than on death. Even the contemplative monastic orders of the Middle Ages used death merely as an impetus to climb from the biological level of life to the indestructible level of spiritual life. Death is not an act by which we are cut off from the stream of life, but rather through it we are enabled fully to enter into the fellowship of God's people. One cannot but admire the wisdom of God when he subjected the creatures of the earth to mortality. If the biological existence of individuals were lasting indefinitely, there would be no room left for propagation and development. By reducing the organisms to a merely passive existence in death, God uses them as food for the living ones. Similarly by transforming human existence into a spiritual one, God has provided for them a mode of living by which the organic world will never be encumbered.

For the Christian, belief in the new spiritual life is no escape from the futility, the horror, and the painfulness of physical death. But in spite of the loss which it entails, it cannot drive the believer to despair. In wide circles, death is treated as an unavoidable biological event. Such an attitude may give mental release. But by robbing death of its spiritual significance, we also deprive life of it. Modern existentialism has the courage to admit that consequence. Human life would then be an incidental biological event, of which man were unable to make sense. From the Christian viewpoint death is a reminder of the fact that the biological life is not sufficient to render existence meaningful. Yet, in the light of Jesus' resurrection, death is the atonement for life and carries the promise of the higher life with it.

2. The Stages of Life

Like other mammals, human beings are not born in their final shape and condition. They grow up, and individuals of different ages live together side by side. Study of human life shows that such arrangement is not a fortuituous one. Rather, it is the device by which the mammals, and above all man, are equipped for developing their full life. Unlike plants and insects they have a future of their own, towards which they are to grow. Like all life, man passes through marked stages of youth, maturity and old age. In human life more than in the animal realm it can be seen that each stage has its definite and necessary function. However, we seem to have entered into a phase of history in which a dream of eternal youth is strangely mixed with the delusion of the equivalence of the generations. The result is a confused and confusing condition of social life, in which the generations operate side by side without reciprocal relationship. In the Christian view of life, youth is the indispensable prerequisite of maturity and the place of learning. The history of mankind would move with pathetic slowness if each generation had to start the process of learning afresh. It is simply untrue to hold that youth harbours all possible knowledge potentially within its mind. It has been endowed, though, with the capability of being taught. Youth is a period of preparation for independent and responsible action. Man is destined for action, and since he, unlike animals, may not rely in large measure on his instincts, learning is an imperative task set before him. It comprises careful observation, speech, skilled use of his limbs, and practical techniques no less than instruction in spiritual things. The contention that all that is required in order to build a new world is protest against and rejection of the established social order, is tantamount to calling down havoc upon the social fabric.

The young generation needs learning. It will be called upon later in life to act in a responsible way. To do so requires a general knowledge of the world in which we live and of our abilities, because responsible action is possible only in knowledge of the consequences of our actions. That difficulty is particularly obvious in the case of juvenile sexuality. The physical maturity antedates mental maturity. As a consequence, juveniles are apt to consider sex as play and are overwhelmed and frightened when it results in pregnancy. The child looks at learning with mixed feelings. He enjoys it inasmuch as his curiosity is thereby satisfied, but he loathes it when special effort for its acquisition is required. The young person is but vaguely able to anticipate the usefulness and necessity of the things to be learned. Thus it cannot be left exclusively to him to decide what and how much he is to learn. It is true to say that in the whole the younger generation has an amazingly wider knowledge of facts than a few decades ago; also that it is often confronted, at an early age, with the necessity to make practical decisions. Yet it is not thereby more mature. For what they have to learn, above all else, is the ability to act responsibly; that is to say, in consideration of the consequences which a contemplated way of action will have, not only for their own future, but also that of the other people involved.

Traditionally the way in which the training of the will for responsible action has been practised has been by teaching children to respect the authority of adults. There seems to be no other way to accomplish the transformation of the child's naïve egotism into regard for other people's rights and interests. Everybody knows that this aspect of education is most difficult. It inevitably causes frictions. Yet, it is also obvious that excessive permissiveness in the early years will increase the child's problem, once he has to act outside of the family. One can understand the impatience of young people and their wish in freedom to participate in the life of the adults. Their unruliness and rebellion against the adults is certainly not exclusively the fault of the youngsters.

In our times the college generation has a high moral sensitivity, especially in social and international affairs. Despite all the disturbance and unrest caused by their noisy demonstrations, those actions fail to have practical success because they act prematurely. They lack political power and support as well as a clear view of their goal. Juvenile unrest in our days is a symptom of the diffidence with which the adolescents look at the adults' moral trustworthiness. How large an amount of credibility can be expected of parental instruction in an age where, on the whole, Christian values and standards are neglected and derided? The attitude of the home is of decisive significance for the young people's moral responsibility. Church life, in like manner, may succeed in having a formative role, yet children are keen observers; moral instruction does not impress them when they notice a contrast between words and conduct. Conversely, what people complain about as the 'immorality of the younger generation' usually reflects the attitude of their seniors. Adulthood is the stage of life in which people normally have reached the ability materially and morally to take care of themselves and of others. The job and/or marriage are the most obvious symbols of that state. Married in their majority, they have to take care of a spouse and frequently of children. The danger of our age lies in the fact that the economic and public concerns of husband and wife are so excessive that the education of the children suffers. The hope that the school and youth organizations will replace the parents' work is fulfilled but partially. Yet, since theirs is the age where people are of the greatest usefulness, the demand made on the adult generation is naturally a considerable one.

The natural obligation of the middle generation is both for the younger ones and for the old-age generation. It seems, however, that that twofold responsibility is shifting in our time. Concern for the old people has moved from the family home to boarding houses or nursing homes. In turn, the strong impact which radio and TV make on the child's mind, just as the influences of the street, place an increased responsibility upon the middle generation. It is up to them to curb undesirable and dangerous impulses and to prevent wanton destructiveness. Likewise, the shift from the three-generation to a two-generation home, which is the rule in our days, makes it incumbent on the middle generation to seek increased public assistance for the economic and health needs of the old people. The heavy burden which is thus laid upon the adults' shoulders makes it imperative for them to keep in a state of physical and mental fitness, and to avoid all excesses by which their health might be endangered and/or weakened. The present general shift from the home to public life has substantially altered the role of adult women. The political and economic equality granted to them requires in exchange their full participation in social and political life. The contribution made by the family to social life of the last century has substantially diminished, with the result that the children get less education and more freedom. Consequently, the nature of responsible action is learned by a hit and miss method rather than on the basis of moral principles.

Old age is often referred to as the stage of life in which people retire from active work, and, on account of their decreasing usefulness, get ready for the end. In modern geriatrics they are frequently treated as though their normal place were among their own age group. Yet, that stage of life has its positive purpose, too. The very fact that older people are but rarely called upon to make decisions gives them an opportunity to reflect upon their life and its experiences in a detached way. They are ready to see the limits within which each of us has to move, and what consequences the various methods of action will entail. Since they are no longer engaged in working for a definite goal, they find it possible to admit their former errors and faults. Out of the experience of their adult life there grows wisdom. They know how to direct the energies available most successfully and with a minimum of waste or friction towards the goal contemplated. There are numerous opportunities today where old people may help others by their experienced counsel and guidance, yet in modern life we notice an opposite tendency, too. Business corporations, schools and public administration are craving for very young men because they possess a maximum of energy and flexibility. But while the result is found in economic growth and rapid development, our social problems get more troublesome all the time.

In assigning specific functions to each of the age groups, God has prepared a means for sound and steady growth in human history. Apart from their interrelation, however, the respective generations are apt to impede historical progress. The adolescents who engage in riot and protest, in defiance of their elders, may be able to disturb the *status quo*, yet prove to be unable to replace it by improved conditions. The activism of today's middle generation has led us into conditions of increased dehumanization, because it lacks wisdom and knowledge of the human heart. In turn, the 'gerontarchy' in politics has left our age with thoughtless political machines. In healthy conditions, youth is questioning the activity of the adults and thus keeps the road open for genuine progress, adulthood is anxious to augment the cultural goods and to avert dangers. Old age finally reminds the activist that his work is under the judgement of the future.

3. Desires and Happiness

Writers on Christian ethics are inclined to look contemptuously down upon eudaemonism. Since the days of Kant, happiness has been expelled from classical ethics. Yet, man's natural craving for happiness cannot easily be bypassed. Man is not able to live a meaningful life without paying attention to joy and pain, and to find full satisfaction in morality. He wants to live a life which gives him satisfaction in the totality of his psychosomatic existence. Hence, he likes what gives him delight, he hates discomfort and suffering, and he feels morally justified in doing so. According to temperament and education, such emotions may primarily concern his physiological well-being, for instance, enjoying a good meal, physical exercise or sexual intercourse, or they may be caused by learning, aesthetic contemplation or friendship. Furthermore, since the individual is a spontaneous being endowed with selfhood, he will not be satisfied with pleasurable things that come to him from the outside; his self, too, craves for satisfaction. The awareness that he is able to act spontaneously is also apt to render him happy. The lady who reaches for the third cocktail thereby indicates that what she cherishes is not simply the intoxicating effect but rather the feeling that hers will be a self-induced drunkenness.

People like their passions because they provide an intensified mode of living which is rendered doubly enjoyable by its irrational character. One seems to be completely free in such actions, because nobody can foretell the outcome. For the same reason, people seek adventures, for their self is at stake therein; one has to be present with the greatest effort of self-affirmation. Advising a person to show moderation in his passion or his quest for adventure is therefore considered an attempt to take the fun out of life. The moral problem of the passions and desires does not lie, as Plato and Aristotle suggested, in the absence of rationality. Of course, it is not advisable to make decisions as long as the heat of emotions prevents us from a clear sight of the consequences of our actions. The moral problem of the passions is not found in the satisfaction they give us, either. Rather, it is their egotistic nature that causes moral concern. Through the passions the ego seeks a violent intensification of himself. Modern psychotherapy has rightly recognized that fact. People whose job compels them constantly to subdue their selfwill and indignation, and who have 'to be reasonable', are encouraged by the psychotherapist to release their inhibitions in bursts of shouting and acts of violence in the company of like patients.

Theoretically, the escape from that egotism would be found in the awareness that the destination for which the Gospel prepares us, is so much more sublime than those offered by our passions, and so permanent that life here on earth could do without them. While that is certainly true, the question must nevertheless be asked, 'Why did God place us into a world whose goods are highly pleasurable, if he did not want us to enjoy them?'

The solution would seem to lie in man's ability to love his fellow man and God. As has been shown above, Christian love is not to be confounded with erotic love, which is an act of passionate self-assertion in which the partner provides merely the opportunity to satisfy our passion. Christian love recognizes other people as being in need of whatever goods are at my disposal and which might be helpful for them. That means that to my passion and its satisfaction something must be added by which its naked egotism is tempered. Erotic lust, for instance, may be supplemented by the awareness that the partner is a person who has aspirations and problems of his own. He is not merely a beautiful and youthful body. The food which we relish should remind us of the kindness of God, who has set so many delightful things so lavishly before us. My hot anger, called forth by injustice, may lead to acts of violence; yet it may also prompt me to join in measures intended to get rid of that injustice. In all such instances, Christian love does not diminish the intensity of passion or water down the satisfaction felt. Yet, I am enabled thereby to experience my contentment in the awareness that I live in God's world and in the company of other people. Apart from Christian love, our passions claim unlimited freedom of indulgence. Our egotism deludes us into thinking that it is the complete freedom we enjoy which accounts for our satisfaction. In love, we experience that it is our ability to apprehend real values spontaneously, which give us the sense of fulfilment. Such an attitude will not reject the desires of the body, such as hunger, thirst, relaxation and sex, nor is it necessary to sublimate them by seeking satisfaction in rational rather than physical pleasures. For, by doing so, our egotism might remain as powerful as previously. Bound by love, we realize that true life does not consist in just being ourselves or engaging in the search for our identity. We are rather aware of our self-transcendence. We realize that we are destined for the service of God and our fellow men.

No general rule can be stated by which love will limit our passions. We can say with the Reformers, nevertheless, that the medieval theologians were wrong in demanding that the goods of this world should be used, yet not enjoyed. While the New Testament writers appreciate wine, they warn against drunkenness; while food and drink are praised as God's gift for which to give thanks, the Christian is not to become the slave of his belly; while sexual intercourse is an essential element of married life, prostitution is to be shunned.

Of course, in the fire of passion, all limitations will appear to be too rigorous to be heeded. Even Christian love is not strong enough from the outset to lead the individual in the right direction. Our only comfort is the fact that God loves those cold or hot, rather than the lukewarm. For even in the misguided passion lies the recognition that God's world is a good one which should be passionately embraced. In no other area of life is the moral confusion greater than in that of the passions. It is often only in retrospect, *ex post facto*, that we learn what standards and principles should have been applied to our situation.

There are people who are discouraged by the constantly repeated, yet unsuccessful, efforts to overcome the excesses of their passions and desires. From their condition they draw the conclusion that the fault lies in the 'Utopian rigorism' of Christian ethics. Consequently, they give up their faith completely or indulge in scrupulous self-accusations. They are victims of a fatal error. What God expects of man is his willingness to serve his Creator within his abilities, as well as to trust in God, who will equip and strengthen people according to the purpose for which he wants to use them.

C. Interference with Nature
1. The Order of Human Life
Man plays an ambiguous role in this world. He is a part of nature and depends on it. Yet, as the creature who is destined for dominion over the universe, he has power to interfere with nature's regular course and to transform it according to his plans. That power implies the possibility seriously to disturb the order of nature. Nature is a system of relationships and affinities, which under normal circumstances is able to restore its equilibrium. As long as the human population was small in numbers, nature could, with relative ease, wipe off the traces of the

disturbing impact man would make upon this earth. The situation has rapidly changed, however, with the tremendous increase of its population during our century, the widespread tendency to urbanization, the technological progress and the ever expanding traffic. In turn, nature provides all that man needs for the sustenance, preservation and improvement of his life. Yet, it does not, as a rule, furnish them in the condition in which they are needed. Man must adjust them for his use. In that process, man himself is transformed. As he manufactures tools and finished goods and makes inventions, his way of life moves away from nature and adjusts itself to his implements.

The changes called forth by this development might be regarded as purely practical and biological ones. Since man has a divine destination, however, it is legitimate to ask the question, 'To what extent does modern man's way of life affect his fitness for the service of God?'

Some have held that the right life demands of man to place himself as far as possible upon the level of original nature. He should abstain from meat and should live of vegetables and fruits, if possible in raw condition, and should shun all technology by which one's environment would be altered. Such view implies a denial of man's dominion over nature. In turn, it postulates that nature has reached its final stage; the evolutionary process has reached its final goal, and in a way has even overshot the mark in making man. Christian thinking has offered an entirely different interpretation of man's role. The evolutionary process has shifted from the biological to the mental realm. Man is the creature who possesses reason and thus is capable of forming notions. Thus, science, technology, philosophy and art are man's legitimate means by which he improves his human existence. It is true to say that modern philosophy takes a sceptical view of human development. In particular, the one-sided way in which the scientists emphasize the predominance of the intellect is considered man's lethal disease. The fault does not lie in the growth of man's intellect, but rather in modern man's failure to relate his discoveries and inventions to the actual needs of his fellow men. As a result, the modern development of human life, instead of tying people together, isolates them from each other.

Furthermore, by neglecting God and his plan, modern man is unable to make the right use of nature's goods. Man is expected to admire nature, beauty, order and wisdom. Failure to notice God's work in nature was the critical fault of the theology of the nineteenth century. It was bound to end in subjectivism. Moreover, man is not the owner or lord of the universe. It is God's property, and man operates within his world upon God's behest. Hence not everything that man is capable of doing is good and legitimate. Take the work of the physician. He understands how to use the powers and substances of nature in order to restore health and to strengthen people's physical and mental powers. Such an ability is a privilege granted to a few members of mankind. Some people contend that to consult the doctor or to use his prescriptions is a sinful interference with the will of the Creator. Actually, such view is a relapse into a primitive religion in which nature, rather than its creator, is worshipped as the supreme deity. In the healing art we see an indication of the fact that God is aware of man's inability to preserve life's health by his own efforts. Moreover, the availability of healers in this world also expresses God's intention to heal man. It is characteristic of Christianity that in the Gospels Jesus' healing activity is so impressively stressed. Yet God's lordship sets limits to what the physician may do with a good conscience. For instance, if an act of abortion saves the life of a pregnant woman, it is a legitimate healing operation. The Roman Catholic view, according to which such abortion is considered a mortal sin, sacrifices the established claims of the family to the putative claims of the unborn foetus. Yet an abortion which is performed for no better reason than to save the unwed mother the inconvenience or embarrassment of extramarital pregnancy can hardly be reconciled with the will of God. Likewise, it is the physicians' privilege to preserve life which, without his assistance, would be doomed. But, in our days, there are doctors who want to keep alive a body which has to be fed artificially, and which gives no hope of recovery or active participation in social life. In such a case the physician would seem to substitute the display of a medical technique for a moral action. The same judgment may be passed on the geneticist who seeks to influence the development of genes by chemical or physical treatment. Such treatment may be applied to animals in experiments. But nobody has a right to influence the nature or character of an individual so that it will suit his own wishes or fancy.

Artificial insemination is a legitimate device for the breeding of animals, because there is no personal relationship between the mating partners. But in human relations it would be a disregard of the reciprocal relationship into which the spouses have entered in marriage. In the case of the husband's incurable sterility, adoption is the appropriate way of having children.

In turn, we do not share the exasperation which some theologians have shown on account of the transplantation of hearts or other vital organs from dying individuals to ailing ones. The case would seem to be similar to blood transfusion. There is no intrusion or transfer of one personality into another; the dying person's heart performs an analogous role to that of a mechanical device. Another hotly debated problem concerns the use of contraceptives. The Roman Catholic Church has been adamant in its prohibition of contraceptives, on the ground that their use was contrary to the nature of sexual life. Yet that argument rests on the assumption that in human relations the sexual act is confined to the transportation of semen into the woman's uterus. It has rightly been pointed out that the way in which nature is thereby understood would render all hygiene and the whole work of the doctor unnatural. The right view would admit that there is a close relation between sexual intercourse and conception. In the light of God's purpose these relations should be interpreted as meaning that God is using man's lust to secure the continuation of the human race. No less important is the fact, however, that in this way God brings personal beings together in the joyful awareness of their belonging together. Husband and wife are not so much the efficient causes by which a child comes into being, but rather the parents of their child, for whose development they are personally responsible. It is up to them to decide what the size of their family should be if the parents were to take responsible care of their children's education. Obviously no general rule can be established for that purpose. The Catholic doctrine, according to which all sexual intercourse is sinful, unless motivated by the desire to have children, is based upon Manichaean dualism. It is not only unsound psychologically, but also incompatible with the Biblical view.

2. *Man's Environment*

Man is ethically confronted by nature in two ways, namely, inasmuch as man himself is a part of nature, and also inasmuch as nature is the environment in which he has to live. Of course, in neither case is nature itself in a position to make claims on man. The moral problem arises from the fact that in either respect man is connected with nature in an inseparable way. Since the days of the Enlightenment – that is to say, since the beginnings of modern technology – Western mankind has looked at nature as the storehouse where the raw materials for man's activities were to be found and fetched. Believing in the self-restoring ability of nature, little attention was originally paid to the consequences which the exploitation of natural resources would have upon man's environment. But nature's resilience has definite limits. Thus, with the rapid expansion of modern industry and technology, the consequences of that exploitation are now visible in a pathetic and frightening way. In history the plains and mountains, forests and lakes, minerals and water supplies, the bottom of the ocean and outer space have been treated as goods without owner. Thus they were at the mercy of those who would discover and seize them. For the early settlers of America there was no problem in utilizing the bounties of nature, because the abundance of the spaces and goods available seemed to be unlimited. With the rapid increase of the world's population, the unbelievable development of industry and technology, and the enormous expansion of traffic, the situation has radically changed. Owing to the speed with which modern science advances, anything found on or in earth, organic or inorganic, has become useful, and is a commercial good. The past century was obsessed by the burning desire, and often the craze, for producing, irrespective of the necessity to manufacture those goods, and without any thought given to the consequences which their use might entail. The intensity with which that process goes on seems constantly to increase. The most important problem which confronts the future of mankind is not that of Capitalism versus Communism; that has shifted from the sphere of ideology into that of cybernetics. The basic issue has thereby been reduced to the question, 'Is the further advance of our technological civilization best served by free enterprise or by centralized control?' The basic moral problem in social life is now this: Does ownership imply the right of an unlimited production and sale of manufactured goods, or is the use of nature's goods to be determined strictly by regard for the best interests of mankind? What right does a man have to manufacture goods whose use will do harm to the customer's physical, mental or moral life? If the answer to these questions is in the negative, as it will be from a Christian viewpoint, its application will infringe on the rights and prerogatives of governments no less than of private business men, and will therefore meet with hostility. People who do not believe that our body has been given to us for God's service will demand that such goods should be in the market on account of the momentary pleasure they provide.

Christianity also holds that this world was made for the mutual benefit of all the creatures. Maintaining the balance of nature is an essential prerequisite of man's well-being. Lack of an appropriate natural environment, especially forests, will adversely affect the mental and physical health of a population. Yet, through thoughtlessness and greed, modern man has already exterminated numerous species of animals and plants. Our forests are depleted, man-made erosion has washed away the fertile humus in large areas, our lakes, rivers and the atmosphere over our cities have been dangerously polluted, and strip mining has transformed the beauty of the countryside into ugly heaps of sterile soil. Our big cities lack the green areas necessary for the recreation of the city dwellers. We are using up our mineral and oil supplies at a pace which will leave our descendants empty-handed in the foreseeable future. That list of man's thoughtless greed might be continued endlessly.

Of course, it would be foolish to decry industrialization as the work of the Devil and to dream of returning to a pre-industrial cottage life. Since God singled out man for a life of the mind, we have no right to condemn industry, which is an offshoot of scientific thinking. It has delivered man from the hardships of direct contact with an inhospitable nature. But, since it is scientific thinking that enables man to foresee the possible consequences of his actions, we must not shut our eyes when our interest is concerned. We should denounce a development in which nature has been treated merely as a source of profit or enjoyment for a small minority, which acts without regard for the needs and interests of the many. God created this world – and hence our natural environment – for the benefit of mankind. The fact that a few of them are more enterprising or more intelligent gives them a chance to derive special advantages. But, in the interest of the totality of man, we are responsible for the restoration of the balance of nature.

D. The Human Races

In continental Europe, ethicists hardly thought of referring to the existence of different races prior to Hitler. No matter whether their background was idealistic or was found in natural law, they would hold that, from a moral viewpoint, all men were equal. Yet the situation changed radically when Hitler challenged the humanism of his countrymen by contending that some races were absolutely superior to others and that some were so pernicious that they had to be exterminated. The problem has freshly gained urgency as a result of the civil rights demand of the U.S. negroes and the colour problem called forth in Great Britain and South Africa as an aftermath of the colonial era.

That there are human races with prominent characteristics should never have been denied, notwithstanding the fact that racial unity is compatible with a remarkable latitude of individual features and peripheral cases which might be attributed to more than one race. The ethnologists know next to nothing about the origin of human races. Races are likely to be temporary groupings. Intermarriage may eventually form new races such as the Eurasians, while ancient ones may long have ceased to exist. Each race has not only specific anatomical and physiological features, but also its specific attitude towards this world and people. Thus there is sense in speaking, for instance, of 'negritude'. Yet historical factors may so strangely operate upon a portion of a race that it forms eventually a group of its own, as for instance the Dutch as a portion of the Germanic race or the American negro as distinct from the African natives. Despite the racial differentiation, mankind forms an integral species in contrast to all animals. Even if mankind should have had a multiple origin, the genetic *morphé* would be the same. Nevertheless, the recent conflict situation has resulted in emphasis placed on the difference. In the Western countries, the coexistence of several races has become a problem through the confusing juxtaposition of two rival ethics. The Enlightenment, referring itself to Natural Law, had postulated that all men were equal by nature and were therefore entitled to equal civil rights. Conversely, the empiricists would emphasize the differences. They would therefore suggest that a patriarchal system would be most appropriate. The problem has not yet preoccupied the thinking of the Churches concerned for a sufficiently long time to allow us to speak of the 'Christian attitude'. Though the two philosophical theories have been adopted by a number of theologians, their very co-existence is a sign of their inadequacy.

It will be good, probably, to start from the fact that God's work in Creation is characterized by diversity in unity. Whatever differences God has laid into nature may not be interpreted as differences of value but rather of function. Each of them is destined to make its specific contribution to the whole of the universe, and by doing so to enrich the whole. One should therefore welcome the recent attempts of negro leaders to emphasize their particularity. The American negro is not simply a human being with a black skin. Rather, he forms one distinct group of Americans. Segregation – that is, enforced separation of the races – is in no way justified; it impoverishes both groups, since it is a denial of the common origin and destination of all men. It is only natural that within the Church Universal, as in any council of Churches, racial differences should not affect equality of standing and rights. One wonders, nevertheless, whether merging white and negro churches is an ideal solution. May it not result in depriving the negro of his specific features? It will not be enough for Christians to combat racial prejudice.

We must work actively for racial reconciliation and co-operation. What the negro has to fear most is not the white backlash, but rather the indifference of the white Christians. Three hundred and fifty years of slavery and a century of discrimination have engendered a deep feeling of inferiority on the part of the negro. The Church has it in its power to restore his self-confidence and self-esteem. No less is required to overcome the destructiveness of mere resentment. Apart from that self-assurance, the negro will not be able to enjoy and effectively to use his civil rights.

A similar approach would seem to be appropriate to the handling of international relations. The unquestionable superiority which the civilization of the Western world has over the rest of nations has resulted in a paradoxical development. All the gifted people of the young nations are anxious in our days to acquire Western knowledge, because through it they hope to be able to meet the Western man on his own level. Yet that development does not mean that the national differences of the earth are disappearing. In a bewildering way, the universal adoption of western civilization is paralleled by a very powerful nationalism and tribalism which is characterized by animosity and rivalry towards other nations, and frequently by hostility. To expect that Western civilization might become the unifying bond of the nations, for instance through UNESCO, would be Utopian. Outside the Western world that civilization has a purely instrumental significance. For the nations who adopt it, it is not the outgrowth of their own national life and aspirations.

A truly reciprocal relationship and interchange of civilizations occur but rarely in history, for instance, in the encounter of Greek and East Mediterranean civilizations in the age of Hellenism, or in the late Roman Empire. Even there, however, the synthesis was followed by a new disintegration into nationalities. One may hope, nevertheless, that in the course of history many more nations may find an opportunity for intimate exchange. However, it seems that the only place where a truly reciprocal relationship is established is in the Church. Every particular Church must necessarily be allied with a civilization, yet without identifying itself with it, because its foundation transcends human history. In turn, for that very reason, any national church is free to choose the most appropriate civilization. In that process they will learn from the example of other Churches. Thereby, all churches are capable of being intrinsically united with a congenial civilization. Such development makes for mutual recognition of the various civilizations, for instance, in theology, exegesis and forms of worship. Through the influence which the Church has on national life, one may hope that mankind will eventually be united in a solid and lasting way.

In conclusion, a word should be said concerning the Jewish problem. That there is a problem is evidently shown in the activities and publications of the Jewish Anti-Defamation League (Bne berith). But, notwithstanding Hitler, it is not a racial problem. Whether the Hebrew tribes that settled in Canaan about the middle of the second millennium B.C. were of a common racial stock is doubted by some historians. The fact is undeniable that, with their Babylonian exile, the Jews have been exposed to frequent intermarriage and racial mixture through proselytizing. In the ethnological sense there is no Jewish race in existence. Today's Jews are a closely knit social group held together by their determination to remain a distinct sociological entity and different from all nations and races. That determination is based upon the awareness that they are God's chosen people, a conviction that is held even by those Jews who for the rest have little use for the Jewish religion.

The Jewish problem is an eschatological one, and thus all attempts to solve it prematurely by social or political means will not have more than provisional success. Like the Church, the Jewish people is a transcendental realisty, tied up with a human association. The glory of its mission is always marred by the inadequacy of its adjustment to this world. Since both aspects are joint in God's plan, the Church, which at present is in a more favourable position than the Synagogue, is the guardian of Judaism. It denounces all defamation and discrimination of the Jewish religion as an affront to God's purpose. Though the younger sister, Christianity will at the same time be Judaism's educator, reminding them that their only hope lies in the faithful practice of their religion.

Epilogue

23 Ethics and Spirit

A. Spirit and Faith

1. *The Problem*

From the description of the Christian life given in the preceding chapters, it should be obvious that, in many respects, the Christian way of life differs profoundly from other ways of life and moral systems. But in view of the fact that all over the world there are so numerous different ways of life, the question arises inevitably, 'Is there any reason why the Christian way should be held in higher esteem than any of the others? Is not the diversity of possible types of ethics a clear indication that all of them have only a relative right of existence, and that an ethical pluralism would be the most consistent way of coping with that diversity?' Christian theology has succeeded in presenting its ethical views in a number of impressively systematized and consistent ways. But that is a merely formal characteristic for which the theologians deserve praise. Yet it does not furnish a special reason why the Christian way of life should be preferred to any other one.

Furthermore, how unique is Christian ethics? Does not its history suggest that the combination of Christian religion and Christian life is a purely incidental one? Is not what we call 'Christian life', in fact, but one type of morality which has grown up in the Mediterranean world and the adjacent countries? Is it not the outcome of common cultural and historical conditions? Finally, should not the modern advocates of 'secular ethics' be on a safer path, since, as Bonhoeffer contended, Western mankind had recently come of age, and was able in its conduct to proceed without the crutches of religion? Of course, there is a diversity of ethical views. Whether this should be the case, however, cannot be decided merely on the basis of their actual co-existence.

These questions are not of yesterday, and they must be raised by us who have embraced the Christian way. The answer cannot be given simply on the basis of a general idea of religion or ethics. The question that concerns us is this: 'Would something substantial be lacking in my life if I dropped my Christian ethical outlook?' Thus the problem is stated on the basis of my personal experience, yet in the perspective of human existence in general rather than in an existentialistic way.

2. *Spirit and Church*

Christian ethics, as has been shown, is faith manifested in human activity. Yet faith is never a purely individual act. It presupposes the individual's membership in the Church of Christ. Though not all acts of faith are collective acts, the activities of faith are nevertheless organically connected with the corporate nature of Christianity. There can be no life of faith outside of the Christian community, notwithstanding the fact that faith is a personal concern. Failure to notice that relationship has resulted in numerous modern misinterpretations of the Christian faith and in erroneous appraisals of the Church's activity.

We started from the fact that the average Christian's life lacks extraordinary features. To the outsider, it will often appear dull, lukewarm and uninspired. No wonder that to Troeltsch and other observers it seemed to coincide with the modern secular morality in general. Nevertheless, watching it more closely and from the inside, one will notice important differences. The Christian life has a special kind of authoritarian structure. The New Testament speak of shepherd and flock, king and subjects, master and disciples, or lord and servants. These and similar metaphors bear witness to the Christian's awareness that in his religious thinking and activity he should not act as his own authority. Though millions of church people are indistinct from each other, as far as their spiritual zeal and vision are concerned, that lack of originality does not result in stagnation. While there may be but few shepherds or leaders, they are never completely lacking. The people to whom those metaphorical titles are applied may or may not be officers of the Church. Their leading position certainly does not come from their office. Men like Tolstoy, George Müller, Hudson Taylor, Bp. Charles Gore, Albert Schweitzer, Robert E. Speer, John R. Mott, the Blumhardts, or Father Bodelschwingh, to mention only a few representatives of recent times, have manifested their leadership ability in and through the lives of hundreds of thousands. They are the persons to whom the Church Universal looks up as the deputies of its heavenly leader.

Other kinds of ethics are aware of ethical dignitaries, too. Yet, in idealism, for instance, the higher ones are at the best regarded as models, not as leaders. Conversely, images like 'shepherd' or 'master' imply an ontic or institutional relationship that determines the correlation between leader and flock. In Christianity, it is a reciprocal relationship. The leader acts in the awareness that full responsibility for the integrity and strength of the flock is incumbent upon him. The flock, in turn, is obligated willingly to be led and fed by the shepherd. All those titles have one feature in common: they designate the leaders as given to a group as a divine gift. Apart from these leaders, the group would not be able to find its way and reach its goal. The diverse titles disclose the various goals implied in the supreme leadership of Christ. The unity of the flock, for instance, submission of the will in the fight against evil, illumination of the mind, help in calamities – all of these are suggested thereby. In other systems of ethics, people are supposed to be either actually or potentially equipped for their goal, and hence will reach it; or they are permanently incapable of reaching their goal. Christians may be assured that, no matter how deficient they may seem to be, they will find divinely-appointed leaders in the Church.

In this connection, the ministry of the Church proves to be an additional help. Unlike the privilege of leadership, which is an occasional and divine gift, the ministry is a human form of organization. In spite of its humble origin, the ministry should not be despised or disparaged. Though it is an office of the human organization of the Church, it has a valuable and important function in the Spiritual life, for it stands in the Church as the symbol of the office of leadership. By means of it, the Church reminds itself of its lack of perfectibility, of its spiritual needs as well as its inability to meet them by its own efforts and resources. In turn, the Church does not abandon the ministry to the subjectivism of the incumbent. It is his task to keep the congregation informed about the ends pursued by its leaders, and to aid them in their endeavours to follow that leadership. Catholicism and Protestantism have this in common – that, through the office of priest or pastor, they provide for the permanency of leadership within a community which otherwise might be in darkness for long periods of time.

The leadership provided in the Church constitutes one of the fundamental differences between contemporary secular ethics and Christian life. Both may be in far-reaching agreement on the things to be done. Yet in secular ethics the moral deeds are ends in themselves, whereas the average Christian wants his actions to be in agreement with a transcendental purpose, namely the attainment of the goals to which the spiritual leaders have pointed. It is the movement towards that aim by which Christian life is rendered meaningful, no matter how small and insignificant our actions may be by themselves.

In this connection special mention must be made of the work of the Holy Spirit in the Church. In spite of the conspicuous place which the Spirit occupies in the creeds of the Church, or perhaps on account of that fact, theologians have usually found it difficult to deal with the role of the Spirit in ethics. If the Spirit were understood as cosmic energy, he might endow human activity with a kind of transcendence, yet it would lack intrinsic connection with the work of Christ and preclude the createdness of this world. In turn, however, when understood as the third person of the Trinity, the Spirit seems to be so far remote from human life that he might be spoken of in relation to such transcendental events as the unity of the Church, pardon of sin, and resurrection, but could hardly be experienced.

B. Faith and Charisma

1. *The Dynamics of the Church*

The relation in which the individual Christian stands to the Church can be described in a number of ways. It can be defined by social and religious values, as is the case of the Christian as member of a congregation or denomination. As has been shown in the preceding section, the church may also be envisaged as a system of order in which the individual is seen standing in relation to a spiritual leader. No less important, and frequently referred to in the New Testament, is the locale of the individual believer in a dynamic field, which forms the history of redemption. It is characterized by the correlation between the ordinary Christian and the charismatics. We started our investigation with the observation that in the congregations we encounter, as a rule, ordinary or average Christians. Occasionally, however, people of extraordinary or outstanding abilities are found. The difference between the two groups is not to be seen in various degrees of spiritual intensity or passion. Of course, there is the possibility of growth implied in what we call average Christianity, though in most instances within a limited range only.

The distinctive mark of charismas lies not primarily in the realm of piety. Rather, the charismatic has a special ability to render those services to the Church by which it is enabled effectively to transform mankind and this world in accordance with God's plan of redemption. Though it is the same Spirit who works in the average Christian and the charismatic, they have different functions which are related to subsequent steps in holy history. Faith manifests to the world that, notwithstanding its opposition and hostility, God is able to win the hearts of men. The charismas are special abilities by which human individuals are enabled actively to participate in the process of redemptive transformation. Average believer and charismatic are both incorporated in the dynamic field of redemption, yet in an asymmetrical relationship like man and animal. The functions are not interchangeable. The presence of the charismatic gives to the believer an opportunity to act spiritually, according to his limited ability. Hence comes the assurance that the work of Christ does not exclusively belong to the past, namely to the earthly ministry of Jesus. Rather in the charismatics' activity that work is seen as going on and moving effectually towards its ultimate goal. As the term 'charisma' indicates, those abilities are not acquired by a special effort of the will or a special mental technique. One simply has them, because it is the Spirit who operates 'in' them. The charismatic, in turn, is aware of the fact that his existence is not an end in itself. Rather he is destined to keep the average Christian's faith alive by turning them to the Spirit's ongoing work.

It is impossible to draw up a complete list of all the varieties of charisma found in the Church. In a way it may even be held that the attempt to distinguish so many clearly defined charismas would be misleading. All of them have this in common, that they serve the spiritual advance of the Church in all the areas that need help. Thus one might say that all charismatics have the same gift, namely the ability to keep the Church moving towards its ultimate goal, while the differences are purely quantitative ones, namely of width, strength and depth. It is not a rare occurrence, for instance, to find people possessing several charismas. There are charismatics who will administer or guide the Church, or who will act as teachers and interpreters of Scripture. Others will be able to heal, to counsel, to exhort or to give comfort. Still others possess ecstatic gifts, and are able in a state of trance to speak in tongues or to compose hymns and songs. Not unknown are also the faculties of telepathy, of prophecy and of discerning false spirits. Of course, all those abilities are more or less well-known phenomena outside Christianity, and are found even apart from all religion. Their specific Christian feature lies in the charismatic's ability to use the material endowment for the fostering of the spiritual ends of the Church.

Greatest and most precious of all spiritual gifts is love. Charismatic love is not an emotion. Rather it is a social attitude which implies willingness to acknowledge the fact that, as God's creature, my fellow man participates as fully as myself in the dignity of the human race. Hence, he has not only a right to live, but also to share in the goods of this world. Thus I am called to come to his support according to my abilities and resources. Charismatic love is practised especially in situations in which the average Christian is reluctant to show sympathy, for it embraces even the enemy and the outcast. Hostility is not obliterated thereby, and meanness is not ignored; yet they are not allowed to deprive love of its ability to care for such people's needs. The attitude of the Quakers and Mennonites, who in a war are concerned with the medical needs of the enemies of their country, is often misunderstood. The majority of Christians identify political frontiers with moral ones. While love of our neighbour is most directly related to our practical contacts, more central is love of God, because in it love of our fellow man has its root. Love of God is first of all readiness to discover his justice, wisdom and love in the apparently unjust or irrational manner in which this world runs its own course. Furthermore, it is willingness to promote God's ends here on earth. Such attitude is espoused in spite of the apparent futility so to do. The charismatic has experienced in his own life that God is able to triumph over all the evils of the universe. Love of God is therefore in a position to rejoice, even in a world in which other people may notice only chaos and destruction. Yet as a factor of constant transformation such charismatic love of God is incompatible with a self-centred adjustment to this world. There is no contradiction in such outlook. Love of God is grateful for all the good things of this world and enjoys them. But the charismatic loves this world because he will discern in it God's saving design. He does not confine his appreciation to the things that are useful for his own ends or that happen to please him.

Within the Church, the charismatics fulfil two functions, that of service and that of witness. Whatever such persons do is not only helpful to the Church; their work is of such a character that in it the divine teleology and the on-goingness of history are manifested. By no means all those who notice a charismatic work will believe that it was inspired by God. Nevertheless, they are unable simply to explain it as the working of natural causes. As a result of their weak faith, the congregation may be tempted to doubt God's existence or his ability to solve our problems. Yet the activity of the charismatics gives convincing evidence of the Spirit's operation and effectiveness.

Jesus compares the gifts of the Spirit to the role of salt for seasoning a meal, or that of light being brought into a dark room. The metaphors would indicate that by themselves the charismatic abilities are natural elements of the human mind, and in no way something supernatural.

Their distinction lies in two facts: they are missing in those who need them, yet they are found in others who will use them for the benefit of the needy. The choicest steak will not be tasty, unless salted. In turn, the gifts of the Spirit appear small in comparison with the natural faculties of man. It requires a mere spoonful of salt to season the whole meal, and though the lamp is tiny in proportion with the size of the room, it makes all that is hidden in its darkness visible. Furthermore, it is the exact correlation between the Church's needs and the charismatic's service which renders the charismas so important. As light and salt are exactly the things required to render room and meat useful or pleasant, so do the gifts of the Spirit in general. They are geared to the predicament of the Church.

The charismatic may not excel over the rest of the Church in intelligence, and if ever he does so, he does not crave for admiration. He realizes that his most precious good is his certainty of faith and his readiness to act accordingly, even in the presence of threats and oppression. Though the charismas are given to individuals, they are not granted as a personal distinction, but rather as God's gifts to be used for the benefit of the Church. Hence the charismatics are not supposed to withdraw from the common Christians, or form a separate group within the Church, an *ecclesiola in ecclesia*, as has been attempted from time to time. In order to irradiate their gifts into this world, the charismatics must be willing to condescend to the level of the congregation and to co-operate with the common church people. In turn, the latter ones must recognize that they need the light of the charismatics in order to perform their share in God's work. The presence of the charismatic is to remind them that they are not destined to engage in merely secular activities. In the co-operation of congregation and charismatic, the latter's vision of the true human life eventually will be adopted by the common Christian. As a result, the spiritual message of God is transformed into a collective human will. Thereby the invisible Spirit acquires concreteness and thus strength to move the minds and wills of thousands of ordinary believers.

What prompts the common believer to accept the challenge of the charismatics is not in the first place their special zeal or religious energy, though they are helpful, but rather the new vision of an aspect of true life that is thereby recognized as being an essential feature of God's people. While the spiritual life of the congregation may not transcend its actual level, their situation has changed, nevertheless, for obstacles and inhibitions are overcome. Thus the charismatic's vision becomes the standard by which they then judge life. Father Bodelschwingh's home for the epileptics, incurables and bums, Robert E. Speer's Student Volunteer Movement for the promotion of Foreign Missions, or John Wesley's appeal to repentance and conversion, are a few instances which exemplify our statement. These men have been used by the Spirit to recall to the Churches permanently the possibilities by which they are enabled to lend a hand in the cosmic transformation.

2. *Church and Charismatics*

While the primitive Church held the charismatics in high esteem and considered the charismas an indispensable manifestation of the Church's election, the Church's outlook changed radically once the official ministry had become a dominant factor in the life of Christianity. Of course, nobody was able to stop the Spirit when he made intermittently his appearance in the Church. Nevertheless, the charismatics were looked upon with high suspicion and occasionally expelled from the official Church. In turn, the theologians were often unable to say much about the work of the Spirit, and the charismatics were at a loss to understand themselves. In recent times, there has been a renewed interest in the charismas, especially in prophetic interpretation of Scripture, healing and glossolalia. Although the 'theological' Churches still frown on these enthusiastic phenomena, there is a growing interest in these gifts among clergy and laity alike. There are spectacular charismas such as glossolalia, ecstasy and healing; there are also inconspicuous gifts such as spiritual teaching, nursing and tending to the indigent. They all have their legitimate place in the work of the Church. The spectacular gifts may prove to be troublesome at times; the inconspicuous ones may seem to be useless because they do not attract public attention. They cater for different kinds of people in the Church, and all of them are therefore indispensable, provided only that the congregation uses them as opportunities whereby to serve God.

The central place which not only Eastern Orthodoxy and Rome but also the leading Protestant churches have assigned to theology has resulted in a trend towards doctrinal and organizational uniformity and a strict insistence upon order. These tendencies it is difficult to reconcile with the Spirit's trend towards diversification and exuberant life. In the wake of the one-sided developments of many centuries, it is not easy to make room in the Church of today for enthusiastic forms of worship sought in experiments of Jazz mass, cultic dance and dramatics, or the ecstatic meetings of the Original Gospel Movement in Japan. Since by no means all the gifts of the Spirit are of the ecstatic-enthusiastic type, one can hardly agree with those advocates of modernity, who would completely abrogate the traditional forms and orders of worship. Equally objectionable, it seems to us, is the outright rejection and condemnation of enthusiastic worship. The two types can hardly be merged, but they have a right to co-exist side by side. Recognition of the place of enthusiastic worship might help to combat the fatal tendency to leave the leadership of the Protestant churches in the hands of the clerical bureaucracy.

Of course, there is also danger, lest in the enthusiastic movements more attention should be paid to the unusual and singular forms in which the charismas manifest themselves than to the function which they serve in God's plan of redemption. A specific charisma may be treated as though it represented the totality of the Spirit's work, e.g. when Pentecostals contend that glossolalia is the sole criterion of salvation, or when the ministry of healing is looked upon as the only genuine work of neighbourly love. Unfortunately, a good deal of what goes on in the Churches as charismatic religion has but an external similarity with the gifts of the Holy Spirit. As was shown above, the charismatic phenomena have their parallels in non-Christian religions. It seems therefore safe to hold that all so-called charismatic phenomena, which are self-induced by means of a mental technique or drugs, should be regarded as lacking spiritual origin. Likewise, it is to be kept in mind that in the charismas it is the Spirit of God who communicates himself to the Church. Though diversity is characteristic of the Spirit's work, no particular ability may be accepted as a fruit of the Spirit when other spiritual abilities are neglected or despised, especially love. The genuine charisma comes to a person as a gift and thus is destined for the execution of the ends which God pursues therewith. The gift is not at our free disposal. One may have it, yet did not engender it. Finally, the charismas are the divine device by means of which the ordinary people, those who form the majority of the Church's membership, are enabled to participate in the service of God. By accepting the charismatic's vision of true life they make it a potent factor in the Church.

In their conduct, the majority of Christians do not differ conspicuously from their secular neighbours. Their moral outlook is, as a rule, dominated by practical considerations of usefulness or pleasure. They differ, however, essentially in one respect. Since the charismatics confront him with the image of truly human life, the Christian will appraise

357

CHRISTIAN ETHICS

his own actions in the light of that standard. Thus with reference to each action he is able to say that it ought or ought not be done. The questions may now be asked, 'How are we to account for the charismatic structure of the Church? Why is it that the Spirit does not impart charismas to all Christians alike?' We suggest that the work of the Spirit, as all of God's works in this world, are arranged according to the law of paucity or parsimony. God wants to attain to the greatest possible effect by means of the smallest amount of energy. Man was created for action rather than to be merely a passive recipient of God's gifts. Activity is not an end in itself, however, man is destined to work for the realization of God's plan. Without the incentive that comes to him through the charismatic's vision, the ordinary Christian would be at a loss what to do for God's sake. The charismatic, too, is not a mere recipient of a gift; the gift implies a task, namely responsibility for the Church people's faith. Thus all the members of the Church, each one according to his ability, are employed for participation in God's work. If all had received the full gift of the Spirit, nobody would have a task, and all would be idle. Now, not only all are busy in mutual responsibility and love, the dynamic field, too, is activated thereby, and keeps on moving towards a higher level of human existence.

Man realizes that, prior to any specifically moral life, his mental and physical faculties assign to him a task which he feels unable to perform. Being a member of the human race, he is expected to act reasonably at all times, to do what is good in all circumstances, to lead a healthy and sober life when he is surrounded by so many pleasurable things. Yet the task surpasses what he is willing and able to do. Under those conditions, it is the presence of outstanding men whereby mankind is prevented from losing completely the sight of their goal and from falling into despair when they try in vain to live a truly human life. Apart from those charismatic examples, the human family would be submerged into mediocrity, dullness and boredom. Yet there is a fundamental difference between the great men of secular society and the charismatics. In the secular sphere the great ones are admired or envied, and people are proud of them, when they belong to their own nation, class or race. But the gap which separates the great man from their followers cannot be bridged. In the spiritual realm, however, the charismatic aims at a specific goal to which the Spirit wants to attain through the whole people of God. Thus there is a common task which the charismatic and the church people are destined to perform. The work of Albert Schweitzer, for instance, has not produced a second Albert

Schweitzer. Yet through his hospital work in Lambarene, millions have understood that the sick in equatorial Africa are our responsibility. To us as Christians they are as close as the people next door.

C. The Power of the Spirit

1. *The Mystery of the Spirit*

In the preceding sections, the role which falls to the Spirit in the mission of Christianity has been strongly emphasized. Yet by doing so our argument seems to lose its force. Of course spiritual leaders and charismatic models are thereby related to an historical congregation. Yet their work is so completely geared to the service of God's transcendental purpose that man's earthly life seems to have only peripheral significance. Of course, there have been Christian theologians who would say that for a Christian that was the only legitimate perspective. One can argue that this world is a realm of futility and meaninglessness, a valley of tears and Hell itself, and that our only hope was the after-life in Heaven. But such view cannot consistently be carried through except on the basis of a Neo-Platonic or Manichaean cosmology. The Biblical idea of a divine Creation, however, is incompatible with such a dualism. We may adopt the Biblical promise of a heavenly reward for the Christian, but thereby this world is not robbed of its goodness. The Biblical promise means that the work of faith which is due in this world, is so important that its significance does not end with the death of our body. Rather the Christian, having surrendered his life to the operation of the Spirit, has become an integral and indestructible factor of holy history.

The idea of Creation is not meant merely to provide a mystical substitute for the notion of a prime cause. It also implies the belief that man is privileged to enjoy all of the world's goods and to co-operate with the Spirit here on earth in the removal of the obstacles which block the possibility of a meaningful life. True life is not confined to the world to come. By God's kindness we are enrolled for service here on earth. It is our willingness or unwillingness to deal with the God who made this world that will decide whether or not the world to come will receive us. Or we may say, looking at life in the opposite perspective, that the true life is the ordinary life lived under the conditions of this world, provided we envisage it in the light of the divine goal thereby to be reached. Through the connection of our life with the divine purpose, our position in the universe is radically altered. While man is from his creation the object of the Spirit, by faith he is rendered fit to contribute to the world's salvation. That is to say, the Christian becomes an active agent

359

of God's work. The recipient of divine life becomes a life-giver, able to bring forth spiritual life in others. He who has been illumined makes light shine in the darkness in which his fellow men live. In the rebirth of man, the mystery of the Spirit is celebrated. The Spirit moves from his origin in God into this world in order to impart life to it. In the genesis of the individual creatures the Spirit seems to have exhausted all its energies. In fact, however, through man's faith, he returns again into the Father's bosom. In that reversal of the Spirit's direction we find the answer to our question.

Incapable as utilitarianism and hedonism are to gauge the depth of spiritual life, they contain nevertheless a valuable element of truth. They postulate that in order to make sense, ethical life must give satisfaction to be experienced under the conditions and in the context of earthly life. Yet, through its egotism, the utilitarian will prepare his own undoing. Christianity does not seek its own profit. Nevertheless it takes it for granted that the goods brought about in and through the Church will be effective and lasting ones. That implies that they will eventually make themselves felt as constructive influences in the believer's life and in the Church's environment, too. Similarly hedonism's error lies in the assumption that the only valuable pleasure is the one provided by our senses. Christian ethics knows two restrictions. Firstly, our enjoyment of pleasurable things is increased when we let others share in our joy. Also, though there is no harm or wrong in sensual pleasure, no pleasure is good when it prevents me from, or interferes with, my service of God.

In order to do justice to God and this world, we have to realize that ours is not a static and unchanging world. In that case it would be correct to designate it imperfect on account of the evils, difficulties and dangers found on earth. Rather this is a world that is on the march. Its changes are not senseless mechanical imitations of its elements. Rather it is on the move toward the goal God has assigned to it. Thus a given moment may be considered meaningful because it contributes an essential element to the completion of that process, though it implies imperfections and lack finality. The teleological character of the world process may be seen in the fact, that in nature and aim, the cosmic changes have throughout the same structure. Thus all the creatures are granted an opportunity to make their contribution to the ultimate goal: namely, a condition of the universe in which all things are united in the praise of their Creator, each one according to its ability, and devote all their energies to the maintenance of the universal harmony.

2. *Personal Changes*
a. SPIRIT AND MIND

To the sociologist it may seem that the so-called spiritual life of the average Christian is but an extraneous and second-hand imitation of the spontaneous spiritual life found in the charismatics and spiritual leaders. Hence there could be no change of level or intensity in that group's spiritual life. Yet, except for the nominal Christian who, in spite of his membership, shuns all contact with church life, Christians are changed by the fact that they belong in an historical field and are affected by the dynamics of divine history. The width of the change through which we pass in our lifetime may go on unnoticed because our moral thought is so heavily conditioned by the perspective of classical ethics. We measure moral progress by the energy of will therein employed and by our facility or difficulty to conform our will with the urge and goal of the moral law. Seen in that light, the common Christian's moral life does not undergo radical changes. Of course, there are ups and downs. It may be possible to excuse the dormant will or to challenge social callousness or to develop habits of prayer and Bible study. That is all for the good, yet it does not alter the Spiritual quality of our life.

Nevertheless, our moral horizon is constantly widened and its faculty of moral judgement is sharpened by the vivid interest which the congregation takes in the theological and ethical movements of its time. The debates on peace and war, the just economic and social order, or on the use of contraceptives, to mention only a few topics, are indications of the Church's spiritual vitality.

In that process the individual's Christian life will be strengthened. Nevertheless only in rare cases, and never by his own efforts, will he thereby become a charismatic. His experience enables him, however, to become aware of the role he plays in God's plans and to admire the wisdom deployed therein. As he realizes how great a privilege he enjoys in becoming conscious of God's purpose, the Christian acquires a sense of superiority, which in turn prompts him to take his moral obligations seriously – that is to say, not as a commandment that hits him from the outside, but rather as a necessity derived from his destination. He grows in differentiating between purely practical activity, in which man wants to assert the superiority of his mind and will over nature on the one hand, and moral activity, whose ultimate aim it is to improve man's relation to the universe in the light of God's design on the other.

In the perspective of the ordinary Christian all that is done by faith appears in a strange twilight. Acting as a Christian seems to be both beautiful and noble, but also appears to be unfit to cope with the conditions of this world. The bifurcation of life, which is characteristic of the common Christian, will disappear nevertheless in charismatic life. Though the inspiration takes place under the conditions of this world, the bifurcation reaches a terminal point where the practical outlook clashes with the spiritual one. The charismatic refrains from activities which may be useful or pleasant, yet would harm the interests of God's people wherewith the charismatic is primarily concerned. On this matter, there is an irreconcilable contrast between the charismatic sense of restraint and moderation on the one hand, and the modern idea of unlimited freedom or self-expansion on the other. The modern sense of life would tell us that, whatever a man is able to do, he should engage in, if some usefulness or profit can be derived from it.

b. EFFECTS OF THE SPIRIT

Critics of the Church have often pointed out the fact that, outside Christianity or at least outside of the great official churches, spiritual life is more intense and challenging than in what is considered the inner core or the ecclesiastical centre of Christianity. That fact should not be denied altogether. Yet by itself the contention has no decisive significance. For what matters in Christianity is not the fact that people are moved by religious ideas, but rather that they should live and act in agreement with God's will and, in particular, with his redemptive purpose. Nevertheless, and notwithstanding the basic difference between true and false religion, the fact is important that in Christianity there are degrees of spiritual experience. They reflect the degree of directness, in which a spiritual attitude stands to the realization of holy history.

In that respect, theology speaks of salvation, sanctification, and participation. In a more psychological terminology, we might refer to them as self-identification, or discovery of one's self, growth and new life. Characteristic of man's natural understanding of himself is the feeling of lostness in a vast universe without a centre. The result is uncertainty, anxiety, fear, and a sense of impotence derived from the evils and difficulties of this world. Man may postulate the existence of an Archimedean point for his life, yet, on account of its subjective nature, he is also ready to replace it by others which are seemingly more satisfactory. Man's main concern is with the avoidance of evils and the pursuit of pleasant things. Through the Biblical message man is confronted with a set of values, whose authenticity is confirmed by historical events in Israel's history, the life of Jesus and the beginnings of the primitive Church. Thus man knows himself as one who in this world learns to distinguish between what renders existence meaningful and what deprives it of meaning. That is the level of experience of the ordinary Christian. The function of the individual is that of a recipient of spiritual illumination.

The ordinary Christian who knows the will of God merely as a commandment may not find real satisfaction in his condition, because he is unable to bridge the gulf between the life he lives, on the one hand, and the standards of true life, on the other. As soon, however, as he begins to realize that in the life of the charismatic it is God's Spirit which is at work, his spiritual condition will give him satisfaction. He discovers that even his weak and purely formal faith is evidence that the Spirit has started his life-giving work in his heart. Looked at from the outside, for instance from a psychological viewpoint, the faith of the common believer may appear to be mere wishful thinking. Viewed from inner experience, however, it discloses the contact in which the believer stands with the activity of the Spirit. By faith he is part of a comprehensive cosmic process, namely the restoration of man's true life.

Nevertheless, on account of the incipient character of sacred history, faith would never give full satisfaction but for the fact that, in the community of God's people, there were persons who directly participate in the process of redemption. In that respect, the earthly ministry of Jesus is of special importance. Whereas in the majority of charismatics the spiritual impulse is confined to a specific ability, in Jesus it is the whole person or the individual in his selfhood that is moved by the Spirit. In such persons, the aim of life is not moral goodness as such but rather, passively no less than actively, conformity with, and participation in, God's redemptive will.

In such a life, human nature has been brought to its completion. That is the reason why Christians look up to Jesus. For what they perceive in him is not a model that confronts them as an alien will. Rather noticing that in him the same Spirit is in operation that works in their faith, they find in Jesus' life the assurance that they, too, are engaged in the final transformation of mankind. That implies the promise that they, with all of God's people, will participate in the world's consummation. Thus the Church is able to ask Jesus to be its guide. In order to move in the right direction, the Church then no longer depends on commandments or moral principles. It relies on the presence of Christ in its midst, or on an inner voice by which it is told what is good and necessary for the harmony of God's work.

The distinction of levels of the spiritual life should not be understood in the manner taught by the medieval mystics. God does not demand of him a discipline of will and thought, by means of which his inner life would be refined and reorientated. Rather we become aware of the fact that God's people, notwithstanding the differences of their spiritual life, form a unit of mutual love and help. Within the Church of Christ there are different modes in which the Spirit operates and manifests his redemptive work. The final aim of the Spirit makes the Church a fellowship of interdependence and mutual correlation. The co-operation of all of them is required, and none can be missed. The process of transformation would not proceed towards its goal except that all engaged in it would perform their specific task faithfully. Thus what imparts meaning and consequence to our life of faith is our participation in the Church's activity rather than our psychological or moral accomplishments.

3. *Spirit and World*

For methodical reasons it seemed to be advisable to discuss first of all the changes which the Spirit calls forth in the lives of individual believers. Yet, as has been shown, the individual Christian's life is not spent in a vacuum. It takes place in the Church, both as an organized institution and as the world-wide fellowship of God's people. Accordingly, the power of the Spirit can be seen at work as an effective factor in the Church. As a result, the Church is an unique institution. It is part of human civilization, and hence not able completely to escape the temptations, weaknesses, and errors of such an institution. Yet, amazingly, the effectiveness of the Church's work is not thereby substantially impaired. The success of its work does not rest in the first place upon the quality of its activities or the abilities of its workers, but rather upon the intrinsic truth of its message and the intrinsic energy by which it aims at the the full realization of that truth. Its well-known shortcomings would be its undoing, nevertheless, unless the charismatics in its midst would emphasize from time to time the necessity of corrective action and improvement. An otherwise unknown inner urge for self-criticism and reform are constitutive elements of the Church.

Equally unique is the Church's sense of mission. In view of the fact that the primitive Church tended towards the formation of national churches, one should expect that after some while national antagonisms would stop the missionary process. Yet the awareness of being the dynamic field of a transcendental power made charismatic people disregard national frontiers and prejudices and spread its message all over the world. We consider the missionary enterprise of the Church to be unique. Both Islam and Communism adopted the idea of evangelism from Christianity, though for different reasons. They lack the Christian transcendence, which alone could truly motivate an universal mission.

Furthermore, even when faith was defined exclusively in terms of moral goodness, the Spirit did not allow Christianity to be satisfied with personal perfection. The very regard for God's purpose makes Christians aware of the obligation to think of their fellows and their needs. Following the Spirit's promptings, Christians have built hospitals, orphanages, homes for the aged and infirm, schools, universities and monasteries. Their value was so obvious that their example was imitated by non-Christian religious and secular groups. The usefulness of those enterprises confirmed the Church's assurance that, with the assistance of the Spirit, the apparently impossible could be performed, and that it was in its power eventually to transform the whole social structure of mankind. Being performed in a world in which faults and shortcomings are the order of the day, the redemptive process, too, will have its setbacks and standstills. Yet in view of the past successes of the Spirit the Christian is sure that those obstacles will not be able to stop the Church's advance completely. Time and again Christians have discovered in themselves unknown and unexpected spiritual abilities by which to cope effectively with the secular powers. They discovered their power to heal both the sick and the incurable without medical training, to ask for relief funds and to receive even more than they had asked for, to brave emperors and generals, to interfere in politics and eventually to prevail. In that way, millions were helped who otherwise would have perished, and many people were stimulated up to a new life. Others were encouraged by their charisma to defy the arbitrariness or injustice of the social order. Master and slave would treat each other with all the respect due to a child of God. Women were no longer regarded as an inferior sex, and sexual intercourse was lifted to the level of a personal relation.

Viewed in the isolation of his individual existence, the Christian may sometimes, in a mood of dejection, be driven to the conclusion that his way of life is futile and Utopian. Of course, since he stands in the midst of an historical process, it is not surprising that his own deeds should not immediately produce visible effects upon world history.

Things are quite different, once we think of ourselves as members of the Church. By moving in the same direction with its masses, we become aware of the fact that the Spirit of God is capable of renewing all things through human agents. Within the frame of world history the changes wrought by the Church cannot be overlooked. Thus not in its own strength, but rather, through participation in the life of the Church, the individual Christian is enabled to attain to the goal for which he has been destined by God.

24 Our Problem

A. The New Mentality

1. The New Quest

The aim of this book is primarily directed towards obtaining a critical understanding of the nature, purpose, and objective of the Christian life. But there are good reasons why such study must reach out beyond Christian introspection; Christianity has a missionary obligation to the non-Christian world, and must therefore familiarize itself with modern non-Christian mentality. In religion as in ethics, ours is an age of transition. Modern man is no longer satisfied with the interpretations which past ages have given of human life. But his perplexity and resentment show also that, neither in the realm of faith nor in ethics, clear insights have yet been gained. One thing is certain, nevertheless. During the last few centuries, Western mankind's primary interest in philosophy and theology has been concerned with Man, especially with his possibilities and limitations. While interest has more recently shifted in the main to sociology and social sciences, the subject matter remains the same.

The spiritual situation is greatly confused and complicated by the fact that the changes which have occurred in Western mentality were originally provoked and solicited by Protestantism. It will therefore be advisable first to give a brief survey of some of the most outstanding features of modern mentality and then to ask ourselves how in their light the ethical objective may be formulated in a manner that is both in agreement with the spirit of the Reformation, and related to the problems and viewpoints of our contemporaries.

2. Principal Perspectives

a. CHANGE

Perhaps most characteristic of modern man's mind is his obsession with change. It seems to be intolerable to him that something should last unchanged for a long while, let alone for ever. Of course, changes have always occurred, and people have realized that they were unable to prevent them altogether. But what was formerly interpreted as an

367

inescapable fate is now considered a moral necessity. Likewise, while formerly change was held to be the exception, it is now accepted as belonging to the very nature of existence. This change in outlook is of relatively recent origin. In the Middle Ages, the people's mentality was dominated by the conviction that the Church was in the possession of an unchanging and unchangeable truth. Thereby not only the thoughts of men, but also the political and social institutions and even the daily life of the people, were strictly regulated.

An entirely new outlook manifested itself simultaneously in the Renaissance movement and in the demand for a reformation of the Church and its theology. Their roots are found in a new view of God, or the universe. God, it was held, is not merely the supreme value or the supreme power. Rather he is above all the source of life, and thus is capable of creating new things in our time without diminishing or wasting his substance. The old order of things, including its shortcomings and errors, is not to last for ever. The novelty expected was conceived of as potentially implied in what has already been acknowledged as truth. Hence it would not only be compatible with the past; it would even be an essential supplement of the treasure of verity. Since the sixteenth century, the non-Catholic sector of the Western world is characterized by its burning expectation of new insights. Just as truth is multiform and not uniform, so is the universe a diversified unity. Innovations may therefore be tolerated and even welcomed rather than be condemned.

The hope for the advent of a new age was originally an eschatological one. The coming newness would deliver mankind from the fetters, errors and prejudices of the past. Yet, in accordance with the general secularization of man's outlook, novelty lost its religious connotation. Man rather than God was believed to be the author of novelty, and what made it desirable was no longer seen in its ontological superiority, but rather in the increased quantity and diversity of the goods produced. That development was intensified in the twentieth century through the use of the various media of mass communication and the industrial mass production of consumer goods. The quantity and diversity of the goods available created a problem of its own, however. The consumer gets tired of the merchandise and the entertainment freely offered to him. Since the consumption must be kept on a high level in order to be profitable, new types of merchandise and new programmes of entertainment must be offered in increasingly rapid succession. Thereby a general mental habit is created, by which novelty and change is demanded in political and social life, in literature and in the arts, too.

In such circumstances, change has to be manufactured. People's sense of life undergoes a strange modification in that process. Instead of starting from a reality which is relevant in itself and demonstrates its relevance through its creativity, modern man finds the meaning of his life in productivity and flexibility, by which he will be enabled immediately to become aware of new productions. Underlying this attitude is the belief that whatever exists is relevant only as long as it is new and has no parallel. Since man considers himself the source of productivity, it is obvious that changes will be brought forth all the time. To the modern man a hypothesis, for instance, will appear acceptable, no matter how absurd it may be, provided only he can believe that it is an utterly new view. By means of television and publicity in the popular magazines the public is persuaded that, whenever a new product is on the market, it is essential that everybody change over to it.

The shift from relevant novelty to mere change or from creativity to productivity has occurred in such a subtle way that modern man is usually unaware of its fallacy. Yet since novelty is no **lon**ger measured by way of reference to an objective reality, modern man feels he has a right to ascribe a value to goods in complete freedom. In that way people will waver helplessly between conventional and subjective evaluations. It is obvious that such attitude will result in the disintegration of the social order. The advocates of 'law and order' seem to be unaware of the fact that social disturbances, riots and violence are not so much the work of a few wicked ringleaders or agitators as the manifestation of a generation which rebels against the contention of those in power that they alone have a right to proclaim their subjective idiosyncrasies as the order of justice. Likewise, education is doomed to be a failure when the child is taught to be his own master, or to make his choice among several sets of ethical conventions while no firm standard is provided by which to make the choice.

The obsession with change, strong as its hold may be on modern man, is an expression of unrest, perplexity and dissastisfaction, nevertheless. At its bottom lies the contention that the world in which we live has no value by itself. Yet modern man pretends that he has the power to render it relevant; but all the attempts made to demonstrate the truth of that bragging ends in disappointment.

Thus modern man is torn between the delusion of a better world that will come out of his productivity, and the cynical contempt of those whom he considers responsible for the evils of this world.

b. SELF-RELIANCE

The way in which modern man as an individual seeks to overcome his cynical view of change and to buttress his hope of final success is by making the future depend on the creative abilities of the human race. The individual man encounters insuperable obstacles on his road to a meaningful life. Nevertheless, mankind has undeniably made enormous progress in its mastery of nature. History seems definitely to refute the medieval belief that nature was the hiding place of malicious forces bent on doing man all kinds of harm. In particular the marvellous accomplishments that have been made by science and technology during the last century claim to be incontrovertible evidence of the unlimited creative powers of mankind. Thus man may for all practical purposes rely on his own abilities, resources and powers. Looking at what he has already discovered, modern man announces confidently that no difficulty can arise in life which will not eventually be taken care of by man. The impossible today is but the possible of tomorrow.

It has been pointed out that man's intellectual abilities have developed during a long history. In the light of that development the hope seems to be legitimate that new abilities will eventually come into being which will greatly surpass all those which man has acquired thus far. From the ancient Greek trust in the self-sufficiency of Reason, the modern attitude differs considerably. The Greeks believed that man's reason had been absolutely the same through all ages. Modern man believes in a historical development of the human mind. It is held that not until our time has mankind a right to believe in its self-sufficiency.

This belief manifests itself most conspicuously in two phenomena. Modern man trusts that, through the powerful ability of his mind, he is able to attain a complete knowledge of the universe. He also believes that he has the ability so to use science that a complete transformation of nature will thereby be accomplished. The whole universe, he hopes, will become a place of happiness and pleasure for the whole of mankind. Closely related to that hope is the new nationalism which differs considerably from past types. The new nationalism is not so much erected on the foundation of past political achievements and national superiority as upon the belief in the nation's self-sufficiency which forms the basis for national sovereignty which, in turn, guarantees international prestige and power. Particularly symptomatic of the new

OUR PROBLEM

nationalism is the almost superstitious anxiety with which the younger nations insist on the sanctity of their borders, notwithstanding the fact that they have been drawn up in more or less arbitrary ways by the former colonial powers.

The self-reliance of the scientists is well-known. The infallibility of science has become one of the basic dogmas of modern mankind. With rare exception, modern scientists deem it inconceivable that they should discuss any relevant problem on any other than a 'scientific' basis. The suggestion that modern science might have by-passed some of mankind's elementary problems is vigorously repudiated.

To the outsider, this self-reliance exhibits a remarkable weakness. Modern science is an open system. The only way in which its positions can be verified is by their effectiveness. Yet the effects lie in the future. No position is ever verified in its totality. The future will eventually disclose its inaccuracy, if not its outright falsehood. One might discount those shortcomings, because the corrective element, which the future brings with it, would seem to make the original inaccuracies tolerable. But this contention loses its cogency when the question is asked, 'Why should man be so proud of his self-sufficiency?' It is true that the volume of natural energies which man has subdued and uses for technological ends increases substantially each year. In a closed system such increase would mean more employment, more pleasant conditions of work, better education, and so on. But man's self-reliance presupposes an open system. In an open system there is no fixed centre or goal; everything is flux and movement. Is not modern man a Sisyphus, who works untiringly without ever accomplishing anything worth his efforts? In order to impart meaning to such an elusive process, modern man seeks refuge in work. The quantity of the things produced seems to be the only tangible standard of meaningful existence. No wonder that modern man makes a cultus of work. Since the process of production is menaced from time to time by strikes and wars, the emphasis is eventually shifted from the creativity of mankind to the individual production measured in terms of ability, material, tools available, and opportunities.

A conspicuous consequence of the prevailing subjectivisim of our age is the lack of a specific style in art or fashion. Former generations were able by devoting themselves to certain values to find a form by means of which they would express common aspirations or evaluations. Our time is characterized by a bewildering multiplicity of personal styles or rather individual forms, none of which strikes one as being necessary or really expressive of the aims of creative mankind.

It is not for the first time that people trusted in the self-sufficiency of mankind or of their nation. But formerly they held that, through the human mind, truth or salvation would gradually manifest itself. In our age, the creativity of mankind finds expression in the individual's sense of self-sufficiency. Yet far from resolving all of man's problems through science and technology, that very trust in self-sufficiency brings into being moral and social problems which tenaciously continue to plague modern man.

C. DEPERSONALIZATION

In his quest for identity, modern man is torn between various modes of self-consciousness. As an individual, he feels himself to be the lord of changes; he is aware of the fact that in his individual life the scope has been enlarged, the abilities refined and the means of expression have grown more articulate. In accordance with that unfolding of human personality, freedom of thought and criticism were regarded as most precious goods. Yet there is another process which has gone on simultaneously during the last hundred years. As the agent of the species, the individual relies proudly on his self-sufficiency. Yet precisely in that capacity he senses the loss of his personality. Realizing that man's creative forces belong to the species rather than to the individual, people will organize their life for the purpose of collective action. In an age when the population of the world has grown to unexpected proportions, the formation of mass organizations seems to be inevitable. There is hardly a single person in the Western world whose life is not incorporated into one or several mass organizations, be it only the audience of a radio station. That development has obviously grown solid roots in our technological civilization. It seems to be the most appropriate method of dealing effectively with the material and social needs of mankind. In view of its undeniable usefulness, technology has grown strong roots in modern society. Mass organization is therefore mechanized life.

Such a development may appear surprising. For the Reformation and the Renaissance, by which modern society was brought into being, were movements which worked for the freedom of the individual over against the collectivism of the Middle Ages. The freedom that the sixteenth century aimed at was freedom within narrow limits. It was freedom in the service of one's fellow man, or freedom of artistic production within the standards of classical beauty, or service within a society whose foundation had been laid by God. Yet, as has been shown, the aspirations of the Reformation were gradually secularized, and thus it was necessary to substitute the sociological form of mass organization for the authority of intrinsic standards.

This development has paradoxically diminished rather than augmented the opportunities for personal contact and intercourse. It cannot be denied that, by incorporating individuals into mass organizations, dealing with them is greatly simplified. No less important is the fact that mass organizations are in the interest of those who rule or want to rule. The listeners of a radio station are a captive audience. There is no way of stopping or interrupting the speaker. By switching over to another station, the listener will find himself in the same predicament. No one can wonder at the increasing tendency to run schools and colleges, relief organizations or political parties, and even churches, after the pattern of a large business organization. Nor is that form of organization confined to the Western world. In the Communist countries the whole life of the people is planned and determined by mass organizations.

Now, however, it is urged that the advantages of such organizations are more than outweighed by the losses incurred. The larger the enterprise, the more difficult it is to initiate any changes. Furthermore, in the big organizations machines will regulate the course of activity. Thus the individual member is no longer treated as a person; he is simply a cog in a gigantic wheel. From being the lord of nature, modern man is thus demoted to the rank of a slave of technology. The urbanization of life has transformed the neighbour next door into the gentleman living at No. 31 in the same block of flats. In harmony with the aggrandizement of business, the boss's office has been replaced by a staff room, and the teacher-pupil relationship has given room to the use of teaching machines. The modern methods of publicity are cleverly-devised techniques by which the customer is persuaded to give up his own judgement and to accept that of the announcer or his patrons. The modern methods of advertising and propaganda constitute a special threat to human dignity, for it is speech by which man is lifted above animals. But in those methods words become empty shells. By pretending to address themselves to man's critical faculty, the public speakers aim at preventing him from forming a judgement of his own.

Strangely enough, however, our generation is far from protesting unanimously against the modern attack on the dignity and personal life of the individual. The consumption of hallucinatory drugs and of alcoholic beverages is still on the increase. Rather than assert themselves against the menace to their personality, many of our contemporaries seem to prefer an existence made tolerable by one's own imagination.

Modern depersonalization is in the first place a social calamity. The spirit of initiative and responsibility is thereby dulled and eventually killed, and the mechanized order is accepted as matter of course, irrespective of its unpleasant or cruel consequences. People hold that what is every man's business is no man's business in particular. That is not surprising, for once the individual has been brought down to the point of social depersonalization he will find it difficult to believe in his cosmic dignity as a person. Rather he will harbour a sense of loneliness in the vast expanses of the universe, or of the meaninglessness of one's infinitesimal smallness. Unless he is a person, that is to say a being endowed with a measure of independence and self-determination, and thus ontologically superior to mere existence, the individual cannot feel secure when he is confronted with this world. Persons only are capable of ethical decisions.

B. Christian Self-assertion

1. *The Christian Vantage Point*

Our survey has shown the confusion and uncertainty with which modern man looks at his life, and his obvious inability to reach a meaningful position. But the difficulty in which Christian self-awareness finds itself is hardly lesser, for the modern mentality is greatly indebted to Protestantism. Some will even go so far as to contend that genuine Protestantism survives in modern mentality rather than in the ecclesiastical institutions. Others, in deference to secular developments, have completely written off the religious element in Protestant ethics. They are satisfied with the manifestations of human creativity. In order to separate the wheat from the chaff, it will be necessary to recognize the role which God plays in history, while discounting those elements in modern mentality in which the divine dynamic is disregarded. Nothing is to be gained by deploring the moral decay of our age. What this world needs is an increase of constructive spiritual energies. For instance, the frequency of lawlessness, crime and vice in the modern world should not be interpreted as indicating an increasing deterioration of the human substance, or an accentuated trend towards unethical life. Without condoning those activities we have to realize that they simply bring to light what has always been in the human heart, and what, by a wrong understanding of freedom, has been given a chance to come to light.

374

A great deal of confusion and perplexity has been created in the field of Christian ethics because the theologians have adopted philosophical notions and patterns of thought and method without sufficiently guarding their use against misunderstandings. Granted that, in order to emphasize the dynamic character of Christian ethics the philosophies of Whitehead or Bergson are in some respects preferable to those of Plato or Aristotle. Nevertheless, the theologian is apt to go astray, unless the basic difference between their immanentist ground of reality and the personal, transcendental God of Christian belief dominates his thinking.

A further reflection will be in order. Whereas in classical philosophy the individual was conceived of as a portion of the species only, modern thinking recognizes the individual as the very agent through whom the species becomes actual. Hence the individuals in their diversity constitute the wholeness of the species. While we reject the finality which Bonhoeffer ascribes to the present period of history, we recognize, nevertheless, the fundamental significance of the fact that within Christianity an emancipation from classical theology is taking place. Ethical predicates like 'right' and 'wrong' are now applied to attitudes and habits rather than to particular actions. That development is paralleled in theology. The doctrine of the attributes of God, for instance, makes room for a pattern of his continual divine work of redemption, which takes place in sacred history; likewise the careful elaboration of the *Ordo Salutis* is replaced by the description of the believer as an object of Christ's ongoing saving activity. That shift explains the affinity in which recent types of Protestant theology stand to philosophers like Jaspers, Whitehead, Bergson, or to Bloch. Yet equally important is the fact that, in Christian ethics, the decisive dynamic is not rooted in man or the universe but rather in the transcendental power of God. The modern nominalism, according to which nothing is able to exist of which no consistent notion can be formed, we deem naïve. It completely overlooks the fact that all scientific knowledge is analogous. For there is always more in the things than we are capable of apprehending and comprehending.

The Christian Emancipation has transformed ethics, too. We do no longer elaborate a series of virtues that have to be realized or a code of commandments that have to be obeyed. The start is made from an image of man, and moral evaluation is based upon the individual's eagerness to let that image guide his thinking, feeling and acting, and thus to become real in one's life.

375

2. Towards a Christian Life

The Church exists and works in a world which to a large extent is non-Christian. Yet the mentality of Western man, which in recent times has been adopted more or less universally, has developed in the presence and under the influence of Protestant Christianity. In turn, modern Protestant theology, thoroughly dissatisfied with the outlook of the post-Reformation divines of the sixteenth century, makes vigorous attempts to come to terms with the ethical outlook of the modern age. The Church finds itself confronted by a twofold task. It has to test the manifestations of the modern mind in order to utilize them to the extent in which they are compatible with the spirit of the Gospel. At the same time it has to point out to the modern man the fatal weaknesses and delusions implied in his moral outlook. Troeltsch was mistaken when he interpreted modern man's mentality as being the logical out-growth of Christianity. Tillich, too, conceded too much to the modern mind; he held that it was basically in agreement with the divine truth, though he recognized its need to be supplemented by other Christian elements.

The principal objection which Christianity raises to modern man's understanding of himself concerns his disregard of the indissoluble relation in which man stands to God. It makes little difference in that respect whether the existence of God is expressly denied or merely treated as irrelevant. For man differs from animals by the fact that his life possesses meaning. Yet there can be no true meaning except when human life is directly related to God as its ultimate determinant. Through the Creator, this world is permanently kept in motion. However, if with Heraclitus, Epicurus or Whitehead we assume that reality is a never ending flux and change while lacking an ultimate goal, human existence will be a mere waste of effort; it would never be crowned by success. Even if the future were always better than the past, our actual existence could make no sense, because its value would inevitably, and in the long run, be infinitely surpassed by subsequent developments.

The self-reliant modern man may look with legitimate pride upon his creativity because he alone has an unlimited capability – through science and technology – to transform this world according to his own intentions and wishes. Yet does he not overlook the fact that he has not made himself and this world? Moreover, what is gained by man's mental superiority is lost again through the success of his abilities, for the development of science and technology has resulted in depersonalizing human life. That consequence is not inevitable, yet Christian faith alone offers a new perspective. By their faith in God, people are able successfully to assert their selfhood and thus personal life. That function faith is capable of performing, because it implies an effective image of true human life. Underlying all ethics is the idea of genuine humanity though it is not apprehended by all men with the same degree of clarity. In the closed systems of ethics – and practically all ethics of antiquity were of that kind – man's actions were guided by the image of an individual who would from time to time perform deeds in accordance with the conditions and needs of the community which required a special effort of the will. The authority of the ethical demand could therefore adequately be expressed by means of commandments. A man's moral value would depend on the number of his good actions. The only threat to personal life in such a closed system was seen in the reckless demands of a tyrant. The situation has changed radically in our age, which considers the universe an open system. Within it, technological civilization has no use for personal actions. Modern man expresses his moral conviction in terms of impersonal projects which are aimed at the material improvement of this world and living conditions within it. The individual himself is held to be actually what he should be, because he has the ability to engage in useful activities.

Christianity, however, will not be satisfied with such a view, though it agrees with it by placing man into an open universe. Faith sees the constant flux of time controlled by God's plan and man's eschatological destination. Experience has also taught the Church that the Jewish image of the righteous man and its medieval equivalent of the saint are not fit to fill the world-wide frame by which our life is conditioned. More or less consciously, the Church has regarded Christ as the representative of true life.

In this connection, the significance which the 'quest of the historical Jesus' has had for Protestant ethics deserves special mention. Modern scholarship, which disparages the historical value of such research, fails to notice that the historical approach was not an end in itself. Starting from the conviction that in Jesus alone Christianity could find effective guidance on the way to a worthwhile personal life, they threw out the medieval picture of a saviour who kept completely aloof from this world, and turned to the Jesus of the Gospels. There they discovered a man who lived in fellowship with actual people and shared with them the plight of a citizen of a world filled with evils. Such a reconstruction was not meant to satisfy historical interest and curiosity, or to find a great man who might be emulated, despite the fact that he had lived nearly two thousand years ago. Rather the Gospel story made those scholars aware of the fact that, by the grace of God, mankind was able to bring forth such a person, and that, notwithstanding the powerful opposition of cosmic forces, God's kindness was working effectively in his people, in order to engender in them true humanity. Thus the image which underlies Christian ethics embraces a man who lived in the historical situation of his time and country, yet never lost sight of God's purpose and redemptive will. The evangelists intended to present the saving role of Jesus rather than to draw an historical picture of a Jewish rabbi called Jesus. The Church in every age has therefore a right to reinterpret afresh the Gospel image of Jesus in the context of its special problems and opportunities. The Gospel story taught the Church that the life for which God has destined man implies a multitude of personal relations with relatives, friends, neighbours and with countrymen, with outcasts and with authorities, with good and with virtuous people; but also with criminals and prostitutes, with plants and animals and seasons, with health and sickness, wealth and poverty and hunger. The quest for the historical Jesus has convinced the Church that the ethical significance of Jesus does not lie in his actual deeds, but rather in the pattern of his ministry and in the power, by which he was enabled so to live. The Christian, who walks on that path, can be sure that he is able to live his life as a person whom no power in this world may permanently restrain. His personal life will not operate with the same intensity all the time; there may be considerable differences of involvement and commitment. But once he has learned to hold the image of the Jesus of the Gospels before himself, he will never again accept the 'realism' of modern civilization as an ultimate.

The importance of the ethical image is most conspicuously illustrated by the 'sexual revolution'. The prevailing naturalism of this age contends that the sexual relation is a physiological process which neither implies nor entails moral obligation, provided only that it was based upon mutual consent. The consistency of such an outlook has been discussed above. That such an interpretation of sex should be adopted at all is explained by the fact that the people concerned have an image in which man is considered a self-contained being. Thereby is overlooked the fact that, being either male or female, the individual is naturally related to the other sex for sexual satisfaction, and that, as potential parents, people who have intercourse with each other have an innate responsibility for possible offspring. That those defective and erroneous views should, nevertheless, be held and advocated by so many of our contemporaries is an indication of the emotional grip that such an image has on modern man.

From a Christian viewpoint, it is easy to disapprove of naturalistic individualism. Yet experience has also shown that neither sex instruction and theoretical indoctrination, nor the authority of mores and parental reprimands, are strong enough to break the emotional hold. It seems that the only effective way by which the Church can cope with the sex revolution is by making articulate its image of true humanity. Since that image dominates the whole of Christian ethics, it will not be necessary to attack the problem in the sexual field directly. One can start in fields in which the attraction of individualism and naturalism is less. In that way, an incipient sense of relatedness and responsibility can be developed, which may gradually spread to all areas of moral life.

The difficulties which we encounter in the field of sexual education remind us of the fact that no Christian life is ever complete morally. During our whole existence we are on the march towards that communion with God which Jesus enjoyed here on earth. Some will see the goal with greater clarity than others, and realization of the concept, formed of the true life will vary considerably according to circumstances, resources and abilities.

All the different representations of life point to the same idea or ideal, however, so that, in spite of particular differences, Christians may realize their basic unity in Christ. For all the ethical images which we devise go back to the image which Jesus impressed on the Apostles. Through it we are enabled consciously to participate in the mystery of our salvation. We were created to be the image of God. In our lives God's saving will and purpose are to be manifested in this world. Yet what we actually do seems to be a denial of God's presence. However, by holding before us Christ as the image of human life God attracts us to himself and challenges us to follow Jesus. Thus not by what we do in our own strength but by what he enables us to become, we are privileged to be his mirror and image.

'It is not to be thought that I have already achieved all this. I have not yet reached perfection, but I press on, hoping to take hold of that for which Christ once took hold of me. ... I press toward the goal to win the prize which is God's call to the life above, in Christ Jesus.'

(Phil. 3:12, 14 – NEB)

Bibliography

History of Ethics

Binkley, Luther John. *Contemporary ethical theories*. New York, 1961.

Bochensky, J. M., *Contemporary European Philosophy. Engl. tr.* Berkeley, Calif., 1956

Brinton, Crane. *A history of Western morals*. New York, 1959.

Broad, C. D. *Five types of ethical theory*. New York, 1930.

Hall, T. C. *History of Christian ethics within organized Christianity.* London and New York, 1910.

Heard, Gerald. *Morals since 1900*. New York, 1950.

Hill, Thomas E. *Contemporary ethical theories*. New York, 1950.

Johnson, F. Ernest, *Patterns of Ethics in America Today*. New York 1960.

Lecky, William E. H. *History of European morals from Augustine to Charlemagne*. New York, 1872.

Long, Edward LeRoy. *A survey of Christian ethics*. New York, 1967.

MacIntyre, Alasdair C. *A short history of ethics*. New York, 1966.

Niebuhr, H. Richard. *The Kingdom of God in America*. Chicago, 1933.

Pike, Edgar R. *Ethics of the great religions*. London, 1948.

Selby-Bigge, L. A. *British moralists*. New York, 1965.

Sidgwick, Henry, *Outline of the History of Ethics*. 7th ed. London, 1939, Paperback, 1960

Sneath, E. Hershey, *The Evolution of Ethics as Revealed in the Great Religions*. New Haven, 1927.

Swapey, William Curtiss. *Ethical Theory from Hobbes to Kant*. New York, 1953

Troeltsch, Ernst. *The social teaching of the Christian Churches*. Eng. tr. New York, 1931.

Tsanoff, R. *The moral ideas of our civilization*. New York, 1942; London, 1944.

Warnock, Mary. *Ethics since 1900*. 2nd ed. London, 1966.

Webb, Clement C. J. *The contribution of Christianity to ethics*. Calcutta, 1932.

Weber, Max. *The Protestant ethic and the spirit of capitalism*. New York, 1930.

Westermarck, Edward A. *The origin and development of the moral ideas*. London and New York, 1906.

Widgery, Alban G. *Christian ethics in history and modern life*. New York, 1940.

Philosophical Ethics

Ayer, A. J. *Language, truth and logic*. Rev. ed. London, 1946.

Barbour, G. F. *A philosophical study of Christian ethics*. Edinburgh, 1921.

Beauvoir, Simone de. *The ethics of ambiguity*. New York, 1948.

Bentham, Jeremy. *Introduction to the principles of morals and legislation*. Oxford, 1879.

Berdiaev, Nicolai. *The destiny of man*. London, 1937.

Bergson, Henri. *The two sources of morality and religion*. Eng. tr. New York, 1935.

Blanchard, Brand. *Reason and goodness*. London, 1961.

Bosanquet, Bernard. *Psychology of the moral self*. London and New York, 1904.

Bradley, F. H. *Ethical studies*. Oxford, 1870 and 1927.

Brandt, Richard B. *Ethical theory: the problems of normative and critical ethics*. Englewood Cliffs (N.J.), 1959.

Brightman, Edgar S. *Moral laws*. New York, 1933.

Buber, Martin. *Good and Evil*. New York, 1953

Carus, Paul. *The ethical problem*. Chicago, 1899.

Corkey, Robert. *A philosophy of Christian morals for today*. London, 1901.

Dahlstrom, Earl C. *Helping human beings: the ethics of interpersonal relations*. Washington (D.C.), 1964.

Dewey, John, and Tufts, James H. *Ethics*. Rev. ed. New York, 1932.

Edel, Abraham. *Method in ethical theory*. London, 1963.

Ewing, Alfred C. *Second thoughts in moral philosophy*. London, 1959.

Findlay, John N. *Values and intentions: a study in value theory and philosophy of mind*. London, 1961.

Fromm, Erich. *The heart of man: its genius for good and evil*. New York, 1964.

Garnett, A. Campbell. *Ethics: a critical introduction*. New York, 1960.

Green, Thomas H. *Prolegomena to ethics*. 2nd ed. Oxford, 1884.

Hare, R. M. *The language of morals*. New York, 1936.

— *Freedom and reason*. Oxford, 1963.

Hartmann, Nicolai. *Ethics*. Eng. tr. London, 1932.

Heart, Gerald. *The third morality*. New York, 1952.

Higgins, Thomas J. S. J. *Ethical Theory in Conflict*. Milwaukee, 1967

Jacques, John H. *The Right and the Wrong*. London, 1965.

James, William. *Pragmatism*. London, 1907.

Jaspers, Karl, *Man in the Modern Age*. Engl. tr., New York, 1933

Joad, Cyril E. M. *Guide to the philosophy of morals and politics*. London, 1938.

Kant, Immanuel. *Critique of practical reason*. Eng. tr. Chicago, 1949.

Kerner, George C. *The revolution in ethical theory*. Oxford, 1966.

MacKinnon, Donald M. *A study of ethical theory*. London, 1957.

Marcel, Gabriel. *Philosophy of Existence*. Eng, tr., New York, 1949

Maritain, Jacques. *Moral philosophy: an historical and critical survey of the great systems*. New York, 1964.

Mill, John Stuart. *Utilitarianism*. 1863.

Moore, George Edward. *Ethics*. London, 1912.

Muirhead, John H. *Rule and end in morals*. Oxford, 1932.

Nietzsche, Friedrich Wilhelm. *Beyond Good and Evil*. Eng. tr. Chicago, 1955.

Prince, Kropotkin. *Ethics. Origin and Development*. Engl. tr., London, 1924

Rashdall, H. *Good and Evil*. 2nd ed. Oxford, 1924.

Reid, Louis A. *Creative morality*. London, 1937.

Ross, W. D. *Foundations of ethics*. Oxford, 1939.

Royce, Josiah. *Studies of Good and Evil*. London, 1892.

— *The philosophy of loyalty*. New York, 1908.

Russell, Bertrand. *Human society in ethics and politics*. London and New York, 1954.

Sartre, Jean Paul. *Existentialism*. New York, 1947.

Scheler, Max, *The nature of sympathy*. Eng. tr. New Haven (Conn.), 1954.

Seth, James. *A study of ethical principles*. 4th ed. New York and Edinburgh, 1894.

Sidgwick, Henry. *The methods of ethics*. London, 1907.

Spencer, Herbert. *Data of ethics*. London, 1879; New York, 1883.

Stace, Walter T. *The concept of morals*. New York, 1937.

Stevenson, Charles L. *Ethics and language*. Oxford, 1944.

Taylor, Alfred E. *The faith of a moralist*. London, 1930.

Teilhard de Chardin, Pierre. *The Phenomenon of Man*. Eng. tr., New York, 1959

Thornton, Lionel S. *Conduct and the supernatural*. New York and London, 1915.

Tillich, Paul J. *The new being*. New York, 1955.

— *Morality and being.* New York, 1963.

Tilus, Harold Hopper. *What is mature morality?* New York, 1943.

Toulmin, Stephen. *An examination of the place of reason in ethics.* Cambridge, 1950.

Tsanoff, Radislov. *Ethics.* New York, 1947.

Urban, Wilbur M. *Fundamentals of Ethics.* New York, 1930.

Wheelwright, Philip E. *A critical introduction to ethics.* New York, 1935.

Williams, Gardner. *Humanistic ethics.* New York, 1951.

Theological Ethics

Beach, Waldo. *The Christian life.* Richmond (Virginia), 1967.

Bennett, John C. *Christian ethics and social policy.* New York, 1946.

Brunner, Emil. *The divine imperative.* London, 1937; Philadelphia, 1942.

Dewar, Lindsay, and Hudson, Cyril. *Christian morals.* London, 1945.

Eavey, C. B., *Principles of Christian ethics.* Grand Rapids (Mich.) 1958.

Elert, Werner, *Christian ethics.* Eng. tr. Philadelphia, 1957.

Fairbairn, Robert B. *Of the doctrine of morality in the relation to the grace of redemption.* London and New York, 1887.

Fletcher, Joseph. *Situation ethics: the new morality.* Philadelphia, 1966.

Forell, George. *Ethics of decision: an introduction to Christian ethics.* Philadelphia, 1955.

Garvie, Alfred E. *Christian moral conduct.* London, 1938.

Gore, Charles. *The philosophy of the good life.* London, 1930.

Harkness, Georgia. *Christian ethics.* New York, 1957.

Heick, Otto W. *Guide to Christian living.* Philadelphia, 1954.

Henry, Carl F. H. *Christian personal ethics.* Grand Rapids (Mich.), 1957.

— *Aspects of social ethics.* Grand Rapids, 1964.

Henson, Herbert Hensley. *Christian morality.* Oxford, 1936.

von Hildebrand, Dietrich. *Christian ethics.* New York, 1953.

King, Winston L. *The holy imperative.* New York, 1949.

Kirk, Kenneth E. *Some principles of moral theology.* London, 1920.

Knudson, A. C. *The principles of Christian ethics.* New York, 1943.

Lehmann, Paul L. *Ethics in a Christian context.* New York, 1963.

Maritain, Jacques. *True humanism.* New York, 1938.

Matson, Alvin D. *Christian ethics.* Rock Island (Illinois), 1938.

Monroe, Warner. *An introduction to Christian ethics.* Anderson (Indiana), 1947.

Mortimer, R. C. *Christian ethics.* London, 1950.

CHRISTIAN ETHICS

Muelder, Walter C. *Moral law in Christian social ethics*. Richmond (Virginia), 1966.

Murray, John C. *A handbook of Christian ethics*. Edinburgh, 1908.

Niebuhr, H. Richard. *Christ and culture*. New York, 1951.

— *The responsible self*. New York, 1963.

Niebuhr, Reinhold. *An interpretation of Christian ethics*. New York, 1959.

— *The Children of Light and the Children of Darkness*. New York, 1944.

Osborn, Andrew R. *Christian ethics*. London, 1940.

Ramsay, Ian T., ed. *Christian ethics and contemporary philosophy*. London and New York, 1966.

Ramsey, Paul. *Basic Christian ethics*. New York, 1950.

Rashdall, Hastings. *Conscience and Christ*. London, 1916.

Rauschenbusch, Walter. *A theology for the social gospel*. New York, 1918.

Robinson, John A. T. *Christian morals today*. London and Philadelphia, 1964.

Sellers, James. *Theological ethics*. New York, 1966.

Sittler, Joseph. *The structure of Christian ethics*. Baton Rouge (Louisiana), 1958.

Strong, Thomas B. *Christian Ethics*. London and New York, 1896

Temple, William. *Christianity and social order*. London, 1942.

— *Man and God*. London, 1934.

Thielicke, Helmut. *Theological Ethics*. Eng. tr., Philadelphia, 1966

Thomas, George F. *Christian ethics and moral philosophy*. New York, 1955.

384

1. Index of Names

Acton, Lord, 229
Adam, 202
Alcoholics Anonymous, 319
Althaus, 16
Ambrose, 5
Anabaptists, 9, 233, 238
Animism, 29
Anselm, 136
Antichrist, 190
Anti-Defamation League, 347
Aristotle, 337
Arnold, Johann, 11
Augustine, 5, 60, 230
Ayer, A. J., 23

Bacon, Francis, 9, 12
Barth, Karl, 19, 93
Beach, Waldo, 22
Beck, Johann T., 18
Benedict of Nursia, 6
Bennett, J. C., 22
Bentham, Jeremy, 12, 23
Bergson, Henri, 20, 34, 89, 100, 375
Bloch, Ernst, 230, 375
Blumhardt, C. G., and J. C., 350
Bonaventura, 7
Bodelschwingh, 19, 350, 356
Bonhöffer, D., 19, 167, 349, 375
Bosanquet, Bernard, 22
Bradley, F. H., 22, 118
Brunner, Emil, 19, 30, 64
Burckhardt, Jakob, 229
Byron, Lord, 29

Caird, Edward, 22
Calvin, Jean, 8, 9, 119, 196
Camus, A., 20
Carlyle, T., 22, 23
Cathars, 7
Clement of Alexandria, 5
Clement of Rome, 5
Cohen, H., 15, 108
Comte, A., 20, 128
COPEC Conference, 24
CORE, 324
Cousin, 20
Cox, Harvey, 30
Cyprian, 5

Dale, B. J., 23
Darwin, Charles, 100

de Beauvoir, Simone, 20
Decalogue, 163
de Chardin, P. T., 20, 110
Descartes, Rene, 9, 106
Determinism, 30, 70
De Wette, W. M. L., 18
Dewey, John, 21
Dike, 201
Dissenters, 10
Dorner, J. A., 18
Duns Scotus, 7

Eden: see Paradise
Edwards, Jonathan, 11, 20
Elert, 16
Emerson, Ralph Waldo, 20
Engels, Karl, 286
Enlightenment, 11, 19, 20, 161, 200, 230, 345
Epicurus, 376
Eucken, Rudolf, 17
Evangelicalism, 23

Fairbain, A. M., 23
Feuerbach, L. A., 17, 128
Fichte, J. G., 14, 118
Finney, 21
Fletcher, Joseph, 30, 42
Forell, George, 22
Forsyth, P. T., 23
Fourrier, 20
Fox, George, 10
France, 19, 188
Francis of Assisi, 7, 331
Franklin, Benjamin, 20
Fromm, Erich, 50
Freud, Sigmund, 29, 59, 62, 114, 128
Fundamentalism, 21

Garvie, A. E., 23
Genet, 20
Görres, J. J. von, 29
Goethe, J. W. von, 142
Gogarten, F., 324
Golden Age, 230
Gore, Charles, 24, 350
Great Britain, 22–4
Gregory the Great, 5
Green, T. H., 22
Grotius, Hugo, 11

2. Index of Subjects